JOURNAL FOR THE STUDY OF THE OLD TESTAMENT SUPPLEMENT SERIES
122

Editors
David J.A. Clines
Philip R. Davies

JSOT Press
Sheffield

IMAGES

OF

EMPIRE

Edited by
Loveday Alexander

Journal for the Study of the Old Testament
Supplement Series 122

Copyright © 1991 Sheffield Academic Press

Published by JSOT Press
JSOT Press is an imprint of
Sheffield Academic Press Ltd
The University of Sheffield
343 Fulwood Road
Sheffield S10 3BP
England

Typeset by Sheffield Academic Press
and
Printed on acid-free paper in Great Britain
by Billing & Sons Ltd
Worcester

British Library Cataloguing in Publication Data

Images of empire.—(Journal for the Study of the Old
    Testament. Supplement series. ISSN 0309-0787; 122)
    I. Alexander, Loveday II. Series
    937

ISBN 1-85075-312-1

CONTENTS

ABBREVIATIONS

AB	Anchor Bible
AE	Années epigraphiques
AJA	*American Journal of Archaeology*
AJPh	American Journal of Philology
ANRW	*Aufstieg und Niedergang der römischen Welt*
AUSS	*Andrews University Seminary Studies*
BA	*Biblical Archaeologist*
BETL	Bibliotheca Ephemeridum Theologicarum Lovaniensium
Bib	*Biblica*
BHT	Beiträge zur historischen Theologie
BJS	Brown Judaic Studies
BMC	British Museum Coins
BMCRE	British Museum Coins of the Roman Empire
BNTC	Black's New Testament Commentaries
BZNW	Beihefte zur *ZNW*
CBQMS	Catholic Biblical Quarterly Monograph Series
CChr. Ser. Lat.	Corpus christianorum series latina
CIL	*Corpus inscriptionum latinarum*
CNRS	Centre nationale des recherches scientifiques
CSEL	Corpus scriptorum eccclesiasticorum latinorum
DJD	Discoveries in the Judaean Desert
HTR	*Harvard Theological Review*
HUCA	*Hebrew Union College Annual*
ICC	International Critical Commentary
ILS	*Inscriptiones latinae selectae*
JACT	Joint Association of Classical Teachers
JJS	*Journal of Jewish Studies*
JRS	*Journal of Roman Studies*
JSNTSup	Journal for the Study of the New Testament Supplement Series
JSOT	*Journal for the Study of the Old Testament*
JSPSup	Journal for the Study of the Pseudepigrapha Supplement Series
JSS	*Journal of Semitic Studies*
JTS	*Journal of Theological Studies*
MAMA	W. Calder and J. Cormack, *Monumenta Asiae Minoris Antiqua*
MGWJ	*Monatsschrift für Geschichte und Wissenschaft des Judenthums*
MNTC	Moffatt NT Commentary
NCB	New Century Bible

New Documents	G.H.R. Horsley (ed.), *New Documents Illustrating Early Christianity* (Macquarie University, NSW: Ancient History Documentary Research Centre)
NICNT	New International Commentary on the New Testament
P&P	*Past and Present*
PBSR	*Papers of the British School at Rome*
PEQ	*Palestine Exploration Quarterly*
PG	J.-P. Migne (ed.), Patrologia Graeca
PL	J.-P. Migne (ed.), Patrologia Latina
RB	*Revue biblique*
RE	Pauly–Wissowa–Kroll, *Realenzyklopädie*
REG	*Revue des études grecques*
RevQ	*Revue de Qumrân*
RG	Augustus, *Res Gestae*
RSA	*Rivista storica dell'Antichita*
SBLDS	Society of Biblical Literature Dissertation Series
SBLMS	Society of Biblical Literature Monograph Series
SNTSMS	Society for New Testament Studies Monograph Series
TLZ	*Theologischer Literaturzeitung*
TWAS	Twayne's World Authors Series
VT	*Vetus Testamentun*

LIST OF CONTRIBUTORS

Miriam Griffin
Faculty of Literae Humaniores, University of Oxford.

Richard Bauckham
Department of Theological Studies, University of Manchester.

Keith Branigan
Department of Archaeology and Prehistory, University of Sheffield.

D.J. Mosley
Department of Classics and Ancient History, University of Warwick, Coventry.

Tessa Rajak
Department of Classics, University of Reading.

George J. Brooke
Department of Biblical Criticism and Exegesis, University of Manchester.

Philip R. Davies
Department of Biblical Studies, University of Sheffield.

Douglas R. Edwards
Department of Religion, University of Puget Sound, Tacoma.

Vernon K. Robbins
Department of Religion, Emory University, Atlanta.

Martin Goodman
Oriental Institute, University of Oxford.

Steven Fanning
Department of History, The University of Illinois at Chicago, Chicago.

Gillian Clark
School of Archaeology, Classics and Oriental Studies, The University of Liverpool.

Philip S. Alexander
Department of Middle Eastern Studies, University of Manchester.

Imperatores!

G. E. Pallant-Sidaway

There is a story that a Roman emperor ordered that the statue of a god should be removed from its own locality to Rome. When the operation began the piece of sculpture burst into laughter.

INTRODUCTION

Loveday Alexander

There can be few topics on which public opinion has changed more radically in the last hundred years than the idea of Empire. Olivia Manning neatly captures a precise moment of change in *The Danger Tree*, published in 1977 but reflecting the shifting moods of the British in Egypt in 1942. A young British officer, freshly arrived from home, is shocked that the more experienced heroine should question what the British have done for the native Egyptians: 'We've brought them justice and prosperity, haven't we? We've shown them how people ought to live.' He and his kind, she reflects,

> believed that the British Empire was the greatest force for good the world had ever known. They expected gratitude from the Egyptians and were pained to find themselves barely tolerated.

Her own view is more cynical:

> What have we done here, except make money? I suppose a few rich Egyptians have got richer by supporting us, but the real people of the country, the peasants and the backstreet poor, are just as diseased, underfed and wretched as they ever were.

Even the role of military protector has to be challenged:

> They don't think we're protecting them. They think we're making use of them. And so we are. We're protecting the Suez Canal and the route to India and Clifford's oil company.[1]

This debate, *mutatis mutandis*, could be paralleled almost exactly in

---

1. O. Manning, *The Danger Tree* (first published Weidenfeld and Nicholson, 1977): quoted from *Fortunes of War*. II. *The Levant Trilogy* (Harmondsworth: Penguin Books, 1982), p. 24.

relation to Rome. It is strange now to read Rostovtzeff's cheerful description of the 'great benefit[s] conferred on mankind by the Roman Empire', 'not for a single inconsiderable aggregation of men but for all who were more or less influenced by civilization', and of the 'civilizing mission' achieved by Rome

> not by constraint or violent means, not by arms or by transferring nations from place to place, but by peaceful methods and by the natural attraction of a higher form of life offered by a dominant state and nation.[1]

In a post-imperial world, there is something rather disturbing about such a positive estimate of the benefits of empire: we expect something cooler and more cynical, along the lines of these words written by Brunt in 1978:

> Under the Principate the worst feature of republican misrule were obliterated; above all, peace and order were better preserved. But exploitation did not end. . . Provincial revenues were spent lavishly on feeding and amusing the inhabitants of Rome and beautifying the city, to say nothing of court expenditure. These privileges were not challenged by provincials in the senate or on the throne. Equality as between Italians and provincials was not attained, until all were sunk in equal misery.[2]

But the twentieth century has no monopoly on scepticism about the imperial ideal. The Babylonian Talmud contains an enigmatic dialogue which provides an uncanny echo to the debates of the historians (which in their turn echo post-war Europe's political unease in relation to its imperial heritage):

> Rabbi Judah (bar Ilai), Rabbi Yose (ben Halafta) and Rabbi Simeon (bar Yohai) were sitting talking. . .
> Rabbi Judah began: 'How splendid are the works of this people [i.e. the Romans]! They have built market-places, baths and bridges.'
> Rabbi Yose said nothing.
> Rabbi Simeon bar Yohai answered him: 'Everything they have made they have made only for themselves: market-places, for whores; baths, to wallow in; bridges, to levy tolls'.[3]

1. M. Rostovtzeff, *Rome* (trans. J.D. Duff; Oxford: Oxford University Press, 1960), p. 215. This edition is based on the 1928 Corrected Impression of the original 1927 publication.

2. P.A. Brunt, *'Laus imperii'*, in P.D.A. Garnsey and C.R. Whittaker (eds.), *Imperialism in the Ancient World* (Cambridge: Cambridge University Press, 1978), pp. 190-91.

3. *b. Šab.* 33b, N.R.M. de Lange (trans.), 'Jewish attitudes to the Roman

This story, though it is not actually discussed in the present volume,[1] goes some way towards explaining the primary motivation for *Images of Empire*. The narrative date of the exchange is around the time of the bar Kochba revolt, the second great Jewish revolt against Rome which took place during the principate of Hadrian. It expresses a range of views of the empire whcich are those of contemporaries, not the projections of modern historians; and it expresses the views (or some of the views) of the ruled to set alongside the better-publicized views of the rulers. The Roman Empire, in fact, provides an almost unique example of a great empire of the past where we have access to a variety of contemporary comment 'from below' as well as 'from above'. Not all of it is easy to decode; ancient apocalyptic, the exegetical techniques of Qumran or the Church Fathers, early Jewish mystical writings or Romano-British archaeology: these and other specialist areas of study all have light to shed on the experience of living in the Roman Empire, but they all require the interpretative skill of an expert in a particular field if they are to be made accessible to the historian. Hence, quite simply, the idea of an interdisciplinary colloquium on the Roman Empire, focusing primarily on the varied images generated by that empire among its subjects. The *Images of Empire* colloquium was held at Halifax Hall in the University of Sheffield in March 1990, under the auspices of the Deparment of Biblical Studies. This volume contains the conference papers, more or less as presented on that occasion.

The first two papers set up what appears to be a neat polarity between the centre and the periphery, and between positive and negative views of the empire. Miriam Griffin starts, appropriately, at the centre, with the 'bread and circuses' of the Imperial City: what effect did the city itself, recipient of so much of the emperors' attention, have on the provinces? What effect was all this expenditure designed to have? Richard Bauckham's paper shows the obverse of this particular image: for one provincial at least, the author of the book of Revelation, the Imperial City is a whore, her luxurious lifestyle supported by military coercion and related directly to economic exploitation of the provinces. Yet things are never as simple

empire', in Garnsey and Whittaker (eds.) *Imperialism in the Ancient World*, pp. 255-81 (p. 268).

1.   See de Lange's article mentioned in the previous note for a discussion of rabbinic views of Rome.

as they seem. As Miriam Griffin reminds us, the creation of an imperial ideology is impossible without some degree of 'collusion of belief and expression. . . between those above and those below'. This insight is echoed in contemporary study of the more recent empires of Europe: Peter Marshall, Rhodes Professor of Imperial History at King's College London, says in a recent article:

> The creation or the operation of empires are now generally seen as depending on interactions between Europeans and other peoples rather than on the simple exercise of European power. Thus when Europeans acquire control they are likely to have been responding to developments within indigenous societies, and their empires appear to a considerable degree to have been shaped by those who were willing to cooperate with them.[1]

Views like this may find some support in Keith Branigan's essay on the archaeological evidence for indigenous views of the Roman Empire from Roman Britain:[2] is the 'Asterix' image of heroic resistance a mirage reflecting the unease of historians rather than the feelings of the ancient Britons? If it is, then it is at least not a modern creation: for whatever reason, one of the most damning indictments of empire, ancient or modern, is that found in the speech composed by the Roman historian Tacitus for the Scottish chieftain Calgacus, discussed here by Derek Mosley. Clearly it was not only provincials who saw the unsavoury underside of the empire—and not only Romans who profited from it.

With the next three essays we return to the eastern empire. If 'the consent of the governed', in Miriam Griffin's phrase, was an essential element in the success of the empire, characters like Agrippa II (and for that matter his chronicler Josephus) are often treated as typical of the 'consenting classes', those locals readiest to support the empire and with most to gain from it. Yet as Tessa Rajak argues, Agrippa's speech expresses the voice of a pragmatic realism rather than of acquiescence in the imperial ideology, and may even be read as 'an implicit, suppressed apocalypse'. Josephus, read in this way, turns out

---

1.   P. Marshall, 'Overseas Expansion and Empire', *History Today* 41 (May 1991), pp. 32-36 (p. 33).

2.   The possible uses of archaeological evidence for this kind of enquiry are explored further in K. Branigan (ed.), *Rome and the Brigantes: The Impact of Rome on Northern England* (Department of Prehistory and Archaeology, University of Sheffield: Sheffield, 1980).

to be more complex than is often thought, and this complexity is even more evident when we look at some of the Hebrew and Aramaic literature produced in the eastern half of the empire around the turn of the era. In a careful analysis of the commentaries found among the Dead Sea Scrolls, George Brooke issues some cautions about the identification of contemporary allusions in exegetical texts which have some implications for the study of parallel phenomena in the New Testament. Nevertheless, Brooke's study shows clearly that Roman power was a fact of life even for minority groups on the fringes of the empire, and that one way to make it manageable was to locate it within the group's indigenous traditions. In Philip Davies's essay this process is seen again: Rome, which was hardly on the horizon when the book of Daniel was written, comes to dominate its exegesis in succeeding centuries through the identification of the empire with the 'fourth beast' of Daniel ch. 7. Moreover, Davies argues, the perspective of these texts is not a narrowly sectarian one: 'it is the extent of Roman rule which is deplored and not any particular wrong done to the Jewish nation', a point made also in Bauckham's study of the Christian apocalypse. Both confirm indirectly that the strongest counterbalance to an imperialist ideology is likely to be a rival ideology; and both also suggest that this rival ideology may provide a foundation for opposition which is broader and deeper than the wrongs of the individual.

Two papers on Luke–Acts shed new light on the vexed question of Luke's attitude to the empire. Luke is widely regarded as the most pro-Roman of the NT writers; both these papers draw attention in different ways to an expected feature of his narrative, what Vernon Robbins calls its 'aggressiveness'. The empire is seen as a proper 'workplace' for the Christian religion, and to that extent is accepted: but may not this very acceptance contain an implied challenge to the empire's claims? Douglas Edwards sets Luke's narrative alongside the novel *Chaereas and Callirhoe* which, he argues, also makes suppressed claims for the author's home city of Aphrodisias and the cult of Aphrodite. Both studies suggest that these apparently naive narratives, like the tales of the book of Daniel, may have more to tell the historian than would at first appear. Intriguingly, there is surprising confirmation for Robbins's use of the social-geographic term 'territoriality' in the patristic writer Hippolytus cited by later Gillian Clark, which brings the 'aggressiveness' decidedly to the fore.

Martin Goodman brings us back to the question of the relationship between text and history. Like the archaeologist, he argues that 'staring at texts can have only limited value' compared with looking for hard evidence of resistance or revolt: behind the rhetoric we must look for the reality, and in this light the Jewish subjects of the empire did not in fact differ markedly from their fellow-subjects in their range of responses to Rome. In the last analysis, however, texts are what we mostly have to go on, and the last three papers in the volume explore the imperial theme in some of the Christian and Jewish literature produced under the later empire. Steven Fanning explores the use of imperial language in Jerome's Vulgate, one of the most influential texts of the Middle Ages, where, for example, he detects a perceptible heightening of the majesty of God through the use of imperial language. Gillian Clark takes us through a selection of Patristic writers, always more complex and less predictable than their reputation allows them to be: even Eusebius's 'starry-eyed report of the Council of Nicaea' should not be dismissed as empty flattery. And finally, Philip Alexander looks at the Jewish mystical tradition, where, he argues, the ritual of the imperial palace is transferred to the heavenly court. His conclusion aptly sums up the ambivalence—and the fascination—of much of the material studied in this volume. Taking over the language and imagery of the empire into the religious vision of the mystic might seem to be a final betrayal of a long and honourable tradition of resistance to the dominant culture. Yet if Alexander is right, that would be a too-hasty conclusion. The mystics, he argues, projected their hopes upward to

> a supra-terrestrial, hidden world in which the relationships that pertain in this world are reversed. . . If they could not speak to the king on earth, they could speak to the king in heaven and be assured of *his* protection.

Like much of the literature studied here, these texts do not present a programme for political action; but this does not mean that they are not subversive.

> Empires can physically coerce their subjects, but they cannot easily compel the imagination or storm the citadel of the mind. . . [These] visions can, consequently, be seen as an effective strategy for resisting the imperialism of 'wicked Rome'.

The papers appear below in the order in which they were presented orally, and broadly in the same manner. No attempt has been made to summarize the findings of the colloquium or to synthesize out a unified position: the papers represent the individual viewpoints of their authors, writing from a variety of distinct intellectual traditions, unified only by their focus on the central theme of the images generated by the Roman Empire. In preparing the material for publication, the authors have been encouraged to preserve as far as possible the freshness of the original occasion, where the sheer dynamics of addressing an interdisciplinary gathering created both an impulse to communicate with specialists in neighbouring disciplines, and a corresponding willingness to grapple with unfamiliar material, which are not always characteristic of academic conferences. It is my hope that, although the book contains a wealth of detailed information, both the freshness and the desire to communicate will come across in print, so that the book will be of interest not only to other specialists in the various disciplines represented at the conference, and to students of the Roman Empire, but also to the general reader with a taste for the ancient world.

My thanks are due, firstly to all the contributors for making the colloquium (and the book) possible, and to George Pallant-Sidaway for the (non-archaeological) illustrations; to all those who helped with the colloquium itself, especially Christina Cockcroft; to Anne Alexander for indexing assistance, and to all those at Sheffield Academic Press who have helped to bring this book to completion. The book is dedicated to the memory of Professor F.F. Bruce, founder of the Department of Biblical Studies at Sheffield, whose own personal odyssey took him through many of the disciplines covered in this volume, and whose support for interdisciplinary study of the NT continued up to his death in September 1990.

Further Reading

This book does not claim to be a complete introduction to the subject, and we have not tried to draw up a comprehensive bibliography on the diverse subjects covered in these essays; but students who wish to read further will find plenty of leads to follow in the footnotes to each paper. Particularly noteworthy are:

P.D.A. Garnsey and C.R. Whittaker (eds.), *Imperialism in the Ancient World* (Cambridge University Research Seminar in Ancient History; Cambridge: Cambridge University Press, 1978).

A. Giovannini, (ed.), *Opposition et résistance à l'empire d'August à Trajan* (Entretiens sur l'antiquité classique, xxxiii; Geneva: Fondation Hardt, 1987).

K. Wengst, *Pax Romana and the Peace of Jesus Christ*, (trans. J. Bowden from the German *Pax Romana. Anspruch und Wirklichkeit. Erfahrungen und Wahrnehmungen des Friedens bei Jesus und im Urchristentum* [Munich: Christian Kaiser Verlag, 1986]; London: SCM Press, 1987).

On the Jews and Rome, see further

G. Stemberger, 'Die Beurteilung Roms in der rabbinischen Literatur', *ANRW* II.19.2 (1979) pp. 338-96.

M. Hadas-Lebel, 'L'évolution de l'image de Rome auprès des Juifs en deux siècles de relations judéo-romaines—164 à +70', *ANRW* II.20.2 (1987), pp. 715-856.

The NT evidence is summarized in

K. Aland, 'Das Verhältnis von Kirche und Staat in der Frühzeit', *ANRW* II.23.1 (1979), pp. 60-246.

See also

W. Schaefke, 'Frühchristlicher Widerstand', *ANRW* II.23.1 (1979), pp. 460-723.

URBS ROMA, PLEBS AND PRINCEPS

Miriam Griffin

It is only right and proper that a colloquium on Images of Empire should start at the centre, where many of the most important and familiar symbols of imperial majesty in the Roman style were first generated. It is also right that it should start, in particular, with the *Princeps* and the ordinary citizens of the city of Rome, for it could be said with justice that the *urbs Roma* itself was one of the most vital images of the Imperium Romanum.

The ambiguity of the word 'Rome' to mean a city and an empire is not just a modern one. In the panegyric *To Rome*, delivered by Aelius Aristides in the mid-second century CE, the Greek orator celebrates her both as πόλις and as ἀρχή, comparing her urban amenities to those of Alexandria and Antioch and her imperial extent and organization to the empires of Macedon and Persia. The ambiguity had also existed for Greek city-states which had acquired empires, but Aristides rightly stresses that Rome's generosity with her citizenship had developed a cohesiveness that made the whole world like the *territorium* of the city of Rome. A Latin poet, when writing a valedictory to the fallen city in 416 CE, was to express the idea in these words: 'You have made a city out of what was once a world'.[1]

Aristides points out that whereas Athens was twice in size what it was in power, while Sparta's power was far greater than its size, Rome's power matched her magnitude. In transforming Rome from a city of brick into a city of marble, Augustus intended, like Pericles,

1. Aelius Aristides, *To Rome*, e.g. 13 fin.; 61; 91. Rutilius Namatianus, *de reditu* 66: 'urbem fecisti quod prius orbis erat'. Something of the same dual conception seems to underlie Marcus Aurelius's description of himself as 'by πόλις and πατρίς, a Roman' (6.44).

that the city should be embellished as befitted the majesty of her empire. Vitruvius felt he could justify sending the *Princeps* a treatise on architecture in view of his concern 'that the state be made greater not only through new provinces, and that the majesty of the empire should find its expression in the eminent dignity of its public buildings'. After the civil wars of 69 CE had shaken the empire, Vespasian felt that, whatever the parlous state of Roman finances, the city must be rebuilt quickly. He wished to be seen personally shifting rubble and initiating the rebuilding of the Capitol: it symbolized his determination 'to put the state on a firm footing, then to embellish it'. The Elder Pliny, in his *Natural History*, which was dedicated to Vespasian's son Titus, appropriately reviewed the 'wonders of our city' to show that, in her buildings also, Rome has conquered the world.[1]

Rome asserted her position as *caput rerum*. In 20 BCE a golden milestone in the forum symbolized her position as centre of the world: it was engraved with the distances from the principal cities of the empire to the gates of Rome.[2] The more imaginative emperors represented the temples and other public constructions of Rome on coins that circulated throughout the empire.

For the most part, however, as Zanker has recently emphasized, the pictorial imagery emanated from Rome mostly through willing imitation, rather than prescription. 'These endless rows of Corinthian columns had become a symbol for one's claim to a share in Rome's imperial culture.' This was particularly true in the western portion of the empire, but even in the east the adornment of cities, a cherished enterprise long before Rome impinged on the Greek part of the world, could now be associated with the grandeur of the capital. Aelius Aristides celebrates the Greek cities, 'some newly founded, others increased by you', whose monuments and embellishments provide the elegant city of Rome with beautiful suburbs.[3]

---

1. Aristides, *To Rome* 9; Suet. *Aug.* 29; Vitruvius I, pref. 2; Suet. *Vesp.* 8.1 ('afflictam nutantemque rem publicam stabilire primo, deinde et ornare'); 8.5; Pliny, *NH* 36.101: 'verum et ad urbis nostrae miracula transire conveniat. . . sic quoque terrarum orbem victum ostendere'.

2. Dio Cass. 54.8.4.

3. P. Zanker, *The Power of Images in the Age of Augustus* (Ann Arbor: University of Michigan Press, 1988), pp. 336-38, 100; Strabo (5.3.8) notes that, whereas the Greeks had always attached importance to having beautiful structures in

Clearly many people visited Rome itself and were then inspired and equipped to imitate her. Members of the local aristocracies could afford to travel, and travel was now safer and easier: even the invalid Aelius Aristides managed it. There were constant embassies to the city, while the Tabula Siarensis from southern Spain now shows us that *municipia* and *coloniae* of Italy and the empire had *legati* stationed in the city ready to transmit messages quickly. There was even a regular guided tour of the sights of the city, for Tacitus tells us that the representatives of the Frisii who visited Rome in 53 CE saw 'the things that are shown to barbarians', including Pompey's theatre, 'where the greatness of the Roman people could be viewed'.[1]

The image of Rome that such visitors carried away included more than grand structures and elegant amenities. Political traditions also were absorbed. The virtual identity of the *urbs*, with its public and religious buildings, and the *res publica* could be taken for granted by Cicero in the Republic and by Cornelius Nepos in the triumviral period.[2] Some clue to the importance of the political ideology radiating out from the city is to be found in chapter 90 of Aristides' encomium, where after discussing the size and military organization of the empire (ἀρχή), he turns to the constitution of the city (πόλις). Seeking to confer the highest compliment a Greek could find, he identifies it with the mixed constitution that had been celebrated by Aristotle and then, in its incarnation as the Roman Republic, by Polybius and Cicero. For Aristides the people are the democratic element, the senate and magistrates the aristocratic element, and the

their cities, the Romans originally concentrated on useful ones but that, in his own time (the early Principate), they had made Rome dazzlingly beautiful; Aristides, *To Rome* 94.

1.   Easy travel: Aristides, *To Rome* 100; Pliny, *NH* 14.2; *Tabula Siarensis* (*AE* 1984, p. 508), frag. II, col. b. 23-25; Tac. *Ann.* 13.54: 'ea quae barbaris ostentantur'.

2.   Cicero (*Rep.* 3.43) is clearly making a paradoxical statement when he says that Syracuse and Athens, despite their great structures, were not *res publicae* when they were ruled by tyrants, because these *res* did not then belong to the people: H.P. Kohns, 'Res publica—res populi (zu Cic. rep. I 39)', *Gymnasium* 77 (1970), pp. 403-404; H. Braunert, 'Zum Eingangssatz der res gestae divi Augusti', *Chiron* 4 (1974), pp. 351-52 (on *Phil.* 3.30, 34). When Cornelius Nepos in *Atticus* 20.5 says of Caesar and Antony 'se uter principem non solum urbis Romae sed orbis terrarum esse cuperet', *urbs* clearly stands for the government of Rome, the usual expression being *princeps civitatis* (cf. the *Atticus* 19.2).

monarchic element (which for Polybius and Cicero was supplied by the consuls) is, of course, the *Princeps*, described as the ephor and Prytanis who, more majestic than a king and without the vices of a tyrant, enables the people to have what they want and enables the few to rule and exercise power. This shows, he says, that the Romans are natural rulers, whose experience of being ruled as free men has made them avoid the arbitrary and tyrannical methods of earlier empires (91). They send out governors in regular succession to protect and care for the governed just like elected magistrates in a city, for they manage the world as if it were one *polis* (36). Rome has established a κοινὴ τῆς γῆς δημοκρατία, a Republic of the world (for δημοκρατία is, of course, the standard Greek translation of *res publica* in that sense) under one excellent ruler and κοσμητής in which each receives what he deserves, the distinctions of rank in this macrocosm being those of citizen and non-citizen (60).[1]

For the argument here, it does not matter if this was not the view of Tacitus, who regarded the Principate as one-man rule and viewed with scepticism even the identification of the Republic with the mixed constitution. Nor does it matter if Aristides' view was not the view of the Principate promulgated from the centre.[2] What is significant here is that Aristides could see the government of the city of Rome as the source of the excellent system of government that obtained in the Roman empire.

The Ideology of Plebs and Princeps

I shall focus here on one aspect of the political ideology of the Principate, namely, the proper relationship between *plebs* and *Princeps*: first because the *plebs*, alone of the citizen population of

1. On δημοκρατία, see G.E.M. de Ste. Croix, *Class Struggle in the Ancient World* (London: Gerald Duckworth, 1981), p. 323, not, however, properly distinguishing its traditional Greek use in *To Rome* 90 for democracy contrasted with monarchy and aristocracy, from its debased use for any constitutional republican government (as in 38), flatteringly extended in 60 to the one-man rule of the Principate.

2. Tac. *Ann.* 4.33 makes the snide comment that the mixed constitution was easier to praise than achieve and, if achieved, never lasted long. See C. Wirszubski, *Libertas as a Political Idea at Rome* (Cambridge: Cambridge University Press, 1960), pp. 161-62.

Rome, had no other status in the empire than as citizens of the city of Rome, so that their relationship to the *Princeps* is unambiguously contained in the image of the city itself; and secondly because that ideology has often been described—wrongly, as I hope to show—in a way quite at odds with the way in which Aelius Aristides was able to perceive the Principate. The examination of how the relationship of *plebs* and *Princeps* was meant to be seen *at Rome* will lead us back to the larger question of the Image of the Roman Empire that the *Urbs Roma* was meant to generate.

As a preliminary, something should perhaps be said about the term 'ideology', a word now very much in vogue with historians. Much of what historians now call 'ideology' we recently called 'propaganda'. But this is not just a change of verbal fashion. 'Propaganda', not in its ecclesiastical origins but as historians use the term, is a kind of official language imposed from above; 'ideology' is more a kind of collusion of belief and expression, not altogether conscious, between those above and those below. It goes with this difference that 'propaganda' is a pejorative term, expressing the standpoint of those at whom the message is aimed, whereas 'ideology' can be used descriptively, without expressing approval or condemnation. Being interested in 'ideology' goes with an interest in rituals, ceremonies and all the symbolic aspects of power—in fact it goes with an interest in the surface of politics and society in itself; whereas to study 'propaganda' suggests that the important thing is the stripping off of that surface to expose the reality beneath.

In his *The Power of Images in the Age of Augustus*, Zanker has developed the notion of a cultural ideology which, though originating at the top and emanating outward from Rome, was neither prescribed nor supervised and gradually became internalized. There are times when phrases such as 'enthusiastic reception of new symbols' and 'general feeling of approval of the new regime' may seem to paint too benign a picture of the system Augustus created, and events in eastern Europe might suggest that 'propaganda' conveys better the sinister side of such a process.[1] But the notion of veneer and reality implicit in that term does not do justice to the element of hypocrisy involved in living under such a regime, to judge from the words of Vaclav Havel

---

1. Zanker, *Power of Images*, pp. 337-38, 100. See A. Wallace-Hadrill's reservations in 'Rome's Cultural Revolution', *JRS* 79 (1989), pp. 162-63.

in his 1990 New Year presidential address. He pointed out that the crucial line of conflict does not run between people and state but rather through the middle of each individual, for everyone in his or her own way is both a victim and a supporter of the system. 'All of us have become accustomed to the totalitarian system, accepted it as an unalterable fact and therefore kept it running...None of us is merely a victim of it, because all of us helped to create it together.'

Tribunicia Potestas—*the Ideological Key?*

The *Principes* from Augustus onwards spent time, money and energy in pleasing the Roman *plebs*: no one would dispute that the amount of evidence available justified Yavetz in writing a book called *Plebs and Princeps*. Also undeniable is the fact that the first *Princeps* had a genius for adopting and adapting the themes of Republican ideology. One might then surmise that, in pleasing the Roman *plebs*, he exploited the rich and ancient rallying cries of the *populares*.

The *popularis ratio*, by which I mean a 'left-wing' political style adopted by individual members of the governing class whether for selfish or idealistic reasons, can be said to have three strands: *exempla* of popular heroes, constitutional views, and characteristic types of legislation.

Relevant to the first is what Ronald Syme said in *The Roman Revolution* about Octavian's flirtation with the idea of becoming tribune of the *plebs* in 44 BCE: 'He might invoke the tribunate, emulating the Gracchi and a long line of demagogues'. He might, but did he? Certainly later as *Princeps*, Augustus was more apt to bore senate and people with the speeches of Metellus Macedonicus and Rutilius Rufus, Optimates and conservatives of the deepest dye, or to set up statues of successful Republican generals. It was the father of the Gracchi who had a statue in his new forum, thus earning, as Cicero had once predicted, eternal honour, in contrast to his nefarious sons. And Augustus paid conspicuous honour to the statue of Pompeius Magnus, which had once been sprinkled with the blood of his deified parent, the most famous *popularis* politician of the late Republic.[1]

---

1. R. Syme, *The Roman Revolution* (Oxford: Clarendon Press, 1939), pp. 119-20. T.P. Wiseman (*New Men in the Roman Senate* [Oxford: Oxford

Caesar was the obvious *popularis* model for Octavian, but, as has often been said, he was also something of an embarrassment and was therefore systematically played down in the publicity and literature of the Augustan age. What is not so often noticed is that Caesar's domestic policies and *popularis* politics are *particularly* ignored in early imperial literature. Even Velleius Paterculus, who, as a historian, had some obligation to recount his political and legislative activities, prefers to dwell on his escape from the pirates, his *clementia*, and his triumphs. The brief disparaging remark of Seneca, 'ille publicola, ille popularis', makes explicit what was clearly the attitude of earlier imperial writers.[1]

Caesar's dictatorship had exposed the difficulty faced by a *popularis* who finds himself in autocratic control of the state. The trouble principally concerned the tribunate, one of the key elements in the *popularis ratio*, whose prerogatives were both a means and an end in *popularis* politics. Up to his dictatorship, Caesar had pursued the longest consistently *popularis* career Rome had ever seen. One of his pretexts for invading Italy was the senate's determination to ignore the veto of the tribunes M. Antonius and Q. Cassius. But within a year, Caesar had threatened to kill a tribune who interposed his sacrosanct body between him and the door of the *aerarium*.[2] Then, in 47 and 45 BCE, he lost his temper with tribunician insolence, until finally in 44 he had two tribunes, who protested that free speech was no more, removed from office by vote of the senate on the proposal of a fellow tribune.[3] This seems an ironic comedown for a man who still perhaps prized his former image enough to accept the right to sit on the tribunician benches and the privilege of *sacrosanctitas* equal to the tribunes.[4]

University Press, 1971], p. 99) points out that in 44 BCE the tribunate, which had no age requirement, would have been attractive to Octavian, who was more than ten years too young to hold a regular magistracy. As *Princeps*: Suet. *Aug.* 89; 31.5. Cicero on the Gracchi: *Off.* 2.43.

1.   E.S. Ramage, 'Augustus' Treatment of Julius Caesar', *Historia* 34 (1985), pp. 223ff. I owe the point about early imperial writers to Laura Duxbury ('Some Attitudes to Julius Caesar in the Roman Republic' [DPhil thesis, Oxford, 1988], pp. 372-77). Sen. *Ben.* 5.16.5.
2.   Cic. *Att.* 10.4; Plut. *Caes.* 35.
3.   Suet. *Divus Julius* 78; Dio Cass. 42.29; 44.10.3.
4.   Dio Cass. 42.20.3; 44.5.2-3.

Octavian learned the lesson of Caesar's assassination in this as in other respects. Very revealing is the one reference, in Augustus's own account of his achievements, to his tribunician power as a basis for action, rather than just as an honour or a date. In chapter 6 of the *Res Gestae*, Augustus says (in an undisputed restoration from the Greek) that he repeatedly refused the offer from the senate and *populus Romanus* to become *curator legum et morum*, which he goes on to describe as a kind of solo censorship (*summa potestate solus*) and contrary to *mos maiorum*. He was surely thinking of the resentment Caesar had provoked by becoming *praefectus moribus*, even in people like Cicero, who had some sympathy with moral reform. His solution was to pass his moral legislation, for which the senate had offered him the *cura*, through his *tribunicia potestas*. The *forum ipsum ac rostra*, in Seneca's phrase, from which the *Leges Iuliae* were passed, no doubt seemed less autocratic and censorious.[1] Yet the phrase 'The measures which at that time the senate wanted me to take', occurring immediately before the mention of *tribunicia potestas*, and the reference immediately after to the colleagues in that position whom Augustus requested and received from the senate,[2] make it hard to agree with Lacey that 'here perhaps is a glimpse of the people's protector'. Lacey tried to defend this suggestion on the grounds that the moral legislation 'curbed the ability of the rich to dispose of their property', but, after all, the regulations on adultery and marriage at least reached far down the social ladder, while those concerning inheritance affected people with capital worth only a quarter of the equestrian census.[3]

In Syme's sinister formulation, 'The two pillars of his rule,

1. *Res Gestae* 6: '(1)...senatu populoque Romano consentientibus ut curator legum et morum summa potestate solus crearer, nullum magistratum contra morem maiorum delatum recepi. (2) quae tum per me geri senatus voluit, per tribuniciam potestatem perfeci, cuius potestatis conlegam et ipse ultro quinquiens a senatu depoposci et accepi.'; Caesar: Cic. *Fam.* 9.15.5; Suet. *Iul.* 76; Sen. *Ben.* 6.32.1.
   2. To the same period belongs the inscription recording the senatorial decrees that authorized the secular games of 17 BCE, where the *tribunicia potestas* of Augustus and Agrippa is mentioned as well as their membership of the quindecimviral priestly college which gave the games (*CIL* 6.32323 ll. 52, 150; cf. *RG* 22.2).
   3. W.K. Lacey, '*Summi fastigii vocabulum*: the Story of a Title', *JRS* 69 (1979), p. 29.

proconsular *imperium* and the tribunician powers, were the Revolution itself—the Army and the People. On them stood the military and monarchic demagogue'. Yet Augustus, while omitting all explicit reference to the *imperium*, did not hesitate to advertise the tribunician power in his self-commemoration. The one apparently had ideological value which the other lacked, but of what kind?[1] According to the *popularis ratio*, the tribunate is there to diminish and control the *consulare imperium* and the *potentia senatus*. When Polybius analysed the Roman Republican constitution as the mixed constitution of Greek political theory, he saw the tribunes as having a duty to uphold the interests of the people against opposition from magistrates and senate. Cicero, as an admirer of the mixed constitution, had defended the tribunate as providing the element of popular liberty essential to it in a controlled form.[2] In *De Legibus* he argued that, without the belief in their equality that this office gave them, the people would be less willing to accept the authority of the senate. Cicero is here engaged in a debate with his brother Quintus, who has been defending the laws of Sulla 'which took from the plebeian tribunes the power of doing mischief and left them only the power to bring help'. The *iniuriae faciendae potestas* here refers principally to their quasi-magisterial powers of legislation; the *potestas auxilii ferendi* refers to the *ius auxilii* and the *intercessio*. These were the powers, Sulla could argue, that were most closely related to the original functions of the tribunes, who had been created by the *plebs* to protect their rights and welfare against the power of their rulers and were themselves protected by the solemn oath, taken by the *plebs* for themselves and their descendants, to avenge any injury to a tribune.[3]

Octavian's first interest in the tribunician power seems to have been in these defensive attributes, which were less threatening to the senate, yet gave him, along with the accompanying privilege of sitting on the tribunician benches, the tribunician image of protector of the

---

1. Syme, *Roman Revolution*, p. 337. Cf. the way in which Tacitus (*Ann.* 1.7) regards Tiberius' use of the *tribunicia potestas* as compatible with being 'ambiguus imperandi', while his use of the *imperium*, which had also been given to him in Augustus's lifetime, is to act 'ut imperator'.
2. Cic. *Rep.* 2.57.9, cf. Tac. *Ann.* 4.32; Polyb. 6.15.7.
3. Cic. *Leg.* 3.23-24, cf. Livy 2.33; 3.55.

underdog, welcome to one who held at the same time the dictatorial office of triumvir. The non-provocative character of the first tribunician attribute he accepted, that of *sacrosanctitas*, which was offered in 36 BCE, is indicated by its being conferred by the senate: its later confirmation by a law of the people is listed by Augustus among his religious honours. Moreover, the non-political significance (in Republican terms) of the *sacrosanctitas* was underlined when it was granted in 29 BCE to Octavia and Livia.[1]

When Dio comes to his general account of the powers of the *Princeps* under the year 23 BCE, it is the *sacrosanctitas* and the *intercessio* that he emphasizes. As for the *ius auxilii*, it is the power that Tacitus indicates in his famous description of Augustus as 'satisfied with the powers of a tribune for defending the plebs'.[2] Whether or not such a power was accepted by Octavian after Actium in 30 BCE, the judicial rights that were granted at the same time—to hold trials on appeal and to intervene with a vote of acquittal in trials before the ordinary courts—are in themselves related to the tribune's *ius auxilii*.[3]

The related right of *intercessio*, the veto, Octavian acquired either at the same time or in 23 BCE, when he finally accepted the full *tribunicia potestas* for life from the senate, a grant also confirmed by a law of the people.[4] One reason why the senate offered him the position of tribune for life, as Cassius Dio puts it (perhaps correctly), was clearly to replace the rights of convening the senate and initiating legislation that he would otherwise have lost when he laid down the office of consul.[5]

1. Dio Cass. 49.15.5; 49.16 (a less plausible tradition in Appian, *Civil Wars* 5.132 and Orosius 6.18.34); *Res Gestae* 10; Dio Cass. 49.38.1.

2. Dio Cass. 53.17; Tac. *Ann*. 1.2: 'ad tuendam plebem tribunicio iure contentum'. The allusion is clarified by Florus (2.1.1): 'specie quidem plebis tuendae, cuius in auxilium comparata est' in a passage condemning tribunician legislation.

3. Dio Cass. 51.19.6, though his assertion has been doubted; A. Lintott, 'Provocatio', *ANRW* 2.1 (1972), pp. 263-67.

4. *Res Gestae* 10; Dio Cass. 53.32.5. Lacey ('Augustus and the Senate: 23 BC', *Antichthon* 19 [1985], pp. 57-67) argues that *RG* 10 refers to a grant of *tribunicia potestas* by the people alone in 30 BCE, which Augustus simply retained in preference to the office of tribune offered by the senate in 23 BCE, but he overlooks the reason for the emphasis on the senate in relation to tribunician colleagues in *RG* 6 (above, p. 26 n.1), and hence makes too much of its omission in *RG* 10.

5. Shown by the upgrading of the tribunician power, which he accepted, to give him priority in these respects over the senior magistrates (Dio Cass. 53.32.5; 54.3.4).

Why he accepted the *tribunicia potestas* in particular is unclear. It was simple and convenient for putting legislation to the people, while the question of immediate and repeated iteration was less certainly against Republican rules than in the case of the proper magistracies. In any case, Augustus, who as a patrician could not take the actual office, could avoid raising the issue. The image of the tribunate was further blurred by his eventually having one colleague like an ordinary magistrate (whereas there were ten tribunes), though, unlike a magistrate, Augustus's colleague in the tribunician power was appointed by the senate. Eventually, by being used to number the years of his reign and then, from 4 CE on, to designate his successor, it became the 'summi fastigii vocabulum'. It might almost be said that the greatest advantage of the *tribunicia potestas* was that nobody knew what the rules were: in Syme's phrase, 'The *tribunicia potestas* was elusive and formidable'.[1]

Was its convenience and vagueness, combined with the air it imparted of non-autocratic *clementia*, the whole reason for taking it? Certainly Augustus and his successors made little practical use of the *tribunicia potestas*. The *sacrosanctitas*, previously useless in protecting Caesar's life, is alluded to only in its puzzling use by Tiberius outside of Rome in Rhodes to defend himself. Indeed the Emperor Vitellius is said to have applied to the *ius auxilii* of the regular tribunes in office to protect himself against the contempt shown him in the senate by Helvidius Priscus.[2] Of the emperor's use of his own *ius auxilii* little is heard. As for legislation, Claudius, like Augustus, initiated *plebiscita*, but comitial legislation soon petered out under the Principate.[3]

In any case, little suggests that this most *popularis* of powers was invoked to secure the support of the people against the senate. It was probably the people of whom Augustus was thinking when he surrendered the consulship in 23 BCE outside Rome in order to avoid opposition, for in 22, frightened by adverse portents, they first forced the senate to offer him the dictatorship with its 24 lictors and then, after he refused to accept the consulship for life, pressed on him the consular insignia.[4] Clearly the people felt insecure when he was no

1. Syme, *Roman Revolution*, p. 377.
2. Suet. *Tib.* 11; cf. Tac. *Hist.* 2.91.
3. Tac. *Ann.* 11.14.
4. Dio 53.32.3; 54.1 (cf. *RG* 5). A.H.M. Jones ('The Imperium of Augustus',

longer seen to be holding the supreme magistracy. Hence, not surprisingly, Augustus made little use of the tribunician image, that is, the lack of magisterial insignia and the use of the low benches (*subsellia*) instead of the magisterial *sella*. In 19 BCE he accepted the insignia of a consul, complete with an escort of lictors, which entitled him to sit in the senate on a curule chair set between the consuls: Claudius too, when he did sit on a tribunician bench, still sat, not with the tribunes, but between the consuls.[1]

Nor did Augustus retain his residence in the Forum: he moved to the Palatine—the opposite move from the one Caius Gracchus had made in his second tribunate.[2] In the end the people got used to his looking like a consul, while numbering his reign according to his *tribunicia potestas*—a system of dating, however, that was not allowed to replace the dating by *consules ordinarii* on public and private monuments: not even, for the most part, on his own *Res Gestae*.[3] We have seen that Augustus was careful not to represent his tribunician legislation as *popularis* in character. Similarly, in the few cases where we see the *Princeps* using his tribunician veto, he is mostly exercising clemency towards upper class defendants in senatorial trials.[4]

Cicero, in the passage of *De Legibus* already discussed (p. 27) notes that the ability of one tribune to stymie the others made the office less troublesome than his brother thinks. Is it too cynical to suggest that Augustus wanted the *tribunicia potestas* largely because his mere possession of it would prevent, in an inoffensive way, the real tribunes

in *Studies in Roman Government and Law* [Oxford: Basil Blackwell, 1960], pp. 10-12) suggested that Augustus assumed the tribunician power in 23 BCE which was 'neither very essential nor very adequate' as a gesture, a guarantee of protection to the *plebs* and a threat of something more demagogic to the Optimates, but he admits that, as the immediate sequel showed, the *plebs* did not consider it adequate. In fact, Augustus seems to have anticipated their discontent by resigning the consulship outside of the city. Moreover, the history of his tribunician powers, as described above, counts against his having such a motive.

1. Dio Cass. 54.10; Suet. *Claud.* 23 reading '<sella> triburniciove subsellio' (cf. Dio 60.16.3).

2. Suet. *Aug.* 72; cf. Plut. *C. Gracchus* 12.

3. Tac. *Ann.* 3.57; see Lacey, '*Summi fastigii vocabulum*', p. 33; and p. 32, n. 3 below.

4. Tac. *Ann.* 3.70; 14.48; 16.11. At 1.10 the senate expects Tiberius, if he refuses its decree granting him full powers, to use his veto. In Dio Cass. 60.4.5, Claudius uses it to protect his predecessor's memory, a form of clemency.

from fomenting and leading political opposition? Caesar's experience may again have weighed with him in this, and Octavian himself had removed a tribune from office in 29 BCE. Tribunes continued to exercise the veto in civil suits and against legislation, usually on behalf of the underdog, such as actors and defendants,[1] but it is perhaps significant that the last attested instance of its use in a political context was an act of sycophancy towards the emperor, just as Vitellius as *Princeps* appealed to the *ius auxilii* of the tribunes to protect himself.[2] Hardly any tribunician legislation is attested except the emperor's, and what there is tends to be measures in his honour which he himself could not propose, such as the idea of renaming the sixth month after Augustus in 8 BCE. Instead we find the tribunes in 2 BCE being sent to approach the *Princeps*, when there was a popular demand for reform, and in Pliny's day the vociferous Nigrinus proposed that the *Princeps* be asked to initiate measures to curb electoral abuses.[3]

The *Princeps* not only formally outclassed ordinary tribunes by his privileges in convening and proposing: his mere possession of the same powers put theirs in the shade. The tribunate became, as Pliny describes it, an 'empty title', a 'sine honore nomen'. The senate gleefully curtailed tribunician prerogatives at the instigation of, and in the interests of, the higher magistrates.[4] Not surprisingly, candidates for the office were hard to find under Augustus, as indeed for those other officers of the *plebs*, the aediles, who had lost their right to give games and their judicial functions to the praetors, their responsibility for fire-fighting and corn distribution to equestrian and senatorial officials. We see them both acting as representatives of the *plebs* in a ceremonial context, e.g. accompanying envoys from the senate and *equites* on a mission of congratulation to Tiberius and Sejanus. Perhaps the only thing that kept these positions going was the fact that they were made alternative but compulsory stages in all but the patrician *cursus honorum*.[5]

The imperial *tribunicia potestas* was in fact deeply subversive of the

1. Dio Cass. 52.42.3; actors: Tac. *Ann.* 1.77; 13.28; defendants: 6.47, cf. 16.26.
2. Tac. *Hist.* 4.9; 2.91.
3. Macrob. *Sat.* 1.12.35 (cf. Dio Cass. 55.6.6-7); Dio Cass. 55.9.10; Pliny *Ep.* 5.13.
4. Pliny *Ep.* 1.23; Tac. *Ann.* 13.28.
5. Dio Cass. 53.2; 58.2.8; cf. *Res Gestae* 12.1.

tribunate itself, just as the imperial *appellatio* 'took over' the *provocatio ad populum*. It is, therefore, not surprising to find Augustus, in the first chapter of the *Res Gestae*, adopting Cicero's version of his actions in 44–43 BCE and using the old Republican slogan, 'rem publicam a dominatione factionis oppressam in libertatem vindicavi', in the Optimate sense to describe his championship of the senate. The oppressor to whom he alludes was Antony who, caught between senatorial disapproval and Caesarian competition, had turned to *popularis* measures and methods.[1] In fact, with the end of the Republic, not only did *popularis* politics disappear, along with all real political conflict, but the use of *popularis* slogans ceased as well.[2] This was their last appearance, and it was not Octavian, but his opponent, who was using them.

The Princeps *as 'Patron of the* Plebs'?

It was characteristic of the *popularis ratio* in the Republic to advocate that material benefits be conferred on the *plebs* as a matter of right and therefore be funded from the *aerarium*. It was characteristic of the *Princeps*, however, that he displayed *liberalitas* from his own resources. The emperor's generosity might seem to be an inheritance from the *principes viri*, rather than the tribunes, of the late Republic.[3]

More justice might seem to be done to this relationship *de haut en bas* by Yavetz's description of the *Princeps* as the 'patron of the *plebs*'. This notion of patron is not, of course, the concept we find in

1. *Res Gestae* 1.1, which Wirszubski (*Libertas as a Political Idea*, pp. 100-105) compared with Cic. *Phil.* 3.5. See also H. Braunert 'Zum Eingangssatz der res gestae', pp. 343-46, who rejects the idea that Octavian was here following Caesar's description of his activities in *Bellum Civile* 1.22.5 as 'ut. . .populum Romanum factione paucorum oppressum in libertatem vindicaret'.

2. J. Martin, 'Die Popularen der Späten Republik' (Inaug. Diss., Freiburg-i-Br., 1962).

3. Augustus's liberality, as documented in the *Res Gestae*, is not associated with the *tribunicia potestas*. In 15 both his tribunician power and his own consulships are mentioned, probably to emphasize that Augustus was not a *privatus* when he exercised his beneficence, for distributions by private citizens were traditionally regarded with suspicion (Cic. *Off.* 1.58; Livy 5.13-15, cf. Dio Cass. 53.28.1-2 where Augustus, even though consul, asks the senate in 24 BCE for permission to give a *congiarium*).

the ancient sources: indeed Suetonius makes it clear that Augustus was a *patronus* to particular free-born individuals and to his own freedmen, as men of standing had always been, and that he defended his own clients in court and was clement to his own freedmen. Pliny similarly distinguishes Trajan's *clientes*, not only from senators and *equites*, but from the crowd of bystanders who surrounded him on his first return to Rome as Princeps.

What Yavetz meant to convey by saying, 'With the commencement of the Principate, the emperors became in a sense patroni of the entire urban *plebs*', was the notion that the *Princeps* showered benefits on the *plebs* with the deliberate aim of freeing the common people from the *clientela* of the aristocratic families and binding them to himself instead: 'henceforth the *Plebs* in Rome were to have only one patron'.[1]

There is some truth in the idea that aristocratic families with their large followings became less a feature of the Roman scene as time went on, though the 'pars populi integra et magnis domibus adnexa' was still a factor to be reckoned with in 69 CE, according to Tacitus. The same author, in his famous passage on the change of lifestyle that took place at that time, notes that the old aristocratic houses had mostly perished because they attracted adverse imperial attention through their conspicuous consumption which attracted large *clientelae* of *plebs, socii* (provincial subjects) and *regna* (client kingdoms). But Tacitus does *not* suggest that this effect was brought about by the deliberate desire of the Julio-Claudian *Principes* to destroy the aristocratic *clientelae* and absorb them themselves. Even the bad emperors who killed off rich and outstanding families were only concerned with aristocratic *clientelae* as one sign of the aristocratic pre-eminence that they felt threatened rivalry and competition with themselves.[2]

Finally, not only does Yavetz's notion of the *Princeps* as unique patron of the *plebs* lack support in the ancient sources: it runs counter to the modern idea of a patronage system which, according to sociologists, involved 'competition between patrons for clients and the ability to change patrons or to have multiple allegiances to them'.[3]

1.   Suet. *Aug.* 56; 67; Pliny *Pan.* 23.1; Z. Yavetz, *Plebs and Princeps* (Oxford: Clarendon Press, 1969), p. 90.

2.   Tac. *Hist.* 1.4; *Ann.* 3.55.

3.   T. Johnson and C. Dandeker, in A. Wallace-Hadrill (ed.), *Patronage in*

There is no harm in describing the *Princeps*, in his role as benefactor of the *plebs* of Rome, as their patron, provided one makes it clear, as does Veyne in *Bread and Circuses*, that this does not denote a real social relationship but is a metaphor. Like Cicero's description of the government of the Roman empire as a 'patrocinium orbis terrarum' or Veyne's own alternative formulations, 'patron of the state' and 'patron of the empire', the metaphor points to the voluntary use of personal resources to help and protect those inferior in power and wealth.[1]

Having rejected the tribunician power and the notion of unique patron as the ideological basis of the *Princeps*' relation to the *plebs*, we might go further and question whether Yavetz was right to suggest that the benefits the *Princeps* conferred on the *plebs* were socially divisive and that the manner in which he conferred them was competitive with the role of the aristocratic houses on the social scene

Bread and Circuses

The closest we come to an analysis of imperial policy towards the *plebs* in an ancient author is the famous passage in a letter of Fronto addressed to Lucius Verus about the middle of the second century CE. It elevates Juvenal's 'bread and circuses' into the highest principle of political wisdom ('summa civilis scientiae ratio'):

> In the arts of peace scarcely anyone has excelled or even equalled Trajan in his popularity with the people (*populus*). He did not neglect actors or other performers of the stage, the circus or the amphitheatre, since he knew that the two primary ways of retaining a hold on the *populus Romanus* are the corn-dole (*annona*) and the shows (*spectacula*), that a government wins approval for amusements as well as more serious things and that neglect of serious matters brings the greater loss, neglect of entertainments the greater discontent. (Fronto, *Princ. Hist.* 17).[2]

He goes on to point out that *congiaria* provide a weaker incentive than shows because they only conciliate the *plebs frumentaria* (those on the

Roman Society (London and New York: Routledge, 1989), p. 240.

    1.   P. Veyne, *Bread and Circuses* (London: Penguin, 1990; English abridgement of the original French edn, 1976), e.g. pp. 246-47; 255-57; 321 (cf. 346, 391), 330, and see p. 37 n. 3 below; Cic. *Off.* 2.27.

    2.   Juvenal *Sat.* 10.81; Fronto, *Princ. Hist.* 17.

corn register), whereas shows appeal to the *universus populus*.

Tacitus, like Fronto, tends to restrict imperial concern with the corn supply to the *plebs frumentaria*, because they are both thinking principally of the corn dole and the periodic free distributions, which could be thought of as peculiarly dependent on the emperor's presence. For emperors saw that the dole was maintained even if the usual sources fell short, out of their own bounty if necessary, as Augustus advertised in *Res Gestae*.[1] Nero only discontinued them in 64 CE because the general hardship caused by the Great Fire in Rome made it necessary to release all stored corn onto the market in order to keep the market price low, and that was doubtless a temporary measure.[2]

The corn dole, however, by no means exhausted the responsibilities undertaken by the *Princeps* in regard to the corn supply. Tiberius reminded the senate how onerous was the obligation borne by every *Princeps* to see that the city was supplied: 'This worry belongs to the *Princeps*', he said. It was in fact a responsibility more likely to earn him popular abuse if he failed than credit if he succeeded. He was the one who was shouted at in the theatre when prices were high; he was the one who was pelted with stale bread when scarcity was rumoured.[3] Even the engineering projects undertaken by Claudius to improve Ostia harbour, and by Nero to construct an inland waterway along the west coast of Italy from Lake Avernus, to protect ships bringing corn to Rome, met with hostility and incomprehension.[4]

These long-term projects and general responsibilities were not intended to benefit only the *plebs frumentaria*, the quarter of a million poor on the list of corn recipients, nor indeed only the lower classes of the urban population. They benefited all the inhabitants of the city. It is true that the rich could get away more easily and retreat to their country villas in times of scarcity, but that was not true of the magistrates or of other senators and *equites* when the senate and courts were in session or they had other official duties. Augustus

---

1. Tac. *Ann.* 15.36; *Res Gestae* 15; 18.
2. Dio Cass. 62.18.5; cf. Tac. *Ann.* 15.72; Suet. *Nero* 10. See M. Griffin, *Nero, the End of a Dynasty* (London: Batsford, 1984), pp. 106-107.
3. Tac. *Ann.* 3.54; 6.13; 12.43; Suet. *Claud.* 18.
4. Pliny *NH* 14.61; Tac. *Ann.* 15.42; *ILS* 207, 5797a; cf. Pliny *Ep.* 8.17. See Griffin, *Nero*, pp. 108, 262 n. 50.

speaks in his *Res Gestae* of liberating the *civitas universa* from fear and danger by taking charge of the corn *supply*, while Suetonius says that Augustus took care to administer the corn *dole* in such a way as to consider the interests of farmers and corn-dealers as well as the populace.[1] This follows citation of a written pronouncement of Augustus, at the time of the great famine of 6 CE, saying that he had thought of abolishing the distributions because they discouraged agriculture and hence worked against solving the general problem of supply, but gave up the idea, knowing that they would one day be restored *per ambitionem*, presumably the desire for popular favour of some succeeding *Princeps*. Though no doubt his hesitation was not real, the pronouncement is noteworthy and supports Suetonius's idea that he behaved like a *salubris* rather than an *ambitiosus princeps*. But even Nero, as we have seen, put the problem of feeding the population in general ahead of the maintenance of the dole.

Fronto's view about shows being pleasing to the whole population is not easy to deny. Though philosophical souls and intellectual snobs had objections to gladiatorial games, the importance attached by senators and *equites* to their special seats in the theatre and circus suggests that this was not the usual attitude among the upper classes.[2]

When Tacitus recounts, in succession, first that Nero provided special seats for *equites* at the circus and then that 'illustrious women and senators were degraded by going into the arena', he makes us wonder if even Nero set out to please the *plebs* at the expense of the upper orders. Dio stresses his use of compulsion in securing upper-class participation in musical and gymnastic performances, and the delight of the spectators at the humiliation of their betters, especially when Nero forbade the use of masks.[3] Yet the same crowds, 'pervilia et sordida plebs' in Suetonius's phrase, enjoyed watching their emperor perform 'per incuriam publici flagitii', according to Tacitus.[4] However Dio felt about it, the truth may be that the chance of seeing the emperor and noted celebrities perform just made the shows more exciting: indeed Suetonius seems to put exhibiting 400

1.   *Res Gestae* 5.2; Suet. *Aug.* 42.
2.   E. Rawson, '*Discrimina ordinum*: The *Lex Julia* Theatralis', *Papers of the British School at Rome* 55 (1987), pp. 83-114.
3.   Tac. *Ann.* 15.32; Dio Cass. 61.19; 61.17.
4.   Suet. *Nero* 21, 22; Tac. *Ann.* 16.4.

senators and 600 knights in the arena on the same level with showing off monsters in salt water. Even Tacitus admits that compulsion and bribery of the upper orders by the emperor was not always necessary, for, as Augustan and Tiberian legislation attests, the problem in the early Principate was to keep men and women of high birth *off* the stage and *out* of the arena.[1]

In the early part of his reign, Nero had, like Augustus, found popularity with the *plebs* perfectly compatible with deference towards the upper classes. The 'good' *Princeps* showed *civilitas* and *comitas* to all orders, respecting the social hierarchy. In the case of the *plebs*, what was expected, in addition to general accessibiliity, was that the *Princeps* should enjoy the games without losing his dignity or showing excessive bloodthirstiness, and that he should allow free expression of public opinion.[2] But emperors disciplined those who insulted members of the upper orders there, while senate and *Princeps* joined in repressing brawls and riots.[3]

There is, moreover, a crucial weakness in the view that the *Principes* set out to curb the influence of anyone who tried to obtain clients among the common people. This is the fact that the *Princeps* did not, indeed could not, confer all his *beneficia* personally and that, as his agents, he customarily chose members of the upper orders: only 'bad' emperors used women and freedmen. This notion, which sociologists call 'second-order patronage', is developed by Saller in his book on *Personal Patronage under the Early Empire*. He points out that, by using senators and *equites* as 'brokers', the *Princeps* accomplished two things: a wide distribution of benefits, and the conciliation of those in a position to do him harm by virtue of their monopoly of military commands.[4]

---

1. Suet. *Nero* 12; Tac. *Ann.* 14.15; cf. 14.21. See B.M. Levick, 'The *Senatus Consultum* from Larinum', *JRS* 73 (1983), pp. 97-115.

2. Tac. *Ann.* 1.76; Suet. *Dom.* 13.

3. Tac. *Ann.* 11.13; 1.77. Veyne (*Bread and Circuses*, pp. 406-408) realizes that 'sultanism', whereby bad emperors tyrannized the senate and appealed to the *plebs*, was not implicit in Roman imperial beneficence to the *plebs*.

4. R. Saller, *Personal Patronage under the Early Empire* (Cambridge: Cambridge University Press, 1982), pp. 68, 73-75. P. Garnsey and R. Saller (*The Roman Empire* [London: Duckworth, 1987], pp. 149-50) try to combine this notion with Yavetz's view that the tribunate and patronage as a specified social relationship were the ideological bases of imperial generosity to the *plebs*.

In considering the application of this idea to the relations of *plebs* and *Princeps*, we have only to note that Augustus, alive to the traditional political importance of the corn dole, entrusted it to ex-praetorian *praefecti frumenti dandi* chosen by lot from a list of nominees drawn up by the magistrates, their duties being regulated by senatorial decree.[1] As I have already noted, the aediles lost their other functions, not to the emperor directly but to equestrian *praefecti* and to senatorial boards who were responsible for the care of the streets and aqueducts on terms laid down by senatorial decree.[2] A glance at Frontinus's *de aquis*, written under Nerva, shows how much power the senior senators who served as *curatores aquarum* had: though the *Princeps* reserved to himself the right of granting water rights, the *curatores* let contracts for repairs, settled liability to payment for water rights, and exercised jurisdiction in connection with the regulations passed from time to time, mostly by the senate. Frontinus notes that, when he was uncovering long-standing violations of existing regulations, he was the *causa impetrati beneficii*, the mediator in securing for some the pardon of the *Princeps*.[3]

Members of the upper orders, notably *equites*, also served as organizers of the emperor's games, and might have their names inscribed on the *tesserae* that perhaps controlled entrance to the games.[4] On the famous inscription honouring the memory of the ambitious Q. Veranius (consul in 49 CE), he is described as 'presiding at his own request over the *Princeps'* games, at which he was the agent of his generosity '. At this date, probably 37 CE, Veranius was an ex-consul and about to become governor of Britain.[5]

Though not concerned with the *plebs* of Rome, I cannot refrain from adducing here, as an illustration of the continuing importance of aristocratic *clientelae*, and in the precise context of imperial *beneficia*, the inscription honouring Pomponius Bassus. The municipality of Ferentinum sent representatives to him to praise his work in implementing the alimentary scheme. While praising Trajan's

1. Dio 54.1.4; 54.17.1.
2. P.A. Brunt, 'The Role of the Senate in the Augustan Regime', *CQ* 34 (1984), pp. 423-44; Frontinus *De Aquis* 2.99.
3. Frontinus *De Aquis* 2.99-100; 103-104; 110.
4. Tac. *Ann.* 13.11; Pliny *NH* 37.45.
5. Smallwood, *Documents Illustrating the Principates of Gaius, Claudius and Nero*, §232c.

generosity and care for the future of 'his Italy', they invite Bassus to become the town's patron, taking it 'in clientelam amplissimae domus suae'.[1]

Why Benefit the Plebs?

Another way of uncovering the ideology that informed the *Princeps'* relationship to the *plebs* is to ask: 'Why were the *plebs* worth cultivating by the *Princeps*?' As Tacitus notes, they were no longer a political force under the Principate.[2] The *Princeps* never required a renewal of his powers after the initial formal ratification by the assembly, and after 14 CE, except for a brief period under Caligula, his favoured candidates for office were not at the mercy of the free vote of the electoral assemblies. Popular legislation rapidly declined, the emperor's own pronouncements and *senatus consulta* gradually assuming the force of law.

The hatred of the *plebs* could not topple Tiberius; their love could not save Nero. To stay in control, the *Princeps* needed to have the loyalty of the army commanders, of the praetorian prefects, of the soldiers themselves, and of his household staff whose physical proximity gave opportunity for assassination. It was only in combination with troops in Rome that the *plebs* could be thought of as a possible support in elevating Calpurnius Piso to the throne in 64, though Tiberius apparently thought that, properly led, they might

---

1. *ILS* 6106. In 32 BCE Octavian excused Bononia from taking the oath of loyalty to his *partes* because the town was in the *clientela* of the Antonii. Suet. *Aug.* 17.2 makes it clear, however, that the conflict of loyalty only existed because Octavian and Antony were opponents in a civil war. That, as Suetonius implies, the relationship with Octavian established by the oath was not *clientela*, is now confirmed by the new oath of 6/5 BCE to Augustus and his sons and grandson from Baetica (J. Gonzalez, 'The First Oath Pro Salute Augusti Found in Baetica', *Zeitschrift für Papyrologie und Epigraphik* 72 [1988], pp. 113ff.): it not only preserves the military language of the original, but also speaks of making the *inimici eorum partibus* one's own.

2. Tac. *Ann.* 4.33.2. For Veyne (*Bread and Circuses,* pp. 259-61; 374; 383-85), the short answer to the question is 'to display his generosity, using the city of Rome as his stage or court'. He rightly rejects (p. 466 n. 305) Yavetz's idea that emperors wanted the support the *plebs* could give them, but wrongly ignores, as I hope will emerge, the importance of displaying the city itself with a view to impressing subjects and inspiring imitation.

cause enough disruption to help Macro and the *vigiles* hold off any attempt by Sejanus to rally the praetorian guard.[1]

Public disorder might, in fact, seem to be the bogey that both the *Princeps* and the upper orders together sought to banish by ingratiation and largesse. Seneca paints a vivid picture of what might happen if the corn supply was neglected: 'destruction, famine, and what follows famine—general revolution. Those in charge would be faced with stones, sword and fire'.[2] It was for this reason that meetings and meeting-places were suspect: hence *collegia* were controlled and discouraged by all emperors, taverns subjected to regulations designed to make them less attractive, theatres provided with guards of soldiers, and actors occasionally banished when the hooliganism of their fans got out of control.

And yet—though plebeian riots certainly had nuisance value, they could be controlled by force. In fact, the threat of force was generally enough. The comparative peacefulness of Rome in the early Empire is rightly ascribed to the deterrent effect of the large forces stationed in, or on the fringes of, the city: possibly six thousand men in the *vigiles* and four to six thousand in the urban cohorts in addition to nine thousand, at times twelve thousand, praetorians (at least on paper)—one soldier for every fifty people on an estimate of one million for the urban population. Even on the most conservative estimate (praetorian cohorts of five hundred, not a thousand), we have one soldier for every hundred people. Tacitus, as Syme noted, emphasized the new situation by replacing the traditional formula 'senatus populusque' with 'senatus milesque et populus'.[3] Nor did emperors hesitate to use these forces against the mob,[4] and, in the period after Gaius's murder, the consuls used them to stop looting.[5] The emperor himself was regularly attended by an armed escort, usually plain-clothes praetorians.[6]

Lampoons and grumbling at street corners, or rather in the large

1. Tac. *Ann.* 15.59; cf. 6.23.
2. Sen. *Brev. Vit.* 18.
3. R. Syme, *Tacitus* (Oxford: Clarendon Press, 1958), I, p. 412, on 'senatus milesque et populus'. For the calculations of numbers, see D. Kennedy, 'Some Observations on the Praetorian Guard', *Ancient Society* 9 (1978), pp. 275-301.
4. Tac. *Ann.* 1.7; Suet. *Tib.* 37; Dio Cass. 59.28.11; Tac. *Ann.* 14.7; 11.61; 15.58.
5. Dio Cass. 59.30.3.
6. Tac. *Ann.* 16.27; *Hist.* 1.38; Pliny *Pan.* 23.4.

and convenient gathering places in which the poorer inhabitants of a Mediterranean city spend most of their time, were hardly a serious threat. The point I am trying to make is that the *Princeps* did not have to conciliate the *plebs* if he was prepared to hold them down by force (as Tiberius was), using the praetorian cohorts, exiling actors and leaders of their fan clubs. Even when he was dead, the *plebs* were thwarted of their plan to burn the body in an amphitheatre in order to make the stingy emperor provide at least one show.[1] Most *Principes* preferred to conciliate them. They respected the tradition whereby complaints were aired at the games, and the *Princeps* listened and responded. When we read of demands about taxes and the corn supply being voiced there and redress often obtained, it is hard to believe that the amusements were largely intended as a means of diverting popular enthusiasm into non-political channels, as the pantomime actor Pylades suggested to Augustus.[2] Indeed it might be said that, through their generosity in giving games, the *Principes* gave more opportunities for shouting matches, and indeed for riots, than was necessary. Of the places Cicero lists as those where the will of the people could be known—the public assemblies, the elections, and the games—only the third now remained, but the emperors allowed it full scope.[3]

Why then did the *Princeps* spend so much money and effort on feeding, housing and entertaining the urban *plebs*? A partial answer lies in the Republican tradition of aristocratic largessse, to which at least the early *Principes*, being themselves of that class and inheriting such traditions, naturally subscribed.

Augustus's allegiance to this Republican tradition is clear in the forms his generosity took, which included the standard types of *liberalitas* and *largitio* enumerated by Lucius Crassus in his famous speech of 106 BCE and by Cicero in *De Officiis*: that is, help to impoverished senators and *amici*, public works, games and distributions: only paying ransom to pirates is omitted, as Augustus had largely done away with them. Also Republican is the way he

1. Suet. *Tib.* 37; 75.
2. Dio Cass. 54.17.5.
3. Cic. *Sest.* 106. See A. Cameron, *Circus Factions* (Oxford: Clarendon Press, 1976), pp. 155-61; J. Deininger, 'Brot und Spiele. Tacitus und die Entpolisierung der plebs urbana', *Gymnasium* 86 (1979), pp. 287-303.

records his expenditure on the state and Roman people in the central chapters of the *Res Gestae* (15–24), specifying booty as the source of his spending on buildings and largesse to soldiers and *plebs*, indicating that he gave the official games or *ludi* as a magistrate, the gladiatorial games and nautical exhibitions (*munera*) as a private citizen.[1] Augustus's munificence naturally exceeded that of his Republican predecessors, and it was important that it should, for, if the Principate itself was accepted by the upper orders as the nearest thing to the Republic compatible with stability and peace, the justification for its tenure by any particular individual rested on his ability and willingness to shine in the traditional ways expected of a senator, a magistrate, and a commander of legions. To be sure, Augustus had taken certain steps to ensure that the *Princeps* was clearly first in these respects: he had, for example, put an end to triumphs outside the imperial house, which ensured its monopoly of booty. His successors found other ways of using political power to increase their revenues.

However, just as this imperial generosity was not confined to the lower orders, so it did not extinguish the generosity and popularity of the upper orders, whom it often involved. Augustus in fact initially encouraged the survival of the Republican tradition among the senators themselves, urging triumphators to spend money on public buildings and roads. He also left the name of the original builders attached to buildings he restored: it was only a Domitian who departed from that tradition.[2] Even after the non-imperial triumphs ended, and with them the erection of public buildings in Rome by men outside the imperial house, they could still restore those constructed by their ancestors. Augustus gave games in the name of other magistrates who were away or lacked the means.[3] Even Nero finally contributed prizes for chariot races when the extravagance of the imperial games encouraged the managers of the circus factions to refuse to provide drivers for less than a full day's racing: one of the emperor's favourites, the senator Fabricius Veiento, had registered his protest

1. Cic. *Brut.* 164ff.; *Off.* 2.55-64.
2. Tac. *Ann.* 3.72.1; Suet. *Aug.* 29, 30, cf. *Dom.* 5. The role of the traditional Roman priesthoods in the euergetism of the senatorial class is stressed by R. Gordon, ('The Veil of Power', in *Pagan Priests* [ed. M. Beard and J. North, London: Gerald Duckworth, 1990], pp. 223-24).
3. *Res Gestae* 22.2; Suet. *Aug.* 43.

by training dogs to run instead of horses.[1]
But why was such a high level of expenditure on *congiaria*, free distributions, public shows with their free gifts, and public amenities felt to be necessary at all? Why did the *Princeps* not confine his largesse to the soldiers and the upper orders and ensure that the latter did the same? Here a different aspect of Republican tradition can be invoked. Neither the emperor nor the upper orders from which he came saw Rome as a police state. Though Tacitus complains about soldiers in the forum and the senate house, neither the emperor nor his praetorian escort wore military dress in the capital.[2] And indeed, even if the city itself could have been controlled by force, Rome's far-flung provinces could not be, given the size of the territory Rome controlled and the relative meagreness of her military forces.[3] The consent of the governed was necessary, and an awareness on their part that revolt was hopeless. Rome itself was the visible manifestation of that deterrent power. She was the showpiece of the Empire, *regina et domina orbis*, in the words of Julius Frontinus in his work on aqueducts. And that model *curator aquarum* goes on to point out that the maintenance of the water pipes of Rome is the best testimony to the greatness of the Roman Empire.[4]

When embassies and visitors from distant provinces, from client kingdoms, or from places even more remote visited the city, it was important that they see a city of marble with all the cultural and recreational amenities, and an array of citizens in togas, at least in the forum and the theatre,[5] looking like rulers of the world. A shabby, starving and obviously discontented population would not have made a good advertisement for Roman rule and for that *consensus universorum* that the Principate claimed to command.

Yet it is important to remember that those same visitors came from towns, provinces, or kingdoms where the social hierarchy with all its

1. Dio Cass. 61.6; Suet. *Nero* 22.
2. See Griffin, *Nero*, pp. 222-23.
3. On Rome's 'economy of force', see e.g. E.N. Luttwak, *The Grand Strategy of the Roman Empire* (London: The Johns Hopkins University Press, 1976), pp. 17-19.
4. Frontinus *De Aquis* 2.88.1; 119: 'ad tutelam ductuum divertemus cum magnitudinis Romani imperii vel praecipuum sit indicium'.
5. Suet. *Aug.* 40; 44.2.

differentials of rank and obligation were carefully respected and upheld by the Roman government. The claim by Aelius Aristeides, that all people of Rome's world republic received their proper due, finds an echo in Pliny's counsel to a proconsul in Spain to respect the *discrimina ordinum*.[1] Therefore it was appropriate that when these visitors to Rome witnessed a festival or public ceremony, they were left in no doubt that between the *plebs* and the *Princeps* came the knights and senators, wearing their emblems of rank, sitting in their privileged seats, and consuming their larger portions of food.

Calpurnius Siculus describes the first glimpse that a rustic visitor to Rome had of Nero's wooden amphitheatre:

> I saw a structure that rose skyward on interlaced beams and almost looked down on the summit of the Capitoline. Passing up the steps and gently inclining slopes, we came to the seats, where in dark cloaks the baser sort viewed the show close to the women's benches. For the parts exposed to the open sky were thronged by knights or white-robed tribesmen [that is, the Roman *plebs* in their white togas].[2]

Senators who now—in lieu of a triumph—received triumphal regalia by vote of the senate (but on the initiative of the emperor) also received a bronze statue in Rome. Indeed the city was full of statues of senators inscribed with all their offices and honours. Monotonous in their similarity they may have been, as Eck has pointed out, but they would have impressed on visitors to Rome the importance of the senatorial order, even if what the *Princeps* thereby authorized was a display of corporate, rather than individual, eminence.[3]

Similarly, when Augustus organized treasury support for gladiatorial games to be given by the praetors, the element of aristocratic *competition* was reduced: both the number of gladiators and of shows and the permitted level of personal topping-up was

1. *To Rome* 60; Pliny *Ep.* 9.5. Zanker (*Power of Images*, pp. 325, 328) shows how theatres and public squares built in Italy and outside in the Augustan period give visual form to the social hierarchy.
2. Calpurnius Siculus *Ecl.* 7.23: for the reading and interpretation here, see Rawson, 'Discrimina ordinum', p. 95.
3. Dio Cass. 55.10.3 with W. Eck, 'Senatorial Self-Representation', in *Caesar Augustus* (ed. F. Millar and E. Segal; Oxford: Clarendon Press, 1984), p. 129. See also Zanker, *Power of Images*, p. 121, for the lack of individual identity of the priestly figures on the Ara Pacis, who rather embody the office.

uniform and specified, senatorial permission being required.[1] Although this was in keeping with senatorial self-protective restrictions in the Republic, there was now a *Princeps* who could, and did, spend far more. He was, after all, the pinnacle of that social hierarchy in which, however, the senators surpassed the other citizens.

Senators indubitably enjoyed more power under the Republic, and the people indubitably preferred the Principate, which held that power in check, to a restoration of the old Republic. That is made quite clear by the account in Josephus of Claudius's accession.[2] But it was the mere existence of the Principate, which inserted the *Princeps* at the top of the social pyramid, rather than any demagogic or patronal favouring of the *plebs* by the *Princeps*, that clipped the wings of the senate, just as it clipped those of the people's tribunes.

Since I have at times been critical of Yavetz's book in this paper, it is only fair that I should end by agreeing with what he says later about the significance of the title *pater patriae* to Augustus. He writes:

Augustus refused to present himself as a leader of one stratum of the population. He wanted to be, and to appear to be, *pater patriae*, and when the title was eventually bestowed upon him in 2 BC, he regarded this as the crowning achievement of his life. When the title was offered to him for the first time by a deputation of the plebs which came to see him at Antium, he declined the honour. Once, when he entered the theatre in Rome, the masses urged him to accept the title, but he declined again.

The evidence comes from Suetonius, who goes on to say that Augustus accepted the honour only when it was conferred in the Senate House and by 'the senate in agreement with the people'. Augustus reserved mention of that title for the last chapter, the climax, of his *Res Gestae*, where he claims to have received it from 'senatus et equester ordo et populus Romanus universus'.[3]

Populus Romanus universus, consensus and *omnes ordines* are phrases used by Cicero when he was countering *popularis* claims to popular support.[4] He liked to argue that the true *popularis* does not

1. Dio Cass. 54.4.
2. Jos. *AJ* 19. 228.
3. Yavetz, 'The *Res Gestae* and Augustus' Public Image', in *Caesar Augustus* (1984), pp. 13-14; *Res Gestae* 35; Suet. *Aug*. 58: 'senatus te consentiens cum populo Romano consalutat patriae patrem'.
4. E.g. *Leg. Agr.* 2.5, 7; *Sest*. 109.

appeal to one section of the *populus Romanus* but to the *consensus omnium ordinum*, the *universi populi Romani iudicium*.[1] Thus this last chapter of the *Res Gestae*, just like the first, belongs to the Optimate tradition of the Republic.

Similarly, the new Tabula Siarensis shows the senate instructing the 35 tribes of the *plebs urbana* to pay public homage to the dead Germanicus and ensuring that the *pietas omnium ordinum* and the *consensus universorum civium* in honour of the *domus Augusta* be broadcast to Roman colonies throughout Italy and the Empire.[2]

This notion of transmitting the image of *urbs Roma*, including the relation of the different social orders to the *Princeps* at the centre, may even help to explain one of the great puzzles of imperial history. Why else should the *Res Gestae*, which concentrates almost exclusively on the traditional Roman organs of government and the inhabitants of the city of Rome, have been thought an appropriate document to be exhibited publicly in the major cities of the distant province of Galatia and possibly elsewhere in the Roman Empire?

---

1. E.g. *Red. Sen.* 20; *Sest.* 107; *Off.* 1.85.
2. *AE* 1984, 508: frag. II, col. b, ll. 22-23, 'pietas omnium ordinum; consensus universorum civium'.

THE ECONOMIC CRITIQUE OF ROME IN REVELATION 18

Richard Bauckham

The book of Revelation is an apocalyptic prophecy written by the Jewish Christian prophet John in the late first century CE, probably during the reign of Domitian, and addressed in the form of a circular letter to the Christian churches in seven cities of the Roman province of Asia. It is one of the fiercest attacks on Rome and one of the most effective pieces of political resistance literature from the period of the early empire. Its thoroughgoing criticism of the whole system of Roman power includes an important element of economic critique. This condemnation of Rome's economic exploitation of her empire is the most unusual aspect of the opposition to Rome in Revelation, by comparison with other Jewish and Christian apocalyptic attacks on Rome, and it has also received the least attention in modern study of the book. Though we shall have to refer briefly to other aspects of Revelation's critique of Rome, this paper will focus on the economic aspect. In particular, a detailed study of the passage 18.9-19 will be offered. Finally, some comparable material in the Jewish Sibylline Oracles will be noticed.

1. *The Literary Structure of the Account of the Aall of Babylon*

The broad structure of the last seven chapters of Revelation[1] is as follows:

16.1-21	The seven last plagues leading to the fall of Babylon
17.1–19.10	Babylon and her fall

---

1. For this structure, see especially C.H. Giblin, 'Structural and Thematic Correlations in the Theology of Revelation 16–22', *Bib* 55 (1974), pp. 487-504.

19.11–21.8	Transition from the fall of Babylon to the arrival of the New Jerusalem
21.9–22.9	The New Jerusalem
22.10-21	Epilogue to the book

The key to this structure is found in the clear parallelism between the major sections 17.1–19.10 and 21.9–22.9, which describe the two contrasting cities: Babylon, the harlot, and the New Jerusalem, the bride of the Lamb. The introductions to each of these two sections, describing how the interpreting angel takes John to see in a vision each of the two women who represent the two cities (17.1-3; 21.9-10), are closely parallel. So are the conclusions to each of these two sections, again featuring the same interpreting angel with which each section began (19.9-10; 22.6-9). Between these parallel introductions and conclusions, however, these two major sections are rather different. In the second section (21.9–22.9) John merely describes his vision of the New Jerusalem. The first section (17.1–19.10) is more complex in structure. The vision of the harlot (17.1-6) is followed by a lengthy explanation of the vision by the interpreting angel (17.7-18). Then a further series of visions and auditions (18.1–19.8) serve to describe the fall of Babylon and its significance. This series of visions and auditions ends with a reference to the New Jerusalem (19.7-8) which serves to connect the two major sections on Babylon and the New Jerusalem. It indicates the relation between the two: that Babylon the harlot must fall in order to make way for the arrival of the New Jerusalem. That connection having been established, the events which intervene between the fall of Babylon and the arrival of the New Jerusalem are described in the transitional section (19.11–21.8).

The passage with which I am here primarily concerned is the series of visions and auditions in 18.1–19.8 (though I shall also have to refer to the initial vision of Babylon in ch. 17). The structure of this passage 18.1–19.8 has been frequently misunderstood, but is important to grasp. It falls into four main parts:

A	18.1-3	An angel pronounces judgment on Babylon
B	18.4-20	A voice from heaven predicts the fall of Babylon
A′	18.21-24	An angel pronounces judgment on Babylon
B′	19.1-8	Voices in heaven praise God for the fall of Babylon

Although ch. 18 has often been treated as a unit in itself,[1] it should be

---

1.   This is a mistake made by K.A. Strand ('Two Aspects of Babylon's

clear that the scene of rejoicing in heaven in 19.1-8 is part of the
depiction of the fall of Babylon and is needed to complete the unit.
Moreover, just as there are links between the passages here labelled A
and A',[1] so there are also between B and B', which show that the latter
is the fourth part of a four-part unit. B depicts the mourning for
Babylon by the kings of the earth, the merchants and the sailors (18.9-
19), and ends by calling on the inhabitants of heaven to rejoice over
Babylon's fall. This call is taken up in B', where the rejoicing in
heaven over Babylon's doom contrasts with the mourning on earth in B.

But section B (18.4-20), which contains the material most relevant
to my theme, needs to be further analysed.[2] It is important to realize
that the whole of this section consists of the words of the voice from
heaven to which 18.4 refers.[3] Most interpreters and translations have
supposed that the words of the voice from heaven end with v. 8, but
there is no reason to suppose this. Rather, the prediction of Babylon's
fall which begins in vv. 7b-8 continues with the prediction of how the
kings, the merchants and the sailors will mourn for her (vv. 9-19).
John is not describing the mourning on his own account, but
continuing to report the words of the heavenly voice. (The future
tenses in vv. 9-10, 15 make clear that the account of the mourners is
prediction; the vividness of the scene accounts for the present and past
tenses in vv. 11, 14, 17-19; for the variation of tenses, cf. 11.7-13.)[4]

Judgment Portrayed in Revelation 18', *AUSS* 20 [1982], pp. 53-60) and
W.H. Shea ('Chiasm in Theme and by Form in Revelation 18', *AUSS* 20 [1982],
pp. 249-56) (both following A. Farrer, *The Revelation of St. John the Divine*
[Oxford: Clarendon Press, 1964], p. 189), who propose a chiastic structure for
Rev. 18. They correctly recognize the parallelism between 18.1-3 and 18.21-24, but
they miss the parallelism between 18.4-20 and 19.1-8. Moreover, their analysis of
18.4-20, which treats 4-8 as a unit, cannot be upheld (see below for my alternative
analysis).
    1. A. Yarbro Collins, 'Revelation 18: Taunt-Song or Dirge?', in J. Lambrecht
(ed.), *L'Apocalypse johannique et l'Apocalyptique dans le Nouveau Testament*
(BETL, 53; Gembloux: Duculot/Leuven: Leuven University Press, 1980),
pp. 198-99.
    2. The following analysis largely agrees with Collins, 'Revelation 18',
pp. 193-96.
    3. So Collins, 'Revelation 18', p. 193; *idem, Crisis and Catharsis: The Power
of the Apocalypse* (Philadelphia: Westminster Press, 1984), p. 117.
    4. Cf. also J. Fekkes III, 'Isaiah and Prophetic Traditions in the Book of
Revelation: Visionary Antecedents and their Development' (unpublished PhD thesis,

Recognizing this removes the problems otherwise caused by vv. 14 and 20. In v. 14 the account of the mourning of the merchants is interrupted by a comment addressed to Babylon, but the speaker does not change. Verse 20 is not part of the lament of the sailors (v. 19): it would be quite incongruous for the sailors who are lamenting the loss of their own livelihood through the fall of Babylon to continue by calling on the inhabitants of heaven to rejoice because of it. But on the other hand, there is no need to supply for v. 20 a new speaker not indicated in the text. Rather, the heavenly voice, after quoting the sailors' lament in v. 19, turns to address the inhabitants of heaven in v. 20. The key to analysing the whole of section B is to recognize the various addressees of various passages and to distinguish the passages addressed to various addressees from those which are predictions addressed to no specified hearers. The section can then be divided as follows:

4a	Introduction
4b-5	A call to the people of God to come out of Babylon
6-7a	A call to the agents of divine justice to execute vengeance on Babylon
7b-8	Prophecy of the fall of Babylon
9-10	Prophecy of the mourning for Babylon: First group of mourners
11-13	Prophecy of the mourning for Babylon: Second group of mourners (a)
14	Interjection addressed to Babylon
15-17a	Prophecy of the mourning for Babylon: Second group of mourners (b)
17b-19	Prophecy of the mourning for Babylon: Third group of mourners
20	Call to the inhabitants of heaven to rejoice over the fall of Babylon

In these divisions there is a logical progression. First, the people of God are warned to leave doomed Babylon lest they share her punishment. Then, the ministers of vengeance[1] are commanded to do their work. Then, the execution of vengeance, the fall of Babylon, is foreseen. Then, as Babylon burns, three groups of mourners are depicted lamenting her fall. Finally, heaven is called on to rejoice

University of Manchester, 1988), p. 221 n. 53.
　　1.　These are unidentified, but are probably heavenly beings: Collins, 'Revelation 18', p. 193.

that God's judgment on Babylon has taken place. The whole of ch. 18 is closely related to Old Testament prophecies of the fall of Babylon and the fall of Tyre, from which it borrows phrases, images, and ideas. But out of these deliberate echoes of the Old Testament John has created a fresh prophecy of considerable literary skill, which appears especially in the vivid portrayal of the three groups of mourners for Babylon (vv. 9-19). This is inspired by and borrows phrases from Ezekiel's prophecies of the fall of Tyre, which include dirges sung for Tyre by two different groups of mourners (26.15-18; 27.29-36) and also a catalogue of the merchandise from various lands in which Tyre traded (27.12-24). But with this inspiration from Ezekiel, John has produced a highly effective description of his own, in which the terms of the description are both repeated and varied in each of the three cases, creating parallelism while avoiding monotony.[1] The function of this description of the mourners will be discussed later, but it is appropriate to note here how the structure of the passage gives special prominence to the merchandise which the merchants import to Rome. The two shorter accounts of the kings (vv. 9-10) and the sailors (vv. 17b-19) frame the longer account of the merchants (vv. 11-17a), which is broken in two by the interjection addressed to Babylon (v. 14). The merchandise is listed at length in the first part of the account of the merchants (vv. 12-13), is the topic of the interjection addressed to Babylon (v. 14), is mentioned again when the account of the merchants is resumed after the interjection (v. 15), and is also portrayed symbolically (as the adornments of Babylon imagined as a woman) in the merchants' lament (v. 16), which ends by lamenting the destruction of so much wealth (v. 17a). We would be justified in supposing that, in his account of the fall of Babylon, John wished particularly to highlight the imported wealth which will perish with the city.

2. *Rome as the Harlot City*

The book of Revelation uses two major, complementary images of the evil power of Rome. One is the sea-monster ('the beast') introduced in

---

1. A. Vanhoye, 'L'utilisation du livre d'Ezéchiel dans l'Apocalypse', *Bib* 43 (1962), pp. 436-77; Collins, 'Revelation 18', p. 199.

ch. 13. It represents the imperial power, the Roman emperors as a political institution, and, in particular, their *military might*, on which the Roman empire was founded. The other image is of the great city Babylon, first named in 14.8, and then portrayed as a woman, 'the great harlot', in ch. 17. Babylon is the city of Rome (built on seven hills: 17.9) and in particular the city of Rome as a *corrupting influence* on the peoples of the empire. Ch. 17 brings the two images together: the harlot is enthroned on the seven heads of the beast (17.3, 9-10). In other words, Roman civilization, as a corrupting influence, rides on the back of Roman military power. The city of Rome grew great through military conquest, which brought wealth and power to the city, and its economic and cultural influence spread through the world in the wake of the imperial armies. John never forgets that Rome's power is founded on war and conquest, but he also recognizes that it cannot be reduced to this. As well as the irresistible military might of the beast, there are the deceptive wiles of the great harlot.

For John, the satanic, antichristian nature of Roman power, as exercised in his time, was demonstrated most obviously by the Roman state religion in which the power of the state was deified. It may be that John's use of the two distinct images of Roman power—the beast and the harlot-city—was assisted by a feature of this state religion. It included not only the worship of the divinized emperors but also the worship of the goddess Roma,[1] who was a kind of personification of the city of Rome.[2] It may be that in the woman of Revelation 17 John's readers would have recognized the goddess Roma,[3] revealed by the vision in her true character: a Roman prostitute, wearing her

---

1. See J.M. Court, *Myth and History in the Book of Revelation* (London: SPCK, 1979), pp. 148-52. For the cult of Roma in the cities of Asia, see D. Magie, *Roman Rule in Asia Minor to the End of the Third Century after Christ* (Princeton: Princeton University Press, 1950), pp. 1613-14; S.R.F. Price, *Rituals and Power: The Roman Imperial Cult in Asia Minor* (Cambridge: Cambridge University Press, 1984), pp. 40-43, 252, 254; R. Mellor, ΘΕΑ ΡΩΜΗ: *The Worship of the Goddess Roma in the Greek World* (Hypomnemata, 42; Göttingen: Vandenhoeck & Ruprecht, 1975), pp. 79-82.

2. Mellor, ΘΕΑ ΡΩΜΗ, p. 199: 'Roma was the deification of the *populus Romanus*'.

3. So Court, *Myth and History*, pp. 148-52.

name on a headband on her forehead (17.5) as prostitutes did in the streets of Rome.[1] John describes the impulse to the imperial cult in 13.4: people 'worshipped the beast saying, "Who is like the beast, and who can fight against it?"' The irresistible military might of Rome seems divine and attracts worship. The verse has a kind of parallel in 18.18, with reference to Babylon. Those who there lament her downfall cry, 'What city was like the great city?' Here the wealth and splendour of the city of Rome evoke admiration, just as her military might evoked spontaneous, if somewhat craven, worship. The point should not be pressed too far. If the picture of the great harlot owes something to the goddess Roma, John does not actually portray her as an object of worship, as he does the beast. His point is more that, through her corrupting influence, she promotes the idolatrous religion of Rome. But Babylon comes close to self-deification in her proud boast, 'A queen I sit, I am no widow, mourning I shall never see' (18.7), which echoes not only ancient Babylon's boast (Isa. 47.7-8)[2] but also contemporary Rome's self-promoted reputation as the eternal city.[3] It was the city which believed, as an article of faith, that she could never fall, whose fall is announced in Revelation 18.

In order to understand why John portrays the city of Rome both as the city of Babylon and as a harlot, we must briefly consider his Old Testament sources. John is very conscious of writing in a long tradition of prophetic oracles[4] and so is constantly echoing and reapplying the oracles of his predecessors. His portrayal of the fall of Babylon is a remarkable patchwork of skilful allusions to Old Testament prophecies of the fall of Babylon and the fall of Tyre.[5]

1. R.H. Charles, *A Critical and Exegetical Commentary on the Revelation of St John* (ICC; Edinburgh: T. & T. Clark, 1920), II, p. 65.

2. For the dependence on Isa. 47.7-9, see Fekkes, 'Isaiah and Prophetic Traditions', p. 227-31. With Rev. 18.7 and 17.18, cf. Frontinus, *De Aquis* 2.88.1: Rome as *regina et domina orbis*.

3. Collins, 'Revelation 18', p. 201.

4. See F.D. Mazzaferri, *The Genre of the Book of Revelation from a Source-Critical Perspective* (BZNW, 54; Berlin/New York: de Gruyter, 1989), especially ch. 10. His positive thesis—John's conscious continuity with Old Testament prophecy—is more convincing than his negative thesis: the contrast between Revelation and apocalyptic.

5. Vanhoye, 'L'utilisation du livre d'Ezéchiel', pp. 475-76; Charles,

There are two major sources: Jeremiah's great oracle against Babylon
(Jer. 50–51) and Ezekiel's great oracle against Tyre (Ezek. 26–28).
But allusion is also made to all of the shorter oracles against Babylon
and Tyre to be found in the Old Testament prophets (Babylon: Isa.
13.1–14.23; 21.1-10; 47; Jer. 25.12-38; Tyre: Isa. 23).[1] It seems that
John has quite deliberately fashioned a prophetic oracle against Rome
which gathers up all that his prophetic predecessors had pronounced
against the two cities of Babylon and Tyre. For John these oracles are
more than a literary source. They are oracles which, because they
applied to Rome's predecessors in evil, apply also to Rome. He sees
Rome as the culmination of all the evil empires of history. Just as the
beast, as portrayed in Rev. 13.1-2, combines in itself the features of
all the beasts which in Daniel's vision symbolized the evil empires
before Rome (Dan. 7.3-8), so the Babylon of Revelation 17–18
combines in itself the evils of the two great evil cities of the Old
Testament prophetic oracles: Babylon and Tyre.[2]

Of the two, Babylon is the city whose name John uses as a cipher
for Rome. No Old Testament city could more truly be called, like
Rome, 'the great city which has dominion over the kings of the earth'
(Rev. 17.18). Rome resembled Old Testament Babylon in being a
proud, idolatrous, oppressive empire, and especially in being the
power which conquered and oppressed the people of God. Rome
declared itself the heir of Babylon by setting itself against God in its
political and religious policies. But it is important to notice that
Ezekiel's oracle against Tyre contributes as much to John's account of
the fall of Babylon as Jeremiah's and Isaiah's oracles against Babylon
do. If Rome was the heir of Babylon in political and religious activity,
she was also the heir of Tyre in economic activity. For Tyre was the
greatest trading centre of the Old Testament period, notable not, like
Babylon, for her political empire, but for her economic empire. So it
is to focus his indictment of Rome for her economic exploitation and
his pronouncement of judgment on Rome for this aspect of her evil,
that John reapplied to Rome Ezekiel's oracle against Tyre. The Old

Revelation, II, pp. 95-113; Fekkes, 'Isaiah and Prophetic Traditions', pp. 83-84.

    1.   Fekkes, 'Isaiah and Prophetic Traditions', pp. 86-88.

    2.   Cf. G.R. Beasley-Murray, *The Book of Revelation* (NCB; London:
Marshall, Morgan & Scott, 1974), p. 264: 'This city summed up in itself and
surpassed the wickedness of the tyrant-powers of the past'.

Testament background therefore helps us to see how central the economic theme is to the condemnation of Rome in Revelation. If Babylon gave Rome its name in John's oracle, it is probably Tyre that supplied the image of the harlot for Rome.[1] The Old Testament prophets do not portray Babylon as a harlot, but Isa. 23.15-18 uses the image of the harlot for Tyre. The reference there is obviously to the vast trading activity through which the city of Tyre had grown rich. Tyre's commercial enterprise is compared with prostitution because it is association with other nations for the sake of profit. Thus we should expect the primary significance of John's portrayal of Rome as the great harlot to be economic. But since the way in which Tyre profited from her purely commercial empire was significantly different from the way in which Rome benefited economically from her political empire, John develops the image of the harlot to suit its specific reference to Rome. The significance he gives to it requires some careful unpacking.

The image of the harlot is so fundamental to John's understanding of Rome that even when he is speaking primarily of the city, as in ch. 18, he does not forget that the city is a harlot. Hence the terms of the description in 17.1-6 are echoed in 18.3, 9 (cf. 17.2) and 18.16 (cf. 17.4), while the image of the harlot recurs explicitly in 19.2. The basic notion, of course, is that those who associate with a harlot pay her for the privilege. And Rome is no ordinary harlot: she is a rich courtesan, whose expensive clothes and jewelry (17.4) indicate the luxurious lifestyle she maintains at her lovers' expense. The meaning of the picture is unpacked for us when the harlot's clothing and jewels are described again, in the same terms, in 18.16. Here they are plainly a metaphor for the wealth of the city of Rome, for all the luxury goods listed in 18.12-13, brought to Rome by the great network of trade throughout her empire. In other words, Rome is a harlot because her associations with the peoples of her empire are for her own economic benefit. To those who associate with her she offers the supposed benefits of the *Pax Romana*, much lauded in the Roman propaganda of this period. Rome offered the Mediterranean world unity, security, stability, the conditions of prosperity. But in John's view these benefits are not what they seem: they are the favours of a

---

1. So Fekkes ('Isaiah and Prophetic Traditions', pp. 219-20), who thinks Rev. 17.3b; 18.3b, 9a allude to Isa. 23.17b.

prostitute, purchased at a high price. The *Pax Romana* is really a system of economic exploitation of the empire. Rome's subjects give far more to her than she gives to them.

There are, of course, those who have a vested interest in the power and the economic dominance of Rome: the kings, the merchants and the mariners (18.9-19). To these people, who share in Rome's profit, we shall return later. But many of Rome's subjects are in fact exploited by her, yet fail to see it. They are taken in by Roman propaganda. They are dazzled by Rome's glory and seduced by the promised benefits of the *Pax Romana*. This delusion John portrays by means of two additional metaphors, which extend the harlot image. When he refers to the harlot's influence, not on the ruling classes of the empire, but over the peoples of the empire, he says that she intoxicates them with the wine of her fornication (14.8; 17.2; 18.3) or that she deceives them with her sorceries (18.23). The latter probably refers to the magic arts used by a prostitute to entice her clients (as in Nah. 3.4),[1] or may simply portray Rome in another guise: as a witch (cf. Isa. 47.12). In any case, it is clear what John means. When Rome's subjects, the ordinary people of the empire, welcome her rule, it is because she has enticed and seduced them. They are taken in by the prostitute's wiles and the tricks of her trade.

We have seen, then, that the primary meaning of the harlot image in Revelation 17–18 is economic. But John was no doubt also aware of a much more common Old Testament use of harlotry as a metaphor.[2] In this usage, idolatrous religion is described as harlotry, because the people of God, when they adopted pagan religious practices, were being unfaithful to their husband, God, and 'played the harlot' with other gods (e.g. Jer. 3.). This Old Testament sense of harlotry could strictly be applied only to the people of God, but it is very likely that John takes advantage of the traditional association of harlotry with idolatrous religion, when he refers to the *corrupting* influence of the harlot city (19.2). When the intoxicating draft from her golden cup is otherwise described as 'abominations and the impurities of her

---

1.   J.M. Powis Smith in J.M. Powis Smith, W. Hayes Ward and J.A. Brewer, *A Critical and Exegetical Commentary on Micah, Zephaniah, Nahum, Habakkuk, Obadiah and Joel* (ICC; Edinburgh: T. & T. Clark, 1912), p. 338; W. A. Maier, *The Book of Nahum* (St Louis: Concordia Publishing House, 1959), p. 302.

2.   Court, *Myth and History*, pp. 140-41.

fornication' (17.4), and when she is described as 'the mother [i.e. the mother-city, the metropolis] of harlots and of the abominations of the earth' (17.5), the reference, following a familiar Old Testament use of the term 'abominations', is to idolatrous religion. *Religious* corruption is offered in the cup whose golden exterior symbolizes the attraction of Rome's wealth and splendour. John will be thinking primarily of the imperial cult. Part of the delusion of the *Pax Romana*—the intoxicating wine from the harlot's cup—was the people's sense of gratitude to the Emperor, who was worshipped as a divine Saviour for the blessings he had brought to his subjects. From John's Jewish Christian perspective, the political religion of Rome was the worst kind of false religion, since it absolutized Rome's claim on her subjects and cloaked her exploitation of them in the garb of religious loyalty. Thus, for John, Rome's economic exploitation and the corrupting influence of her state religion go hand in hand.

Finally, the portrait of the harlot in Rev. 17.1-6 ends with a fresh and even more sinister use of the image of drunkenness: she who made the earth drunk with her seductive wiles is herself 'drunk with the blood of the saints and the blood of the witnesses of Jesus' (17.6). The accusation recurs, this time with a judicial image, in 18.24: 'in her was found the blood of prophets and of saints, and of all who have been slain on earth'. Here the prophets and saints are the Christian martyrs, and many commentators understand 'all who have been slain on earth' also as Christian martyrs, but this is not the natural sense, and it robs the verse of its climax. Rome is indicted not only for the martyrdom of Christians, but also for the slaughter of all the innocent victims of its murderous policies.[1] The verse expresses a sense of solidarity between the Christian martyrs and all whose lives were the price of Rome's acquisition and maintenance of power. John has not forgotten that Babylon rides on the beast with its bear's hug and its lion's teeth (13.2). He knows that the *Pax Romana* was, in Tacitus's phrase, 'peace with bloodshed',[2] established by violent conquest, maintained by continual war on the frontiers, and requiring

---

1.   The fact that the verb σφάζω is used of the Lamb in 5.6, 9, 12; 13.8 and of Christian martyrs in 6.9, is no proof to the contrary, for it is also used of general slaughter in 6.4.

2.   Tacitus, *Ann.* 1.10.4.

repression of dissent.[1] Like every society which absolutizes its own power and prosperity, the Roman empire could not exist without victims. Thus John sees a connection between Rome's economic affluence, Rome's idolatrous self-deification, and Rome's military and political brutality. The power of his critique of Rome—perhaps the most thoroughgoing critique from the period of the early empire—lies in the connection it portrays between these various facets of Rome's evil.

Thus it is a serious mistake to suppose that John opposes Rome only because of the imperial cult and the persecution of Christians. Rather, this issue serves to bring to the surface evils which were deeply rooted in the whole system of Roman power. In John's perspective, the evils of Rome came to a head in her persecution of Christians, because here Rome's self-deification clashed with the lordship of the Lamb to which the Christian martyrs bore witness, and so what was implicit in all of Rome's imperial policies here became explicit. Hence Revelation most often portrays the fall of Rome as vengeance for the death of the Christian martyrs (16.6; 18.24; 19.2; cf. 18.6). But this is certainly not the whole story: God's judgment of Rome is also seen as a result of her slaughter of the innocent in general (18.24; cf. 18.6), her idolatrous arrogance (18.8), and her self-indulgent luxury at the expense of her empire (18.7). The economic element in this critique is probably the one which has received the least attention in previous scholarship, but, as I have noted, it is very prominent in ch. 18, and to the detail of this element I now turn

3. *The List of Cargoes (Revelation 18.12-13)*

John's list of twenty-eight items of merchandise imported by sea to the city of Rome has not received the attention it deserves. Although, of course, it lists no more than a small selection of Rome's imports in this period, it is, to my knowledge, much the longest extant list of Roman imports to be found in the literature of the early empire. This rather remarkable fact suggests that we pay rather careful attention to the significance of this list for Revelation's polemic against Rome.

Some commentators have been content to remark that the list is

1. Cf. K. Wengst, *Pax Romana and the Peace of Jesus Christ* (trans. J. Bowden; London: SCM Press, 1987), pp. 11-19.

modelled on Ezekiel's list of forty foreign products in which the city of Tyre traded (27.12-24), as though John's list were sufficiently explained by this source.[1] No doubt it was Ezekiel's list which suggested the idea of such a list to John, but it can have contributed little more than the idea of a list of cargoes. It is true that a number of items of merchandise are common to both lists, but no more than would be practically inevitable in any two lengthy lists of items traded in the ancient world. Each list also has a significant number of items which do not occur in the other. But the feature of the lists which shows that John's was formulated largely independently of Ezekiel's is that the principle by which each list is arranged is different. Ezekiel lists the products with which each named country traded with Tyre: the arrangement is geographical. John does not indicate the sources of the merchandise, but arranges his list according to types of cargo. Closer study of John's list will reveal that what he has done is to substitute for Ezekiel's list, which is an accurate account of Tyre's trade in the sixth century BCE, a list which is just as accurate in representing the imports of the city of Rome in the first century CE.

With the exception of William Barclay's popular commentary on Revelation,[2] H.B. Swete in his commentary of 1906[3] was the last New Testament scholar who made any attempt to gather information about individual items in the list and to comment on their significance as Roman imports.[4] No doubt this lack of interest in the concrete detail which John so deliberately provides reflects not only the average exegete's preference for theology over concrete history, but also a failure fully to recognize the thoroughly contextualized nature of John's prophetic message. For all its visionary symbolic form, John's attack on Rome is aimed at the concrete political and economic

1. Charles, *Revelation*, II, p. 103; I.T. Beckwith, *The Apocalypse of John* (Grand Rapids: Baker Book House, 1967 [1919]), p. 715.
2. W. Barclay, *The Revelation of John* (Daily Study Bible; Edinburgh: Saint Andrew Press, 2nd edn, 1960), II, pp. 200-12.
3. H.B. Swete, *The Apocalypse of John* (London: Macmillan, 2nd edn, 1907), pp. 232-35.
4. Later commentators, such as Charles (*Revelation*, II, pp. 103-105) and Beckwith (*Apocalypse*, pp. 716-17) do no more than select information from that collected by Swete and, long before him, Wetstein. R.H. Mounce (*The Book of Revelation* [NICNT; Grand Rapids: Eerdmans, 1977], pp. 329-31) gives more detail than most recent commentators, by following Barclay as well as Swete.

realities of the empire in his time.[1] The symbolism is not a way of abstracting from these realities but a means of prophetic comment on their significance. By neglecting the list of cargoes, interpreters of Revelation have neglected one of the best pieces of evidence for John's engagement with the realities of Roman power as experienced by his contemporaries.

In order to redress the balance, though still in a rather provisional way, I offer here some comment on each item in the list. Of particular importance will be evidence that the merchandise in question was generally seen as a feature of the newly conspicuous wealth and extravagance of the rich families of Rome in the period of the early empire.

Gold. Rome imported gold especially from Spain,[2] where most of the mines had become state property during the first century (Strabo 3.2.10), sometimes by highly dubious means of confiscation (Tacitus, *Ann.* 6.19). The use of gold was one of the commonly noticed features of the growth of extravagant luxury among the wealthy families of Rome in the first century (e.g. Tacitus, *Ann.* 3.53; Pliny, *NH* 33.39-40; Martial 10.49; 11.95), and in one of the periodic attempts to curb this, in 16 CE, a law prohibiting the use of gold plate at private dinner parties was passed (Tacitus, *Ann.* 2.33). Pliny complains that now the ceilings of private houses are commonly covered in gold (*NH* 33.57), that today even slaves use gold for ornament (*NH* 33.23), and reports that since even plebeian women now wear shoe-buckles of gold, they are thought old-fashioned and silver ones are preferred by the aristocracy (*NH* 33.152). With the place of gold at the head of John's list, it is worth comparing the fact that it is the first object of Roman greed mentioned in Eumolpus's account of the insatiable desire for wealth and luxury which motivated Roman imperial expansion: 'if there were... any land that promised a yield of yellow gold, that place was Rome's enemy, fate stood ready for the sorrows of war, and

1. Cf. D. Georgi, 'Who is the True Prophet?', *HTR* 79 (1986), pp. 121-26, especially p. 123: 'John's work is anything but the product of an esoteric quietist piety. Here a prophetic consciousness which has a hold on historical reality expresses itself.'

2. T. Frank, in *idem* (ed.) *An Economic Survey of Ancient Rome* (Baltimore: Johns Hopkins University Press, 1940), V, p. 292.

the quest for wealth went on' (Petronius, *Sat.* 119). Pliny (*NH* 36.6) considered the private use of ivory, gold and precious stones the evidence of the luxury (*luxuria*) he so regularly condemns as moral degeneration in the Rome of his day.

Silver. The case of silver, also imported mostly from Spain,[1] was similar to that of gold (cf. e.g. Tacitus, *Ann.* 3.53). Pliny strongly associates silver with the luxury of the Roman rich in his time, remarking on the fashions for silver-plated couches and baths made of silver, the common use of silver for serving food (cf. Martial 11.97), the rage not only for vast quantities of silver plate but also for silver art objects by particular artists (Pliny, *NH* 33.145-53). In the use of gold and silver, as with so many of these imported luxuries, Nero and Poppaea provide examples of the current extravagance taken to absurd extremes (Pliny, *NH* 33.54, 140; Suetonius, *Nero* 30.3).

Precious stones. Most came from India, as part of the eastern trade in luxuries which flourished from the reign of Augustus onwards.[2] Indian jewels were widely used in Rome throughout the first century.[3] That they came from beyond the bounds of the empire explains why the emperor Tiberius, in his letter to the Senate about Roman extravagance in 22 CE, referred to 'that special feature of Roman extravagance, the transfer of Roman currency to foreign, often hostile nations, for the purchase of jewelry' (Tacitus, *Ann.* 3.53). But, of course, Rome owed it to her empire that she could afford these expensive imports from beyond the empire. Pliny, who thought that the fashion for the extravagant use of precious stones in Rome dated from Pompey's triumphs, in which fabulous jewels were exhibited (*NH* 37.11-13, 17), considered the human love of them had grown into a violent passion in his time (*NH* 37.2). They were not only worn by women in large quantities (cf. *NH* 9.117-118 for an extreme example), but also set in rings for men (Pliny, *NH* 33.22; Martial

---

1. Frank, in *idem* (ed.), *Economic Survey*, V, p. 292; J.J. van Nostrand, in Frank (ed.), *An Economic Survey of Ancient Rome* (1937), III, pp. 150-51, 158.
2. E.H. Warmington, *The Commerce between the Roman Empire and India* (London: Curzon Press/New York: Octagon Books, 2nd edn, 1974), part 2, chapter 3.
3. Warmington, *Commerce*, pp. 40, 90.

5.11) and frequently used to inlay expensive drinking vessels (Pliny, *NH* 33.5; 37.17; Juvenal 5.37-45; Martial 14.109, 110).

Pearls. Inferior pearls came from the Red Sea, the finest quality from the Persian Gulf, and the most abundant supplies from India. Pearls were one of the imports from India and the east which were increasing considerably in the late first century, and they may have made up the largest part of the oriental trade. Romans valued the pearl after the diamond, but for the largest and best would pay more than for any other piece of jewelry.[1] Pliny calls pearls the most costly product of the sea (*NH* 37.204). Nero, who scattered pearls among the people of Rome (Suetonius, *Nero* 11.2), exemplifies the Roman obsession with pearls (Pliny, *NH* 37.17), including the practice of swallowing them, dissolved in vinegar, at banquets for the sake of the thrill of consuming such vast expense at a single gulp (cf. Pliny, *NH* 9.121-22). During the first century it became common for wealthy Roman women to wear pearls in great quantities, to the fury, once again, of those who blamed feminine extravagance for the outflow of Roman currency from the empire (e.g. Pliny, *NH* 12.84). Pliny constantly treats pearls as the epitome of extravagant luxury (*NH* 9.105, 112-14, 117-22; 37.14-17; cf. Petronius, *Sat.* 55).

Fine linen (βυσσίνον). During the first century linen was tending to replace wool as the material for clothing in Rome. John refers to the expensive linen worn by the wealthy, imported mostly from Egypt, but also from Spain and Asia Minor.[2]

Purple. The list of four textiles (fine linen, purple, silk, scarlet) is made up alternately of types of cloth (fine linen, silk) and cloths characterized by their dyes (purple, scarlet). Silk, linen and woollen cloths (in order of expense) were all dyed with purple, the expensive dye obtained from shell-fish which were fished in various places around the Mediterranean and which was much prized in the ancient world in general. Reinhold calls it 'the most enduring status symbol of

---

1.   Warmington, *Commerce*, pp. 89, 167-71.
2.   Frank, in *idem* (ed.), *Economic Survey*, V, p. 156; T.R.S. Broughton, in Frank (ed.), *Economic Survey*, IV, p. 822.

the ancient world'.[1] Because of the vast number of tiny shellfish needed to make small quantities of the purple dye, the dye was much more expensive than any of the materials which it was used to dye and accounts for the exorbitant price of purple cloth.[2] Because of its price, it was used not only as a mark of official status, political or cultic, but also by private individuals as a deliberate, conspicuous display of affluence. From the late Republic onwards, it was increasingly in evidence in Rome for this purpose, and regularly appears as a symbol of extravagance in writers of the first century BCE and first century CE.[3] From Julius Caesar to Nero, attempts were made to limit the use of purple, but after the death of Nero apparently no restrictions were in force.[4] According to Pliny, first-century Rome developed an insane craze for purple clothing ('purpurae insania': *NH* 9.127; cf. 8.197; 9.137), which, he says, 'the same mother, Luxury, has made almost as costly as pearls' (*NH* 9.124). Because both pearls and purple dyes derive from shellfish, he calls shellfish the greatest single source of moral corruption and luxury (*NH* 9.104). From at least the time of Nero, there was an imperial monopoly in the purple dye,[5] and an inscription from Miletus indicates that those involved in the purple trade were freedmen of the *familia Caesaris*.[6] This connection with the emperors gives an extra significance to the appearance of purple in the list in Revelation. Moreover, in view of the geographical area to which the book of Revelation is addressed, it is worth noting that some of Rome's purple cloth would probably have come from the clothing and dyeing industries of Miletus, Thyatira, Laodicea and Hierapolis.[7]

1.   M. Reinhold, *History of Purple as a Status Symbol in Antiquity* (Collection Latomus, 116; Brussels: Latomus, 1970), p. 71.
2.   For the price, see M.G. Raschke, 'New Studies in Roman Commerce with the East', in H. Temporini (ed.), *Aufstieg und Niedergang der römischen Welt*, II.9.2 (Berlin/New York: de Gruyter, 1978), pp. 624, 725 n. 305.
3.   Reinhold, *History of Purple*, pp. 41-44, 51-52, 72.
4.   Reinhold, *History of Purple*, pp. 45-47, 49-50.
5.   G.H.R. Horsley, 'The purple trade, and the status of Lydia of Thyatira', *New Documents 1977*, pp. 26, 28, against Reinhold, *History of Purple*, p. 72.
6.   Horsley, 'The purple trade', p. 28.
7.   For these, see C.J. Hemer, 'The Cities of the Revelation', *New Documents 1978*, pp. 53-54; *idem, The Letters to the Seven Churches of Asia in their Local Setting* (JSNTSup, 11; Sheffield: JSOT Press, 1986), pp. 109, 181-82, 199-201;

Silk. Silk,[1] imported at great expense[2] from China, some by the overland route through Parthia, most via the ports of northwest India, was used in Rome to any extent only from the reign of Augustus.[3] Romans, who thought silk grew on trees, considered nard and silk the most expensive things derived from trees.[4] The sumptuary laws of 16 CE prohibited, as an effeminate custom, the wearing of silk by men (Tacitus, *Ann.* 2.33), but the extent to which silk became common for both male and female dress (though clothing was not usually made wholly of silk)[5] is indicated by Josephus's account of Roman soldiers dressed in silk at the triumphs of Vespasian and Titus (*War*.126).

Scarlet (κοκκίνον). Since the scarlet dye was obtained especially from the kermes oaks (from the 'berry' [κόκκος]—in fact an insect parasite) in various parts of Asia Minor (the best was said to come from Galatia),[6] John may be thinking especially of the clothing industries of his own province of Asia. Petronius's Trimalchio, who represents the excesses of the first-century Roman rich taken to ludicrous absurdity,[7] had cushions with crimson (*conchyliatum*: a

---

Broughton, in Frank (ed.), *Economic Survey*, IV, pp. 817, 819-20; H.W. Pleket, 'Urban elites and business in the Greek part of the Roman Empire', in P. Garnsey, K. Hopkins and C.R. Whittaker (eds.), *Trade in the Ancient Economy* (London: Chatto & Windus/Hogarth Press, 1983), pp. 141-42. As well as the true purple, the term was also used for less expensive dyes (Reinhold, *History of Purple*, pp. 52-53), such as that made from the roots of the maddar plant in western Asia Minor: see Hemer,'The Cities', pp. 53-54, for the suggestion that it was in this that Lydia of Thyatira (Acts 16.14) traded.

1. On the silk trade, see now especially Raschke, 'New Studies', pp. 605-37. He denies that it was responsible for Rome's adverse balance of trade with the East.

2. For the price of silk, see Raschke, 'New Studies', pp. 624-25.

3. Warmington, *Commerce*, p. 175 n. 32.

4. Warmington, *Commerce*, p. 177.

5. Raschke, 'New Studies', p. 623.

6. See Pliny, *NH* 16.32; 9.141; Broughton, in Frank (ed.), *Economic Survey*, IV, p. 617.

7. Trimalchio, a freedman who has made a fortune from sea-borne commerce, apes the ostentatious symbols of wealth of the Roman upper classes. On locating Trimalchio in his social and economic context, see J.H. D'Arms, *Commerce and Social Standing in Ancient Rome* (Cambridge, MA: Harvard University Press, 1981), pp. 97-120.

variety of the purple dyes derived from shellfish) or scarlet (*coccineum*) stuffing (*Sat.* 38). Typically, it is Nero who nearly matched this fictional absurdity in fact: the cords of his golden fishing net were of purple and scarlet thread (Suetonius, *Nero* 30.3).

All kinds of citrus wood (πᾶν ξύλον θύϊνον). The phrase may mean 'all articles made of citrus wood', or 'all kinds of citrus wood',[1] since different specimens of the wood were valued for their various colours and the various patterns created by the veining (resembling the eyes of the peacock's tail, the spots of the panther or the stripes of the tiger: Pliny, *NH* 13.96-97; Martial 14.85). The wood[2] came from the citrus tree (*Callitris quadrivalvis*), which grew along the whole north African coast from Cyrenaica westward, but had been much depleted so that by Pliny's time the best quality trees were largely confined to Morocco. Tables made from the wood became one of the most expensive fashions of early imperial Rome, indispensable at the banquets of the wealthy, so that largely with reference to these tables, Pliny could say that 'few things which supply the apparatus of a more luxurious life (*nitidioris*) rank with' the citrus tree (*NH* 13.100). Seneca, contrary to his own principles, possessed five hundred of them, with ivory legs (Dio Cass. 61.10.3). Because trees large enough to provide a table top in one piece took a very long time to reach that size and were rare, these tables were vastly expensive. Even Cicero paid 500,000 sesterces for his, which was said to have been the first recorded citrus wood table in Rome (Pliny, *NH* 13.102), while Petronius's Eumolpus writes of

> tables of citrus wood dug out of the soil of Africa and set up, the spots on them resembling gold which is cheaper than they, their polish reflecting hordes of slaves and purple clothes, to lure the senses

(Petronius, *Sat.* 119; cf. Martial 14.89: a table worth more than gold). Certainly, the record price which Pliny quotes for one table would

---

1. So Swete, *Apocalypse,* p. 233; Beckwith, *Apocalypse,* p. 716.
2. On Roman use of citrus wood, see especially R. Meiggs, *Trees and Timber in the Ancient Mediterranean World* (Oxford: Clarendon Press, 1982), pp. 286-92; and *idem*, 'Sea-borne Timber Supplies to Rome', in J.H. D'Arms and E.C. Kopff (eds.), *The Seaborne Commerce of Ancient Rome: Studies in Archaeology and History* (Memoirs of the American Academy in Rome, 36; Rome: American Academy in Rome, 1980), pp. 185-86.

have been enough to buy a large estate (*NH* 13.95). These tables were therefore standard in references to first-century Roman excess. According to Pliny, when Roman women were accused of extravagance in pearls, they pointed out the equally extravagant mania of men for citrus wood tables (*NH* 13.91). But the wood was also used on a smaller scale in furniture and works of art, doorposts (Statius, *Silvae* 1.3.35) or even writing-tablets (Martial 14.3).

All articles of ivory. The Roman consumption of ivory was one of the earliest stages of the process which now so notoriously threatens the survival of the elephant. In the first century CE the Syrian elephant (once one of the three species) was already well on the way to extinction (Juvenal 11.126-27 refers to Nabataean elephants as a source of ivory). When Pliny was writing (*NH* 8.7), the extravagant Roman use of ivory had led to the severe depletion of elephants within the accessible areas of north Africa, and the shortage of African ivory was made up by the increasing trade in Indian ivory throughout the first century.[1] As examples of its use found in ancient literature, Warmington lists statues, chairs, beds, sceptres, hilts, scabbards, chariots, carriages, tablets, bookcovers, table-legs, doors, flutes, lyres, combs, brooches, pins, scrapers, boxes, bird-cages, floors:[2] a list to which it would be easy to add (e.g. Juvenal 11.131-34: dice, draughts, knife-handles; Suetonius, *Nero* 31.2: ceilings). For Pliny, it was a striking indication of modern luxury that ivory had replaced wood for making images of the gods and table-legs (*NH* 12.5; cf. 36.6), while Juvenal complains that nowadays a rich man cannot enjoy his dinner unless the table is supported by a leopard carved in solid ivory (11.120-24). In their race for conspicuous luxury, the Roman rich of the early imperial period had whole articles of furniture covered in ivory. The increased use of ivory is reflected in the increased literary references to ivory in the late first century.[3] Lucian on one occasion regards gold, clothing, slaves and ivory as the constituents of wealth (*Dial. Meretr.* 9.2).

---

1. Warmington, *Commerce*, pp. 40, 89, 162-65. Raschke ('New Studies', p. 650) contests this, but probably incorrectly.
2. Warmington, *Commerce*, p. 163.
3. Warmington, *Commerce*, p. 164.

All articles of costly wood. Expensive woods might include ebony, from Africa and India, but there is hardly any evidence for its use in Rome.[1] The best maple wood, used for furniture, could be very expensive.[2] Cedar and cypress were used for furniture, boxes, sarcophagi, doors and sculpture.[3] The expensive woods were also used for veneering,[4] a practice Pliny regards as a new-fangled extravagance (*NH* 16.232; 33.146).

[All articles of] bronze. The reference will be especially to expensive works of art made from Corinthian bronze and perhaps also Spanish bronze.[5] Petronius's Eumolpus gave as an example of the way Romans acquired a decadent taste for luxuries from overseas: 'the soldier out at sea would praise the bronze of Corinth' (Petronius, *Sat.* 119). Pliny speaks of a mania for Corinthian bronze, which he claims is more valuable than silver, almost more valuable than gold (*NH* 34.1). The frequently mentioned 'Corinthian bronzes' were statuettes, which seem to have been a Roman fashion throughout the first century and extremely expensive (Pliny, *NH* 34.6-8, 36; 36.115; 37.49; Martial 9.59.11; 14.172, 177; Suetonius, *Aug.* 70.2; Petronius, *Sat.* 50). When Tiberius set price limits for household furnishings, his particular complaint was that the price of Corinthian bronze vessels had risen to an immense figure (Suetonius, *Tiberius* 34). Vastly expensive bronze lamp-stands (not of Corinthian bronze) were also popular, as were such items of furniture in bronze as banquetting couches (Pliny, *NH* 34.10-14).

[All articles of] iron. Articles of iron and steel would be, for example, cutlery, swords and other armaments, ornamental vessels, imported especially from Spain[6] and Pontus. The Seric iron mentioned by Pliny has often been thought to be high quality Indian steel, but Raschke

1.   Meiggs, *Trees*, pp. 285-86, against Warmington, *Commerce*, pp. 213-14.
2.   Meiggs, *Trees*, pp. 291-92.
3.   Meiggs, *Trees*, pp. 292-94; cf. R.M. Hayward, in Frank (ed.), *Economic Survey*, (1938), IV, p. 53.
4.   Meiggs, *Trees*, pp. 296-97.
5.   Van Nostrand, in Frank (ed.), *Economic Survey*, III, p. 163.
6.   Van Nostrand, in Frank (ed.), *Economic Survey*, III, p. 162; Frank, in *idem* (ed.), *Economic Survey*, V, p. 292.

thinks it more likely to be cast iron from China or central Asia.[1]

[All articles of] marble. Rome imported marble mainly from Africa,[2] Egypt[3] and Greece.[4] Augustus's famous boast that he found Rome brick and left it marble (Suetonius, *Aug.* 28.3) was relatively justified,[5] and heralded the beginning of a period of lavish use of fine marble in Rome, not only for public buildings but also for the ostentatious palaces of the rich (cf. Pliny, *NH* 17.6). The major marble quarries of the empire were annexed to imperial ownership in the early first century so that they might more efficiently supply the needs of Rome.[6] Of course, marble was used not only for building but also for such things as statuary, sarcophagi and baths (Martial 9.75). John's reference to articles of marble presumably refers to such articles, as well as, for example, to columns already cut and shaped in standard lengths before shipment to Rome.[7] Pliny treats the private use of marble as an absurd and indefensible luxury (*NH* 36.2-8, 48-51, 110, 125).

Cinnamon. The term most likely refers both to cassia (the wood of the plant), which was often called cinnamon and formed the bulk of the trade in cinnamon, and also to cinnamon proper (the tender shoots and delicate bark), which was extremely expensive.[8] The common modern view is that they came from somewhere in south Asia (India, Ceylon, Indonesia or south China), but that the merchants of south Arabia, the middlemen in the trade, succeeded in keeping the Romans ignorant of the true source in order to keep the trade in their own hands, with the result that the Romans continued to believe that cinnamon came from

1. Raschke, 'New Studies', pp. 650-51, against Warmington, *Commerce*, pp. 257-58.
2. R.M. Hayward, in Frank (ed.), *Economic Survey*, IV, pp. 53, 62; J. Ward-Perkins, 'The Marble Trade and its Organization: Evidence from Nicomedia', in D'Arms and Kopff (eds.), *Seaborne Commerce*, p. 326.
3. Ward-Perkins, 'Marble Trade', p. 326
4. J.A.O. Larsen, in Frank (ed.), *Economic Survey*, IV, pp. 488-49 n. 35.
5. Frank, in *idem* (ed.), *Economic Survey*, V, p. 19 n. 30.
6. Ward-Perkins, 'Marble Trade', pp. 326-28.
7. Ward-Perkins, 'Marble Trade', pp. 327-28.
8. For the reasons for the high prices of spices in Rome, see Raschke, 'New Studies', p. 670.

Arabia or east Africa.[1] Raschke, however, maintains that ancient cassia and cinnamon were not the same spices as are known by those names today and that they probably did in fact come from east Africa (Somalia).[2] In any case, cinnamon was valued as incense, medicine, perfume and a condiment in wines. In common with the rest of the eastern trade, the trade in cinnamon probably increased considerably in the later first century CE.[3]

Amomum (ἄμωμον). This was another aromatic spice, certainly from south India, though the Romans thought it came from various places along its trade routes.[4]

Incense. Incense, made in various parts of the east from a combination of ingredients, often very expensive, was not only used in religious rites, but also valued for perfuming the rooms and the funerals of the rich.

Sweet-smelling ointment. Despite many translations, μύρον refers generally to aromatic ointment, not exclusively to that made from myrrh (σμύρνα). Myrrh, imported from the Yemen and Somalia at great expense,[5] was certainly one of the most prized of such perfumes (Pliny, *NH* 13.17), and was also an ingredient, as were cinnamon and amomum, in perfumes, some vastly expensive (Pliny, *NH* 13.15), made from a variety of ingredients. Such unguents were considered typical features of the good life in imperial Rome,[6] and therefore Pliny treats them as one of the expensive feminine—or, if used by men, effeminate—indulgences which were ruining the society of his time (*NH* 13.20-22; cf. 12.83-84).

Frankincense. Frankincense from the Sabaeans (of southern Arabia) is one of Virgil's examples of the imports to Rome from distant parts of

1. V.M. Scramuzza in Frank (ed.), *Economic Survey*, III, pp. 350-51; Frank, in *idem* (ed.), *Economic Survey*, V, p. 293.
2. Raschke, 'New Studies', pp. 652-55.
3. Warmington, *Commerce*, pp. 186-88.
4. Warmington, *Commerce*, pp. 184-85.
5. G.W. van Beek, 'Frankincense and Myrrh', *BA* 23 (1960), pp. 86-88.
6. See the revealing funerary inscriptions from Rome in A.L. Connolly, 'Frankincense and Myrrh', *New Doccuments 1979*, pp. 130-31.

the world (*Georgics* 1.57). Like other aromatics, it was used as perfume. Frankincense and myrrh[1] are the prime examples of the perfumes of Arabia (Pliny, *NH* 12.51), on which Pliny blames in part the drain of Roman currency to the east (*NH* 12.82-84). They are also the kind of perfumes which were consumed in vast quantities at the funerals of the rich, illustrating for Pliny the *luxuria* of mankind even in the hour of death: 'the perfumes such as are given to the gods a grain at a time...are piled up in heaps to the honour of dead bodies'. As so often, Nero supplies the most outrageous example: Pliny thinks he must have used at the funeral of Poppaea more perfumes than Arabia produces in a whole year (*NH* 12.82-83). According to Warmington, 'So great was the use of aromatics at funerals that the death of any living thing tended to call forth from the poets reference to Indian and Arabian perfumes'.[2]

Wine. Rome imported wine especially from Sicily[3] and Spain.[4] Trimalchio's first business enterprise was to send five ships loaded with wine from Asia to Rome: he lost thirty million sesterces when they were wrecked (Petronius, *Sat.* 76). However exaggerated the sum, it indicates that the wine trade with Rome could be considered highly profitable.[5] It seems that by the end of the first century CE, the Empire had a serious problem of a surplus of wine and a shortage of grain (cf. Rev. 6.5-6). With the extension of the large estates (*latifundia*) owned by wealthy Romans in the provinces, vines were cultivated at the expense of corn, because the wine trade was the more profitable. An edict of Domitian therefore attempted to reduce by half the cultivation of vines in the provinces, but it was apparently quite

1. On frankincense and myrrh, see van Beek, 'Frankincense and Myrrh', pp. 70-95; Connolly, 'Frankincense and Myrrh', pp. 129-31; Raschke, 'New Studies', p. 652.
2. Warmington, *Commerce*, p. 90.
3. V.M. Scramuzza, in Frank (ed.), *Economic Survey*, III, p. 350; Frank, in *idem* (ed.), *Economic Survey*, V, p. 293.
4. Van Nostrand, in Frank (ed.), *Economic Survey*, III, pp. 177-78; Frank, in *idem* (ed.), *Economic Survey*, V, pp. 220, 297.
5. The qualities of wine from various places are discussed in Athenaeus, *Deipnosophistae* 1.32-34, but the discussion is so literary it would be hazardous to conclude that they were all drunk in Rome.

ineffective in the face of commercial considerations.[1]

Oil. Africa and Spain were at this time taking over from Italy as the major suppliers of olive oil to Rome.[2] Vast quantities were imported.[3]

Fine flour. Although the other three items of food (wine, oil, wheat) grouped together in the list were staples for all inhabitants of Rome, it is noteworthy that the list's general emphasis on luxury is maintained by this reference to fine flour imported for the wealthy. According to Pliny, the Egyptian product was not as good as the Italian (*NH* 18.82), but the most esteemed fine flour was imported from Africa (*NH* 18.89).

Wheat. The sheer size of first-century Rome's population (estimated at 800,000 to 1,000,000)[4] made its corn supply a vast economic operation. Under the early empire, Sardinia and Sicily declined in significance as suppliers of grain to Rome, while Africa and Egypt supplied the bulk of Rome's needs (cf. Josephus, *War* 2.283, 386). Thousands of ships must have been involved in shipping the grain across the Mediterranean.[5] As Tiberius put it, 'the very life of the Roman people is daily at the hazard of wind and wave' (Tacitus, *Ann.* 3.54). The immense importance of the corn supply meant that the state increasingly supervised the system, but private merchants and shippers continued to run it.[6] It was financed not only by the sale of grain to consumers but also by the government which bought supplies to

---

1. Wengst, *Pax Romana*, p. 224; Hemer, *Letters*, p. 158.
2. Van Nostrand, in Frank (ed.), *Economic Survey*, III, p. 177; R.M. Hayward, in Frank (ed.), *Economic Survey*, IV, p. 61; Frank, in *idem* (ed.), *Economic Survey*, V, pp. 221, 292, 297. On the olive oil trade in Rome, see S. Panciera, '*Olearii*', in D'Arms and Kopff (eds.), *Seaborne Commerce*, pp. 235-50.
3. For the volume of Spanish oil imported, see P. Garnsey and R. Saller, *The Roman Empire: Economy, Society and Culture* (London: Gerald Duckworth, 1987), p. 58.
4. See K. Hopkins, *Conquerors and Slaves* (Sociological Studies in Roman History, 1; Cambridge: Cambridge University Press, 1978), pp. 96-98.
5. G. Rickman, 'The Grain Trade Under the Roman Empire', in D'Arms and Kopff (eds.), *Seaborne Commerce*, pp. 263-64.
6. Rickman, 'The Grain Trade', pp. 268-72; P. Garnsey, 'Grain for Rome', in Garnsey, Hopkins and Whittaker (eds.), *Trade*, pp. 126-28.

distribute as the free corn dole, though much of the latter was also made up of the supplies of corn which came from the provinces as tax in kind. This makes the inclusion of wheat in John's list significant, as well as inevitable. Whereas many other items in the list illustrate how the wealth which rich citizens of Rome gained from the empire was spent on conspicuous luxuries, this item shows how the general population of Rome survived only at the expense of the rest of the empire. A city of a million people—the largest city in the western world before eighteenth-century London—could not have grown and survived without the resources of the whole empire to support it.[1] This was one respect in which the harlot (the city of Rome) rode on the beast (the imperial power). There is some evidence of bread riots in the cities of Asia Minor around the time when Revelation was written,[2] and since Rome had first claim on Egyptian wheat, before the other cities of the empire,[3] resentment could well have been directed by the poor against the system of corn supply to Rome. The economic background to Revelation is in this respect vividly portrayed in Rev. 6.5-6: shortage of the most basic foodstuffs (wheat and barley), but a surplus of wine and oil.[4]

Cattle. The import of animals to Rome by sea might at first sight seem surprising, but in fact methods of transporting livestock on ships must have been well developed in the imperial period, when large numbers of wild animals of all kinds were transported to Rome for the entertainments in the amphitheatres.[5] Wild bulls and wild sheep were among such animals,[6] but the references to cattle and sheep in the list in Revelation are unlikely to be to these, since if the supply of animals to the amphitheatres were in mind, more obvious species such as

1.   Garnsey and Saller, *Roman Empire*, p. 83.
2.   Collins, *Crisis*, pp. 94-97; Wengst, *Pax Romana*, p. 224.
3.   Garnsey and Saller, *Roman Empire*, pp. 98-99.
4.   Wengst, *Pax Romana*, pp. 223-24; Hemer, *Letters*, pp. 158-59.
5.   J.M. Frayn, *Sheep-rearing and the Wool Trade in Italy during the Roman period* (ARCA Classical and Medieval Texts; Papers and Monographs, 15; Liverpool: Francis Cairns, 1984), p. 164.
6.   On bulls: J.M.C. Toynbee, *Animals in Roman Life and Art* (London: Thames & Hudson, 1973), pp. 149-51; G. Jennison, *Animals for Show and Pleasure in Ancient Rome* (Manchester: Manchester University Press, 1937), pp. 59, 70. Sheep: Frayn, *Sheep-rearing*, pp. 42, 164; and cf. Columella 7.2.4.

elephants or lions would surely have been referred to. Nor is the import of cattle likely to have been for food:[1] beef was not a very important item even in the banquets of the rich.[2] Cattle were kept primarily as working animals and for milk. But one breed of cattle not native to Italy, the Epirote, was highly regarded by Roman farmers (Varro, *Res rust.* 2.5.10; Pliny, *NH* 8.45)[3] and cattle of this breed were imported from Greece to Italy for breeding purposes, to improve local breeds (Strabo 7.7.5, 12). The first century was the period in which Roman aristocracy had acquired large sheep and cattle ranches (*latifundia*) both in Italy and, by conquest and confiscation, in the provinces.[4] Cattle were also imported to Italy from Sicily (Strabo 6.2.7).

Sheep. Since the reference is to the animals, it can hardly be the wool trade that the author had in mind.[5] Some sheep may have been shipped from Sicily to Rome for meat for the rich,[6] but the reference is probably again to the import of sheep for breeding purposes. Roman estate-owners were no doubt anxious to improve the amount and quality of the wool produced by their flocks and would import good foreign breeds for this purpose.[7] Although his meaning is not quite clear, Strabo (3.2.6) probably refers to the transport of rams from southwest Spain to Italy for breeding.[8] John's first readers might well have been familiar with the transport of sheep to Rome, since the Romans rated Milesian sheep as the third best in the world (Pliny, *NH* 8.190).[9]

1. Pigs were shipped live from Spain to Rome: van Nostrand, in Frank (ed.), *Economic Survey*, III, p. 181.
2. K.D. White, *Roman Farming* (London: Thames & Hudson, 1970), pp. 276-77.
3. Cf. White, *Roman Farming*, p. 279.
4. Frayn, *Sheep-rearing*, pp. 111-13, 164-65.
5. For the wool trade, see Frayn, *Sheep-rearing*, pp. 162-71. I am grateful to Dr Frayn for advice on this paragraph.
6. V.M. Scramuzza, in Frank (ed.), *Economic Survey*, III, pp. 351-52 ; cf. Frayn, *Sheep-rearing*, pp. 3, 24; Columella 7.2.1; 7.3.13.
7. Cf. Frayn, *Sheep-rearing*, pp. 32-33; and cf. Columella 7.2.4-5; M. Hilzheimer, 'Sheep', *Antiquity* 10 (1936), pp. 205-206.
8. Frayn, *Sheep-rearing*, p. 165. The context, referring to Turdetanian exports, favours this interpretation.
9. Frayn, *Sheep-rearing*, pp. 34, 167-68.

Horses. Race horses for chariot racing in the circuses were imported from Africa, Spain, Sicily, Cappadocia and parts of Greece famous for their horses (Laconia, Thessalia, Aetolia).[1] There were imperial stud farms in Spain and Cappadocia for the supply of such horses. Since Italy was short of the high quality pasture needed for breeding racing horses and the demand for them was considerable, there must have been a sizeable overseas trade.[2]

Chariots. (ῥεδῶν = Latin *raeda* or *reda*, apparently the same as the *carruca*: see Martial 3.47.). These were the four-wheeled, horse-drawn, private chariots used by the rich for travel in Rome and to their country estates. Presumably the chariots themselves, like the word *raeda* (Quintilian 1.5.57), were imported from Gaul. In order to satisfy the taste for ostentatious extravagance, there were silver-plated (Pliny, *NH* 33.140) and gilt (Martial 3.62) chariots of this kind.

Slaves. The significance of the way John refers to slaves and their place at the end of the list will be discussed below. Increasing numbers of slaves in Rome were a feature of the growing prosperity of the rich and the increasing size of the city.[3] The demand was by no means met by the offspring of existing slaves. The enslavement of prisoners taken in war, which had been the normal source of slaves under the Republic, continued to be important in the first century CE, when wars on the frontiers continued and the Jewish war alone produced 70,000 slaves (Josephus, *War* 6.420), but it cannot have been as productive a source as it had been during the period of continuous foreign wars. Harris argues that of the other sources (foundlings, children sold by their parents, adults selling themselves into slavery, slavery through debt, victims of kidnapping, some criminals), much the most important source, because of the common practice of exposing children, must have been foundlings.[4] In any case, slave trading was a

1. Van Nostrand, in Frank (ed.), *Economic Survey*, III, p. 180; R.M. Hayward, in Frank (ed.), *Economic Survey*, IV, p. 52 ; J.A.O. Larsen, in *ibid.*, p. 485; Frank, in *idem* (ed.), *Economic Survey*, V, p. 293; White, *Roman Farming*, p. 289.
2. White, *Roman Farming*, p. 298.
3. Hopkins (*Conquerors*, ch. 1) discusses the increase in slaves in Italy generally.
4. W.V. Harris, 'Towards a Study of the Roman Slave Trade', in D'Arms and

profitable business, and Asia Minor was evidently the most important source of those slaves who were not taken in war.[1] Ephesus, one of the seven cities of Revelation, must have played a major role in exporting slaves from Asia Minor to Rome.[2] It should be noted that, whereas slaves as such were certainly not regarded as a luxury, the vast numbers of slaves acquired by the Roman rich and the huge prices paid for slaves of particular beauty or skill were considered extravagances (e.g. Tacitus, *Ann.* 3.53; Juvenal 5.56-60; Martial 11.70).

These detailed notes on the merchandise enable us to draw some general conclusions about the list. In the first place, most of the items were among the most expensive of Rome's imports. At the end of his *Natural History* (37.204), Pliny has a list of the most costly products of nature in various categories. It has twenty-seven items in all, or twenty-nine if gold and silver, which he mentions as an afterthought, are included. Including gold and silver, thirteen of the twenty-eight cargoes in Revelation occur in this list of Pliny's (gold, silver, precious stones, pearls, purple, silk, scarlet, citrus wood, ivory, cinnamon, amomum, aromatic ointment, frankincense), and these in fact account for eighteen of the items in Pliny's list. These cargoes were expensive in themselves. Others in the list in Revelation (oil, wheat) were not expensive as such, but were imported in such vast quantities that in total they must have cost a very great deal. Thus the list is very representative of Rome's more expensive imports.

Again, while the list includes some items (wine, oil, wheat) which illustrate how the survival of the whole city depended on such imports, it features especially the luxury items which fed the vulgarly extravagant tastes of the rich. In this respect, perhaps the most surprising omission is a reference to the exotic foodstuffs imported from all over the empire for the banquets of the rich, which are regularly the special target of Roman writers' complaints or satires on the excesses of first-century Roman indulgence (e.g. Petronius, *Sat.* 38; 55; 119; Juvenal, 5.80-119; 11.138-144; Seneca, *Ad Helviam* 10.2-11; *De vita beata* 11.4; *Ep.* 60.2; 89.22; Pliny, *NH* 12.4; 15.105). But

Kopff (eds.), *Seaborne Commerce*, pp. 118-24.
1. Harris, 'Study', p. 122.
2. Harris, 'Study', p. 127.

it may be that no *single* item of this kind was important enough to belong in a list like this. However, the import of many of the luxury items which are listed had very considerably increased during the period since Augustus. It is not surprising that several of the items belong wholly or partly to the eastern trade with Arabia, east Africa, India and beyond (jewels, pearls, silk, ivory, iron, cinnamon, amomum, incense, aromatic ointment, frankincense), which flourished especially under the early empire.[1] Imports from the east are regularly prominent among the luxury goods mentioned by Roman writers critical of the conspicuous extravagance of the Roman rich in that period. It is true that Tacitus claims (*Ann.* 3.55) that the fashion for expensive excess gave way to simpler tastes again from the time of Vespasian, but neither the literary nor other evidence (e.g. in 92, Domitian constructed warehouses for oriental spices in Rome)[2] bears this out, at least with regard to the kind of items included in the list in Revelation.[3] As a critique of Roman wealth, John's list will still have accurately made its point in the reign of Domitian (if we accept this traditional and most widely accepted date for Revelation).[4]

As the notes on each cargo have shown, many of the items in the list are specifically mentioned as prime examples of luxury and extravagance by Roman writers critical of the decadence, as they saw it, of the wealthy families of Rome in the early imperial period (gold, silver, jewels, pearls, purple, silk, scarlet, citrus wood, bronze, marble, cinnamon, amomum, aromatic ointment, frankincense, slaves). This same verdict is effectively expressed in the comment on the list which is made by the voice from heaven in Revelation 18.14:

> The ripe fruit (ὀπώρα) which your soul craves has gone from you,
> and all your luxuries (λιπαρά) and your glittering prizes (λαμπρά) are
> lost to you, never to be found again [my translation].

The first line evokes Rome's addiction to consumption, while the two words chosen for the merchandise in the second line suggest both the

---

1. Warmington, *Commerce*, pp. 79-80.
2. Warmington, *Commerce*, pp. 89-90.
3. According to M.T. Griffin (*Nero: The End of a Dynasty* [London: Batsford, 1984], pp. 206-207), what happened under Vespasian was a change of imperial style (away from extravagance), a change later reversed under Domitian.
4. For recent defences of this date, see Collins, *Crisis*, ch. 2; Hemer, *Letters*, pp. 2-12.

self-indulgent opulence (λιπαρά) and the ostentatious display (λαμπρά) of Roman extravagance. This is not to say that John's objections to Roman luxury are necessarily the same as those of Roman moralists. The list in Revelation is part of a thoroughgoing, comprehensive critique of the Roman empire as such. Many of the Roman writers I have mentioned were primarily concerned with the way wealth has corrupted the upper classes of Rome. They are nostalgic for the traditional austerity and simplicity of the old Roman aristocratic lifestyle. This is not likely to be John's perspective. Nor will he have shared the anxieties of Pliny and the emperor Tiberius about the empire's disadvantageous balance of trade with the lands to the east. But occasionally the Roman sources indicate moral sensitivity to the fact that the wealth of the Roman rich derived from the conquest and plunder of the empire, and that the economic exploitation of the empire was by no means always to the advantage of the people of the empire (e.g. Petronius, *Sat.* 119). Lucan, for example, clearly recognizes that it was not the ordinary people of Mauretania who benefitted from the high price of the tables made from the citrus trees they themselves had valued only as shade from the sun (9.426-30). Seneca inveighs against 'the wretches whose luxury overleaps the bounds of an empire that already stirs too much envy' (*Ep.* 10.2), and rather similarly suggests the danger to Rome from greed for the spoils of conquered nations: 'whatever one people has snatched away from all the rest may still more easily be snatched by all away from one' (*Ep.* 87.41).

That John saw Rome's wealth as her profit from her empire, enjoyed at the expense of the peoples of the empire, is left in no doubt by the literary connection between the list of cargoes and his portrait of the harlot Babylon. In 17.4 he had described the harlot as

περιβεβλημένη πορφυροῦν καὶ κόκκινον, καὶ κεχρυσωμένη χρυσίῳ καὶ λίθῳ τιμίῳ καὶ μαργαρίταις.

In 18.16 the merchants, in their lament for the great city, describe her (implicitly as a woman who is)

περιβεβλημένη βύσσινον καὶ πορφυροῦν καὶ κόκκινον, καὶ κεχρυσωμένη ἐν χρυσίῳ καὶ λίθῳ τιμίῳ καὶ μαργαρίτῃ.

The description is practically identical in each case except for the addition of βύσσινον ('fine linen') in 18.16. The addition of βύσσινον serves to link the description in 18.16 more closely with the list of Roman imports in 18.12-13. All the six items of finery mentioned in 18.16 occur among the first eight items in the list of cargoes (18.12). (The addition of βύσσινον also serves to link 18.16 with 19.8: just as Babylon, the harlot, is clothed in fine linen, so is the New Jerusalem, the bride of the Lamb, but the varying significance of the fine linen highlights the contrast between the two cities.)

Clearly the expensive adornments of the harlot (17.4; 18.16) represent symbolically the imports listed in 18.12-13, the wealth of Rome (18.17a). The luxuries Rome imports are like the extravagant lifestyle which a rich courtesan maintains at the expense of her clients. They are the price which the kings of the earth have paid for the favours of the harlot (17.2; 18.3). But we must assume that while it is the kings who associate with the harlot—bringing their lands under her dominion and ruling in collaboration with her—the price is actually paid by their peoples. In the case of some of the items of merchandise, the trade was probably perceived by most provincials who, like John, did not benefit from it, as directly exploitative, drawing resources to Rome which were needed in the provinces (such as wheat and slaves), or using local labour to extract expensive products at little benefit to local people (for example, marble). I shall later provide evidence that anti-Roman sentiment in Asia Minor perceived the slave trade in that way (*Sib. Or.* 3.353-55, discussed in Section 5 below). But the trade with the east cannot have been seen as part of Rome's exploitation of the empire in that way. Rather, the point will be that the wealth Rome squanders on luxuries from all over the world was obtained by conquest, plunder and taxation of the provinces. Rome lives well at her subjects' expense. Of course, John recognizes that *some* of her subjects also benefitted from the vast network of trade which fed the huge appetite and expensive tastes of the capital. To those beneficiaries I shall shortly turn.

The way in which the list of cargoes ends still requires comment. The last cargo, slaves, is described thus: σωμάτων, καὶ ψυχὰς ἀνθρώπων. σώματα was in common use with the meaning 'slaves', and John has taken ψυχὰς ἀνθρώπων from Ezek. 27.13 (MT: *bᵉnepeš 'ādām*; LXX: ἐν ψυχαῖς ἀνθρώπων),[1] where it also refers to slaves. It

---

1. This phrase is a literal Greek rendering of the Hebrew, with which John agrees by coincidence. Rev. 18 is not dependent on the LXX of Ezekiel: see Vanhoye,

is just possible that John intends two categories of cargo ('slaves and human lives') and that whereas the former refers to the regular slave trade, the latter refers to those slaves who, along with some prisoners of war and certain criminals, were destined to die fighting for their lives in the amphitheatres of Rome. This would make a telling climax, but more probably, as most commentators and translations agree, the καί is epexegetical: 'slaves, that is, human persons'. This gives considerable emphasis to the reference to slaves at the end of the list. That John gives both the common term for slaves in the slave markets (σώματα) and a scriptural description of slaves (ψυχαὶ ἀνθρώπων) must mean that he intends a comment on the slave trade. He is pointing out that slaves are not mere animal carcasses to be bought and sold as property, but are human beings. But in this emphatic position at the end of the list, this is more than just a comment on the slave trade. It is a comment on the whole list of cargoes.[1] It suggests the inhuman brutality, the contempt for human life, on which the whole of Rome's prosperity and luxury rests.

4. The Mourners (Revelation 18.9-19)

Some commentators on Revelation suppose that in 18.9-19 John betrays some admiration for the opulence of Rome and some regret at its destruction: 'it is with infinite pathos that John surveys the loss of so much wealth' (Caird).[2] That this is a misunderstanding is already made likely by our study of the list of cargoes. It becomes quite certain when we observe that John attributes the laments for Rome's destruction to three very definite classes of people: the kings of the earth (v. 9), the merchants of the earth (v. 11), and the mariners (v. 17). These are precisely the people who themselves benefitted from Rome's economic exploitation of her empire. What they lament is the

---

'L'utilisation du livre d'Ezéchiel', pp. 447, 449-50, 453. For Revelation's general dependence on the MT rather than the LXX, see Mazzaferri, *Genre*, pp. 42-45.

1. J. Sweet, *Revelation* (SCM Pelican Commentaries; London: SCM Press, 1979), p. 271.

2. G.B. Caird, *A Commentary on the Revelation of St John the Divine* (BNTC; London: A. & C. Black, 1966), p. 227. Against this view, see Collins, 'Revelation 18', especially p. 203; also A.A. Boesak, *Comfort and Protest: Reflections on the Apocalypse of John of Patmos* (Edinburgh: Saint Andrew Press, 1987), pp. 121-22.

destruction of the source of their own wealth.

'The kings of the earth'—whom John brands as having 'committed fornication with' the harlot (17.2; 18.3, 9)—is a stock phrase in Revelation (1.5; 6.15; 17.2, 18; 18.3, 9; 19.19; 21.24; cf. 16.14), with which John probably intends an allusion to Ps. 2.2. Psalm 2, with its account of the victory of God's Messiah over the nations who set themselves against God and his Messiah, is one of the Old Testament texts which John made fundamental to his work and to which he alludes throughout it (cf. 2.26-27; 11.15, 18; 12.5; 14.1; 19.15). He may also have noticed the occurrence of the same phrase in Ezekiel's oracle against Tyre (27.33: 'with your abundant wealth and merchandise you enriched the kings of the earth'; cf. also Isa. 24.21). Thus the phrase itself is determined by its scriptural sources; the class of people John uses it to designate need not be literally kings.[1] It will refer not just to the client kings who put their kingdoms under the umbrella of the Roman empire, but more generally to the local ruling classes whom, throughout the empire, Rome co-opted to a share in her rule. John's readers in the province of Asia Minor will have thought most obviously of the local aristocracy who sat on the councils of their cities. For such people Roman authority served to prop up their own dominant position in society. Naturally, therefore, it is the destruction of Rome's *power* that they lament (v. 10), whereas the other two laments mention her wealth (vv. 17, 19).

However, the power they shared with Rome certainly had economic advantages,[2] to which John alludes in v. 9: οἱ μετ' αὐτῆς πορνεύσαντες καὶ στρηνιάσαντες ('those who committed fornication and indulged themselves with her'). As part of the metaphor, along with πορνεύσαντες, στρηνιάσαντες may here refer to the sensual indulgence of the harlot's clients, but it will also suggest the luxury of material wealth. This is the sense of ἐστρηνίασεν in v. 7, where it refers to Babylon's own indulgence in luxury, while in v. 3, στρῆνος is used of Babylon's luxury which has enriched the merchants of the earth (τῆς δυνάμεως τοῦ στρήνους αὐτῆς: 'her excessive luxury'). Thus in v. 9 the meaning must be that the kings' association with Roman power brings them a share in

1.   Note also that in Psalm 2.2 (cf. 10) 'the kings of the earth' appear in parallel with 'the rulers'.
2.   Cf. Wengst, *Pax Romana*, p. 26.

Rome's luxury. It may be worth remembering here that the aristocracies of the cities of the empire, while they did not engage directly in commerce like the merchants of v. 11, often invested in and profited from trading enterprises.[1] So they too had a direct stake in the vast trade with Rome which is described in connection with the second group of mourners, the merchants. Roman rule increased the prosperity of the cities of the eastern Empire, but it was only the ruling classes who benefited and the gap between rich and poor widened.[2]

The 'merchants of the earth' (18.3, 11) are also described as 'your [i.e. Babylon's] merchants' (18.23). This does not mean that they were Romans, but simply that they did business with the city of Rome. Most of the merchants engaged in the trade with Rome, even those resident in Puteoli, Ostia and Rome, were provincials, citizens of the exporting cities from which the merchandise came[3] (though some of these would be Roman citizens).[4] Thus citizens of the cities where John's readers lived, especially Ephesus, will be included. It is also relevant to note that even the eastern trade, which is prominent in the list of imports, was largely in the hands of Roman subjects.[5] John's term for the merchants (ἔμποροι) no doubt includes both the *negotiatores* and the *navicularii* (ναύκληροι), i.e. the independent shipowners who bought and sold their cargoes at the ports. (Thus the ship*owners* are not included among the seafarers of v. 17, who are all their employees). According to v. 23, Babylon's merchants were 'the great men [μεγιστᾶνες] of the earth'. The phrase is drawn from Isaiah's oracle against Tyre (Isa. 23.8: 'whose merchants were princes, whose traders were the honoured of the earth'),[6] but John must have selected it as corresponding to the reality of the Roman empire. Although

---

1. Pleket, 'Urban elites', pp. 131-44; Raschke, 'New Studies', p. 646. Note the example of Damian in mid-second-century Ephesus: D'Arms, *Commerce*, pp. 164-65.

2. Cf. C.S. Walton, 'Oriental Senators in the Service of Rome: A Study of Imperial Policy down to the Death of Marcus Aurelius', *JRS* 19 (1929), pp. 51-52: the resulting discontent of the poor evidently increased under the Flavians.

3. Frank, in *idem* (ed.), *Economic Survey*, V, p. 242.

4. Raschke, 'New Studies', p. 833 n. 770.

5. Raschke, 'New Studies', pp. 643-45.

6. For the dependence on Isa. 23.8, see Fekkes, 'Isaiah and Prophetic Traditions', pp. 231-33.

merchants were not of high social status,[1] John refers accurately to
their wealth, which put many of them among the richest men of their
time, and to their considerable economic power, as banded together in
the trading companies and associations.[2]

The third group of mourners are so described as to include all who
were employed in the maritime transport industry (v. 17). When they
refer in their lament to the fact that 'all who had ships at sea grew
rich by her wealth' they are probably referring to the shipowners who
employed them. They themselves made a living, but presumably not a
fortune, from the trade with Rome. Of course, partly for obvious
geographical reasons and partly because transport by land was much
more expensive than transport by sea, all the imports listed in vv. 12-
13 reached Rome by sea,[3] in John's time mostly through the port of
Ostia whose harbour had been constructed by Claudius.[4] The
mariners' sense of indebtedness to Rome for their livelihood,
expressed in their lament, finds an interesting parallel in a story
Suetonius tells about the emperor Augustus shortly before his death.
He happened to sail into the gulf of Puteoli just as a ship from
Alexandria was docking. The passengers and the crew honoured him
with festal dress, incense and the highest praise, 'saying that it was
through him that they lived, through him that they sailed the seas, and
through him that they enjoyed liberty and their fortunes (*fortunis*)'
(*Aug.* 98.2).[5]

Thus v. 9-19 allow us to see the fall of Rome from a very definite
perspective which was certainly not John's: the perspective of those
who depended for power and wealth, or simply for a living, on their
involvement with Rome and her economic system. For such people, of
course, Rome's downfall is also their own, and their lamentation is
only to be expected. The perspective John shares is not that of these

1.   A few merchants in highly profitable trades did rise into the urban elites:
Pleket, 'Urban elites', pp. 139-43.

2.   M. Rostovtzeff, *Rome* (New York: Oxford University Press, 1960), p. 264;
G. Rickman, 'The Grain Trade Under the Roman Empire', in D'Arms and Kopff
(eds.), *Seaborne Commerce*, pp. 270-71; D'Arms, *Commerce*, pp. 167-68.

3.   Cf. Aelius Aristides, *Oratio* 26.11-13, quoted below. Wengst's comments
(*Pax Romana*, p. 130) on the Mediterranean sea as a negative image in Revelation
are worth considering in this connection.

4.   Frank, in *idem* (ed.), *Economic Survey*, V, pp. 236-41.

5.   I owe this reference to Dr Samuel Barnish.

people of the *earth* and the *sea* (vv. 9, 11, 17), but that of heaven (18.20; 19.1), where Rome's victims (the martyrs) rejoice in the triumph of God's justice over Rome's exploitation of the earth. In the last section, I cited evidence from Roman writers who shared something, if not all, of John's condemnation of Rome's luxury imports. But admiration for the wealth and luxury which Rome drew from all over the known world, such as is expressed in the laments John attributes to provincials who benefited from it, can also be paralleled, significantly in writers from the provinces. For example, Plutarch refers to

> all the things which the earth contributes, and the earth and the sea and islands, continents, rivers, trees, living creatures, mountains, mines, the first-fruits of everything, vying for beauty in the aspect and grace that adorns this place (*Mor.* 325e).

It is worth quoting at some length from Aelius Aristides the orator, who came from Smyrna, one of the cities of Revelation. In a speech (*Oratio* 26) delivered before the imperial court in Rome, probably in 155 CE,[1] his admiration for the city of Rome was naturally unbounded. But he is especially impressed by the visual evidence of its character as 'the common trading center of mankind and the common market of the produce of the earth' (26.7), a description which rather obscures the fact that Rome was the consumer of all the goods which arrived at Ostia and the exporter of rather few. But Aristides continues:

> Here is brought from every land and sea all the crops of the seasons and the produce of each land, river, lake, as well as of the arts of the Greeks and barbarians, so that if someone should wish to view all these things, he must either see them by travelling over the whole world or be in this city. . . So many merchants' ships arrive here, conveying every kind of goods from every people every hour and every day, so that the city is like a factory common to the whole earth.[2] It is possible to see so many cargoes from India and even from Arabia Felix, if you wish, that one imagines that for the future the trees are left bare for the people there and that they must come here to beg for their own produce if they need

---

1. C.A. Behr (trans.), *P. Aelius Aristides: The Complete Works* (Leiden: Brill, 1981), II, p. 373.
2. On this expression (a rhetorical topos), see R. Klein (ed.), *Die Romrede des Aelius Aristides* (Texte zur Forschung, 45; Darmstadt: Wissenschaftliche Buchgesellschaft, 1983), p. 71.

anything. Again there can be seen clothing from Babylon and ornaments from the barbarian world beyond, which arrive in much larger quantity and more easily than if merchantmen bringing goods from Naxus or Cythnus had only put into Athens. Your farmlands are Egypt, Syria, and all of Africa which is cultivated. The arrivals and departures of the ships never stop, so that one would express admiration not only for the harbor,[1] but even for the sea. Hesiod said about the limits of the Ocean, that it is a place where everything has been channeled into one beginning and end. So everything comes together here, trade, seafaring, farming, the scourings of the mines, all the crafts that exist or have existed, all that is produced or grown. Whatever one does not see here, is not a thing which has existed or exists, so that it is not easy to decide which has the greater superiority, the city in regard to present day cities, or the empire in regard to the empires which have gone before (26.11-13).[2]

This is, as it were, Revelation's list of imports to Rome seen from the perspective of the kings and the merchants.

Why then does John give us the perspective of Rome's collaborators in evil: the ruling classes, the mercantile magnates, the shipping industry? Part of the reason may be that, although the perspective was certainly not John's, it could rather easily be that of some of his readers. If it is not likely that many were among the ruling classes, it is not unlikely that John's readers would include merchants and others whose business or livelihood was closely involved with the Roman political and economic system. For such readers John has set a kind of hermeneutical trap. Any readers who find themselves sharing the perspective of Rome's mourners—viewing the prospect of the fall of Rome with dismay—should thereby discover, with a shock, where they stand, and the peril in which they stand. And for such readers, it is of the utmost significance that, prior to the picture of the mourners, comes the command:

> Come out of her my people,
> lest you take part in her sins,
> lest you share in her plagues (18.4).

The command, whose language is borrowed from Jer. 51.45 (cf. 50.8; 51.6, 9; Isa. 48.20), is not meant in the literal geographical sense it had in Jeremiah. None of John's first readers lived in the city of Rome. The command is for the readers to *dissociate* themselves from

1. I.e. of Ostia.
2. Translation from Behr, *Aelius Aristides*, II, pp. 74-76.

Rome's evil,[1] lest they share her guilt and her judgment. It is a command not to be in the company of those who are then depicted mourning for Babylon.

Revelation's first readers, as we know from the seven messages to the churches in chs. 2–3, were by no means all poor and persecuted, like the Christians at Smyrna. Many were affluent, self-satisfied and *compromising*, and for them John intended an urgent revelation of the requirements and the peril of their situation. Most of the seven cities were prosperous communities with significant stakes, as ports or as commercial, administrative and religious centres, in Roman rule and Roman commerce.[2] But in order to participate in the business and social life of these cities, and so in the prosperity of their wealthier citizens, Christians had to participate also in idolatrous religion, including the Roman state religion. The Nicolaitans, apparently active in several of the churches (2.6, 15), and the prophetess Jezebel at Thyatira, were evidently advocating that such compromise was quite permissible (2.14, 20).[3]

We should note, as the Christians at Thyatira would certainly have noticed, the resemblance between Jezebel, as John portrays her in the message to Thyatira, and the harlot Babylon, as he portrays her in chs. 17–18. Of course, Jezebel is John's symbolic name for the prophetess, just as Babylon is his symbolic name for Rome. It serves to compare her with the Old Testament queen who seduced Israel into idolatry in the time of Elijah. Once reminded of the Old Testament Jezebel's 'harlotries and sorceries' (2 Kgs 9.22) and her slaughter of the prophets of the Lord (1 Kgs 18.13), we can see that the harlot of Babylon is also in part modelled on Jezebel (cf. 18.7, 23, 24).[4] Thus it appears that the Thyatiran prophetess, who was encouraging her followers to participate without qualms of conscience in the thriving commercial life of the city,[5] was, so to speak, the local representative

1. Note that the reference to Babylon's *sins* here is not in John's Old Testament sources but has been deliberately added by him: cf. M. Kiddle, *The Revelation of St John* (MNTC; London: Hodder & Stoughton, 1940), p. 363.
2. See especially Hemer, *Letters* .
3. See Hemer, *Letters*, pp. 87-94, 117-123.
4. It may also be relevant to remember Jezebel's connexion with Tyre (1 Kgs 16.31: daughter of the king of Sidon), the Old Testament city which Revelation takes as typical of Rome's economic evil.
5. Cf. W.M. Ramsay, *The Letters to the Seven Churches of Asia* (London:

of the harlot of Babylon within the church at Thyatira. Through her the seductive power of Rome's alliance of commerce and idolatrous religion was penetrating the church. Some of her followers—who have 'committed adultery with' her (2.22)—might therefore find themselves, with a salutary shock of recognition, among 'the merchants of the earth [who] have grown rich with the wealth of [Babylon's] wantonness' (18.3).[1] Thus John's prophecy against Rome could also become a painful and demanding challenge to some of his Christian readers, who needed to 'come out of her'.

John's critique of Rome therefore did more than voice the protest of groups exploited, oppressed and persecuted by Rome. It also required those who could share in her profits to side with her victims and become victims themselves. But those who from the perspective of the earth and the sea were Rome's victims John saw from the perspective of heaven to be the real victors. Hence his account of the fall of Babylon climaxes not in the laments of the kings, the merchants and the mariners, but in the joyful praises of the servants of God in heaven (19.1-8).

5. *Additional Note on the Economic Critique of Rome in the Jewish* Sibylline Oracles

Jewish apocalypses roughly contemporary with Revelation, which also predict the fall of Rome, criticize Rome for her violence, oppression and pride (*4 Ezra* 11.40-46; *2 Bar.* 36.8; 39.5), but not for her wealth (though cf. *4 Ezra* 3.2). For any parallels at all, in prophetic oracles, to John's economic critique of Rome we must turn to the *Sibylline Oracles*.

The most important passage is *Sib. Or.* 3.350-80, of which it will be sufficient here to quote lines 350-68:

> However much wealth Rome received from tribute-bearing Asia,
> Asia will receive three times that much again
> from Rome and will repay her deadly arrogance to her.
> Whatever number from Asia served the house of Italians,

Hodder & Stoughton, 1909), pp. 316-53; Hemer, *Letters*, pp. 120-23.

1. One could also link the complacent, arrogant affluence of the church at Laodicea (Rev. 3.17) with that of Babylon (18.7): cf. Collins, 'Revelation 18', p. 202.

twenty times that number of Italians shall be serfs
in Asia, in poverty, and they will be liable to pay ten-thousand-fold.
O luxurious golden offspring of Latium, Rome,
virgin, often drunken with your weddings with many suitors,
as a slave will you be wed, without decorum.
Often the mistress will cut your delicate hair

(360) and, dispensing justice, will cast you from heaven to earth,
but from earth will again raise you up to heaven,
because mortals are involved in a wretched and unjust life.
Samos will be sand, and Delos will become inconspicuous,
Rome will be a street. All the oracles will be fulfilled.
Smyrna will perish and there will be no mention of it. There will be
an avenger,
but for the bad counsels and the wickedness of its leaders. . .
Serene peace will return to the Asian land,
and Europe will then be blessed.[1]

With the exception of Nikiprowetzky, all scholars regard this as an
independent oracle, inserted into the third book of the *Sibylline
Oracles* along with other independent oracles (381-488) which did not
belong originally with the bulk of the material in this book.[2] The
latter is a product of Egyptian Judaism, probably of the second
century BCE.[3] The oracle in lines 350-80 has been assigned to two
specific geographical and historical contexts, both in the first century
BCE. Collins argues for a context in Cleopatra VII's campaign against
Rome,[4] but there does not seem to be sufficient evidence for this view.
The 'mistress' of line 359 need not be Cleopatra identified with Isis,[5]
but can be understood as either Asia or Fortune.[6] The former is the
most obvious reading of the passage: line 359 depicts a reversal of the
situation in which Rome is the mistress and Asia the slave. Moreover,

---

1.   Translation from J.J. Collins, 'Sibylline Oracles', in J.H. Charlesworth
(ed.), *The Old Testament Pseudepigrapha* (London: Darton, Longman & Todd,
1983), I, p. 370.
2.   See J.J. Collins, *The Sibylline Oracles of Egyptian Judaism* (SBLDS, 13;
Missoula, MT: Scholars Press, 1974), pp. 21-24, 27-28.
3.   Collins, *Sibylline Oracles*, pp. 28-33.
4.   Collins, *Sibylline Oracles*, pp. 57-64; followed by A. Yarbro Collins,
Crisis, p. 91.
5.   Collins, *Sibylline Oracles*, pp. 61-62.
6.   V. Nikiprowetzky, *La troisième Sibylle* (Etudes juives, 9; Paris/La Haye:
Mouton, 1970), p. 342.

although Collins does produce evidence that the conflict between
Cleopatra and Octavian was perceived in terms of the traditional
theme of the conflict between East and West, Asia and Europe,[1] and so
is able to explain the use of the name Asia in lines 350-55 as a
reference to the East led by Cleopatra,[2] he ignores the place names in
lines 363, 365, which make a reference to Asia Minor much more
plausible. Even if the oracle in lines 363-64, with its wordplay on the
three names Samos, Delos and Rome (Σάμος ἄμμος...Δῆλος
ἄδηλος...Ῥώμη ῥύμη), was already known in the Sibylline
literature (it recurs in 8.165-66) and was inserted here for the sake of
its reference to Rome, the specific mention of Smyrna in line 365
would be strange in an oracle originating in Egypt. Moreover, the
oracle in lines 400-88, with its many references to places in Asia
Minor, can be located with some confidence in Asia Minor and
probably assigned to the Erythrean Sibyl.[3] It would not be difficult to
suppose that 350-80 comes from the same geographical area.

The alternative proposal locates the oracle in Asia Minor in the
context of the campaign of Mithridates VI against Rome.[4] The
strength of this proposal is that lines 350-55 do resemble a theme of
Mithridates' anti-Roman propaganda: the depiction of the Romans as
latrones gentium, driven in their imperial conquests by not only the
love of power but also greed for material gain. The prediction of
peace and reconciliation for Asia and Europe beyond the conflict
(367-68) would also fit Mithridates' campaign against Rome, in which
he stressed his role as a unifier of East and West. However, it is
perhaps, as Collins points out, more difficult to place the prediction of
Rome's restoration after destruction (361) in the context of
Mithridates' campaign.[5]

---

1. On this theme in the Jewish Sibyllines, see E. Kocsis, 'Ost–West Gegensatz
in den jüdischen Sibyllinen', *NovT* 5 (1982), pp. 105-10.
2. Collins, *Sibylline Oracles*, pp. 59-60.
3. Collins, *Sibylline Oracles*, pp. 27-28.
4. B.C. McGing, *The Foreign Policy of Mithridates VI Eupator King of Pontus*
(Mnemosyne Supplements, 89; Leiden: Brill, 1986), pp. 102, 105; followed by
H.W. Parke, *Sibyls and Sibylline Prophecy in Classical Antiquity* (London/New
York: Routledge, 1988), pp. 136-37, 148 n. 1. Cf. also H. Fuchs, *Der geistige
Widerstand gegen Rom in der antiken Welt* (Berlin: de Gruyter, 1964), p. 36.
5. Collins does not advance this argument against the Mithridatic origin of the
passage in *Sibylline Oracles*, pp. 60-61, but does in 'Sibylline Oracles', p. 358.

The association of the oracle with Mithridates' campaign is probably too specific. The oracle makes no reference to a king. There is no reason to connect it with any specific historical occasion. But the parallel with Mithridates's propaganda is illuminating. Both Mithridates and the oracle no doubt take up popular resentment in Asia Minor against Roman plunder and taxation.[1] In view of the large numbers of slaves which Asia Minor supplied to the Roman slave trade, lines 353-55 would be particularly appropriate in an anti-Roman oracle from Asia Minor. It is not entirely clear whether the oracle is pagan or Jewish in origin. The Jewish *Sibylline Oracles* were deliberately written within the same literary tradition as pagan Sibylline Oracles, and some fragments of the latter have very probably been incorporated into the extant Jewish Sibyllines.[2] However, lines 357-60 do seem to contain echoes of Old Testament prophecies of the fall of Babylon (Isa. 47.1; Jer. 51.7; Isa. 14.12; 47.5, 7).[3] None of these can be regarded as certain allusions which definitely establish the oracle as Jewish, but in combination they make it likely.

As happens not infrequently in the *Sibylline Oracles*, this oracle is echoed or imitated in later books, especially in 4.145-48:

> Great wealth will come to Asia, which Rome itself
> once plundered and deposited in her house of many possessions.
> She will then pay back twice as much and more
> to Asia, and then there will be a surfeit of war.[4]

In its present form at least, the fourth *Sibylline Oracle* is a Jewish work of the late first century CE, more or less contemporary with Revelation.[5] If this passage is dependent on 3.350-65, it shows that the latter was known in Jewish circles by the time John wrote. It is

1. Cf. also Antisthenes' story of the Roman consul's prophecy after the Roman victory over Antiochus III at Thermopylae (191 BCE), predicting that a great army from Asia would defeat Rome, devastate Italy, and take women, children and wealth as booty to Asia: Fuchs, *Der geistige Widerstand*, pp. 6-7; Collins, *Crisis*, p. 89.

2. Parke, *Sibyls*, pp. 13, 132-33. The fall of Rome was predicted even in Sibylline oracles which circulated in first-century Rome: Parke, *Sibyls*, pp. 142-43.

3. Other parallels suggested by Nikiprowetzky (*La troisième Sibylle*, p. 342) are even less close. For Isa. 14.12 applied to Rome, cf. *Sibylline Oracles* 5.177-78; 8.101.

4. Translation from Collins, 'Sibylline Oracles', p. 387-88.

5. Collins, 'Sibylline Oracles', p. 382.

also of interest that the fourth *Sibylline Oracle* uses, in close connection with the passage just quoted, the legend of the return of Nero (4.137-39), which is also connected with the fall of Rome in Revelation (16.12-14; 17.11-13, 16-17).

A Sibylline passage later than Revelation (8.68-72, which probably refers to and should be dated in the reign of Marcus Aurelius)[1] predicts that the wealth Rome has taken from Asia will be restored to her by the returning Nero:

> One, an old man, will control dominions far and wide,
> a most piteous king, who will shut up and guard all the wealth
> of the world in his home, so that when the blazing
> matricidal exile returns from the ends of the earth
> he will give these things to all and award great wealth to Asia.[2]

Another fragmentary passage in the same eighth book evidently referred to Rome's sumptuousness (8.123-24) and predicts that, when destroyed, Rome will have to repay all she has taken (129). *Sibylline Oracles* 2.18-19 and 8.40 merely predict that, in Rome's coming destruction by fire, her great wealth will perish. We may further note that the adjective χλιδανή (luxurious), applied to Rome in both 3.356 and 8.50, appears to be part of the Sibylline tradition of criticism of Rome's luxury. Finally, the picture of the people of Rome foreseeing her imminent fall and mourning for her with dirges by the banks of the Tiber (8.60-64) is reminiscent of Rev. 18.9-19, but contains no reference to Rome's wealth (and might be dependent on Rev. 18).[3]

Some contact between Revelation and the Jewish Sibylline tradition of criticism of Rome's economic oppression of Asia is therefore possible, but no parallel exists in the latter for Revelation's focus on trade with Rome.[4]

---

1.   Collins, 'Sibylline Oracles', p. 416.
2.   Translation from Collins, 'Sibylline Oracles', p. 419.
3.   This confirms the verdict of Georgi, 'True Prophet', p. 125: 'The recognition of Rome as a world trade center in the Book of Revelation is a new idea in early Christian literature and has no parallels in Jewish apocalypses'.
4.   Cf. also *4* (*5*) *Ezra* 15.44. Some of the material in this paper was published in a more popular form as ch. 6 of my book, *The Bible in Politics: How to read the Bible politically* (London: SPCK, 1989).

IMAGES—OR MIRAGES—OF EMPIRE?
AN ARCHAEOLOGICAL APPROACH TO THE PROBLEM

Keith Branigan

In the northwest corner of Rome's empire we have few written
sources by which to trace even the outline of historical events, let
alone allow us to examine the images of Rome held by the native
populations of the region. Yet among the sources that do survive we
do have a few tempting morsels. Dio Cassius (62.6.4) puts the following words into the mouth of the British queen Boudicca in 60 CE:

> men who are aggressive, dishonest, greedy and irreligious—if indeed we
> should call 'men' those who bathe in warm water, eat exotic dishes, drink
> unmixed wine, smear themselves with oil, lie on soft cushions and sleep
> with boys (who are in any case past their prime), being slaves to a lyre-
> player (and a bad one at that) (trans. John Wade).

What a contrast to the welcome given to Constantius Chlorus by the
citizens of London following his defeat of the usurper Allectus in
296 CE, and recorded in the Panegyric (8.19.1-2) which saluted his
achievements:

> And so when you landed, the long hoped-for avenger and liberator, it was
> right that a triumphal procession poured on to that shore to meet your
> Imperial Highness. . . finally free, finally Romans, finally restored by the
> true light of the Empire (trans. John Wade).

There are of course two and half centuries between these events, and
it would be easy and simple to argue that the remarkable difference in
attitude to the Romans and their Empire, which is portrayed in these
speeches, was indeed a product of 250 years of Roman rule and
occupation. But we know, of course, that these speeches and
sentiments are no more truly representative of what the Britons

thought of the Romans, than are the words of Caractacus before
Claudius (Tacitus *Annals* 12.37), or of Calgacus before the battle of
Mons Graupius (Tacitus *Agricola* 30–32). In trying to identify and
understand the native perception of Rome in the northwest corner of
her empire, we cannot unfortunately have direct access to the words
and thoughts of those natives.

In the study of the northwest provinces of the Roman Empire, we
do not have a wealth of written documentation and historical sources
of any kind. We scavenge for scraps of historical information casually
dropped from the classical sources gathered around the Mediterranean
dining table, and because such scraps are insufficient to satisfy us, we
turn to the dustbin of history—archaeology—to eke out our meagre
diet. But dustbins can be remarkably informative, and they can tell us
things about those who fill them that they would never willingly
divulge, and so it is with archaeology.

In trying to identify and understand the images of empire held or
created by the people of the northwest provinces, archaeology has, I
suggest, at least three advantages over written materials as a source of
evidence. First, archaeology does not suffer from the deliberate
biases, even untruths, that permeate historical writings. Archaeology
has its intrinsic biases, of course, but they result from the accidents of
discovery and the differentials and chance of preservation. Except
perhaps on the tombstone, the archaeologist does not have to grapple
with bias, prejudice and the manipulation of evidence that faces the
reader of Tacitus. Secondly, the written sources available for the
study of this topic are, of course, Roman sources. They are unlikely
even to reflect, let alone understand, the native Celtic reaction to the
Roman occupation and Roman civilisation. Archaeological evidence,
on the other hand, is the testimony left, albeit unconsciously, by the
indigenous population who peopled the northwest provinces. Thirdly,
our written sources are the product of a small and narrow social
group within the Roman world, whereas our archaeological evidence
can speak for the common man as well as the king and the nobility.

This does raise the question: whose attitudes to, and perceptions of,
the Roman Empire are we, as archaeologists, attempting to identify?
There is a danger in Roman archaeology, to which many have
succumbed in the past, of concentrating the spotlight on the public
buildings, and the well-furnished town-house or villa, rather than on
the lock-up shop, the suburban cottage, or the village hovel. In doing

so we learn something about the attitudes and aspirations of the estate-owners, the successful merchants and the upwardly mobile entrepreneurs. But what of the rural peasantry and the industrial labourers in the potting fields, the mines and quarries? Were the demands made, and the opportunities offered, by the occupying power the same to both of these indigenous groups? If not, to what extent did the differences generate different attitudes to the Romans and their Empire? Ideally, we should be trying to assess the impact of Roman occupation across the whole social spectrum of the native population of a northwest province like Britain or Gallia Belgica, and to begin such an assessment we must try to appreciate what demands and opportunities were generated by the Roman occupation.

The demands on the old tribal elites may have been more onerous than they were on the peasantry, simply because they were demands which in native society had largely fallen on the latter. Taxation under the Romans was certainly more complex and all-pervading than any likely system of tithes or dues used by Celtic communities. The 'annona' or corn tax may well have been matched by a native tithe on produce, but the property tax, the poll tax, and death duties appear to have no Celtic equivalents. Equally the loss of power and prestige by the native nobility must have been a serious blow initially, even though the establishment of local self-governing authorities enabled some of both to be recovered in due course. As to loss of land and property, this is more problematic. There were undoubtedly some instances where both were confiscated, the best documented example being the treatment of the Iceni on the death of Prasutagus, and the seizure of Trinovantian land for the benefit of the legionary veterans settled in the colony at Colchester (Tacitus *Annals* 14.31). In the areas under permanent military garrison or those seized as imperial estates, the native population would again have lost land either to the *territoria* of the forts or to the estates under procuratorial control. But vast parts of the northwest provinces would have been totally unaffected by such confiscations, and in Britain and Gaul the archaeological evidence suggests that many native estates continued to operate uninterrupted by the Roman conquest and occupation.

Against these losses must be set the opportunities and benefits offered by the Roman occupation. The maintenance of long-term peace and stability should not be underrated for the owners of wealth and land, and the Roman occupation must have put an end to the frequent intertribal warfare referred to by several Roman authors, and to the endemic cattle rustling of Celtic societies as portrayed in early Irish sources. Another economic benefit for nobility and peasantry alike was the much greater range and quantity of manufactured consumer products that empire-wide commerce made available. A few products, such as wine, bronze vessels, pottery, and silverware had reached southeast Britain in small quantities in the century before the Roman conquest, and are represented in the graves of the elite. But these same products are found in much greater quantities after the conquest, and as might be expected these increased quantities are more widely spread across the social spectrum. So too the range of imported products is much wider—foodstuffs, for example, now include olives, olive oil, fish sauces. Exotic products such as Egyptian glassware and Chinese silk, albeit in very small quantities, demonstrate the far-reaching commerce to which the people of the northwestern corner of the empire now had access. At the same time, the quantity of home-produced manufactured products also appears to have increased significantly, and to have been available to a much wider segment of society than previously.

Where towns had replaced *oppida* and hill-forts as nucleated centres of population, there are also clearly visible benefits in terms of both domestic housing and communal provision of facilities. Even the meanest of the urban houses usually possessed several rooms, with separate access, providing opportunities for functional differentiation and for privacy not found in pre-conquest homes. Many houses, almost certainly too numerous all to belong to members of the former tribal nobility, possessed hard, clean floors and walls, and at least one or two hypocaust-heated rooms. The provision of a piped water-supply and, perhaps more importantly, a decent sewage system must also have added to what we can most conveniently call 'the quality of life'. These benefits, at different levels of intensity, seem to have been widespread, although in the more remote parts of Britain and in some rural settlements in the lowland zone, there appears to have been little change in domestic accommodation.

It is in the towns, too that we can perhaps most readily appreciate what I believe to be the greatest opportunity offered by the Roman occupation: namely the opportunity for social mobility. Here, the rows of shops that line the high streets and surround the forum, and the market halls that offer specialist outlets for various foods, visibly demonstrate the opportunities that existed in a Roman province for the small-businessman, the entrepreneur, and the middleman. Whether through craft specialism, through buying and selling, or simply through providing a fast food outlet, it was possible in a Roman town to accumulate wealth. Not, perhaps, a fortune, but enough to acquire a certain status, to invest in civic amenities, and thereby to win election to the local council and open doors to further social advancement.

Another route to higher social status was recruitment to the army, with its ultimate goal of citizenship and its secondary benefits of acquiring useful skills and knowledge. These were opportunities open to the population at large, and in themselves they offered nothing to the former tribal nobility. But at least in the earlier years of the Roman province, there can be little doubt that it was these families who provided the majority of the decurions for the local council, and that it certainly was these families from whom the holders of magisterial power emerged. Given that they were a defeated people, the Roman system of local government at least provided them with a means to retain their status and prestige, albeit with greatly reduced powers.

Weighed in the balance, it is difficult, I believe, to avoid the conclusion that for the bulk of the population of a province like Britain the Roman Empire offered more than it demanded. If that was so, then we might expect the native image of Empire to have been far nearer to that expressed by the Panegyric for Constantius Chlorus than to the words put into Boudicca's mouth by Dio Cassius. Given the paucity and the biases of our written sources, we can only test that affirmation against archaeological evidence, which is essentially the evidence of material culture. It will not, therefore, be able to tell us whether the Britons or the Gauls thought the Roman system of taxation or justice was fair (does anyone ever think any system of taxation or justice is fair?), or whether they thought that Roman moral values were superior or inferior to their own. At best I think we can seek to answer one simple question: did they believe the Roman way of life was worth emulating?

At a superficial level the answer to this question is plainly yes, for the native Britons and Gauls built towns, public buildings, and houses in the Roman style, with for the most part no governmental coercion to do so and only modest governmental assistance. Equally, they sought and acquired a wide variety of manufactured and imported goods and foodstuffs, as we have already noted. At the upper end of the social spectrum, this involved very substantial investment of wealth. Some of the large town houses, and even more of the large villas, possessed twenty, thirty or forty rooms, sometimes as in the Keynsham villa[1] of quite remarkable elaboration and paved with mosaics of sufficient size or quality (and occasionally both) to have cost large sums of money. Public and private funds alike were poured into building baths, theatres, and amphitheatres for the entire adult population, of whatever rank or class, to indulge in peculiarly Roman forms of leisure and entertainment. It is clear that these buildings were utilised—they were not just empty showpieces—for they were remodelled, repaired and improved over two or three centuries, and rare but precious scraps of direct evidence exist for those who provided the entertainment in these public places.

But these are all material comforts and improvements, which anyone with the opportunity to indulge in them would be likely to accept regardless of what they thought of those who introduced them. Furthermore, they are essentially the material comforts and tastes of the upper elements of society, and the Roman empire was neither the first nor the last in which a native elite sought to emulate the material lifestyle of the conquerors. I believe that if we are to attain even an approximate understanding of the deeper responses of the Gauls and the Britons to the empire, we have to assess to what extent they began to think like Romans—and to do that from the material evidence recovered by archaeology is obviously difficult in the extreme.

We might begin by looking briefly at one aspect of material culture where the acceptance of Roman innovations may be regarded more as examples of a conscious choice to 'be Roman' than as the adoption of innovations which were in themselves clearly beneficial. In the matter of clothing, for example, there were certainly few, if any, material benefits or comforts to be gained by adopting Roman sandals and tunics designed for a Mediterranean climate, yet both seem to have been popular in Britain and northern Gaul. The tunics survive mainly on tombstones and other sculptures, and although the toga is rare, other Roman garments can be frequently identified. As for sandals, they are widely attested, and where preservation conditions are

---

1. K. Branigan, *The Roman Villa in South West England* (Bradford-on-Avon: Moonraker Press, 1976), pp. 56-57.

appropriate they occur in sufficient quantity to suggest that they were very common indeed. Thirty were represented in the collection from Lullingstone villa, and many were identified at Scole in Norfolk.

Turning to another aspect of fashion, namely hair styles, it is clear that the latest fashions, transmitted to the furthest reaches of the empire through the portraits of the imperial house on coins, were quickly adopted by both men and women. They appear on tombstones and busts, and occasionally on smaller items of personal jewellery such as jet pendants, within a short time of their appearance in Rome. It is not difficult to believe, in looking at the famous portrait bust from Lullingstone villa, that we are looking at a man who thought of himself as Roman; yet there is not a scrap of evidence that second and third century Lullingstone was owned by anything other than a native family.

That is true also of the vast majority, if not all, of other Romano-British villas, yet in the farmyards and outbuildings of these rural estates we may find clues that attest more effectively to the adoption of Roman attitudes and thought patterns than do the mosaic-floored and hypocaust-heated houses to which so much attention is usually paid. There is nothing in the archaeological record, nor in the writings of Caesar and Tacitus on the Britons and the Germans, to suggest that the land was regarded as a resource to be exploited to the full, for profit. Roman farmers, on the other hand, were extolled by such writers as Columella, Varro, Cato and Martial to maximise their profits from the land by utilising its resources to the full. Martial's description of Faustinus's estate at Baiae (*Epigrams* 3.58) boasts that here no land is wasted. The estate produces corn, grapes, cattle, pigs, sheep, geese, partridge, pheasants, chickens, pigeons, fish, deer, garden produce, and timber. The interest of this list is that, with the exceptions of partridge, pheasant, and grapes, it is matched by the archaeological evidence from Shakenoak villa in Oxfordshire. Nor is it very different from that of the Frocester Court villa in Gloucestershire.[1] In fact, wherever Romano-British villas have been subjected to extensive excavation and detailed study of bio-archaeological material, we find evidence for a farming strategy based on maximization of the estate's

---

1. K. Branigan, 'Specialisation in Villa Economies', in K. Branigan and D. Miles (eds.), *The Economies of Romano-British Villas* (Sheffield: University of Sheffield Department of Archaeology & Prehistory, 1989), pp. 42-50 (43).

resources. Maximization of resources and the seizure of profit-making opportunities as and when they arose may have applied to resources other than purely agricultural ones. The substantial tile kilns built at Park Street villa and at Eccles villa[1] were almost certainly far larger than were needed for new roofing and hypocaust-building at these two villas. The former seems most likely to have been constructed to exploit the short-term high demand for tiles in St Albans at the beginning of the fourth century, and the latter to supply the tile requirements of other villas in the Darenth valley.

A more unusual example still, but one which perhaps most neatly encapsulates the new thinking of the Romano-British farmer, is the redevelopment of the Gadebridge Park villa early in the fourth century.[2] A swimming pool was built here, larger in size than any in the province except that in the great spa centre at Bath, and completely dwarfing the other three private villa swimming pools known in Britain. The excavator has plausibly suggested that since the site is fed by saline and chalybeate springs, it too may have been a small spa, serving the needs of the nearby town of St Albans. A very large heated wing, added to one side of the villa at the same time as the swimming pool was built, may have provided the accommodation for visitors to this 'health farm'.

The entrepreneurial attitudes that may be detected at Gadebridge and Park Street villas are neatly reflected also in St Albans (fig. 1), and nowhere better than in insula 28.[3] Here, on the corner of a side street which formed a short cut between the forum and the theatre, a building plot was redeveloped around 200 CE. A neat little dwelling house with eight or nine rooms, three of them heated, stood at one end of the plot. Two lock-up shops fronting onto the street were constructed at the opposite end, and no doubt provided the owner with a useful income, whether from rents or from his own retailing activities. But the real clue to the attitudes of this landowner is found

1. B. Rawlins, 'A Roman Tile Kiln at Park Street, near St. Albans', *Herts Archaeology* 2 (1970), pp. 62-66; A. Detsicas *The Cantiaci* (Gloucester: Alan Sutton, 1983), pp. 166-67.

2. D. Neal, *The Excavation of the Roman Villa in Gadebridge Park* (London: Society of Antiquaries, 1974), p. 68.

3. S.S. Frere, *Verulamium Excavations* (London: Society of Antiquaries, 1983), II, pp. 244-65.

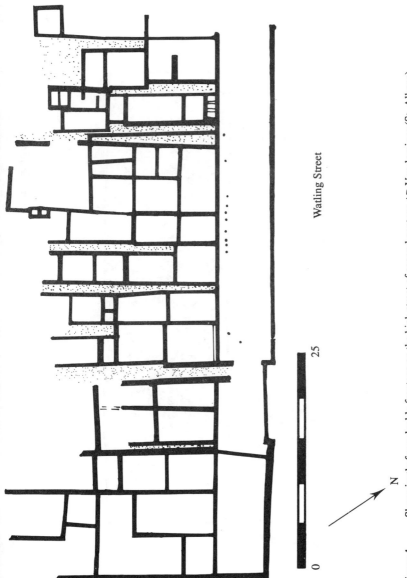

Watling Street

N

0   25

Figure 1   Shops jostle for valuable frontage on the high street of second century AD Verulamium (St. Albans)

Figure 2   An incomplete writing tablet from London with the impression of a letter written in its wax writing surface.

sandwiched between two shops. Here, where another shop could have been accommodated, we find instead a large latrine, so large in fact (probably a 20-seater), that it must have been for public use—and private profit. There would have been a charge for this facility, and given its strategic position between the market place and the theatre, it must have done good business on the public holidays that packed the late Roman calendar.

Given these entrepreneurial attitudes amongst the villa-owners and urban property-owners, we might expect to find further evidence of related Roman behavioural patterns, of which a demand for formal education might be the most obvious. There is much debate as to the extent to which Latin was written and spoken by the native population of Roman Britain. Evidence for the presence of teachers is very limited, confined in fact to the brief mention by Plutarch of the Greek *grammaticus*, Demetrius, whose visit to Britain might just be commemorated by the two bronze plaques dedicated by a Demetrius at York.[1] But suggestive evidence of Latin lessons is provided by a handful of graffiti which appear to be survivals of writing or grammar lessons, and more indirectly but perhaps more powerfully by the mosaics at Lullingstone and Low Ham villas, which respectively carry written and pictorial allusions to Virgil's *Aeneid*.[2]

More convincing still to my mind are the handful of surviving writing tablets which reveal the fluent if heavy-handed Latin of the London-based entrepreneur on the one hand (fig. 2), and the Chew Valley villa owner on the other.[3] And more surprising is the collection of 168 lead curse tablets found in the rural sanctuary at Uley in Gloucestershire.[4] All the evidence from the shrine, and from those tablets which have been deciphered, suggests that the temple was patronized by the local farmers. Unless subsequent investigation reveals the tablets all to be the work of only a few priestly hands (and

1. R. Collingwood and R. Wright, *Roman Inscriptions in Britain* (Oxford: Oxford University Press, 1965), I, §§662-63.

2. A. Barrett, 'The Literary classics in Roman Britain', *Britannia* 9 (1978), pp. 307-14.

3. H. Chapman, 'Letters from Roman London', *The London Archaeologist* 2 (1974), pp. 173-76; E. Turner, 'A Roman Writing Tablet from Somerset', *JRS* 46 (1956), pp. 114-18.

4. A. Ellison, *Excavations at West Hill, Uley* (Bristol: Western Archaeological Trust, 1978).

there is no suggestion of this in the studies so far published), we must assume that the rural population around Uley was also well capable of expressing in Latin both their piety and their wrath. I believe that, increasingly, the evidence suggests that an ability to speak, read and write Latin was much more widespread—socially as well as geographically—in Roman Britain than has previously been believed. Given that, for the rural population in particular, there can have been little material benefit or financial reward to be gained by mastering the language of the imperial power, it surely suggests a willingness, even an enthusiasm, for thinking and expressing oneself like a Roman.

The interest of the site at Uley goes beyond the inscribed curse tablets found there, however, for it is of course a typical example of the Romano-Celtic temples that sprang up in Britain and the northwestern provinces during the empire. About 130 such temples are now known in Britain (and rather more in Gallia Belgica), so that they clearly formed an important expression of popular ideology. That ideology seems to represent a conscious attempt to conflate Roman and native gods; and on the rare occasions where inscribed altars and votives survive, we certainly find that the names of Roman and Celtic deities are presented as a hyphenated unity—Mars-Lenus, Mars-Toutatis, Silvanus-Calirius, and Apollo-Cunomaglus, for example. Since there is no reason whatever to think that there was any pressure from the Imperial government to establish temples to these conflated deities, we must assume that they represent a widespread and popular ideological stance freely adopted by the native population.

In the later Roman empire, the adoption of Christianity is surely a similar phenomenon. There has been a great deal of debate about the extent of Christianity in the northwest provinces in the fourth century, and opinion has generally favoured a very restricted church in terms of both numbers and social class. The rarity and intrinsic value of such discoveries as the Hinton St Mary mosaic and the Water Newton treasure have certainly encouraged such a view. But a steady stream of far less impressive finds, from ChiRo graffiti to the crushed lead baptismal tank from Ashton, continue to add to the collective evidence for Christianity at a lower social level.[1]

Far more important has been the excavation and study of late

---

1.   C. Thomas, *Christianity in Roman Britain to AD 500* (London: Batsford, 1981).

Roman cemeteries at Icklingham, Ashton and Poundbury (Dorchester, Dorset). Icklingham's Christian connections have been posited and generally accepted for some time, based largely on the discovery there of no less than three baptismal tanks, but also the recognition of a mortuary chapel and a font at the centre of the cemetery.[1] Ashton, on the other hand, is a much more recent discovery. The neatly arranged cemetery of unaccompanied east–west burials contrasts strongly with contemporary burials elsewhere in the settlement that are haphazardly oriented, and the lead baptismal tanks from the site add weight to the argument that we may be looking at a Christian cemetery.[2] As for Poundbury cemetery at Dorchester, there are several reasons, collectively very persuasive, for seeing this as a Christian burial ground. The importance of this, if the interpretation is correct, is that a simple calculation suggests that the town of Dorchester may have had a Christian church numbering, at the very least, about 500 or 600 persons in the fourth century.[3] In other words, a substantial part of the urban population, at least in this corner of the province, may have adopted Christianity.

Whether such adoption was by reason of firm religious conviction or by way of fashion is to some extent irrelevant to our particular concern here. The important point is that substantial parts of the native population of Britain can be seen to be adopting Roman patterns of behaviour and belief which, in most cases at least, can have offered no immediate material benefits. I suggest, then, that in so far as we can begin to discern human behaviour and human attitudes from the mute testimony of archaeological evidence, it suggests that in a distant province like Britain there were many people—not just a handful—who thought like Romans, perhaps thought of themselves as Romans, and who viewed the Roman way of life as, on the whole, beneficial to them and worth emulating.

A final test of this proposition might be to look briefly at what happened in the last decades of the Roman occupation, when it must

1. S. West and J. Plouviez, 'The Romano-British site at Icklingham', *East Anglian Archaeology* 3 (1976), pp. 63-125.
2. C. Guy, 'The lead tank from Ashton', *Durobrivae* 5 (1977), pp. 10-11.
3. C. Green, 'The significance of plaster burials', in R. Reece (ed.), *Burial in the Roman World* (London: CBA, 1977), pp. 46-53; K. Branigan, 'Counting Christians in Roman Britain', *JACT Bulletin* 4 (1985), pp. 3-5.

have been clear to many, if not all, that the empire was in the terminal stages of decay and collapse. St Albans, or Verulamium, may be taken as a case study. Here, some years after the traumatic barbarian incursions of 367 CE, house owners were still erecting substantial new town houses. The most impressive yet discovered, found in insula 27, had nearly twenty rooms arranged in three wings around a small courtyard.[1] It was built sometime after 370 CE, and was later remodelled and two of its rooms enlarged. These two rooms were provided with new mosaic floors at a date which must lie very close indeed to the end of the fourth century at the earliest. That expertise was still available to lay new mosaics at this time must surely imply that there was still a greater demand for these expensive floors than that represented by these two floors alone. The impression of Verulamium at this time is one of a town in which the Roman way of life was tenaciously maintained. Long after this house had eventually fallen into decay, and been overlain by a large barn-like building, the streets of Verulamium were being maintained, and at an even later date we find a typical Roman municipal water main of wooden pipes with iron collars being laid across the site. So we have a picture that suggests that here at least, not only the Roman life style but also Roman governmental institutions were being upheld well into the fifth century, if not beyond. This is indeed implied by Bede's account of St Germanus's visit to St. Albans in 429 CE—and so historical and archaeological record here come together at the end of our excursus.

The proposition which I have argued here—that many natives of Rome's northwestern provinces, from all points on the social ladder, perceived the Romans and their empire as broadly beneficial to them—is one which I know would be hotly disputed by many other Romano-British archaeologists. There is at present an attitude abroad which is perhaps best summed up not by the writings of an archaeologist, but by those of the Monty Python team. Recall the scene in *The Life of Brian* where the People's Front of Judaea are framing their demands to Pontius Pilate. Reg, their leader, sums up their feelings about the Romans:

---

1. S.S. Frere, *Verulamium Excavations* (London: Society of Antiquaries, 1983), II, pp. 214-16.

They've bled us white. They've taken everything we had. And what have
they ever given us in return?[1]

Someone mentions the aqueduct, and someone else sanitation. Five
minutes and a dozen interventions later Reg is still undeterred. He
grudgingly concedes the better sanitation, medicine, education,
irrigation, public health, roads, freshwater system, baths and public
order, but he still demands to know 'what have the Romans ever done
for us?' There are many Romano-British archaeologists who believe
that the Britons, like Reg, never really cared for Roman culture at all,
and that their mosaic-floored town houses and country villas were
little more than a facade. I have tried in this paper to go beyond the
mosaics and the baths to gain some insight, some impression, of what
the natives thought *about* the Romans and, in particular, whether the
natives ever thought *like* the Romans. But our only evidence is
archaeological, the evidence of material culture, and it is all too easy
to read it wrongly and misinterpret its message. The images of Rome
which I have tried to grasp here may themselves be nothing more than
mirages.

---

1. G. Chapman, *et al.*, *The Life of Brian* (London: Eyre Methuen, 1979),
p. 20.

'Expendite denarium vestrum et. . .
An entrepreneurial R-B. installed a 24-seater latrine between two shops.

CALGACUS: CLASH OF ROMAN AND NATIVE*

D.J. Mosley

Calgacus, the Caledonian chieftain who led the resistance to Rome at the Battle of Mons Graupius, is known to us only for his role in that one battle in 83 or 84 CE. Of course our noble hero was on the losing side, but defeat elevated him, like others such as Hannibal, to the halls of fame rather than to the dustbins of history.

In the biography of his father-in-law, Agricola (the Roman governor of Britain who organized the defeat of Calgacus and his allied forces), Tacitus devotes one quarter of the whole work to the episode of Mons Graupius. In it he assigned to Calgacus a notable speech of three chapters[1] which arguably puts into the shade the speech delivered by Agricola to the Roman troops before the battle. Agricola's speech occupies only two chapters[2] and, to my mind, constitutes little more than a perfunctory performance, whether on the part of Tacitus or Agricola.

The irony of the circumstances surrounding and following Agricola's victory was plain to Tacitus. He, if not Agricola himself, bore a grudge against the latter's imperial master, Domitian, for allowing Britain to slide beyond full control on the morrow of the dramatic victory. We need no reminder of his aphoristic judgement: 'Perdomita Britannia et statim missa'.[3] In that verdict Tacitus did exaggerate, for in no sense did Rome let Britain slip from her grasp,

---

*My thanks are owed to my colleagues Dr S. Ireland and Dr S.J. Hill for help in discussion, and to Mrs E.A. Greenwood for making the illegible legible.

1. Tac. *Ag*. 30–32.
2. Tac. *Ag*. 33–34.
3. Tac. *Hist*. 1.2.

but there was an even greater irony in the situation. Of Calgacus, as of others in defeat, it might be said that he lost the battle but did indeed win the war.[1] A forward glance or two in history will show that when late in the second century the Romans faced problems in the far north under the governor Virius Lupus, the Caledonians (in contravention of their treaty with Rome) were prepared to assist the Maeatae.[2] Whatever the nature of that treaty, the relationship between Rome and the Caledonians had been regulated by formal terms and not as between conqueror and conquered. The immediate crisis then was solved through the payment of a hefty bribe by Lupus to the Maeatae. In his subsequent campaigns the Emperor Severus had rather less success than had Agricola, failing to manoeuvre the Caledonians into open battle and settling for the cessation of territory.[3] After the death of Severus at York in 211, Caracalla was glad to be able to make a treaty to extricate himself from enemy territory on terms which amounted to no more than receiving promises of good behaviour.[4] A century or so later, the confederacy of the Picts, which embraced the Caledonians, continued to present problems to Constantius.[5] These and related problems were never solved by the Romans.

Perhaps it is only just that history should render what is due to Calgacus. In a way history does so through Tacitus, but, as in many instances, his broad sweeps of the brush leave us frustrated, with an apparent neglect that has prompted the question whether Tacitus cared about Britain.[6] For what it is worth, I believe that he did.

Agricola, too, had to be given what was due to him. His career might have ended with an anticlimax, but the lengthy period of his governorship had to end with a climax suitably presented to warrant Tacitus's eulogy of Agricola and the criticism of the emperor who had been deemed to have failed him. The verbal picture of the Caledonian defeat is one of the most graphic and evocative pieces of writing.[7]

1. A.R. Burn, *Agricola and Roman Britain* (London: English Universities Press, 1953), p. 19.
2. Cassius Dio 75.5.4.
3. Cassius Dio 76.13.
4. Herodian 3.15.6-7.
5. *Panegyric on Constantine* 7.1-2.
6. W.S. Hanson, *Agricola and the Conquest of the North* (London: Batsford, 1987), p. 22.
7. Tac. *Ag.* 30.

Who can verify the figures given for the loss of men on either side, three hundred and sixty Roman auxiliaries and ten thousand natives (the latter in itself a figure of suspicion)? The picture is one of severed limbs lying on bloodstained earth, of lamentation and self-destruction among the defeated, which on the following day gave way to silence among the deserted hills, where houses smouldered and Roman reconnaissance made no contact with the enemy either fleeing or regrouping. That picture is reminiscent of the one portrayed by Sallust on the defeat of the Moors in the Jugurthine War, a defeat which left the field of battle for as far as the eye could see littered with weapons, armour and corpses highlighted by the bloodstained earth between them.[1]

Tacitus's description of the course and outcome of the Battle of Mons Graupius may or may not be characterized by literary commonplaces: the conduct of many Roman battles and the defeats suffered by their enemies will have had elements in common. However, the apparently overwhelming defeat suffered by the Caledonians should not blind us to the elements of political and military skill which lay behind their preparation for battle and the way in which as a group they did survive to fight another day. Indeed, in the absence of any Roman claim to the contrary, we must assume that Calgacus, whether to his credit or his shame, did survive the defeat. If we follow Tacitean versions, then Domitian's jealousy of Agricola, or his sheer neglect of the problem, let the Caledonians off the hook. Alternatively, if we pierce the Tacitean smokescreen, other pressing priorities elsewhere in the empire would have had the same effect. Perhaps, too, geography was on their side. Nevertheless to regroup with such effect as to be able both to cause problems for the Romans and to keep them at bay required a degree of political and military skill, of which we have seen some evidence for the second and third centuries and for which Tacitus himself provides some evidence in the first century, if we read him carefully.

In his penultimate season of campaign, Agricola apparently credited the various northern tribes with the ability to join together in organizing a threat to him by land,[2] and Caledonian resistance materialized on a large scale. After an initial and successful assault on

1. Sallust, *Jugurthine War* 101.11.
2. Tac. *Ag.* 25.

a Roman fort, some Romans were made to recognize the risk in maintaining extended lines of communication, and advocated withdrawal to a position south of the Forth–Clyde line. Agricola cast aside such counsels, but we can see that in the ensuing manoeuvres the military intelligence of Romans and Caledonians alike was of a high order and enabled flexibility of response on each side. Before Agricola realised what was happening, his enemy had concentrated for a night attack on the Ninth Legion. It was too close a call for comfort by the time Agricola arrived with his relief column. Then, rather than incur the risk of being caught between two Roman forces, the natives melted away, and not for the last time at that. Tacitus's assertion, that the boglands and forests covered the enemy's retreat to deny the Roman victory that would have won the war,[1] fails to credit the Caledonian skill in using intelligence, tactics and terrain in pursuit of deadly guerrilla tactics. Certainly the Britons were undaunted and in high morale. They affirmed their alliance with the formalities of conferences and sacrifices.

For the following season's campaign, the British communities managed to agree on a change of strategy. Instead of pursuing guerrilla tactics, they took the initiative in making an organized stand at Mons Graupius, agreeing to meet in concert the common danger. By the despatch of embassies and conclusion of treaties, they amassed the strength of all the tribes, whether or not that amounted to as many as thirty thousand men or even more.[2] It may be argued that the words that Tacitus uses should not be taken to imply all the formality and dignity of diplomacy, but we should cast our minds back to events on the Continent in 69–70 CE. Then, it will be remembered, Civilis the noble Batavian successfully hijacked the rebellion of Antonius Primus and the pro-Vespasianic forces against the Emperor Vitellius.[3] With breathtaking skill he organized a massive Gallo–German conspiracy in revolt against Rome. A close reading of Tacitus's account reveals in a north-European and non-Roman the qualities of a superb practitioner of the skills of political intelligence and

1. Tac. *Ag.* 26.
2. Tac. *Ag.* 29.
3. Tac. *Hist.* 4.13, 14, 16-19, 21, 22, 24-26, 28-30, 32-37, 54, 55, 58, 60, 61, 63, 65, 66, 70, 71, 73, 75-79; 5.14-17, 19-26. On this topic see now P.A. Brunt, *Roman Imperial Themes* (Oxford: Oxford University Press, 1990), pp. 33-52.

diplomacy. Ultimately Petilius Cerealis, like Agricola, showed what could be achieved through superior weapons and training allied to knowledge of tactics and strategy. Agricola's victory, granted the fact that an encomiast must allow him to have shown his mettle and genuinely earned it, was no walkover. There was a considerable deployment of tactical skill on both sides, the more so on the native side in view of their only recently established coalition. Even on Tacitus's own admission, of at least thirty thousand Britons, twenty thousand did not fall in battle.[1] The survivors deliberately broke ranks and reverted to their earlier guerrilla tactics by retreating in small groups to render pursuit difficult. The Romans did well to exercise caution in their pursuit, for in the initial stages of following up their victory they were caught in ambush by the natives, who had superior knowledge of the territory.

Let us now return to the earlier question as to whether Tacitus cared about Britain. It is a question which is not susceptible of an answer in precisely such terms. His own career took him to provincial governorship, he was on good terms with Pliny the Younger, who served as governor of Bithynia, and he was the son-in-law of Britain's best-known governor, Agricola. In the *Agricola* he writes in broad terms more about Britain, and in particular about problems created by the Romans, than was imposed on him by the necessity of his subject. Furthermore, in the *Annals* and *Histories* we find accounts of affairs in Britain, even when they are of quite minor importance by comparison with events in the empire as a whole. A repeated theme is his interest in the native customs of the Gauls and Britons, and, as we have seen in the account of the rebellion of Civilis, he has detailed interest in the tribes of Germany. That we could expect of the author of *Germania*, which takes a social rather than a politico-military theme. There is, too, much comment in the *Agricola* on social and economic affairs in Britain.

The question is worth pursuing in other terms, for when it comes either to speeches or to reported speech, Tacitus does rather well for Britain. It may serve our purpose to look at a selection of them insofar as they may provide some evidence for the attitude of some of those inside or just outside the province to Rome, and attitudes of Romans to them. Plainly, at this point there is no need to raise the

---

1. Tac. *Ag.* 37.

whole issue of the nature and role of speeches in ancient historical writing or even the question of whether the inclusion of speeches in the *Agricola* elevates that work to the realms of history rather than biography. Obviously Tacitus has the whole repertoire of stylistic and rhetorical devices at his disposal, his works abound with themes which are apt topics for *declamatio*, but that does not remove the themes from the realms of reality. Orators practised on themes that were topical as well as on others, such as *The Beauty of Helen*, that were rather less so.

A look at a selection of those speeches may provide some indication of what particular groups such as the Caledonians or Calgacus and his fellow-aristocrats were likely to have felt. We may also see that it is unsafe to address the question of attitudes to Rome in terms that are universal with reference to time, place, nationality, or class. It is also useful to be able to understand why Calgacus may have held views of Rome different from those expressed by (for example) Aelius Aristides of Mysia, Galen of Pergamum, or Dio of Prusa, let alone Polybius, who had been so impatient with the moral inferiority of the Greeks and their carelessness with their liberty. Calgacus plainly could share nothing with Dio through the experience of absorption of the upper classes of the eastern parts of the empire into the Roman system of society and government.

Among the speeches set down by Tacitus with reference to Britain we have:

1. *Annals* 12.34 in which Caratacus exhorts his troops against Ostorius Scapula.
2. *Annals* 12.37 in which Caratacus gives an honourable account of himself in captivity in Rome.
3. *Annals* 14.35 in which Boudicca incites revolt against Rome.
4. *Annals* 14.36 in which Suetonius rallies his troops against Boudicca.
5. *Agricola* 15 in which the thoughts are reported of the Britons as they are about to rebel under Boudicca.
6. *Agricola* 30–32 in which Calgacus addresses his troops.
7. *Agricola* 33–34 in which Agricola exhorts his troops. (The *Agricola* contains no mention of Caratacus.)

All the episodes to which these speeches refer relate to the course of the Roman conquest of Britain within the brief span of one generation

or so, little over thirty years, and before the process was as complete
and settled as it was ever to become. Why should Calgacus prefer not
to be incorporated but to remain outside the *Pax Romana*?

Liberty, self-determination, independence was the prize, and the
dawn of liberty was at hand for the whole of Britain. Calgacus
represents his forces as the last of the free, the carefully conserved
reserves, shielded by their remoteness but with nowhere to retreat.
They have to stand and be counted.

The Romans are arrogant and greedy; they have exhausted the land
and now turn to the northern waters of the sea. They have pillaged
East and West but remain insatiable. For those who think in terms of
the equation of empire with peace, robbery, butchery, and pillage are
the obverse of empire, and desolation and ruin are the obverse of
peace.

Conscription takes away sons and kinsmen; tribute is exacted on
goods and possessions; lands and harvests are used to supply Romans;
forced labour is exacted for constructing roads through woods and
swamps; wives and sisters, if not raped, are seduced as if by guests
and friends; masters normally provided for their slaves, but Britons as
slaves pay for and keep their masters; Britons as the most recent to be
enslaved are treated as the butt in the manner of the newest slaves in
the household; they have no fertile lands, harbours or mines in which
the Romans would spare them to work. In the wake of Roman arms
are tribute, service in the mines (note the apparent inconsistency) and
whips for slaves.

Plainly Calgacus's speech as written by Tacitus contains
inconsistencies, as noted above. Calgacus's own unconquered people
have not yet suffered the indignities to be expected at the hands of the
Romans, but refugees and others who had fled to join the resistance
had experienced them. His speech contains one glaring error (whether
deliberate or not is for others to argue) in stating that the Brigantes
(led by Cartimandua) instead of the Iceni (led by Boudicca) came near
to casting off the yoke of Rome but for their own carelessness.[1] The
speech too contains all of the stock rhetorical devices with which one
might suppose that an unromanized chieftain would not be conversant.
Nonetheless, a recent commentator remarks that the speech seems to

---

1. Tac. *Ag.* 31.

have a bite that goes beyond the purely conventional[1] and that Tacitus is not simply making debating points for Calgacus.

The themes raised in that speech echo some of those that occur earlier in the *Agricola* in the representation of the grievances which led to Boudicca's revolt.[2] Roman control brings repression and slavery in place of freedom, heavy burdens and exploitation, robbing of homes, kidnapping of children, and subjection of men to levies for military service. Curiously nothing is said here about the ravishing of women, though there is emphasis on the greed and lust of the occupying forces, and the violence and insults meted out by centurions and even by the slaves of the Romans.

In the *Annals* Tacitus represents Boudicca as claiming that she is taking up arms, not to recover her kingdom or wealth which had been plundered, but to assert liberty.[3] She, too, seeks revenge for her ravished daughters and for the stripes that have been inflicted upon her, for the Romans held nothing sacred, scourged the old and deflowered native virgins.

For Caratacus, who had fled west to lead the resistance, Tacitus remarks that peace with Rome meant slavery. Caratacus's speech before battle puts the issue at stake as one of liberty or bondage.[4] He argued that when Julius Caesar had been chased away in 54 BCE, wives and daughters had been rescued from violation, land had been freed from taxation, and the symbols of external authority had been banished. After his transfer to Rome for the dubious compliment of honourable display in the Roman victory parade, he made a plea for clemency, stating that he had fought because he did not want to lose his wealth, his arms, men and horses.

Among the Roman provincial auxiliaries serving in Britain were Batavi, who served under their own aristocratic commanders. In spite of their alliance with the stronger power, says Tacitus,[5] they were not subjected to financial exploitation by Rome. Nevertheless they did contribute arms and men to the Empire.

Shortly Civilis was to call them and others in Gaul and Germany to

---

1. R.H. Martin, *Tacitus* (London: Batsford, 1981), p. 44.
2. Tac. *Ag.* 15.
3. Tac. *Ag.* 14.35.
4. Tac. *Ann.* 12.33.
5. Tac. *Hist.* 4.12.

revolt. Among the complaints registered was the claim that the old and the unfit were called up for military service by recruiting agents who expected to be offered bribes to excuse their victims from the levy. Furthermore, young men were called up to gratify the lust of the troops. At a secret meeting of nobles and commoners, Civilis argued that Roman prefects and centurions, when satiated with spoils, were replaced with others who sought fresh plunder. The Roman army camps, which in any case contained odd levies and men too old for effective service, were full of loot. Under these circumstances it was wrong to describe as peaceful development what was in effect servitude. So much for Civilis's argument.

What was the alternative to either enduring such sufferings, or engaging in war the superior might of Roman arms? Perhaps a treaty relationship? Co-operation was not without its own risks, whether in the short or the longer term. In Germany the Ubii, based on Cologne, who changed their name to Agrippinenses, were regarded by their fellow Germans as Quislings. The Treviri, based on Trier, undertook service that was unrewarded, and endured taxation, flogging, the block, and whatever sufferings were devised by their masters.

In Britain the Caledonians did manage to exist under terms of treaty, but the precedent had hardly been promising. As Tacitus records, the Iceni at their own request lived at peace with Rome, but subsequently disarmament was forced upon them.[1] Their king, Prasutagus, in his will shared his estate between his daughters and the Roman emperor. As his reward, centurions ran amok over the estates, slaves pillaged houses, Boudicca was disgraced by being beaten, his daughters were ravished, and his relatives cast into bonds.

The Trinovantes too had co-operated with Rome only to see part of their population driven from their lands, which were appropriated as the site of the Roman colony of Camulodunum. There a temple was constructed and its priests devoured the natives' substance. Common soldiers and military veterans who settled there insulted them: they called them slaves and captives, and they used other terms of opprobrium.[2] There is little wonder that the Trinovantes felt cheated. Their spirit remained unbroken, and they determined to resume their

---

1. Tac. *Ann.* 12.31.
2. Tac. *Ann.* 12.31; cf. *Ag.* 15.

liberty.[1] When, too, they joined in the cause of the Iceni for liberty, one can comprehend Suetonius's appreciation of the ferocity displayed by the Britons in the cause of liberty.[2] Even after Suetonius had restored Roman authority in a bloody battle, the Romans remained uncertain in their policy. Nero's freedman Polycletus was sent out to conduct an enquiry, but in spite of his authority the Britons treated him with contempt and derision. The flame of liberty was not extinguished,[3] and throughout the following decade Rome's governors in Britain proceeded gently.[4] The rage of a population which had sacked Camulodunum, Verulamium, and London, and had slain seventy thousand Roman citizens and allies (whose pleas for Roman protection went unheeded) could scarcely be imagined. The Roman procurator Catus Decianus[5] fled and the military second-in-command Poenius Postumus[6] fell on his sword. Such was the indignation of a people driven to desperation by rapine and oppression.

There was little hope of being able to ride the Roman tiger successfully after making a treaty with it. The risk was not merely from Rome. Cartimandua lost credibility within her own tribe, the Brigantes, for succumbing to the temptation.[7] Livy had explained the essential realities through the mouth of the Carthaginian leader Hannibal nearly three centuries before. The proud and merciless Romans lay claim to universal dominion: they circumscribe the liberties of others and lay down the bounds beyond which they may not pass.[8]

In the light of the catalogue of Roman crimes set out by Tacitus both in his narrative and in the speeches, it is well to remind ourselves of some touchstones of imperialism. Six were set down by Finley in

---

1. See J.F. Drinkwater, 'The Trinovantes: Some Observations on their Participation in the events of AD 60', *Rivista Storica Dell'Antichita* 5 (1975), p. 53-57.
2. Tac. *Ann*. 14.38.
3. Tac. *Ann*. 14.39.
4. Tac. *Ag*. 16.
5. Tac. *Ann*. 14.32.
6. Tac. *Ann*. 14.37.
7. Tac. *Ann*. 12.36; 40; *Hist*. 3.45.
8. Livy 21.44.

his discussion of Athenian imperialism in the management of the Delian League:[1]

1. Restrictions on freedom of action in inter-state relations.
2. Political, administrative and judicial interference in local affairs.
3. Compulsory military or naval service.
4. Payment of tribute.
5. Confiscation of land with or without emigration of settlers.
6. Forms of economic subordination or exploitation ranging from control of seas... to compulsory delivery of goods...

Others can be set down, but we need not labour the point. The fact is that even after the periods of office as governor in Britain of such men as the distinguished jurist Petronius Turpilianus (61–63), the careful conciliator Trebellius Maximus (63–69), and the outstanding general and administrator Julius Frontinus (74–77), Agricola faced administrative problems created by the Romans. Early in the *Agricola* (ch. 13), Tacitus remarks that the Britons readily accept military levies, tribute and other imperial exactions provided that there is no abuse, for while ready to obey orders (but not to accept slavery) they bitterly resent abuse. That observation prepares the ground for the start of Agricola's administration.[2] Although the province was sufficiently well pacified and acquiescent for him to spend most of his governorship on military operations in the north, with none of the worries faced by Suetonius on distant campaigns, he imposed firm discipline on the army and administration. Roman racketeers had exacerbated the levy of corn and tribute by unfair practices, including the exaction of additional charges which caused more resentment than the actual tax. The provincials had to queue up at the granaries to buy back their own corn at inflated prices for shipping to distant destinations instead of to the nearest appropriate point of delivery. Allegedly the neglect and arbitrary conduct of previous governors caused peace to be feared no less than war.

Much of the discussion prompted by examination of the speeches in

---

1. M.I. Finley, 'The Fifth-Century Athenian Empire: A Balance Sheet', in P.D.A. Garnsey and C.R. Whittaker (eds.), *Imperialism in the Ancient World* (Cambridge: Cambridge University Press, 1978), p. 107.

2. Tac. *Ag.* 19.

Tacitus is rendered the more difficult by the rhetorical opposition of *libertas* to *servitus*.[1] Whatever happened to communities incorporated by Rome, they were not enslaved in the legal sense. They were left personally with free status, in communities enjoying local self-government, with a political role and a path for provincials to work their way into the Roman social and political hierarchy, and under common impartial justice.[2]

Without doubt, on one side of the balance sheet there could be substantial benefits for the provincials, but we should not ignore the cultural shock of contact between native and Roman. In the West the cultural shock was greater for both sides than in the East, where the Greeks could afford to remain passive and indifferent to Roman rule.[3] Garnsey remarks that, traditionally, upper-class Romans had entertained little respect for the quality of life of the peoples of the underdeveloped West.[4] Cassius Dio, Balsdon reminds us,[5] thought that in Scotland the unclad Caledonians and Maeatae, during flight from their enemies, lived for days on end in marshy bogs with only their heads protruding above the surface and sustained themselves on a diet of marsh weeds.

Increasingly, with the development of the imperial system of administration, governors were kept under tighter control, and the worst excesses of the Republican era tended to be avoided. The more careful and well supervised the legal and administrative system, the more personnel were required and the more obtrusive the system risked becoming. Some evidence for such developments may be attested by the posting of two distinguished Roman lawyers to Britain soon after 80 CE with the title of *Legatus Juridicus*, Javolenus Priscus[6] and Salvius Liberalis.[7] New forms of religion, some officially inspired

1. E.g. Tac. *Ann.* 12.34.
2. See V. Nutton, 'The Beneficial Ideology', in Garnsey and Whittaker (eds.), *Imperialism in the Ancient World*, pp. 309-22.
3. A.H.M. Jones, *The Roman Economy* (ed. P.A. Brunt; Oxford: Basil Blackwell, 1974), p. 102.
4. P.D.A. Garnsey, 'Rome's African Empire Under the Principate', in Garnsey and Whittaker (eds.), *Imperialism in the Ancient World*, p. 252.
5. J.P.V.D. Balsdon, *Romans and Aliens* (London: Gerald Duckworth, 1979), p. 59; Cassius Dio 76.12.4.
6. *ILS* 1011.
7. *ILS* 1015.

such as the Imperial Cult, were imported, but there is little attempt to interfere with native religion. In Augustus's German campaigns, the Romans did lose centurions and tribunes to native sacrifice.[1] In Africa they banned the worship of Saturn associated with human sacrifice,[2] and in Britain Suetonius Paulinus struck for Anglesey the Druid centre which fed native resistance[3] and which some associated with human sacrifice. Cassius Dio especially associates with religious fervour the mass slaughter wrought by Boudicca's forces.[4]

The shock of Claudius's invasion produced its initial reactions of relief and accommodation between the parties, as for example between King Prasutagus and the Romans. The awakening came later. As Nutton has shown in another context, citizens and local holders of office were promoted by commanders and emperors for services rendered; *beneficia* too were granted, not so much as a reward for services rendered, but as incentives for future obedience and acquiescence, and the process of Romanization and assimilation was by no means a necessary prelude to the promotion of individuals. That, he argues, implies a background not of continuity but of upheaval engineered by the occupying power. Two generations of Britons had been made aware of that since 43 CE, and some of those who objected had fled to Calgacus as the last bastion of freedom. Accelerated acculturation under the legate Varus had precipitated the revolt of Arminius in Germany. It was native institutions and especially their leadership that were threatened by absorption into the Roman system. The initial threat to the basic social order was perceived too late.[5] Royal families were extirpated and the members of the aristocracy were sucked into an alternative system, with recognition coming from Rome rather than from their own people.[6]

Tacitus remarks on the progress in Britain of Romanization,[7] to which Agricola had given both private and official encouragement.

1. Tac. *Ann.* 1.61.5-6.
2. M. Legley (*Saturne Africaine: Histoire* [Paris: CNRS, 1966], pp. 61-62, 314-15) Tertullian (*Apol.* 9.2-3), cited by Garnsey, 'Rome's African Empire', p. 252.
3. Tac. *Ag.* 14.
4. Cassius Dio 62.7.3.
5. See S.L. Dyson, 'Native Revolts in the Roman Empire', *Historia* 20 (1971), pp. 239-374, esp. pp. 256, 258 and 268.
6. Garnsey, *Imperialism in the Ancient World*, pp. 252-53.
7. Tac. *Ag.* 21.

There is archaeological evidence to support his picture of the construction of new types of buildings, temples, civic centres, and town and country houses. As in Bithynia, the local inhabitants competed in the rush to undertake projects, even borrowing capital from Roman lenders to do so.[1] Agricola praised the natural ability of the Britons in public speaking in preference to that of the Gauls. The Latin language was widely adopted. If the German Arminius was bilingual,[2] so could British chiefs have been. Such developments were complemented by the construction of baths (note the alleged disparaging remarks of Boudicca on the effeminacy of warm Roman baths)[3] and porticos, and the preoccupation with the elegance of civic receptions. Roman fashions of dress were adopted, and the toga was in evidence everywhere. The sons of chiefs were educated, or perhaps re-educated, in Roman ways. At one level credit was due officially to Agricola (and no doubt to some of his predecessors and their subordinates) for such developments, but Tacitus notes them as if in sorrow for the loss of innocence which he records in the natives.

The implications were, of course, much wider than Tacitus suggests even in those early years. The tribal map of Britain was substantially redrawn, new tribes were created, old tribal centres such as those of the Trinovantes and Catuvellauni were moved, and new tribal administrative centres were built with their emphasis on public institutions rather than on the authority of chieftains and 'royal' families. Camulodunum had been built by the Romans both to overawe (potential) insurgents and to serve as an example of law and civil policy.[4] In another barbed comment Tacitus observed that Roman governors busied themselves with improvements of taste and elegance but omitted what was useful. They embellished the province but took no care to defend it.[5] Camulodunum was left with no defences against Boudicca. We must remind ourselves through Boudicca and Cartimandua that the Britons did not take gender into account in choosing their leaders.[6] Things were otherwise in Rome.[7]

1. Cassius Dio 62.2.1.
2. Tac. *Ann.* 2.10.3.
3. Cassius Dio 62.6.4.
4. Tac. *Ann.* 12.32.
5. Tac. *Ann.* 14.31, 32.
6. Tac. *Ag.* 16.
7. Note the ostensibly chauvinistic remark attributed to Calgacus (Tac. *Ag.* 31.4).

Those of us who have not endured occupation or the creeping threat of it should not underestimate the phenomenon of cultural shock. We should, in our societies, bear in mind the opposition to plans for urban redevelopment or construction of roads; we should reflect on the scale of opposition even to minor changes as in the denomination of coinage, weights, and measures, as if they represented the adoption of alien values. The passage of a decade or so brings the shock wave from joining such an inter-state or supra-state body as the EEC, of which membership was gained after more than a decade of the full processes of negotiation, consultation, parliamentary process and even, unprecedentedly, national referendum. There was no compulsion, let alone threat of violence or savagery such as the Romans could unleash on natives even under the empire and under an 'Optimus Princeps', as the scenes of the Dacian Wars attest on Trajan's Column.[1] For the natives of the West, which lacked the institutional stability and traditions of the more urbanized East, the shock was all the greater.[2]

Note, however, the respect with which even Cerealis treated the German priestess Veleda, who was held in high regard by both Germans and Romans, although a legionary commander had been despatched to her, seemingly for sacrifice (Tac. *Hist.* 4.61, 65; 5.22-25).

1. On this point, see J. Clarke, 'Roman and Native, AD 80–122', in I.A. Richmond (ed.), *Roman and Native in North Britain* (Edinburgh: Nelson, 1958), pp. 38-39.

2. On matters arising from the *Agricola*, the reader should consult the standard commentary *Cornelii Taciti DE VITA AGRICOLAE* (ed. R.M. Ogilvie and I.A. Richmond; Oxford: Clarendon Press, 1967); also W.S. Hanson, *Agricola and the conquest of the North*, p. 22. After the preparation of this paper, notice appeared of the publication of G.S. Maxwell, *A Battle Lost: Romans and Caledonians at Mons Graupius* (Edinburgh: Edinburgh University Press, 1990).

FRIENDS, ROMANS, SUBJECTS:
AGRIPPA II'S SPEECH IN JOSEPHUS'S *JEWISH WAR*

Tessa Rajak

Authorial Choices

I have not yet found, in any illustrated version of Josephus, a portrayal of that extraordinary scene which took place in the summer of 66 CE, when Marcus Julius Agrippa (the Great King), great-grandson of Herod, standing with his sister, Queen Berenice, addressed the people of Jerusalem from the roof of his palace and tried to persuade them to step back from the brink and not to rush into any action which could be taken as revolt against Rome[1]. But the picture is an arresting one. The exact date cannot be pinpointed—it falls between the beginning of June and the beginning of August. At any rate, while, in early June, Berenice was still appearing in public in the attire of a Nazirite with her head shaven and (perhaps as a suppliant) with her feet bare,[2] it seems likely that by now the period of her dedication had come to an end. We may rather imagine the pair, as they had appeared at Caesarea with Festus for Paul's interrogation, presenting themselves, as Acts so splendidly puts it, μετὰ πολλῆς φαντασίας (Acts 25.23). The drama, in Josephus's story, was high, and the speech ended with the royal couple in tears and the crowd, though not unmoved, we learn (*War* 2.402), still clamouring for rebellion.

The episode, obviously not wholly invented, is given great prominence by Josephus, serving as that turning point which marked the transition from peace to war. It is preceded by the fruitless pleas

---

1. Josephus, *War* 2.345-401.
2. On the meaning of her attire, S. Schwartz, *Josephus and Judaean Politics* (Leiden: Brill, 1990), p. 136.

to the people and their lay leaders, of the entire priesthood, their clothes ripped, their breasts exposed, their heads covered in dust (322), for an end to provocation of the Romans: all were to disregard the desecration of the Temple Treasury perpetrated by the procurator Florus when he had extracted tribute money. The episode is also preceded by the second horrifying clash between Florus's cavalry and unarmed Jews in the narrow alleys of Jerusalem; by the deliberate Jewish destruction of the porticoes which linked the Antonia fortress (Florus's headquarters) with the Temple; by an investigation conducted on behalf of Cestius Gallus, the legate of Syria; and, most crucially, by the refusal of the high priests and notables, strongly supported by Agrippa, to send an embassy to Nero and to lodge a formal complaint against Florus. Agrippa's speech is followed by his ejection from the city, by the killing of the Roman garrison on Masada, and by the decision not to accept any further sacrifices by foreigners in the Temple, which, as Josephus says, meant discontinuing the offerings made on the emperor's behalf and was tantamount to a declaration of war (πολέμου καταβολή: 409). The speech, a long and discursive one, creates a break amidst crowded and precipitous events. So, as well as the speech lending emphasis to those events, the special position of the words highlights their content.

Here, we enter the realm of choices made by the historian, Josephus. He *chose* to put Agrippa centre stage and to make his oration central to the history. He also chose the words themselves that Agrippa uttered: for there is no doubt, in view of their recurrent themes and patterns, that Josephus (in common with other writers of his time) invented his speeches for the most part and used them to communicate or to set off his own interpretation of what happened.[1] In this major performance, content matches context, for here is the one extended consideration, in the *Jewish War*, of the pros and cons of revolt against Rome, and it sums up a realist position rather different from any which the speaker is likely to have held, as we shall see. Indeed it represents a voice which must have been heard among Rome's subjects far from the confines of Judaea, but which is rarely found in the literature. It is somewhat ironic that, when the speech has

---

1. See T. Rajak, *Josephus: The Historian and his Society* (London: Gerald Duckworth, 1983), pp. 80-81; P. Villalba i Varneda, *The Historical Method of Flavius Josephus* (Leiden: Brill, 1986), pp. 89ff.

been closely studied, it has usually been for what it has to say, in its great survey of the peoples subjected to Rome, about the disposition of the legions which controlled the provinces.[1]

There is, in fact, much of Josephus throughout the composition; which is not to say that it is anything so simple as an apologia for his own conduct. Among recurrent Josephan ideas, we find the insistence that the enthusiasts for revolt were a vocal minority among the population; that misgovernment by individual bad procurators should not be allowed to reflect on the emperor at Rome or on the image of the empire as a whole; that Fortune has transferred her favours to the cause of Rome over all other peoples, or in a different formulation, that God has been behind the growth of her empire (360; 390-91); that for the Jews it is now too late to fight; and that they will be responsible for the destruction of their own Temple if they start a war:

> take pity at least on your mother city and its sacred precincts. Spare the Temple and preserve for yourself the sanctuary and its holy places (400).

This last exhortation is linked with Josephus's controversial claim in a later part of the *Jewish War* that not Titus but the Jews had burned down the Temple.[2] Much of this complex of arguments will be reiterated, with little change, in the declamation in book 5 which Josephus makes from the walls of besieged Jerusalem,[3] though the heart of that utterance has a biblical orientation.

A presentation of Agrippa by Josephus cannot be a simple affair. While Josephus's general ideas about revolt may play a large part, he is also saying something about Agrippa specifically, and that has to be understood in the light of Agrippa's highly dubious role in the surrounding events. It is also relevant that Josephus and Agrippa had close connections, certainly from 69 on, when both were involved in

---

1. The classic discussion is in *RE* II.2, s.v. 'legio' (by Kubitschek-Ritterling), arguing that the disposition of troops in the speech reflects Vespasian's arrangements and not Nero's.

2. Rajak, *Josephus*, pp. 206-11; M. Goodman, *The Ruling Class of Judaea* (Cambridge: Cambridge University Press, 1987), pp. 237-38.

3. *War* 5.362ff.; see M. Stern, 'Josephus and the Roman Empire as reflected in the *Jewish War*', in L.H. Feldman and G. Hata (eds.), *Josephus, Judaism and Christianity* (Detroit: Wayne State University Press, 1987), p. 77.

Vespasian's accession and in the fortunes of the Flavian dynasty.[1] Agrippa was an important patron for Josephus, and apparently wrote sixty-two letters testifying to the accuracy of the *Jewish War* (*Life* 364-67). Admittedly, we do find a quite open statement of Agrippa's unpopularity with his subjects in the mid-sixties in *Antiquities* 20, as well as one or two episodes which show the king in a fairly dubious light;[2] and it may be that, if these are to be explained by the fact that Agrippa was dead by the time that this passage was written[3] and that Josephus was, therefore, able to be open about certain earlier reservations, then the relationship was not an entirely unclouded one. Still, the overall picture of mutual cordiality over the years is not much affected by such hypotheses, nor by the fact that Agrippa became the employer of Josephus's enemy and rival, Justus of Tiberias (Josephus would have us believe that the secretary was constantly in disgrace with his master!). Then there is the added twist of the notorious affair between Titus, Josephus's principal protector and first patron, and the Jewish 'mini-Cleopatra' (as Mommsen called Berenice), which lasted at least until her second dismissal from Rome, probably in 75, and therefore almost until the appearance of the *Jewish War*, normally dated between 75 and 79. I do not believe that we can make much progress by reviving the methods of earlier scholarship and seeking to locate strands in Josephus which reflect these various and sometimes contradictory interests. But it is important to be aware that he is performing a balancing act when he writes and that there is often more than one sub-text.

Apart from all this, a speech must, of course, be appropriate to its dramatic situation and not import incredible elements. In this case, addressing a volatile and hostile audience, Agrippa had to display tact and there are many sentiments in favour of Rome which he might have uttered were it not that the needs of the moment, to calm a raging mob, would have made it absurd for him to be shown doing so.

1.   J. Crook, 'Titus and Berenice', *AJPh* 72 (1959), p. 163 n. 9; Rajak, *Josephus*, p. 187.

2.   Especially in relation to the high priests: S. Schwartz, *Josephus and Judaean Politics*, pp. 131, 150-52 and n. 138.

3.   The date of death of Agrippa II remains a vexed question; on Josephus's unfavourable comments in connection with that date, see S.J.D. Cohen, *Josephus in Galilee and Rome: His Vita and Development as a Historian* (Leiden: Brill, 1979), pp. 177-80.

Why Agrippa? The Troubles of a 'Client King'

These are very real complications, and there is no magic formula to help us categorize this, or indeed any other of Josephus's set pieces. We have to deal with the problems as they arise. But it is worth looking a little more closely at the question of why it should be Agrippa who receives the dubious benefit of making the central statements that appear in this speech. The fact that he made a memorable appearance on this occasion is clearly not sufficient explanation; nor even the consideration that what he said was sufficiently disturbing to provoke his expulsion from the city soon afterwards, and, about a month later, the burning of his palace and that of Berenice by Eleazar's rebel group in company with the *sicarii*.

The speech, as well as some of Josephus's surrounding comments, shows Agrippa as putting everything into a last-ditch attempt to persuade restraint. Opening himself and his sister to derision, risking life and limb to make a long and detailed address in that exposed position up on the roof (security arrangements in first century Jerusalem can hardly have been up to modern standards), there was, on this account, just nothing more that he could have done to prevent war. The stance at this point is an accentuated version of the one which Josephus claims to have taken up himself, although Agrippa, unlike Josephus, abandoned the Jewish cause as soon as a revolt was seen to be inevitable. The king was to be found supplying Cestius Gallus with infantry and cavalry for the abortive march on Jerusalem, although it was only *after* Cestius's withdrawal that the first sizeable crop of Jewish desertions to the Roman side is recorded by Josephus.

In various ways, Agrippa needed exculpation far more desperately even than ever Josephus did, and from both sides. It is not only a question of the aftermath. For what Josephus manages to conceal through focusing our attention on the speech, and, quite likely, deliberately, is that Agrippa's incompetence could well be regarded as the single major cause of the breakdown in Jewish–Roman relations, and therefore of the war. We need only recall that this was the man who, at the age of seventeen, had not been considered fit to inherit the position of his popular father, Agrippa I, as ruler of the Jews. Four years later, the son had to be content with the kingdom of Chalcis, an area around Damascus, together, it would seem, with an uncertain role as what A.H.M. Jones calls 'controller of the Temple': this had been briefly possessed by Agrippa's predecessor, his uncle Herod of Chalcis, and it involved the right to appoint high priests. Later, Claudius enlarged the domains, adding what can best be described as 'bits and pieces', including towns in the Galilee. But Judaea remained under procurators, and perhaps the limitations of Marcus Julius Agrippa were evident to those who had known him well in Rome. The *Antiquities* version of the dealings which followed on the sudden death of Agrippa I in 44 CE seems conscious of the need to explain away the rejection:

> Caesar, on hearing of the death of Agrippa. . . was grieved for him and angry at his ungrateful subjects. He had accordingly resolved to send the younger Agrippa at once to take over the kingdom, wishing at the same time to maintain the treaty he had sworn. He was, however, dissuaded by those freedmen and friends whose influence with him was great, who said that it was hazardous to entrust a kingdom so important to a really young man, not yet out of boyhood: he would find it impossible to carry the cares of administration, when the kingdom was a heavy burden even to a grown man. Caesar felt that what they were saying was reasonable. He therefore despatched Cuspius Fadus as procurator of Judaea and of the whole kingdom (19.362).

The text does not tell us why there was no question of waiting for Agrippa to grow up a little. Whatever Agrippa's personal merits, the crisis of 66 reveals that he was the first and foremost to be held accountable by the Romans for good order among the Jews, and only after him came the lay and sacerdotal leaders. For Agrippa had the power to order the magistrates and the notables to collect tribute, and that is exactly what he did on the conclusion of his speech, because the arrears had evidently been a major point of dispute with Florus, and even more, no doubt, because non-payment of tribute was an unequivocal signal of revolt (407).

There is valuable testimony, in Josephus's narrative, to the seriousness with which the duty of maintaining order was taken by the Romans (332) and the merciless penalties to which the native authorities were subjected when they failed to do so. In short, at a time of trouble, Roman rule was no blessing, even to the prosperous elite. We may be sure the dispensation was not very different in other parts of the empire, though we rarely have evidence of this quality. It was under Florus that Jewish members of the equestrian order were crucified in Jerusalem (308). This explains why it was such a risky matter to send to Rome an embassy of protest, even supposing it were allowed to leave: such an embassy drew the emperor's attention to the loss of control and was a declaration of failure on the part of the local administration before ever it was a reproach on the procurator. A case which collapsed would bring disaster. The point is made explicitly in Agrippa's speech:

> the powers that be (τὰς ἐξουσίας) should be conciliated by flattery (θεραπεύειν) and not irritated; for when you indulge in exaggerated reproaches for minor errors, you only injure yourselves by your denunciation (350-51).

On a lesser scale, though potentially just as dangerous, was the fraught question of forms of reception: would an official greeting (ἀσπασμός) be taken as impertinent and provocative, a blatant εἰρωνεία in the context of native bad behaviour, as happened when Florus brought troops to Jerusalem after taking the 17 talents from the treasury of the Temple (298)? Or was it fatal discourtesy not to offer a greeting, as the priests insisted, temporarily at odds with the lay notables, and desperate to protect the Temple when the second wave of troops was due (323). The notables were at this point less compliant, for they had been ordered earlier to hand over agitators to Florus, something which we know to be deeply abhorrent to pious Jews, and which they had therefore refused to do.[1] Any action, or lack of action, could be taken as insubordination. Thus, when Cestius sent the tribune Neopolitanus to Jerusalem as his representative, the soldier may have politely paid his respects to the Temple from the court of the Gentiles (341), but his task was the grim one of checking that all Jews were obedient to the Romans in their midst.

All this puts into perspective Agrippa's inability to do the one job that the Romans were expecting him to do. His consciousness of failure made him desperate to prevent any Jewish representatives going to Rome and complaining about Florus, however strong the case. It is interesting that, some fifteen years earlier, Agrippa *had* been prepared to support the Jews against the Samaritans in a hearing before Claudius at Rome, thereby setting himself against the procurator Cumanus. Josephus seems at that stage to congratulate

---

1. See the classic discussion of D. Daube, *Collaboration with Tyranny in Rabbinic Law* (Oxford: Oxford University Press, 1965).

Agrippa on not being intimidated by the freedmen at court, who allegedly had rallied round Cumanus; and in the end the procurator had been condemned and exiled (*War* 2.245-46; *Ant.* 20.125-36).

In the crisis of 66, Berenice, who could not yet, of course, have been Titus's mistress, had identified herself more closely with the agonies of the Jews than had Agrippa, and, though a queen, she had even been prepared to abase herself in front of Florus, begging him to call off his troops (310-14). Her religious adherence was perhaps stronger, though Agrippa too followed Jewish practices, as we know.[1] This did not, however, detach her for long from her brother's side or from his position. As for Agrippa, at that crucial moment of Berenice's intervention, he had been away in Alexandria, offering his congratulations to his relative by marriage, the renegade Jew Tiberius Julius Alexander, erstwhile procurator of Judaea, on being appointed to the prestigious prefecture of Egypt. Agrippa's conduct after his hasty return from Egypt could hardly be acceptable to any element in the population, and it made his stoning and banishment from Jerusalem unsurprising and his position forthwith untenable until after the revolt. It is amazing that he was allowed even to finish his speech—if indeed he was. We have reason to be sceptical.

The Realist Argument for Roman Rule

Yet the speech according to Josephus is, weeping apart, a reasoned and polished affair, improving rather than realistically depicting the hapless Agrippa. Its content, as we have already begun to see, transcends the need to distract the mind from the monarch's mistakes. In several obvious ways, it carries the voice of Josephus. And at a deeper level, too, the question with which it is essentially concerned is Josephus's own question (and that of those others, most of them non-survivors, who had followed paths similar to his, if rather less tortuous): could the revolt have succeeded? The premises plainly set

---

1. S. Schwartz, *Josephus and Judaean Politics*, pp. 112, 135-137. It must be admitted, however, that the Nazirite vow is the only firm evidence of Berenice's piety and that the Herodians tended to placate their Jewish subjects with token gestures: see D.R. Schwartz, *Agrippa I: The Last King of Judaea* (Tübingen: Mohr, 1990), p. 134 and n. 116.

out are, first, that freedom is unquestionably the state in which it would be desirable to live:

> passing to your present passion for liberty, I say that it comes too late. The time is past when you ought to have striven never to lose it. For servitude is a painful experience and a struggle to avoid it once for all is just (356, Thackeray's translation).

There are shades of the Tacitean Calgacus here, and of the Roman rhetoric of revolt, but this is distinctly not a rebel speech, and so these echoes cannot be taken as just the conventional sentiments. The second premise is that to live under Rome *is* to live in slavery, and no bones are made about the Jews being slaves (356; 357). One might find these admissions somewhat surprising, whether coming from Agrippa or from Josephus. From these premises follow the stated view that it would be natural and right for a people to revolt at the moment of provincialization; and indeed that is when the majority of revolts against the imposition of the *pax Romana* did occur, in the history of the empire. The Jews had, then, simply missed their chance.

As Menahem Stern pointed out, the speech is notable for the absence in it of any of the *laus imperii* which we might have expected in so major a statement of support for Rome; Stern draws a contrast with the pacifying oration of the legate Cerealis in Tacitus's *Histories*.[1] In Josephus, the *pax Romana* appears in an ambivalent light and not as a benefit to the subjects: 'do they not live at peace, under one Roman legion?', asks Agrippa about the Dalmatians (371). It could be argued that a more enthusiastic note would be so glaringly inappropriate in the situation, so provocative to the assembled Jews, that Agrippa simply could not be allowed it by the author. It could also be suggested that in the first century CE such themes did not drop as readily from the lips of Rome's subjects, even from members of their governing classes, as they did from Aelius Aristides, a century later. Thus, Plutarch's tone is less rapturous than Aristides', for all his connections with important Romans. Nonetheless, the underlying negative evaluation, embedded in a plea on behalf of Rome, remains a remarkable feature, and, in my view, it cannot wholly be explained away in terms of the requirements of text or context.

The claims of quiescence are expressed in the recitation, which is

---

1. Stern, 'Josephus and the Roman Empire', p. 76.

far from a eulogy, of the roster of distinguished and strong peoples who have yielded to Rome. This occupies the bulk of the oration. It is high Greek rhetoric, with the Athenians, 'the men who once consigned their city to the flames to maintain the liberty of Greece' (358), being given pride of place. It is an indirect compliment to Rome, perhaps, through its depiction of the staggering scope and the natural and human resources of the empire. Yet this emphasis, too, is double-edged, for there is an underlying critique in terms of exploitation:

> though encompassed by such formidable barriers, though swarming with a population of three hundred and five nations, possessing, so to say, in their native soil the springs of prosperity and irrigating well-nigh the whole world with the overflow of their products, the Gauls are yet content to be treated as a source of revenue to the Romans and to have their own prosperous fortune (εὐδαιμονίαν) meted out to them at their hands (372, Thackeray's translation).

It is instructive to contrast the twist given to the same idea by Aelius Aristides in his panegyric *To Rome* (11), when he declares that

> the lands around the Mediterranean provide the Romans abundantly with whatever is in them. Produce is brought from every land and every sea, depending on what the seasons bring forth.

Here, the notions of Roman appropriation and of Roman control are missing. Still less is there any implication of submission. Agrippa, on the other hand, speaks openly of the Gauls being

> overawed at once by the fortune of Rome and by her power, which brings her more triumph even than her arms. That is why they submit to the orders of 1200 soldiers.

There is almost a modern theory here of deterrent power deriving from success, and the limited military force involved is in no sense a palliation.

But the true nourisher of Rome is Africa, subdued by a vast effort: apart from the corn which 'feeds the populace of Rome for eight months in the year', there is tribute and every kind of contribution to the empire (382-83). These may be given ungrudgingly, but the stress on the sheer size of the transaction leaves us in no doubt that it is exploitative.

Josephus's roster of the regions and provinces, while emphasizing, in almost Thucydidean fashion, the irresistible claims of sheer power, can hardly be meant to intimidate Jewish readers to submission in the 70s, as some have liked to think. So soon after the loss of Temple and city, after the destruction of the last few forlorn hopes in Palestine and abroad, who would have had the heart for new conflict? The argument looks back and not forwards. It is intended loudly and clearly to make one point: that those Jews who had been opposed to resistance had had every practical justification, as well as the logic of history on their side. The moral balance sheet was, on the other hand, a separate issue. Under the Greek bombast, lies some sharp questioning.

But what is interesting is not the author's personal position—and, indeed, others may form a different impression of our historian's stance.[1] Significance lies, rather, in the voice represented in this speech, the voice of the realists, who knew exactly what living under an empire was about, but also that at most times it was necessary to knuckle under, to dig in and wait. Such realists well understood why their fellow countrymen hated Rome, however intensely they deplored their actions; and glimmerings of this understanding, too, come out in Agrippa's speech, even if it is not the author's overt purpose to convey them.

But that was not the end of the matter. The implication of the Josephan doctrine that God is siding with the Romans must surely be that the day will come when the tables will be turned, when he will change sides once more. But for the realists, that distant day was not something to dwell on. Klaus Wengst regards this motif in Josephus as 'an endorsement of the right of the stronger'.[2] In fact, however, there is what might be called an implicit, suppressed apocalypse in what has been taken as being the most shameless of Josephus's doctrines, the corruption at the heart of his writing. A close comparison has been noted[3] between Josephus's interpretation and the sentiments towards

    1.   On these issues, a useful guide is P. Bilde, *Flavius Josephus between Jerusalem and Rome: His Life, His Works and their Importance* (Journal for the Study of the Pseudepigrapha Supplement Series, 2; Sheffield: JSOT Press, 1988), pp. 173-81.
    2.   K. Wengst, *Pax Romana and the Peace of Jesus Christ* (Philadelphia: Fortress Press, 1987).
    3.   N.R.M. de Lange, 'Jewish Attitudes to the Roman Empire', in P.D.A. Garnsey and C.R. Whittaker (eds.), *Imperialism in the Ancient World* (Cambridge: Cambridge University Press, 1978), p. 268.

the Romans attributed in the Babylonian Talmud (*b. 'Abod. Zar.* 18a) to the dying Rabbi Yose ben Kisma. These were spoken to a fellow rabbi, Hananiah ben Teradion, who is known in the tradition as one of the Ten Martyrs tortured and killed in the wake of the Hadrianic revolt, and they were words which counselled patience:

> do you not realize that it is Heaven who has ordained this nation to rule? For even though they have laid waste His home, burnt down His temple, slain his saints and persecuted His servants, still (the empire) is firmly established.

For Josephus, as for many rabbis, the conception of a cycle of sin, punishment, and salvation, with an eventual new beginning, lay beneath the doctrine of the transference of God's favour.[1] In his own tirade from the walls of Jerusalem, Josephus castigates the Romans at length for their sins; he then compares the Romans to the Assyrians, and reminds his hearers that God had known exactly how to destroy the Assyrians and to rescue the Jews, when once the Jews had deserved it (*War* 5.403-406). But for Josephus, as for the rabbis, apocalyptic ideas are rarely, if ever, to be freely enunciated: other speakers will, I know, be commenting on Josephus's curious reticence over the identity and fate of the fourth beast in the visions of the seventh chapter of Daniel.

It is all the more striking that we find the historian suggesting deep reservations about the power of Rome, through a speaker whose object was precisely the opposite, to justify and recommend that power. Unless we wish to take the oration as an exercise in rhetorical ingenuity, a piece of tight rope walking, in which Agrippa is made to put before an agitated populace just enough anti-Roman innuendo to gain himself a hearing, we are obliged to treat Agrippa's words as evoking the ambiguous stance of the native governing class, superficially pre-Roman (in varying degrees), but harbouring doubts and even deep resentments.

It thus becomes easier for us to understand how one section of that class could be dragged into a revolt which it did not desire or approve of, as happened to Josephus and his like: many such people later

---

1. The leading discussion is H. Lindner, *Die Geschichtsauffassung des Flavius Josephus im Bellum Judaicum* (Leiden: Brill, 1972), ch. 2. See also, E. Gabba, 'L'impero romano nel discorso di Agrippa II (Joseph., B, II, 345-401)', *RSA* 6–7 (1976–77), pp. 189-94.

deserted. It is at the same time clear why Agrippa joined Vespasian straight after being expelled from Jerusalem, and then supplied the Romans with manpower for the siege (Tacitus, *Histories* 5.1.2). His personal predicament, if nothing else, made it necessary for him to seek to restore his reputation with the government—and he was lucky to be reasonably well received. But the revolt's outcome, with the Temple destroyed, Jerusalem in ruins and Roman coins depicting *Judaea capta* as a woman weeping, crouched beneath a palm-tree, and overshadowed, sometimes, by a Roman soldier, will not have been more tolerable to Agrippa than it was to Josephus. It is usually emphasized that the 'colonial elites' of the Roman provinces benefited from and therefore tended to approve Roman rule. This is not untrue. But it is easy to forget that even for such people foreign domination remained at best a dubious benefit. Local dignitaries were often directly in the firing line, and, when times were difficult, they could suffer first and most.

THE KITTIM IN THE QUMRAN PESHARIM

George J. Brooke

1. *Introduction*

The overall problem addressed by this paper concerns the description from ancient texts of historical events and personages. The problem is particularly acute in relation to the study of the Kittim in the Qumran pesharim (biblical commentaries) because until relatively recently there was no scholarly agreement concerning the genre of the pesharim themselves. Now that there is an emerging consensus that the pesharim are not the straightforward narration of historical events, more or less loosely attached to biblical prophecy, but are better characterized by reference to types of dream interpretation,[1] their literary style and composition can be better appreciated and also their purpose.

For the most part, the characters mentioned in the pesharim are named only with ciphers and epithets. Surprisingly, instead of understanding this as a clue that some of the parties mentioned in the commentaries might be contemporaneous with the author, scholars set about reading historical events directly from the surface of the text in order to identify the characters involved. For the identification of the Kittim, the two main contenders were the Seleucids[2] and the

---

1. M.P. Horgan, *Pesharim: Qumran Interpretations of Biblical Books* (CBQMS, 8; Washington: Catholic Biblical Association of America, 1979), pp. 229-59; G.J. Brooke, 'Qumran Pesher: Towards the Redefinition of a Genre', *RevQ* 10 (1979–81), pp. 490-91; I. Fröhlich, 'Le genre littéraire des *pesharim* de Qumrân', *RevQ* 12 (1985–87), pp. 383-84.

2. E.g. H.H. Rowley, 'The Kittim and the Dead Sea Scrolls', *PEQ* 88 (1956), pp. 95-97.

Romans.[1] The assumption behind the debate was that, if sufficient attention was paid to uncovering and dating the historical allusions and military tactics in the sections of the pesharim which mentioned the Kittim, then the argument could be settled. A key text in this debate was the Nahum Pesher (4QpNah), which alone named actual historical characters, though their precise identification remains only highly probable, not proven.

The widely accepted conclusion, that in the Qumran commentaries, and indeed in the final redaction of the War Scroll too, the Kittim are the Romans, permitted the emergence of a second phase in scholarly endeavour. Characteristic of this second phase has been a much greater awareness of the problem of the definition of the genre of the pesharim, an awareness that limits how history can be discerned in the texts, and an increased appreciation of the methods of biblical interpretation that the commentators adopted in linking their interpretations with their chosen texts.[2] This more subtle and more cautious approach to the texts has been linked with the recognition that not all the texts found in the caves at Qumran necessarily describe the same community, and that in any case the archaeological evidence for the occupation of the site points to the end and not the middle of the second century BCE.[3] In other words, there has been less concern to discuss the early history of the community against a Seleucid backdrop, and consequently less need for supporters of the Kittim as Romans to interpret every detail in the pesharim as pointing to the Romans, since a later date for the Qumran community sets everything more obviously within, or within reach of, the Roman period.

1. E.g. R. Goossens, 'Les Kittim du Commentaire d'Habacuc', *La Nouvelle Clio* 4 (1952), pp. 155-61.
2. E.g. I. Fröhlich, 'Caractères formels des pesharim de Qumrân et la littérature apocalyptique', in M. Augustin and K.-D. Schunk (eds.), *Wünschet Jerusalem Frieden: Collected Communications to the XIIth Congress of the International Organization for the Study of the Old Testament, Jerusalem 1986* (Frankfurt: Peter Lang, 1987), pp. 453-55; B. Nitzan, *Pesher Habakkuk: A Scroll from the Wilderness of Judaea (1QpHab). Text, Introduction and Commentary* (Jerusalem: Bialik Institute, 1986 [Hebrew]); B. Nitzan, 'The "Pesher" and Other Methods of Instruction', in Z.J. Kapera (ed.), *Mogilany 1989: Papers presented at the Second International Colloquium on the Dead Sea Scrolls* (Kraków: Z.J. Kapera, 1991).
3. See P.R. Callaway, *The History of the Qumran Community: An Investigation* (JSPSup, 3; Sheffield: JSOT Press, 1988), pp. 29-51.

The purpose of this paper is to reconsider all the references to the Kittim in the pesharim, taking the debate a stage further in the direction it is already heading through a detailed source analysis of the commentators' phraseology. To this end, there are several working assumptions behind this paper. First, all the manuscripts of the pesharim can be dated to the turn of the era or later. Though only a single copy of each of the pesharim has survived, a fact that strongly supports the opinion that they are actual autographs, they may not be so. But if not autographs, the date of composition of any of them need not predate the actual manuscripts by much. Secondly, they must be considered as exegesis, not as records of events. They belong to a particular kind of exegetical tradition, a tradition which controls both their method and to some extent their content. Any history they represent is in the first instance the history of the period of their composition: say, at the turn of the era, or even later. We have no reason to suppose that their author or authors had actually lived through the earlier events they may purport to describe. In fact, the heavy dependence on scripture suggests just the opposite. So the image of empire in the pesharim is primarily suggested by exegetical tradition and contemporary experience, elements of which may be read back into an earlier period. Thirdly, if the pesharim probably belong to what archaeologically is Period II of Qumran, then although their author or authors may well have been Essenes, they may not have been the direct heirs of those who had occupied the Qumran site in Period I. In other words, we should watch out for particular polemics in the pesharim that might reveal more precisely both who may have been responsible for them and also who may have been their intended readership.

2. The Texts

(A) 4QpNah. Of the four pesharim which mention the Kittim, 4QpNahum, a manuscript certainly datable towards the end of the first century BCE, has been the most regularly cited in favour of their identification with the Romans.[1] In 4QpNah frgs. 3–4, 1.2-4, the interpretation of Nah. 2.12b is given:

---

1.   See Horgan, *Pesharim: Qumran Interpretations of Biblical Books*, pp. 160-62.

2) The interpretation of it concerns Deme]trius, King of Greece, who
sought to enter Jerusalem on the advice of the Seekers-After-Smooth-
Things, 3) [but God did not give Jerusalem] into the power of the kings
of Greece from Antiochus until the rise of the rulers of the Kittim; but
afterwards [the city] will be trampled 4) [and will be given into the hand
of the rulers of the Kittim][1]

As has been widely noted, this comment is one of the most explicit
historical references in any of the scrolls. The Demetrius mentioned is
probably the Seleucid Demetrius III Eukerus (95–88 BCE) who
attacked Alexander Jannaeus at the incitement of the Pharisees
(= Seekers-After-Smooth-Things). The text describes nothing of the
author's attitude to the Kittim, merely that they will be the first after a
certain Antiochus (probably IV) to enter Jerusalem and trample
(תרמס) it, a word chosen possibly because of its proximity to the
sound of the name Rome itself.[2] As many commentators have noticed,
possibly without justification, the pesher seems to reflect correctly that
in 63 BCE the Romans merely had rulers (מושלי), not kings. There is
nothing in the text of Nah. 2.12b that requires mention of the one who
is to wreak destruction. Nineveh of Nahum is taken to be a typological
cipher for Jerusalem, whose destruction is the result of its harbouring
the wicked of the nations. Though historically correct because written
with hindsight, the interpretation in the pesher, like the text it
interprets, is presented as a future matter. The description of the
Kittim is matter of fact, though clearly with military overtones.

It is possible that the Kittim are also mentioned in 4QpNah frgs. 1–
2, 2.3-5a.

3) He rebu[ked] the sea and dried [it up (Nah. 1.4aα). The in]terpretation
of it: 'the sea'—that is all the K[ittim, whom God will rebuke,] 4) so as to
ren[der] a judgment against them and to wipe them out from the face of
[the earth. And he dried up all the rivers (Nah. 1.4aβ).] 4a) [The
interpretation of it: 'the rivers' are the Kittim,] 5a) with [all] their [ru]lers,
whose dominion will be ended [[3]

---

1. Trans. M.P. Horgan, *Pesharim: Qumran Interpretations of Biblical Books*,
p. 163.
2. It is just possible that 1QpHab 4.14 might be restored to include רומם, 'their
haughtiness', as a play on the name of Rome: see W.H. Brownlee, *The Midrash
Pesher of Habakkuk* (SBLMS, 24; Missoula: Scholars Press, 1979), p. 83.
3. Trans. M.P. Horgan, *Pesharim: Qumran Interpretations of Biblical Books*,
p. 162.

If the restorations are correct, then in both the pesher proper and in the supralinear addition there is mention of the Kittim. In the first instance, rather than simply being used to designate a historical period, as in 4QpNah frgs. 3–4, 1.2-4, the Kittim are the object of the rebuke of the avenging God (Nah. 1.3-4) who will eventually wipe them out. This would indicate that the author lives during the period of the continuing domination of the Kittim and looks for divine vindication. The term 'rebuke' (גער) also occurs in a similar context in 1QM 14.10, and the two words 'judgment' (משפט) and 'wipe out' (כלה) feature in close proximity in a nearby context, 1QM 14.5. This section of 1QM is a victory song with a complex history,[1] but it portrays the eschatological defeat of Belial's forces in stereotypical language.

If the rivers of Nah. 1.4 are to be identified as the Kittim, providing us with a second reference to them, then the interpretation of the parallelism of the prophecy is consistent, but it must also be noted that in frgs. 3–4, 3.9 the rivers are identified with the great ones of Manasseh. Once again, the ending of the dominion of the Kittim is described in language also to be found in the victory song of 1QM 14.7: 'all the nations of wickedness have come to an end'. In other words, though the restorations are not all sure, it seems as if the language used of the Kittim, if not taken directly from the text of Nahum, reflects the poetic liturgy of 1QM 14. As such 4QpNah frgs. 1–2, 2.3-5a tell us nothing specific about the Kittim, simply that the author of 4QpNah probably perceived them as the ultimate eschatological foe. There are images of military might, but the chief concern is with the God of Israel's victory.

(B) 4QpIsa[a]. There are several references to the Kittim in 4QpIsa[a] frgs. 7–10. Isaiah 10.33-34 is cited; suitably it is part of an oracle against the advancing Assyrians. The verses are given interpretation in

---

1.   4QM[a] contains much text that is close to 1QM as well as some elaborate poetic sections; 1QM 14 is matched in 4QM[a] frgs. 8–10: see M. Baillet, *Qumrân Grotte 4 III (4Q482–4Q520)* (DJD, 7; Oxford: Clarendon Press 1982), pp. 20-21. The text's significance has yet to be assessed fully; Baillet writes 'Il est peu probable qu'on ait affaire à une recension plus ancienne que celle reproduite par 1QM. On remarquera en tout cas que le texte suit parfois de près celui de la grotte I, que parfois il semble le résumer, et qu'il a des passages non attestés jusqui'ici' (*Qumrân Grotte 4 III*, p. 12).

short sections, each of which is preceded by a requotation of a section of the Isaianic text. In the order of the commentary, the Kittim are identified first with the mighty one of Isa. 10.34 who will fall, according to the commentator, by the hand of Israel. Then the lofty in stature who will be cut off (Isa. 10.33b) are identified with the warriors of the Kittim (4QpIsaᵃ 3.9). Thirdly, the thickets of the forest which will be cut down with an axe (Isa. 10.34a) are interpreted; all that remains of the interpretation is 'for the battle of the Kittim' (למלחמת כתיאים; 4QpIsaᵃ 3.11). Lastly there is an inclusive repetition of the mighty one who will fall (Isa. 10.34b); he is identified once again as the 'Kittim, who will be given into the hand of his great ones' (4QpIsaᵃ 3.12). There is virtually nothing in these very brief interpretations which does not come directly from the text of Isaiah 10 itself. We cannot reconstruct historical events, only observe the use of scripture.

(C) 1QpPs. In this very fragmentary manuscript, fragment 9 contains a certain reference to the Kittim within the interpretation of Ps. 68.31. The whole fragment can be restored and translated as follows:

> 1) [From your temple at Jerusalem, king]s [bring] gifts [to you (Ps. 68.30)]. The interpretation of it concerns all the ru[lers of] 2) the Kittim, who]before him in Jerusalem. You rebuked [the beasts of the reed thicket] 3) [a herd of bulls among calves of peoples, trampling] silver [ore (Ps. 68.31)]. The interpretation of it: the beasts of the r[eed thicket are] 4) [the K]ittim *l* . .[¹

Horgan's restoration of 'rulers of the Kittim ([מש]לי הכתיאים)' in the interpretation of Ps. 68.30 is preferable to J.T. Milik's original proposal² of 'kings of the Kittim ([מל]כי כתיאים)' because it suits better the traces of ink that remain, because it reflects the terminology of 1QpHab 4.5, 10 and 4QpNah 1.3, and also because it leaves open the question whether the pesher must be describing the Kittim, if Romans, of the imperial age.³ More generally, though the opening word of the

---

1. Trans. M.P. Horgan, *Pesharim: Qumran Interpretations of Biblical Books*, p. 67.
2. J.T. Milik, 'Textes non bibliques', in D. Barthélemy and J.T. Milik (eds.), *Qumran Cave I* (DJD, 1; Oxford: Clarendon Press, 1955), p. 82.
3. M.H. Segal comments on Milik's restoration of 1QpPs: 'The expression, if Milik's restoration is correct can only mean: kings of various Hellenistic states. If

quotation of Ps. 68.31 in line 2 (נערת) may contain a variant from the
MT (גער), it is intriguing to see that the object of the divine rebuke is
identified with the Kittim, just as in the interpretation of Nah. 1.4a in
4QpNah where the same word for rebuke occurs (גוער). Here then is a
literary motif, applied to the Kittim in two contexts. It is noteworthy
that Psalm 68, which is interpreted in 1QpPs, and the poem in 1QM
14, which seems to have influenced the phraseology of the
corresponding section of 4QpNah, share the same genre: both are
victory songs providing stereotypical language to describe the
vanquished. The distinctive aspect of Ps. 68.30-31 is the way it makes
explicit not just the destructive nature of the military aggressor, but
also his purpose in exacting tribute (כסף). The enemy can be
conceived as both a military and an economic threat. Psalm 68.30
identifies the temple at Jerusalem with wealth; perhaps it is there that
the threat is perceived most obviously. However, not enough of the
interpretation survives for us to know precisely how the author
understood the verse.

(D) 1QpHab. Numerous references to the Kittim are to be found in
the Habakkuk Commentary (1QpHab). The author of this commentary
was clearly well aware of the original structure and purpose of
Habakkuk 1–2, which forms the sequential basis for the commentary,
for with only one exception, he confines his references to the Kittim
to the dialogues of Habakkuk 1. The exception is in 1QpHab 9.7 in the
interpretation of Hab. 2.8a, part of the first woe: the plundering
'remnant of the peoples' is identified with the Kittim who will receive
all the riches and booty which the last priests of Jerusalem have
amassed through their own plundering activity.

More extensively, the Kittim are the principal subject of the
interpretation which is given for Hab. 1.6-11 in 1QpHab 2–4 and Hab.
1.14-17 in 1QpHab 6. In the first case Hab. 1.6-11 contains God's
answer to Habakkuk's cry. God declares that he is rousing the
Chaldeans with their mighty army, which is characterized by its
horses and horsemen; the army is violent, terrifying, destructive,
rapacious, and full of scorn for any kind of military or fortified

however כתיאים refers to Romans, we should perhaps restore in 1.1: 'מל[כי הגואים]
('The Qumran War Scroll and the Date of its Composition', *Scripta Hierosolymitana*
4 [1965], p. 142 n. 10).

resistance. Naturally the army of the Kittim and its commanders share these same characteristics, as the typological exegesis identifies the various phrases of the biblical prophecy with the subject of the interpretation. In the second dialogue, Habakkuk begins by praising the character of God and asks why the faithless remain silent in the face of the destruction of the righteous by the wicked (Hab. 1.12-13).[1] Habakkuk then muses over the activity of the wicked, who like a successful fisherman makes a large catch and worships his net in appreciation; the prophet wonders how long this can keep on (Hab. 1.14-17). It is this section which is interpreted of the Kittim. As warmongers rather than fishmongers they gather booty and then sacrifice to their standards and worship their weapons of war through which they have caused many to perish without pity.

3. *The Sources*

This preliminary survey of the texts shows that, although some of the interpretation of the biblical passages in the pesharim is atomistic and seems arbitrary, in fact much in the pesher proper is straightforwardly derived typologically from the biblical text, whose original content and context is more or less properly appreciated by the interpreter. Thus, when one turns to the question of what sources the interpreter used, it is clear that the primary source is the prophetic text being interpreted. However, in addition to this primary source, other literary source material is used, mostly biblical, leaving little room for the direct narration of historical events or circumstances. It is from the analysis of the sources used in the interpretations that the author's picture of the Kittim, his image of empire, can be reconstructed. Close study of 1QpHab can demonstrate this forcefully. There are eleven lemmata to consider.[2]

---

1. In the MT of Hab. 1.12-13 the Hebrew is rightly understood as raising the question of theodicy directly by asking why God remains silent when the wicked attack the righteous; the Hebrew of Hab. 1.12-13 has to be construed differently in 1QpHab.

2. The full Hebrew text of 1QpHab is readily available in K. Elliger, *Studien zum Habakkuk-Kommentar vom Toten Meer* (BHT, 15; Tübingen: Mohr, 1953), after p. 304; E. Lohse, *Die Texte aus Qumran: Hebräisch und Deutsch* (München: Kösel, 1971), pp. 227-43; Horgan, *Pesharim: Qumran Interpretations of Biblical Books*, Part I, pp. 1-9; Brownlee, *The Midrash Pesher of Habakkuk*, pp. 37-219;

(A) 1QpHab 2.10-16 (Hab. 1.6a). In Hab. 1.6a the Chaldeans are described as 'bitter' (מר) and 'hasty' (נמהר). In the pesher the Chaldeans are identified as the Kittim and also described with two epithets, 'swift' (קלים) and 'mighty in battle' (גבורים במלחמה). The first is a simple synonym for 'hasty', the second is probably derived from the biblical text through the interpreter deliberately taking 'bitter' as either 'lord' (מר), a synonym for 'mighty', or as from the verb 'to be fat, strong' (מרא/מרי), as L.H. Silberman has suggested,[1] or even from both. The pesher can be construed as saying that these Kittim will destroy two groups, though the poor state of the text does not allow their clear identification. W.H. Brownlee has ingeniously proposed that these two groups can also be derived from the biblical epithets of 'bitter' and 'hasty' taken additionally as describing those addressed in Habakkuk's oracle.[2] Probably with such an understanding the rest of the pesher can been seen as describing those faithless people on the basis of other biblical texts linked by catchword. All that is learnt further about the Kittim is that they will have 'dominion' (ממשלת), a term also derivable from the מר of the biblical text, one which corresponds with them having 'rulers' (משלי) as in 4QpNah frgs. 3–4, 1.3. The history represented in this interpretation is only perceptible indirectly; the description of the Roman military might is all derived from the biblical text itself.

(B) 1QpHab 2.16–3.2 (Hab. 1.6b). Though the term Kittim has to be restored in the opening of the pesher at the bottom of col. 2, it is clear that the pesher concerns them. Habakkuk 1.6b describes how the Chaldeans will 'march through the breadth of the earth to seize habitations not their own'. The pesher uses the same word for 'march' as the biblical text, and makes a synonymous substitution of 'plain' (מישור) for 'broad places' (מרחבי). In addition the Kittim are described as smiting and plundering the cities of the land. The 'habitations' of Hab. 1.6b are interpreted as 'cities' also in the Targum; their definition as 'of the land' is an unforced deliberate displacement of the same

---

Nitzan, *Pesher Habakkuk: A Scroll from the Wilderness of Judaea (1QpHab)*, pp. 149-98.

1. L.H. Silberman, 'Unriddling the Riddle. A Study in the Structure and Language of the Habakkuk Pesher (1QpHab)', *RevQ* 3 (1961–62), pp. 336-37.

2. Brownlee, *The Midrash Pesher of Habakkuk*, pp. 59-62.

word (ארץ) of the biblical text. There are two plausible ways of deriving 'smiting and plundering' from the 'seizing' of Hab. 1.6b. First, the interpreter took לרשׁת to be from the root רשׁשׁ, meaning 'to beat down, shatter' as in Jer. 5.17, part of an oracle against the faithless,[1] and then in his own choice of words echoed Zech. 11.6 where the root כתת means 'to crush an enemy'; it is noteworthy both that in the targum to Zech. 11.6, כתת is interpreted by בזז 'to plunder'[2] and also that the choice of synonym may have been an attempt to provide an etymology for the term Kittim itself. Or, secondly, לכות can be derived from the root נכה 'to be beaten'[3] and appeal can be made to 2 Chron. 14.13 (Heb. 14) where נכה and בזז are used together, both with 'cities' as their object. There is nothing in the pesher that cannot be derived somehow from the scriptural text, either directly, or through the proper appreciation of the exegetical technique being used, or through appreciation of other related biblical passages which may have informed the author's choice of words.

(C) 1QpHab 3.2-6 (Hab. 1.7). Like the biblical verse, the pesher has two parts. In the first, the 'dreadful and fearsome' of the biblical text are taken as 'terror and dread' (cf. 1QS 10.15), one synonym and one direct transfer of vocabulary, a virtual paraphrase.[4] In the second part there are two elements: on the one hand the biblical 'judgment' (משׁפט) is understood as 'counsel' (עצא), a synonymous usage attested in 1QS 6.22-23; on the other hand שׁאתו, usually translated as 'dignity', from the root נשׁא, is understood in the pesher as 'cunning and deceit', that is as from the root נשׁא, and given a double interpretation probably

---

1. Silberman, 'Unriddling the Riddle. A Study in the Structure and Language of the Habakkuk Pesher (1QpHab)', p. 337.
2. O.H. Lehmann, 'Materials Concerning the Dating of the Dead Sea Scrolls, I-Habakkuk', *PEQ* 83 (1951), p. 36.
3. Brownlee, *The Midrash Pesher of Habakkuk*, p. 65.
4. The structure of the interpretation of Hab. 1.7 thus matches that of Hab. 1.6b showing a neat stylistic device, the A elements remaining the same in both text and commentary, the B element having a substitution:

Hab. 1.6b: A ההולך, B מרחבים   Pesher: B′ משׁר, A′ ילט
Hab. 1.7: A אים, B ונרא   Pesher: B′ פחד, A′ ואימתם

Attention to details like these shows how carefully the commentary has been constructed overall; we should take seriously the author's choice of every word.

because the commentator realized that he was adjusting the usual way of reading Hab. 1.7. The opening phrase of the pesher cites as object of the fear 'all the nations'; by way of stylistic inclusion the interpretation's final phrase makes 'all the peoples' the object of the 'cunning and deceit'. The 'counsel' of the Kittim is for the intention of doing evil (מחשבתם להרע), a phrase reflecting the language of several biblical passages,[1] notably Ezek. 38.10, in which the eschatological foe from the North is described as having just such an intention of devising an evil scheme.[2] Though not all derivable from the text of Habakkuk, the words and phrases of the interpretation can all be derived from relevant scriptural passages. They say little or nothing about the people who may be the Kittim,[3] but much about what the commentator thought of them and was trying to convey to others about them.

(D) 1QpHab 3.6-14 (Hab. 1.8-9b). In this extensive passage, many of the words of Hab. 1.8-9b are reused in the interpretation: the Kittim have 'horses', they come 'from afar', 'they devour like an eagle'. Other words in the biblical text are interpreted with relevant synonyms: as in Hab. 1.8 the horsemen 'trample and scatter',[4] so the Kittim's horses 'thresh the land'; as in Hab. 1.9a the Chaldeans come 'for violence', so the Kittim come 'with wrath and vexation'; as in Hab. 1.9b the Chaldeans mutter, so the Kittim 'speak'; as in Hab. 1.9b these mutterings come from the Chaldeans' face like the east wind, so the Kittim speak with 'hot breath' and 'angry storm'.[5] Thus much derives from the biblical text.

All that remains unexplained in the interpretation are a few words and short phrases. Together with horses, the commentary notes that

1. Ps. 56.6; Prov. 15.26; Est. 9.25; Isa. 59.7; Jer. 18.12.
2. The language of Ezek. 38 lies behind several sections of 1QpHab involving the Kittim: סוסים ופרשים (Ezek. 38.4; 1QpHab 3.6-10); מחשבת רעה (Ezek. 38.10; 1QpHab 3.5); הלם בזז/לבז בז (Ezek. 38.12-13; 1QpHab 3.1; 4.2, 5).
3. Contra Nitzan, *Pesher Habakkuk: A Scroll from the Wilderness of Judaea (1QpHab)*, p. 158.
4. Brownlee, *The Midrash Pesher of Habakkuk*, p. 69.
5. There is an interesting parallel to 1QpHab 3.6-14 in *T. Mos.* 3.1: '[. . .] in those days a king against them from the east and his cavalry will overrun the land' (trans. J. Priest, 'Testament of Moses', in J.H. Charlesworth [ed.], *The Old Testament Pseudepigrapha* [London: Darton, Longman & Todd, 1983], I, p. 928).

the Kittim have beasts (בהמה); this may be a way of representing the leopards and wolves of Hab. 1.8, but through a word which could refer to the beasts of burden of the army of the Kittim.[1] In fact this word provides us with a classic case of historian's abuse of the text. Early in the debate the beasts were identified as elephants, and since the Romans were not known to have used elephants in the eastern Mediterranean, so this piece of commentary was made to refer to the Seleucids who did.[2] That reflects stage one in the history of scholarship. Stage two, based on the acceptance of the identification of the Kittim with the Romans, has still not given up the reference to elephants. B. Nitzan, for example, suggests that the elephants are not real, but reflect what the commentary's author thought of the might of the Roman army.[3] But really בהמות is needed for such an understanding, not the collective singular 'cattle'; further, when בהמות does occur in Hab. 2.17, it is interpreted in 1QpHab 12.4 as 'the simple of Judah who keep the Law', and as far as I know, nobody has tried to suggest that they were elephants!

Not only do the Kittim come from afar, but this is further defined as 'from the isles of the sea'; this picks up an allusion to the Kittim in Jer. 2.10, part of an oracle against the apostasy of Israel. As for the interpretation of the eagle as one who is 'without being satisfied' (ואין שבעה), while Brownlee comments without any evidence that this is 'inspired by the nature of the Kittim',[4] Nitzan more helpfully notes that it is an anticipation of a phrase in Hab. 2.5, in which the arrogant man like death 'has never enough' (לא ישבע),[5] a phrase which is left intriguingly uninterpreted when it features in 1QpHab 8.4. Once again, there is virtually nothing here which cannot be accounted for on the basis of the text of Habakkuk or other biblical passages; there is only a general picture of the Romans, not a reference to any particular campaign.

---

1. Brownlee, *The Midrash Pesher of Habakkuk*, p. 70.
2. E.g. by E. Stauffer, 'Zur Frühdatierung des Habakukmidrasch', *TLZ* 76 (1951), col. 671.
3. Nitzan, *Pesher Habakkuk: A Scroll from the Wilderness of Judaea (1QpHab)*, p. 160.
4. Brownlee, *The Midrash Pesher of Habakkuk*, p. 71.
5. Nitzan, *Pesher Habakkuk: A Scroll from the Wilderness of Judaea (1QpHab)*, p. 160.

(E) 1QpHab 3.14-17 (Hab. 1.9c). This pericope has virtually all perished, though it is likely that the gathering of 'captives like sand' of the biblical text was applied to the activity of the Kittim in some way derived from the biblical text. We need not suppose that here lies the key to either the historical identification of the Kittim or some particular activity of theirs.

(F) 1QpHab 3.17–4.2 (Hab. 1.10a). The brief interpretation given to Hab. 1.10a does not explicitly mention the Kittim, though it is clear enough that they are to be understood as the subject. One appropriate explanation for the lack of a formula mentioning the Kittim would be that the interpreter is here citing a source. M. Burrows noted immediately that the passage was poetic;[1] L.H. Silberman has similarly commented that the interpretation is 'a perfect bi-cola with chiastic parallelism and could be a quotation from some as yet unknown source'.[2]

To find this unknown source, it is helpful first to list the verbs of the interpretation: ילעיגו 'deride', בזו 'scorn', יתעתעו 'mock', and קלסו 'scoff'. For the background to this sequence, we need to take into account both that the targum to Habakkuk renders 'scoff' (יקלס) of Hab. 1.10 by מתלעב, 'to mock', and that it is not uncommon to find in the pesharim examples of the use of an interpretative technique involving a single letter substitution, such as might occur between לעג and לעב, though in any case both words are virtual synonyms. The fourth verb in the sequence (קלס) can be found in Hab. 1.10 itself, so is an example of a direct use of the biblical text. For the three remaining verbs we can turn to 2 Chron. 36.16 where we read: 'they kept mocking (מלעבים) the messengers of God, despising (בוזים) his words, and scoffing (מתעחעים) at his prophets'. Once the possible variation of לעג for לעב is acknowledged, then the fact that the three verbs occur in the same order in both 2 Chron. 36.16 and 1QpHab 4.2-3 is striking, all the more so since תעע occurs as a verbal form only here and at Gen. 27.12 in the Hebrew Bible.

The context of 2 Chron. 36.16 is also relevant. Although the mockery is performed by the people against God's representatives,

---

1. See the remarks in Brownlee, *The Midrash Pesher of Habakkuk*, p. 76.
2. Silberman, 'Unriddling the Riddle. A Study in the Structure and Language of the Habakkuk Pesher (1QpHab)', p. 340.

God raises for their punishment the king of the Chaldeans (2 Chron. 36.17), who attacks both young and old alike, but especially removes the treasures of the house of the Lord and the treasures of the king and his princes (המלך ושריו), two words also to be found in the commentary of 1QpHab. Thus the commentator takes the vocabulary associated with what the Chaldeans act against and makes them, as Kittim, the subject of it themselves. Through using 2 Chron. 36.16, he also underlines that he perceives the Kittim as a particular threat to the temple treasury, a matter which we have seen as also lying behind the interpretation of Ps. 68.30 in 1QpPs.

All that remains to be explained in this section of interpretation are the 'many' or 'great' (רבים), the 'esteemed' (נכבדים), and the 'great army' (עם רב). The plural substantive 'esteemed' features together with the Hebrew root בזה/בוז, with which it is also associated in 1QpHab 4.2 (בוז על נכבדים), in 1QM 14.11-12 (= 4QMª frgs. 8–10, 1.9): 'And to their esteemed you give a reward of shame' (ולנכבדיהם חשיב לבוז). The vocabulary of this poetic passage might well have influenced other sections of the interpretation in 1QpHab (e.g. 'many' in 1QpHab 2.12-15) and 4QpNah frgs. 1–2, 2.3-5a, as was mentioned above. So the first of the objects of this series of verbs of derision can be accounted for on the basis of an earlier exegetical comment, the second by reference to a poetic passage preserved in two manuscripts, and the third, 'kings and princes' by reference to 2 Chron. 36.16, which has provided the string of verbs in the first place. The fourth object, 'great army', which in some measure acts as an *inclusio* through its use of רב, is a not uncommon biblical phrase for army, but more significantly this technical term can be found twice in the Temple Scroll (58.6, 7), in part of the so-called Law of the King, a passage whose vocabulary and subject matter may have influenced the interpretation of 1QpHab 8.3-13.[1] All in all we are able to account for all the elements in this poetic interpretation of Hab. 1.10a through reference to other texts, both biblical and non-biblical. There is no need to resort to a review of historical events to see when the Romans behaved in this way. In fact, the poetic presentation itself points the reader away from historical recitation towards appreciating that the Romans can simply be typecast as military plunderers and that,

---

1. See G.J. Brooke, 'History and Hermeneutics at Qumran', *Bulletin of the Institute for Antiquity and Christianity*, 16.3 (1989), pp. 9-11.

significantly, their plunder may include the contents of the temple treasury.

(G) 1QpHab 4.3-9 (Hab. 1.10b). The interpretation of Hab. 1.10b falls into two interrelated parts. In the first (1QpHab 4.5-7a) two words from the biblical verse are used directly ('fortress', 'laugh'), three words or phrases are repeated from the previous interpretation ('scorn', 'derision', 'great army'), and the only other major word in the interpretation is a synonym for the biblical 'seize' (לכד). The synonym used, חפש, may point to how the second part of the interpretation should be best understood. The term occurs in CD 4.16, 18, and 20, in the saying of Levi concerning the three nets of Belial, the second of which is riches, the third being profanation of the temple; the same word is found in 1QS 10.19 and 1QH 4.12 and 19, all poetic passages. 1QH 4.12 is part of a section of 1QH which overtly reflects the language of Hab. 2.15 and which has been considered to be the source for the interpretation of that verse in 1QpHab 11.2-8.[1] 1QS 10.19 is part of the concluding hymnic material of the Manual of Discipline, a phrase from which has already been noted in the interpretation of 1QpHab 3.4. That same phrase, פחד ואימה, but in inverted word order, is now repeated in 1QpHab 4.7. The fear and dread of 1QpHab 3.4 was interpreted in part in light of Ezek. 38.4, which mentions the 'horsemen and their riders', and 38.10, a passage which mentions the 'evil scheme'; the root חפש also occurs in Ezek. 38.4, in a phrase that is difficult to comprehend. Yet another link with Ezekiel 38, this time 38.20, may be in the occurrence there of the verb הרס, 'to tear down', which occurs also in this section of the interpretation of Hab. 1.10b. It also occurs in Exod. 15.7, yet another poetic passage associated with military victory, the only biblical passage to combine 'fear and dread' (Exod. 15.16, אימתה ופחד) and precisely in the distinctive word order of this section of 1QpHab. The language discloses the cultic and eschatological concerns of the author, rather than the actual deeds of the Romans.

Two other biblical passages may help to explain the rest of the vocabulary of this section of interpretation. The first is Deut. 20.1-20, the rules for waging holy war, a concern of which is that the Israelite

---

1. See P.R. Davies, *Behind the Essenes: History and Ideology in the Dead Sea Scrolls* (BJS, 94; Atlanta: Scholars Press, 1987), pp. 93-97.

troops should not be afraid in any way; those that are should be sent home. In this passage the enemy army is described as עם רב, as in 1QpHab 4.7, but the significant word for fear is neither אימה nor פחד (but cf. Deut. 28.66-67), but a form of the verb רכך, 'to be timid'. The substantive from the same root occurs only once in biblical texts, in Lev. 26.36, part of a key passage for understanding what would happen because of the iniquity (עון) of Israel, a passage which also refers to the inhabitants of the land.[1] Not only is it becoming possible to argue forcefully that biblical and non-biblical Jewish texts can explain the choice of nearly all the vocabulary in the interpretation, but also it is becoming apparent that certain passages are reflected in a number of different interpretations concerning the Kittim, notably Exodus 15, Leviticus 26, Deuteronomy 20 and 28, 2 Chronicles 36, Ezekiel 38, 1QS 10, 1QM 14, and 1QH 4. It is the vocabulary and broad context of these predominantly cultic passages that controls the image of empire in the interpretation, not detailed knowledge of the Roman army and its tactics.

(H) 1QpHab 4.9-16 (Hab. 1.11). Most of the interpretation in this section of 1QpHab derives from the biblical text of Hab. 1.11. To begin with, this is more or less direct and straightforward. 'Spirit' or 'will' (רוח) of the biblical text is interpreted as 'counsel' (עצה). For this sense Brownlee points very suitably to the parallelism in Isa. 40.13 in the uncorrected 1QIsaᵃ:[2]

> Whoever fathomed the mind of (רוח) the Lord,
> or, as for his counsel (עצתו), has made it known?

The 'counsel' takes place in a 'house of guilt' (בית אשם), which may indeed be a reference to the Roman Senate.[3] This designation seems to be based on all three verbs of Hab. 1.11: חלף understood as 'transgress', עבר understood similarly, and וישם taken as from אשם, as

---

1. Lev. 26 lies behind 11QTᵃ 29.7-10, CD 6.11–7.6, and possibly other texts found at Qumran. One wonders whether traditions associated with Levi and with Jacob at Bethel provide some clue concerning the identity of the cultic group who may have been disaffected, perhaps during the reforms of John Hyrcanus I, but found kindred folk amongst the Qumran community with whom they associated.

2. Brownlee, *The Midrash Pesher of Habakkuk*, p. 81.

3. See K.M. Atkinson, 'The Historical Setting of the Habakkuk Commentary', *JSS* 4 (1959), p. 243.

it is in the MT, with an elided *aleph*, meaning 'to be guilty'. עבר is then used in its plain meaning of 'pass on', as the succession of the rulers of the Kittim is mentioned. This is repeated in the next sentence, 'one after another their rulers come', directly using the demonstrative זה. וישם is then used a second time, this time understood as the *hiphil* of שמם, 'to lay waste', and interpreted as 'to devastate, lay waste' (לשחית) in the commentary. Habakkuk 1.11b is then repeated so that וישם is taken in still a third way as from שים, 'to set, appoint'; the commentary on the repeated half verse is too fragmentary to be identified precisely. Brownlee has proposed that in the interpretation of what the Kittim appointed as their god could have been the term 'haughtiness' (רומם), a possible pun in Hebrew on the name of Rome itself.[1] Whatever the case, in the commentary that survives, there is once again nothing that cannot be derived directly or indirectly from the text of Hab. 1.11 itself. We cannot point to a particular decree of the Senate, only to careful multiple exegesis of a biblical text.

(I) 1QpHab 5.12–6.8 (Hab. 1.14-16). The next passage in Habakkuk to be referred to the Kittim is Hab. 1.14-16. The interpretation is in three parts, clearly delineated by the repetition of two sections of the biblical text. In the first section much is lost at the bottom of column 5, but what survives at the top of column 6 shows that the catch of the 'fish of the sea' is compared with the gathering of wealth and loot by the Kittim. The word-pair 'wealth and loot' (הונם עם כול שללם) is not found anywhere in biblical texts, but features in both 1QpHab 9.6 (הונם עם שללם) and loosely in CD 6.16 (בהון מקדש...שללם). More specifically, 'wealth' (הון) is the second of the three nets of Belial described in CD 4.17; in 1QpHab it appears to be qualified by 'loot' (שלל) to make it specifically a matter of the acquisition of wealth by military means. Perhaps it is not surprising that 'loot' is referred to both in Deut. 20.14, the section on the waging of holy war to which reference has already been made, and Ezek. 38.12-13, part of a section that has also already provided vocabulary for other parts of 1QpHab.

The second section of interpretation begins with the repetition of the verb 'sacrifice' from Hab. 1.16. Then, by using the pronoun, the interpreter identifies the nets of Hab. 1.16 as 'signs' of 'standards' and

---

1. Brownlee, *The Midrash Pesher of Habakkuk*, p. 83.

the seine as 'vessels of war', which are also held in awe. Both 'signs' and 'vessels of war' are common enough terms, but the basis of the allegorical interpretation cannot be easily discovered, since it does not appear to rest in any biblical or Qumran text.[1] Yet, before concluding that at last there seems to be some actual historical practice reflected in 1QpHab, it is important to recall that this same interpretation of Hab. 1.16 is to be found in *Targum Jonathan* in relation to the Chaldeans themselves. Though we should not alter 1QpHab to bring it exactly into line with the Targum,[2] we can emphasize that since the Targum is actually concerned with the practice of the Chaldeans, it is likely that the interpretation in 1QpHab belongs in a long exegetical tradition. As Brownlee notes, 'the *pēšer* would not have taken this up, if its author had not believed it also applied to the Kittim of his own day. Yet in this he may have stretched a point; for it was probably the exegetical tradition rather than any specific event which suggested the interpretation'.[3]

In the third section of the interpretation, two words from the text of Hab. 1.16 are repeated and given objects which make their meaning more explicit. First, the fatness of the portion of the Chaldeans is identified with the apportionment of a yoke. The shift from fatness to yoke may be accounted for through an allusion to Isa. 10.27 in which the yoke and fatness of the Assyrians are challenged by the God of Israel. Second, the food or sustenance is associated with the tribute derived from forced labour which was levied on all peoples annually, 'year by year', a temporal note which underlines that the interpretation is concerned with taxation. In fact the phrase 'year by year' occurs in biblical texts describing annual cultic acts (Deut. 15.20; 1 Sam. 1.3; Est. 9.21, 27; Zech. 14.16) or annual payments (1 Kgs 5.25; 10.25; 2 Kgs 17.4). In 2 Chron. 24.5 the Levites are instructed to gather money year by year for the repair of the temple, and in Neh. 10.35-36 the phrase is used of firstfruits offered annually. Thus the use of the phrase 'year by year' in 1QpHab 6.7 implies that

---

1.   Two texts may help, though neither is very close to this passage of 1QpHab. 1QH 6.28-31 speaks of the mighty vessels of war, from which there shall be no escape; CD 6.15 mentions the חרם, through which unclean riches have been acquired.

2.   See N. Wieder, 'The Habakkuk Scroll and the Targum', *JJS* 4 (1953), pp. 14-18.

3.   Brownlee, *The Midrash Pesher of Habakkuk*, p. 102.

the author considered the Romans to be an economic threat, precisely in cultic terms, perhaps even as a threat to annual payments made for the Levites.

The doublet in the interpretation of 'yoke' and 'forced labour' can be found in Ben Sira 40.1, a text that bemoans the fate of man in general. The closing note that this involves the 'ravaging of many lands' may be an attempt to explain 'fatness' (ברי) of Hab. 1.16 through a play on words, since ב and ר occur in both the verb used for 'ravaging' (חרב) and in the 'many' (רב) describing the lands. The verb also anticipates the use of the 'sword' (חרב) in both Hab. 1.17 and its interpretation in the next section of 1QpHab. The phrase 'ravage the land' (חרב ארץ) also occurs in the liturgical text 1QSb in the blessing of the Prince (1QSb 5.24). Overall, once again the interpretation is closely tied to the biblical text and, because biblical and other cultic terminology is used so stereotypically, the commentator hardly gives any information about the Romans that could not also apply to almost every other conquering nation in any age. However, the hints of their presence as both a cultic and an economic threat may be significant.

(J) 1QpHab 6.8-12 (Hab. 1.17). For the interpretation of Hab. 1.17, three matters need to be discussed. To begin with, what is most certain is that there is a clear citation of a biblical text other than Habakkuk in the final phrase. 'Who take no pity on the fruit of the womb' is a quotation of Isa. 13.18, suitably part of an oracle against Babylon, according to the version of 1QIsaᵃ, as Brownlee has noted.[1] Secondly, for the list of those who are put to the sword three biblical texts seem to have played some part. The difficult word אשישים, 'grown men', is most closely paralleled in biblical texts by the similar ישש of 2 Chron. 36.17. That verse describes how there will be 'no compassion on young man or virgin, old man or aged' (ולא חמל על-בחור ובתולה זקן וישש). Both here and in the previous half verse there are verbs that recall Hab. 1.17, 'slay' (הרג) and 'be merciful' (חמל), further encouraging us to see an allusion to this verse in 1QpHab, though a major factor behind seeing such a connection is the use of this section of 2 Chron. 36.16 in 1QpHab 4.1-3, as noted above. But both those verbs also occur in Ezek. 9.5-6, part of a divine command concerning

---

1. Brownlee, *The Midrash Pesher of Habakkuk*, p. 105.

the punishment (from out of the north) of the wicked, which also contains a list of those to be slain, 'old men, young men and maidens, little children and women' (זקן בחור ובתולה וטף ונשים). A third biblical text that may be reflected in the list in 1QpHab 6.11 is Deut. 20.14, part of another text which we have noticed may have influenced other parts of the commentary. In the rules for waging war in Deuteronomy 20 the males are to be put to the sword (חרב) whilst the women and little children (הנשים והטף) are taken as booty. More generally, as Brownlee correctly notes,[1] the thought of the commentary reflects Deut. 28.50 and its context: a nation will be brought against disobedient Israel, which will 'not regard the person of the old (זקן) or show favour to the young (נער)'.

It is Deuteronomy 28 which may help to explain the change of verb in the opening clause of the interpretation: 'concerning the Kittim who will destroy many with the sword'. In place of the 'drawing' (יריק) of the sword of Hab. 1.17, the commentary reads 'destroy' (יאבדו). According to Deut. 28.51, the same nation who will show favour to neither young nor old will cause Israel to perish (האבידו). Leviticus 26.38 uses the same verb to describe the similar fate of the disobedient who have been exiled, not necessarily a significant point apart from the fact that Leviticus 26 seems to lie behind other sections of the commentary of 1QpHab, and at 26.33 divine punishment comes through the unsheathed sword (והריקתי אחריכם חרב), language which parallels Hab. 1.17 (יריק חרבו). A similar phrase can be found also in Exod. 15.9, part of yet another passage to which I have referred earlier: the enemy said 'I will draw my sword' (אריק חרבי). In fact the idiom occurs elsewhere in biblical texts only in Ezekiel (5.2, 12; 12.14; 28.7; 30.11).

For this tenth section on the Kittim, not only is it possible to identify several biblical texts that have provided the vocabulary for the commentary, including one quotation, but also those are the texts that have largely already featured in providing the phraseology of previous sections of commentary. A pattern of source material has begun to emerge, a sufficiently obvious pattern that it becomes all the more clear that any reference to the past historical experiences of the community faced by the Romans are secondary. All is controlled by the commentator's sources, though the motivation for using such

1.	Brownlee, *The Midrash Pesher of Habakkuk*, p. 106.

sources may indeed rest in either the commentator's present experiences of the Romans (i.e. at the turn of the era at the earliest), or in what he thought should have been the experiences of his forebears because of what the ancient texts said or implied about the Kittim. Before commenting on this emerging pattern of source material, it is necessary to mention the last occurrence of Kittim in 1QpHab.

(K) 1QpHab 8.13–9.7 (Hab. 2.7-8a). The commentary on this passage is concerned with the rebellious priest and with other priests of Jerusalem. The Kittim are mentioned incidentally in the closing part of the commentary. They are the ones through whom justice will be meted out on those leaders who have been unjust. The Kittim are identified as the 'remnant of the peoples' (Hab. 2.8) who will plunder the plunderers. Although the passage is not necessarily speaking favourably of the Kittim's action, several scholars have interpreted this reference to the Kittim as depicting them in a good light as the ones through whom God punishes his wicked people. This portrayal is then contrasted with that of the War Scroll (1QM), in which the Kittim feature as the eschatological enemy, and the difference is explained by describing different settings for each work. But this process of reconstruction is not entirely valid. For one thing, it tends to minimize or omit reference to the role of the Kittim in devastating the land as described earlier in 1QpHab in the interpretations of the dialogue sections of Habakkuk; for another, it tends not to allow 1QM to speak of the Gentile destruction of any Israelites, even though this may be part of the broader eschatological plan of the scroll.

4. *The Pattern in the Sources*

In grouping the sources that seem to lie behind the interpretation of Hab. 1.6-11, 14-17, and the other biblical texts in pesharim which mention the Kittim, it is possible to identify five kinds of material.

(A) Basic implied texts. To begin with three texts are implied in the very use of the term Kittim, texts which confirm that we are dealing principally with a biblical stereotype.[1] The first is Gen. 10.4, in which

---

1. See W.H. Brownlee, 'Kittim', in G. W. Bromiley (ed.), *The International*

the Kittim are one of the sons of Javan (Greece). The second is Num. 24.23-24, which it is possible to read as:

> Sea-peoples shall gather from the north;
> and ships, from the district of Kittim.
> I look and they afflict Eber;
> but they too shall perish for ever!

Since this text lacked any literal fulfilment, it became (along with other parts of Numbers 24) a prophecy about the future. As such, the author of Dan. 11.30, the third text, seems to have used it to speak of Roman intervention against Antiochus Epiphanes (as the LXX of Daniel certainly understood; Theodotion retaining Kittim). Apart from providing the cipher, these texts do not seem to give any significant items of vocabulary to the author of the sections of the pesharim which deal with the Kittim. The lack of the use of Daniel 11 and its context may be highly significant for how the setting and purpose of the pesharim should be reconstructed.[1]

(B) Military manuals. Behind several sections of 1QpHab can be seen the vocabulary and concerns of certain sections of military law. Most obvious is Deuteronomy 20, which is military law declared by the priest. Cultic military material is also apparent in the use of poetic sections from the War Scroll (1QM).

(C) Exhortations. Two exhortatory passages have been referred to more than once. These are Deuteronomy 28 and Leviticus 26. Deuteronomy 28 describes how God will bring a nation against the disobedient of Israel, a nation as swift as the eagle flies (28.49). In its present place the material in Deut. 28.47-68 is widely recognized as an expansion that appears to describe the Babylonian destruction of Jerusalem. In using the terminology of this section, it is likely that the author of 1QpHab also recognized this, and so the passage became an appropriate source for describing the actions of the Chaldeans/Babylonians.

Lev. 26.27-45 contains several very close parallels with

Standard Bible Encyclopedia (Grand Rapids: Eerdmans, 1986), III, pp. 45-46; Nitzan, 'The "Pesher" and Other Methods of Instruction'.

1. See the essay by P.R. Davies in this collection for an indication of a satisfactory explanation for this.

Deuteronomy 28, a factor in itself which may explain why the passage is used by the author of 1QpHab in describing the punishment that will come upon Israel if there is disobedience. Once again, the text seems to be aware of the Babylonian destruction of Jerusalem (26.33), and so may have been considered highly suitable for commenting on the Chaldeans. However, more interestingly, it is Leviticus 26 which concludes the Holiness Code (Lev. 17–26), a text which appears to have been particularly influential in certain other texts found at Qumran, notably the Damascus Document (esp. 6.11–7.6) and the Temple Scroll, especially col. 29 which speaks of the covenant with Jacob, a matter only to be found in Lev. 26.42 in the Pentateuch. CD and 11QT share many other characteristics, and parts of CD have been noted as possible influences on 1QpHab. Elsewhere I have argued that the Temple Scroll has acted as a source for 1QpHab.[1] Was the author of 1QpHab a Levite whose concerns are described in these texts in particular? The use of 1QM in general and 1QM 14 in detail would suggest as much, as also the intriguing fact that the LXX of Bel and the Dragon, in which Habakkuk strangely features, introduces Habakkuk as from the tribe of Levi; to a Levite who knew of this association, the oracles of Habakkuk would therefore be especially worth interpreting.

(D) Materials directly reflecting the Chaldeans/Babylonians. The fourth category of material that is reflected in the language of 1QpHab in the sections that interpret the Chaldeans as the Kittim are some biblical passages which also speak of the Chaldeans. Foremost amongst these is 2 Chronicles 36, whose language appears to provide nearly all the phraseology of the commentary that is not directly derivable from Habakkuk itself in items 3.F and J above. The oracle concerning Babylon of Isaiah 13 is apparently actually cited in 1QpHab 6.11-12. In addition the eschatological oracle against the unidentifiable Gog and Magog, possibly Babylon, of Ezekiel 38, is used to provide some further motifs. The use of the Babylon materials shows how far-sighted is the author's perception of the Roman presence, since like Babylon, Rome was shortly to destroy the Temple.[2]

1. G.J. Brooke 'History and Hermeneutics at Qumran', *Bulletin of the Institute for Antiquity and Christianity* 16.3 (1989), pp. 9-11.
    2. As argued by D. Flusser, 'The Kingdom of Rome through the eyes of the Hasmonean House and the Essenes', *Zion* 48 (1983), pp. 159-74 (Hebrew).

(E) Victory songs. In several places I have noticed that the language
and phraseology of the victory song of Exodus 15 is used. In some
places this is to assert that the victory belongs to God, in others to
imply that the punishment of the Egyptians is turned against the
disobedient Israelites themselves. 1QpPs, as an interpretation of Psalm
68, may be a direct reflection upon a song taken as cultically
endorsing God's military supremacy and showing that the Kittim
themselves will not escape from God's rebuke. But further than these
biblical texts, we have noted both in 4QpNah and in 1QpHab that there
is a considerable reflection of the poetry both of 1QS 10, and more
especially of 1QM 14. This latter text may almost certainly be seen as
the source for some of the language of the pesharim because it is also
preserved in 4QM^a, a text which appears to offer an abbreviation of
the regulatory aspects of the War Scroll but an enhancement of the
poetic material. Even in 1QM it is noticeable that the victory song of
1QM 14 occurs between two passages that mention the Levites, the
second of which (1QM 15) also introduces the Kittim. Levites and
Kittim dominate the material in 1QM 1 and 15–18. Another paper
could be written on all these intricate interrelationships between the
War Scroll and the pesharim.

5. Conclusion

This paper has tried to show why and how it is important to pay
detailed attention to the kinds of sources which seem to lie behind the
sections of interpretation in the commentaries which speak of the
Kittim. Such attention reveals a collection of source material that is
remarkably consistent in itself in applying cultic military texts to the
fate that Israel will suffer, that is, has suffered and is suffering, at the
hand of the Kittim.

These sources have a leaning towards concerns with cultic
obligation and cultic practice, especially in the singing of victory
songs, and the place of the Levites. To derive history from the use of
such texts in a commentary like 1QpHab seems foolhardy. The
commentaries are written to demonstrate that the period in which the
author and his readership live has indeed an eschatological character.

The writing of some of the pesharim may well have been motivated
in part by uncertain memories of Pompey's action in Jerusalem, or by
contemporary experience of Roman occupation, such as events

surrounding Sabinus and Varus or even Pilate's introduction of iconic representations into Jerusalem. We can learn little or nothing of the history of the Qumran community from these texts,[1] and little enough about the Romans. Rather, the image of empire is controlled by biblical and non-biblical texts used intricately to show that the words of Habakkuk and others speak directly, if not always in great detail, to the author's contemporary and eschatological generation; they speak especially of the cultic threat posed by the Romans, particularly through what the Romans have taken or might take from Levites by demanding regular tribute from the temple treasury.

In 1968 B. Roberts wrote of the scholarly interpretation of the pesharim and the Kittim in particular: 'By becoming over-concerned about their "historicity" we might be losing sight of the real significance of the scrolls'.[2] This paper has tried to put historicity in its proper context by showing that the image of the empire in the pesharim is controlled by literary motifs which are used to portray the Romans as part of a broader eschatological scenario; within that scenario they are militarily mighty, economically threatening, but ultimately cultically no match for the God of Israel.

---

1. Despite the arguments of J.D. Amusin ('The Reflection of Historical Events of the First Century BC in Qumran Commentaries [4Q161; 4Q169; 4Q166]', *HUCA* 48 [1977], pp. 123-34) and of Fröhlich ('Caractères formels des pesharim de Qumrân et la littérature apocalyptique', in Augustin and Schunk [eds.] *Wünschet Jerusalem Frieden: Collected Communications to the XIIth Congress of the International Organization for the Study of the Old Testament, Jerusalem 1986,* pp. 453-54).

2. B.J. Roberts, 'Biblical Exegesis and Fulfilment in Qumran', in P.R. Ackroyd and B. Lindars (eds.), *Words and Meanings. Essays presented to D. Winton Thomas* (Cambridge: Cambridge University Press, 1968), p. 199.

DANIEL IN THE LIONS' DEN

Philip R. Davies

1. The Ideology of Imperium in Daniel

The book of Daniel provides some of the most vivid images of empire to be found in the Bible, and possibly in ancient literature. It is a political document through and through, dealing explicitly with the relationship between the religion of the Jews and foreign imperium.[1] This book provided one of the foundations for the articulation of Jewish and Christian attitudes to Rome, as its influence on later literature attests. The traces of this influence appear largely in predictions of the future. But why were these predictions of the book of Daniel influential? Why, indeed, did the book, alone of its genre, acquire a canonical status? That its attribution to Daniel, an otherwise rather obscure figure possibly related to other (non-Jewish) Daniels and Dan'els, guaranteed its status is implausible; most writings of this genre had much better qualified pseudoauthors. No: the answer, I suspect, lies in its exilic setting and its powerful and persuasive ideology of imperium. The exile in Babylon (and Persia) was for many Jews not merely a potent symbol of their own long-established status, an archetypal predicament, but, as Daniel 9 itself insists, that exile itself was their exile: it had not ended. Daniel was not a figure of their past, but a fellow-exile, a fellow victim (if also beneficiary) of foreign rule. The appeal of the book of Daniel is intensified by an explicit yet sophisticated ideology of empire and a philosophy of history, and one that, so long as it was preserved, could permit the specific predictions

---

1. On the political function of Daniel, see J.J. Collins, *The Apocalyptic Vision of the Book of Daniel* (Missoula, MT: Scholars Press, 1977), pp. 191-218. On the general political background of much apocalyptic writing, see D. Hellholm (ed.), *Apocalypticism in the Mediterranean World and the Near East* (Tübingen: Mohr [Siebeck], 1983).

to be amended without discredit to its own reputation. A careful look at the ideology of the book is thus an indispensable prerequisite of this paper.

The first point to be made about the ideology of Daniel is that it is not univocal. There is no single image of empire or of reaction to it; the reader will find within it an unresolved tension between qualified approval and outright condemnation, between obedience and resistance, between co-operation and opposition. These oppositions are partly mediated by a further opposition between present and future dimensions: what will be already imposes itself on what is and determines its nature. The ambivalences in this book will have served well (and helped to create?) the attitudes of Jewish subjects to Rome, which we know very well to have been ambivalent also. And that ambivalence lay, of course, not simply in the material well- or ill-being that Rome bestowed upon them, but in the very fact of a non-Jewish empire claiming certain allegiances of the chosen people of the lord of history (as they were inclined to see it) and ever threatening more. Josephus himself affords an obvious instance: if his account of the Jewish war of 66 may be suspected of emphasizing such a polarity of attitudes to Rome, his own understanding of the feelings and logic of either pole emerge clearly enough; there is in his own career and writing abundant evidence of the realization of that ambivalence in his own self.

The first six chapters of Daniel comprise a series of tales probably originating in Jewish communities of the eastern diaspora during the Persian and perhaps early Hellenistic period—more specifically, from the region of ancient Mesopotamia between the middle of the sixth century and the end of the third century BCE. These tales project, in an idealistic way, both the practical accommodations to life under imperium and also, though less prominently, the dream of the ultimate destruction of that imperium with release for the subjugated people in the advent of an eternal divine imperium.[1]

---

1. There is no Hebrew/Aramaic word in Daniel strictly equivalent to 'empire' or 'imperium', the word used being 'kingdom'. For the book of Daniel, the problem and the nature of imperium are largely bound up with the character of the king—though a benign king can be the victim of imperium (as in Dan. 6), and the book can also speak (ch. 11) of imperium being passed from one nation to another, the nation being represented by its patron deity/angel.

These tales can be categorized into two kinds: those that describe the decipherment of a sign that the king has been given, and those that narrate the deliverance of the hero or heroes from persecution.[1] Each type of tale prescribes in its own way the limits of human imperium in both wisdom and power. Human monarchy is set forth as being both ordained and circumscribed by 'the Most High', who truly 'rules the kingdom of men and gives it to whom he will' (Dan. 4.32). The decipherment tales show how the future course of history is predestined by the will of this deity, so that only he can reveal its secrets to whom he chooses, while the deliverance stories demonstrate the deity's control of history by chronicling his intervention to frustrate the intentions of the monarch. Thus the argument that the events of history dance to the tune of the Almighty is demonstrated both theoretically and practically; theoretically by the revealing of secrets and practically by direct intervention, where necessary, in the workings of *Realpolitik*.

Let us reflect on the psychology of such tales. Both kinds of tale generate a conflict between Jewish values and the values of the monarchs to whom they are subject (and it is worth noting again that imperium is bound up with the individual figure of the monarch; as in the books of Kings, the conduct and character of the king both determines and is determined by the 'kingdom'). The conflict may be on more than one level. First, it may appear at the level of insight, in which the whole apparatus of the royal administration is shown to be defective, by failing to understand that, in the last analysis, monarchs and their empires are victims of history and not makers of it, a defect that the Jewish sage can provisionally repair but that must remain as it were systemic, and the true insight that the 'Most High', the true lord of history, offers to his chosen in the form of a secret. At this level, the conflict is hermeneutical, and in the life of the Jewish subject its resolution will find expression in an opposition of public and secret: public acknowledgment of sovereign power and secret denial of its reality, the psychological opposition, the polarity, whose code of secret versus overt the stories themselves assume into their narrative design. Resolution of this type of conflict in the narrative is

---

1. This classification, with some variation, is widely adopted. For an elaboration of the position adopted here see P.R. Davies, 'Eschatology in the Book of Daniel,' *JSOT* 17 (1980), pp. 33-53.

harmonious—the king gratefully acknowledges the power of the sovereign of heaven and appropriately elevates the bringer of revelation to political office—the secret is made open, the revealer of secrets publicly acclaimed.

The conflict may also be engaged on a more explicit level: a clash of will, in which the monarch vainly tries first to impose his policy on the Jewish subject and subsequently to destroy him, whether by furnace or by lions. This conflict is manifest as a trial, but a trial of two kinds. It is a trial of strength, of course, between two competing imperia; but it is also a trial of the Jew, for sovereignty depends ultimately on its acknowledgment. (In the psychology of the individual Jewish subject this kind of story possibly responds to fear, the fear of trial; but this point cannot be developed here.) Again, the resolution itself is harmonious, though it is achieved in different ways in the two examples we have. In ch. 3, where the monarch is the instigator and supervisor of the proceedings, the deliverance of the three youths from the furnace converts him; he acknowledges that their god has the power to thwart his own plans and decrees that this god must not be opposed. In the story of the den of lions, the villain is not the monarch Darius, but rather, as in the case of the Esther story, his officials. Here the monarch greets the rescue of Daniel with relief.

The suggestion in these stories that Jews could rise to high political office under the Persians, and possibly Seleucids, is not fanciful. But everything else is. The historian finds little evidence of religious persecution or enforced emperor-worship in the eastern diaspora under Neo-Babylonians, Persians or Seleucids. These tales of conflict have been manufactured for ideological reasons. These reasons may be quite complex,[1] but we can presume that the preservation of distinct values and identity by a subculture in an imperial cultural milieu, whether hostile or not, requires conflict in order to sustain itself; lack of conflicts aids assimilation. Those members of that subculture determined upon its preservation must inevitably hold it to be superior to the culture of the imperial host. The contradiction between the cultural and political relationships, as perceived by the subculture, then requires to be resolved, if not in real life then through the production of narratives in which such a reversal takes place so as to

---

1. On the social psychology of the tales, see H.-P. Müller, 'Märchen, Legende und Enderwartung', *VT* 26 (1976), pp. 338-50.

project the 'real' or 'correct' hierarchy. In the stories of Daniel it is the monarchs who need the Jews, and the Jewish heroes generally end by being appointed to high political office, with the Jewish god acknowledged by the monarch as the lord of history. It is important to attend to this narrative resolution, to note that it is harmonious, with no immediate residue of conflict left—the monarch is not beaten, but won over. His rule is not broken, but preserved. Together with the need for conflict as a means of articulating values, the culture which produced the Daniel tales also desired harmonious resolution, achieved by asserting that the Jewish god has appointed the monarch, and that so long as the monarch does not overreach his derived authority, he deserves the loyal service of Jewish subjects. In short, conflict aims at reconciliation, the inescapable reality of life in the eastern diaspora, where indeed most Jews who had the opportunity to emigrate to Yehud chose to stay.

So far, however, it would seem that 'rendering unto Caesar' and 'rendering unto God' are at least both possible and desirable without contradiction in principle. But at another level, even these relatively accommodating tales propose a quite different aspect to the conflict they mediate. The superficial accord between Jew and monarch satisfies practical requirements, but the deeper fears and desires also urge to be expressed. After all, the very fact of a cycle of such stories, in which the resolution of one chapter is followed by the crisis of the next, reinforces the impression, which the book—as it seems to me—deliberately cultivates, that harmonious resolution is forever provisional, and, like the repeated hardening of Pharaoh's heart, the whim of a monarch—whether, as in the case of Pharaoh, prompted by deities or otherwise (and here is a matter for further analysis!)—is in the last resort not to be gainsaid. The conflict and the resolution are thus cyclic. Hence we seek another level within the stories, a level which transcends the cycle.

The second Daniel story (ch. 2) introduces the theory of history that is central to the book, namely that human history is a succession of empires (kingdoms). In Daniel these number five, including the final one, which will be eternal. As presented, these empires will be successively degenerate, until finally an empire will be established which will bring all empires to an end and stand for ever (2.44). No doubt is left that in some way this empire pertains to the Jews ('not left to another people' [2.44]). The Jewish people, therefore, subject to foreign monarchs, are not content with episodic victories in romantic tales about individual heroes, but wish to represent themselves as the victors of revealed, and not just hidden, history. This desire and its expression underlie and subvert the intercourse between monarch and Jewish subject. In the interim, the monarch may either co-operate with Jews or oppress them, in either case reaping the due reward from the 'Most High'. But ultimately 'empire' has neither option, its predetermined fate being extinction in the face of the eternal supremacy of the empire of the Jews and their god (and here another ambiguity emerges, which we cannot explore: whether the final empire is of the Jews, for the Jews, or for the righteous [Jews?]; the book of Daniel includes all three at different points). Thus, when Nebuchadnezzar promotes Daniel and his friends to high political office (chs. 2, 3) and confesses the lordship of the 'king of heaven' (chs. 2, 4), when Darius, in ch. 6, even decrees that all peoples shall 'tremble and fear before the god of Daniel', we witness the proleptic demolition of the present political order and a glimpse of the true state of affairs, as seen from the perspective of history's goal.

We are afforded a more vivid glimpse of this vision in the famous tale of Belshazzar (ch. 5), which ends not in reconciliation, but in the death of the monarch, after being told that he is found wanting and that his kingdom's days are numbered, his death sentence having been read out to him by Daniel. The tale concludes, 'Darius the Mede received the kingdom', a phrasing which alerts us to the recognition that for the book of Daniel, while there may be four empires, there is also in a different sense only one empire, that of the 'Most High'; it is he who gives and takes it, and hence monarchs can only 'receive' it from him.

If we turn now to the visions which comprise the second part of the book of Daniel, we encounter a different argument about the sequence of empires from that in ch. 2. These empires are now represented not as ever less glorious but as ever more violent. This change is not necessarily a contradiction, but certainly a clear switch of perspective. The sequence culminates in a particular ruler who challenges the 'Most High' and his people in an unprecedented way. The depiction of non-Jewish monarchs here is in no way sympathetic, as it is in most of the tales, but ranges between dismissive and thoroughly negative. The very graphic images of empire which are found in ch. 7 are those of great and weird beasts, whose bestiality is underlined by symbolizing the final kingdom that will replace them as a human being (literally: 'son of man').[1] According to Daniel 7–12, human monarchy is now not an expression, but implicitly a denial of divine monarchy, a challenge which can only culminate in an eschatological conflict between the two forces, with the god inevitably victorious, and the monarchs destroyed. While in chs. 1–6 empires are 'received' by divine disposition, in Dan. 10.20–11.1 they emerge as the outcome of angelic warfare, each patron angel representing its own nation, as if now to deny the direct working of divine providence in the imperial sequence. As in Daniel 2, an everlasting empire will be established, but according to ch. 12 it will be inaugurated by the victory of the patron angel of Israel, Michael, after which the wicked will be punished and the virtuous rewarded. Thus we witness in the visions two important changes in the image of empire—the notion of cosmic struggle in succession rather than the orderly progress implied by divine gift; and attention to the ethics of empire in the eschatological judgment of the empires and the vindication of righteous individuals (ch. 12).

It is not difficult to explain this change of image. The tales reflect life in a non-Jewish environment with a generally benign monarchy, while the visions, and indeed the production of the book of Daniel as a unified composition, emerge from the experiences of Jews in the territory of Judah who witnessed measures by the Seleucid monarch Antiochus IV (in 167–163 BCE) to proscribe certain traditional religious practices, abolishing the Jewish Temple sacrifice and erecting an altar, probably to Zeus (which Daniel, followed by 1 Maccabees and the New Testament called the 'abomination of desolation', or better, 'desolating sacrilege'). In the later chapters of Daniel, we see reflected an assault on the cult of the 'Most High' by the monarch, portrayed as an act of deliberate aggression, and interpreted as demonic, implying a more chaotic view of history and thus a more dynamic resolution of the problematic of imperium.

The book of Daniel, then, reflects two different political experiences and two different strategies. Overarching these is a common belief that non-Jewish earthly sovereignty, whether benign or hostile to Jews, was under the control of their own god, who would in the

---

1. For a fascinating study of the cultural and psychological aspects of Danielic bestiality, see P.A. Porter, *Metaphors and Monsters* (Lund: Gleerup, 1983).

course of time remove it and restore the Jews to that place which their fidelity to him deserved. I have suggested that the ideology of empire expressed in Daniel is a function of political and social experience and not merely some theological abstract. The same considerations will apply to its interpretation under the Roman empire, which I will now begin to consider.

2. Rome as the Fourth Kingdom

According to Daniel 2 and 7, the final and eternal empire would follow the fourth empire after Nebuchadnezzar, and the book implies that the four empires are those of the Babylonians, Medes, Persians, and Greeks.[1] The last act preceding the final intervention of Michael is the death of the 'king of the north', namely Antiochus IV. World history thus was anticipated to end around the middle of the first century BCE. What in fact happened was that Jewish resistance to Antiochus IV led eventually to a Jewish mini-empire, ruled by the Hasmonean dynasty, which lasted nearly a hundred years, and whose territory exceeded in actual fact what King David had ruled only in theory. Possibly Daniel's final empire was thought by many at the time to have been inaugurated. But the Hasmoneans soon adopted the garb of Hellenistic monarchs, and their popularity waned. In the middle of the first century BCE, by a combination of internal squabbling and encroaching Roman military power, the dynasty fizzled out and gave way to direct or indirect Roman rule. Nevertheless, Daniel's theory of history continued to be nurtured. Inevitably, the final and most terrible of the four earthly empires described in Daniel now came to be seen as Rome and not Macedonia/Greece. For Christian writers, at least in the West, additional confirmation of Daniel's scheme was obtained by recognizing in the final kingdom the church founded by Jesus Christ. Accordingly, under the Romans, the book of Daniel promised for Jews the future destruction of Rome and its replacement

---

1. The theories of world ages/kingdoms/empires in ancient literature have been widely treated. See e.g. J.W. Swain, 'The Theory of the Four Monarchies: Opposition History under the Roman Empire', *Classical Philology* 35 (1940), pp. 1-21; M. Hengel, *Judaism and Hellenism* (London: SCM Press, 1974), pp. 181-83 and corresponding bibliography. Among the ancient texts treating such a theory are Hesiod, *Works and Days*; *Sibylline Oracles* 4.49-101; the Persian *Bahman Yasht* (preserving an earlier source); and numerous Latin writers (discussed in Swain).

by the promised eternal kingdom, while for Christians the process was already under way. This contrast characterizes in general terms the difference between Jewish and Christian readings of Daniel under the Romans. Though in either case Daniel gave warrant for the hope of Rome's imminent demise, attitudes towards Rome were determined by direct experience of imperium rather than simply by appeal to Daniel. In the remainder of this essay, I shall sample some readings of Daniel which throw light on the experiences of imperial rule. My treatment must then be necessarily selective, illustrative and sparing of detail.

3. *Reading Daniel in Differing Circumstances*

Before the War with Rome: The Dead Sea Scrolls
I shall treat Daniel in the Dead Sea Scrolls with especial brevity, since George Brooke has in part addressed the subject elsewhere, and in any case not every use of Daniel here is necessarily indicative of a particular stance towards Rome. Hence the discovery of a legend about Nabonidus, which appears to be an earlier form of the story in Daniel 4, is of no concern to us, though of great importance for the pre-history of the book of Daniel.[1] Our major interest in the Scrolls lies with the use of the term 'Kittim' to denote the Romans. For some time, the identification of 'Kittim' for Romans in the scrolls was disputed, on the grounds that in the Bible the term applies to the Greeks. However, in Dan. 11.30 the term 'ships of Kittim' almost certainly refers to Rome—though these 'Kittim' are not pejoratively treated and indeed of only incidental concern to Daniel as players in the drama of the 'king of the north', Antiochus IV. Since Daniel is used in the opening column of the War Scroll, one of the two scrolls in which the Kittim figure prominently, it is highly possible that the term 'Kittim' for the Romans is inspired by the usage of Daniel.

Relationships between Rome and the inhabitants of Judah evolved from almost one extreme to the other. According to 1 Maccabees, Judah Maccabee made an alliance with Rome, an alliance that perhaps

---

1.   On this text (4QPrNab)—and other Qumran texts related to Daniel—see J.T. Milik, '"Prière de Nabonide" et autres écrits d'un cycle de Daniel, fragments de Qumrân 4', *RB* 63 (1956), pp. 407-15; for the text, see B. Jongeling *et al.*, *Aramaic Texts from Qumran* (Leiden: Brill, 1976), pp. 123-31.

persisted for some time.[1] Whatever the actual motives on each side, it is likely that at least the supporters of the Maccabees, and subsequently the Hasmoneans, regarded Rome as a distant, though increasingly less aloof, protector. Indeed, according to Josephus, Pompey was invited to Jerusalem in 63 BCE to adjudicate between the rival claimants to the Hasmonean throne. Although anti-Roman feeling is often dated by modern scholars from Pompey's arrival in Jerusalem, Antipater came with a Jewish army to the assistance of Julius Caesar in Egypt during the wars of the triumvirate, and in return for this favour, the Jews throughout the empire were granted considerable favours. It was only the experience of direct Roman administration (which, again, was requested by Jewish leaders) that seems to have led to violent anti-Roman feeling and ultimately to war. In this context, the difference of attitude towards Rome between the Habakkuk Commentary and the War Scrolls might be instructive. The former would seem to date from a period before Rome was perceived, at least by the authors, as the inevitable enemy of the righteous. It describes the Kittim in fierce terms, indeed hostile ones, since they deal in 'cunning and guile' and act on instruction from their 'house of guilt' (= Senate?). But attention is throughout focused on their imperium and not on its destruction, of which there is no explicit mention. Their visitation upon Judah is taken for granted, though this visitation is portrayed as a punishment upon its wicked rulers. Apart from the use of the term 'Kittim', there is no hint of Danielic influence and no correspondence with its ideology of empire; the connections are rather with the frequent biblical motif of foreign armies as instruments of divine punishment upon the chosen but disobedient people.

The case is entirely different in the War Scroll, where the Kittim are the final enemy, the 'sons of darkness' whose defeat, in col. 1, is modelled in Daniel's description (ch. 11) of the 'king of the north', who will fight the 'king of the south' and then perish 'between the sea and the glorious holy mountain'. (Daniel seems to refer to Antiochus IV's Egyptian campaign, though the prediction of his death is inaccurate.) In the War Scroll the 'king of the Kittim' enters Egypt and then wages war with the 'kings of the north'. It seems that the scenario of Daniel 11 (and including Daniel 12) has been adapted,

---

1. On the Maccabean/Hasmonaean contacts with Rome, see 1 Macc. 8.1-32; 12.1-23; 14.16-24.

with some freedom, for the Romans.[1]

The date and setting of the War Scroll remains disputed, but my own opinion[2] is that it betrays a period in which these writers perceived clearly that war with Rome was inevitable and that this war would indeed be the eschatological cosmic war of which Daniel 11–12 speaks. Yet, unlike Daniel, which hints at angelic intervention,[3] this document envisages a full-scale human battle, followed by a forty years' war—fulfilling the prediction in Daniel 2 and 7 of an empire of the Jewish people or of their god (the War Scroll shares the ambiguity of Daniel over this). The Habakkuk Commentary, on the other hand, may reflect the views of a slightly earlier period. But this is not necessarily the case, for their respective perceptions of the role of Rome can be traced over a long period, and remain, even after 70, in that literature that sees the disaster as punishment for Jewish rebellion against its god. But this perception is not that of the book of Daniel.[4]

The Late First Century

Here I invoke a pair of contemporary Jewish authors, each writing in the aftermath of the suppression by the Romans of the Jewish war of 66, in which the Temple had been destroyed and, as far as we know, the cult thereafter abandoned. I shall also allude, though very briefly, to the use of Daniel in the New Testament, chiefly in the book of Revelation.

1. For discussion of this influence, see P. von der Osten-Sacken, *Gott und Belial* (Göttingen: Vandenhoeck & Ruprecht, 1969), pp. 30-34.
2. See P.R. Davies, *1QM, the War Scroll from Qumran* (Rome: Biblical Institute Press, 1977), pp. 123-24.
3. Note especially the appearance in 1QM 9.15(?); 17.7; (cf. 13.13!) of Michael (possibly, though not certainly, to be equated with the 'prince of light', 1QM 13.10) and the same figure in Dan. 12.1 (possibly, though not certainly, to be understood as the human figure ['son of man'] of Dan. 7).
4. Dan. 8 can be invoked, of course, as a recognition that the misfortunes of the Jews arise from their own sin. This contradiction of the ideology of the rest of Daniel has long provoked discussion of the originality of this prayer, which can hardly be excised from the chapter without leaving an implausibly stunted rump, though it can certainly be read as a deuteronomistic 'quote' and possibly a well-known liturgical item. Even cursory discussion is out of the question here; let it simply be remarked that the sin of Israel is perhaps to be understood as causing the delaying of the arrival of the final kingdom rather than as the reason for the sovereignty of non-Jewish kingdoms in the first place.

The fall of Jerusalem in 70 could be seen as the fulfilment of the 'prediction' of Daniel as the 'desolating sacrilege', the culminating outrage of the fourth kingdom against the Jewish people and their deity. *4 Ezra*[1] is a Palestinian work dating from the decades after this destruction, and comprising a series of visions and meditations on the catastrophe. It is probably a composite work, and its fifth vision (10.60–12.35) is perhaps an originally independent composition modelled on Daniel 7, which described the four successive kingdoms of the world as four beasts, the first a lion with eagle's wings, the second a bear, the third a winged leopard. Of the fourth we are told in Daniel only that it had iron teeth and ten horns, with one little horn. The fifth vision of *4 Ezra* is of an eagle that, like the beasts in Daniel 7, arises from the sea. It has twelve wings and three heads. The eagle reigns over the earth, but its wings and heads drop successively from it, until one head is left. Finally a lion speaks to the eagle: 'Hear, O eagle, I will speak to you: the Most High says to you, are you not the one remaining of the four beasts which I made reign in my world, that the end of my times might come about through them? But you, the fourth to have come, have overcome all of the previous beasts'. After describing the eagle's cruel deeds, the speech ends: 'so you shall disappear, O eagle... and so the whole earth, free from your violence, shall be refreshed and hope for the judgment and mercy of him that made it'.

By apocalyptic convention, the near-transparent symbolism is made explicit by a subsequent interpretation that, almost by convention too, does not exactly match the vision—presumably because the interpretation is really a re-interpretation and fits slightly different data. But at any rate the eagle is Daniel's fourth beast, the fourth kingdom, and the wings and heads its rulers, though not necessarily all emperors. One development from Daniel is the appearance of a messiah descended from David, who is the lion, and will first judge and then destroy

---

1. For the text of *4 Ezra* see B.M. Metzger in J.H. Charlesworth (ed.), *Old Testament Pseudepigrapha* (Garden City: Doubleday, 1983), I, pp. 517-59; the older translation and commentary of G.H. Box in R.H. Charles, *Apocrypha and Pseudepigrapha of the Old Testament* (Oxford: Clarendon Press, 1913), I, pp. 542-624 is dated but provides a fuller, and very useful commentary. See also A. Thompson, *Responsibility for Evil in the Theodicy of IV Ezra* (Missoula, MT: Scholars Press, 1977), and T.W. Willett, *Eschatology in the Theodicies of 2 Baruch and 4 Ezra* (Sheffield: JSOT Press, 1989).

them. In *4 Ezra* 13 appears the figure of a man coming out of the sea who will judge and destroy the nations from Mt Zion. The vision combines elements from Daniel 2 and 7, but while in Daniel 7 it seems that the human figure is a symbol of the Jewish people, the Holy Ones, here it is taken as an individual redeemer, the 'messiah'. The same is true in the book of Revelation, which I shall not treat in detail, since it is well represented elsewhere. I shall merely note that both it and *4 Ezra* bring into prominence the idea of Daniel 12 (itself perhaps a development of the deliverance tales of chs. 3 and 6) that extreme distress, including death, immediately precedes the end: 'there shall be a time of trouble, such as never has been since there was a nation, till that time' (Dan. 12.1). By the time of which we are now speaking, the overthrow of the Roman empire is not seen as a politically realistic eventuality except by means of a celestial agency, which Daniel 12 provides in the figure of Michael (as remarked earlier, perhaps introduced into ch. 12 as the referent of the human figure of ch. 7).

The 'messianic' interpretations of Daniel in *4 Ezra* and Revelation call for some explanation, though in either case the explanation will be different. In Revelation, where the influence of Daniel 7 is well known,[1] the Danielic figure is of course Jesus Christ, who, according to Acts 1.9 went up to heaven with the clouds of heaven instead of coming down with them, and whose second coming is shortly expected. In the case of *4 Ezra* we may prefer to conclude that the recent experience of defeat by Rome caused the author to reflect on the desirability of such an interpretation: victory over Rome must come only from God and his appointed agent, not be taken by the Jewish people (and we may note that while messianic pretensions do not seem to have been explicit in the war of 66–70, the leaders of the Bar Kochba revolt did invoke a messianic ideology, including of course the taking of the name 'bar Kochba' by Simeon bar Kosiba).

The contents of *4 Ezra*, including its eagle vision, were composed in Hebrew or Aramaic and in Palestine. Clearly the weight of Roman oppression is heavily felt, though as with the Dead Sea Habakkuk Commentary it is the extent of Roman rule which is deplored and not any particular wrong done to the Jewish nation. Although the

---

1.   On the use of Daniel by the author of Revelation, see G.K. Beale, *The Use of Daniel in Jewish Apocalyptic Literature and in the Revelation of St John* (Lanham: University Press of America, 1984).

specifically Jewish context is entirely evident, it seems to me unlikely that any particular event alone inspired the vision—whether the fall of Jerusalem under Titus or the war of Quietus or the measures of Hadrian such as road-building or the founding of Aelia Capitolina or the controversial edict against castration (which is now thought not to have included circumcision in any case). The argument lies indeed rather in the very power of Rome than in any act of sacrilege. Daniel 7 avers that each successive empire grows fiercer and bigger until the end of the entire sequence. According to this logic, the very might of the Roman empire itself is the guarantee of its own destruction, and those who resented this empire could thus take some grim delight in that very thing which they most feared. Such an attitude is similar, though not identical, to that found elsewhere in *4 Ezra* and, again, in the biblical book of Revelation (this time perhaps inspired by Daniel 12, not Dan. 7) that the greater the suffering, the closer the end.

The second author to be studied in this section is Flavius Josephus, who provides a contrasting perspective. His circumstances and his outlook are on the face of it quite different from those of the author(s) of *4 Ezra*. Although Josephus had initially fought against Rome as a general in Galilee, he had later attached himself to Vespasian, and ended up in the closing years of the first century CE not too uncomfortably as a resident of Rome, where he chronicled first the course of that war, then later the entire history of the Jews. In this larger work, the *Jewish Antiquities*, he deals with the 'prophet' Daniel in the course of describing the period of deportation in Babylon. Mindful of the recent events and of his task in persuading non-Jews of the antiquity and venerability of his own people, not to mention their lack of real antagonism toward Rome, what can he say of the book's predictions about the fourth kingdom, its destruction and replacement by the rule of the Jewish god? Daniel's interpretation of Nebuchadnezzar's dream in ch. 2 concludes with the statue representing the four world empires being smashed by a stone that has been cut, without human hands, from a mountain. Having explained the four empires, Josephus concludes thus:

> And Daniel also revealed to the king the meaning of the stone, but I have not thought it proper to relate this, since I am expected to write of what is past and done and not of what is to be; if, however, there is anyone who has so keen a desire for exact information (or 'truth': ἀκριβείας, var. ἀληθείας) that he will not stop short of inquiring more closely but

wishes to learn about the hidden things that are to come, let him take the
trouble to read the Book of Daniel, which he will find among the sacred
writings.[1]

We may justly smile at this diplomatic restraint. But, probing deeper,
we may also ask, even if we cannot answer, what Josephus really
believed. For indeed, Josephus's own political attitudes are not distant,
it seems to me, from those of Daniel. Certainly he is anxious to
criticize those hot-headed countrymen of his who were dragged
unwillingly into a conflict which they cannot have won, as Josephus
elsewhere states through the mouth of Agrippa, in the speech
discussed by Tessa Rajak elsewhere in this volume.[2] Josephus sided
with the ideology of Daniel 1–6 rather than of Daniel 12, and accepted
that non-Jewish rulers were placed in authority by his god, and hence
that resistance to them was futile, even wrong. Yet he also knew the
reality of abused authority—indeed, he assigns some blame for the
war to inept and callous Roman administration. He had after all once
taken up arms in the revolt, and it was he who had placed in the
mouth of Eleazar, the zealot leader on Masada, those words which the
modern visitor to that place can hardly avoid, words which breathe
the preference of liberty and death to slavery and life.[3] I doubt
whether Josephus did not believe, or at least hope, that this fourth
kingdom, this Roman empire, would succumb to the final kingdom,
that its days were numbered. Josephus was an avowed believer in
prophecy (claiming the gift himself), and his description of Daniel as
prophet leaves me, at least, in no doubt that in this most pro-Roman of
ancient writers toleration, and even enjoyment, of Rome was
sweetened by the belief that it was the master of the Jews only for the
time being and that its fall and judgment awaited it. But like Daniel,
Josephus knew how and when to be cryptic. He also knew, as I
suggested earlier, the ambivalence that I have argued must have been
characteristic of the Jewish attitude to Rome generally.

Rabbinic Literature
It is well known and often remarked that, by comparison with early
Christian writing, there is rather little by way of rabbinic treatment of

1.   Josephus, *Ant.* 10.210; the translation is from the Loeb edition.
2.   Josephus, *War* 2.345-401.
3.   Eleazar's Masada speech is given in Josephus, *War* 7.323-36.

Daniel. This is easily understood. After the failure of the second Jewish war with Rome in 132–35, political aspirations went underground and were either suppressed or transformed into other modes. It can be argued that the entire rabbinic programme was the creation of a reality different from the external and political, focusing on the internal, on the social, on the ideal, a view argued extensively and compellingly by J. Neusner and widely accepted. This programme, at all events, is generally traced back to the establishment of the academy at Yavneh after the fall of Jerusalem, and the founder of this academy, Yohanan ben Zakkai, is credited with the aim of offering a leadership of the Jewish nation that both Jews and Romans would accept, one in which messianic elements were marginalized almost to the point of obliteration. As a very broad generalization this seems to be acceptable; certainly there is no evidence for the oft-repeated claim that the rabbis supported the second Jewish revolt in 132–35.[1]

Among the rabbinic literature there are retellings and elaborations of the biblical tales of Daniel and also of the two stories, now in the Apocrypha, in which Daniel figures. But I have discovered no treatment of the visions. In general, rabbinic exegesis of Daniel is characterized by a lack of political comment, for obvious reasons. But one aspect of Daniel does reflect the rabbinic image of empire, namely the attitude toward Persian monarchs. The Persian empire was overrun by Alexander the Great in the fourth century BCE, after which his successors divided the territories, and the eastern part of the empire was ruled by the Seleucids. But in 240 BCE came the Parthians, who ruled until 226 CE, during which time their empire stretched occasionally as far as the borders of the Roman empire itself. During the first century CE the Roman triumvir Crassus was killed trying to defeat them, they briefly invaded Palestine, and they remained a threat to the eastern part of the Roman empire well into the first century. Roman policy towards Judaea was strongly influenced both by the proximity of the province to Parthia, and also by the fact that numerous Jews lived under the Parthians. Until the arrival of the

---

1. On the rabbinic non-participation in the Bar Kochba revolt, see P. Schäfer, 'Hadrian's Policy in Judaea and the Bar Kokhba Revolt: A Re-Assessment', in P.R. Davies and R.T. White (eds.), *A Tribute to Geza Vermes. Studies in Jewish and Christian History and Literature* (Sheffield: JSOT Press, 1990), pp. 281-303, esp. pp. 289-90.

Sassanians (226), the Jews in the eastern diaspora were rather well treated; thereafter religious persecution broke out not infrequently.[1] Now, a good deal of otherwise lost rabbinic interpretation of Daniel is preserved in Jerome's commentary of 407. Among the items of interest is the following, on Dan. 7.5, in which the second beast 'was raised up on one side'.[2] Jerome comments:

> And what is said, that 'it was raised up on one side' the Hebrews interpret thus, that they inflicted no cruelty on Israel. Hence they are also described in the prophet Zechariah as 'white horses'. . .

For both the 'Hebrews' and Jerome, of course, this second beast represents Persia and not, as probably originally intended, Media. Now the Persians, as well as being an imperial nation of the past were, for Jews in the Roman empire, also an imperial nation of the present, and Rome's chief enemy, as I have just indicated. This is perhaps why the word 'Parthians' is scarcely used in rabbinic literature, 'Persians' being preferred. However, much rabbinic literature, and especially the Talmud, contains material originating from under the Sassanids, who were hated. One needs caution, therefore, in seeking indications of the rabbis' attitudes towards the Roman–Parthian conflict. In *b. Berakhoth* 55b there is a discussion about dreams, and at a certain point Dan. 2.29 is cited, in which Daniel began to tell Nebuchadnezzar what his dream was. Now comes the following story, prompted by an obvious association:

> The Emperor [usually thought to be Trajan] said to R. Joshua b. R. Hananiah, 'You [plural] profess to be very clever. Tell me what I shall see in my dream.' He said to him, 'You will see the Persians making you do forced labour, and despoiling you and making you feed unclean animals with a golden crook'.

Trajan, if it was he, was defeated by the Parthians in 116. Another Talmudic passage (*b. Yoma* 10a) argues as follows: Rome will fall into the hands of the Persians, as inferred by *qal wahomer (a minori ad maius)*: The sons of Shem built the first sanctuary, the Chaldeans

---

1. The best recent treatment of this topic is still J. Neusner, *A History of the Jews in Babylonia*. I. *The Parthian Period* (Leiden: Brill, 1969; repr. Chico, CA: Scholars Press, 1984).

2. Fuller treatment of this lemma is given by J. Braverman, *Jerome's Commentary on Daniel: A Study of Comparative Jewish and Christian Interpretation of the Hebrew Bible* (Washington: CBA, 1978), pp. 84-86

(Babylonians) destroyed it, then the Chaldeans fell into the hands of the Persians. How much more so when the second Temple was built by the Persians (according to the Bible, Cyrus decreed and funded it), and destroyed by the Romans, will the Romans fall into the hands of the Persians?

The tales of Daniel invite comparison of the various kings and empires, making Nebuchadnezzar a hero, Darius the Mede kindly, distressed, and trying to rescue Daniel from the lion's den (6.14), Belshazzar irredeemably wicked, and the fourth kingdom the most vicious of the series, the one to be most dramatically destroyed. For two hundred years, Jews under the Roman empire could read in Daniel that not all empires were necessarily bad, and that perhaps, after all, the Persian empire would be the agent of Rome's destruction. Whether it is possible to quantify how much better (if at all) was the position of Jews under the Parthians than the Romans, we can derive from this circumstance the lesson that the empire on the other side of the frontier is always greener. Thus one can find in other rabbinic statements (most probably from the Sassanian period) a marked anti-Persian feeling, often expressed in opposition to Cyrus.[1]

4. *Concluding Remarks*

I have inevitably omitted much of interest: on Christian reading of Daniel I have said nothing of substance, and Porphyry is conspicuously absent. I have, in the space available, attended to Jewish reading, and attempted to argue that despite the striking variety of approaches to the book there lie those tensions and ambiguities, accommodations and aspirations which themselves inform the ideology of Daniel itself. Reading Daniel under the Romans invited a choice of which strategy, which philosophy, which image, of all those presented, was proper to one's own society, one's own inclination, and one's own experiences. The balance between toleration—even co-operation—and the wish for imminent destruction of the empire could be struck differently.

On the whole, Daniel's influence within Judaism has become ideologically weak, even while the stories remain popular. The burgeoning literature on the Holocaust draws surprisingly little on these

1.   Dislike of Persia is reflected in several texts from the Talmud, for example *b.* *Ber*. 8b, 46b; *b. Qid*.49b, 72a; *b. Sanh*. 98b.

stories. By contrast, Daniel has informed Christian historical philosophy, political theory (e.g. Calvin), and still fuels the eschatological fervour of certain Christian and meta-Christian groups and individuals. I ought not, then, to abandon this topic without the expression of a great irony, namely that with the victory of Christianity in the West, with the choice of state religion made after Constantine, the terrible fourth empire of Danielic tradition and the eternal empire that was, by that tradition, destined to succeed it, become one and the same. The Church's image of empire was thereafter for centuries to be one projected from the inside.

SURVIVING THE WEB OF ROMAN POWER:
RELIGION AND POLITICS IN THE ACTS OF THE APOSTLES,
JOSEPHUS, AND CHARITON'S *CHAEREAS AND CALLIRHOE**

Douglas R. Edwards

By the second century CE, the Greek East had dealt with Roman power for at least three hundred years and with imperial power for over one hundred years. Response to Roman power ranged from turbulence and violence to general acquiescence and assimilation. The type of response depended on an array of factors, including an individual or group's status, local and regional history, and location within the empire.[1] The Greek East promoted hellenic culture, with local and regional variations, and for the most part the Romans made no attempt to undermine or replace it. Indeed cities that were expanded or built in the Greek East during the Imperial period of Rome generally did so using Hellenic not Roman culture.[2] Nevertheless, members of the Greek East, especially the aspiring élite classes or their representatives, had to respond to Roman power if they wished to participate in the 'web of power'[3] that linked localities, regions, and groups with Rome.

Local ruling classes and their representatives in the Greek East

*   My thanks to Joyce Reynolds, Simon Price, Fergus Millar, Martin Goodman, Tessa Rajak, Richard Pervo, Ronald Hock, and Howard Kee for reading portions of this paper. The final product, however, remains my responsibility alone.
    1. E.S. Gruen, *The Hellenistic World and the Coming of Rome* (2 vols.; Berkeley: University of California Press, 1984).
    2. P. Garnsey and R. Saller, *The Roman Empire: Economy, Society and Culture* (Berkeley: University of California Press, 1987), p. 189.
    3. The term 'web of power' is used by S. Price, *Rituals and Power: The Roman Imperial Cult in Asia Minor* (Cambridge: Cambridge University Press, 1984), pp. 239-47. Cf. K. Wengst, *Pax Romana and the Peace of Jesus Christ* (Philadelphia: Fortress Press, 1987), pp. 38, 51-54.

sometimes found themselves between two powerful and sometimes competing forces: the rule of the outside political power, Rome, and the peculiar values, traditions, and culture of their group or region.[1] To maintain or acquire status and power they often promoted both widespread and local traditions. Because Roman rule was often passive, though sporadically reactive, as Fergus Millar has persuasively argued,[2] such efforts helped shape the nature of the web of power.[3] Religion played an important role in the Greek East's response to Roman power. By the second century CE, as Peter Brown notes, 'the public worship of the traditional gods still activated strong collective images of concord and parity...'[4] Even deities or religions that had no future salvific significance for their adherents played a powerful role in the social, cultural, and even political identities of persons and groups in the Greek East. S.R.F. Price correctly criticizes the 'Christianizing theory of religion' that stresses only the role of religion as a guide through the personal crises of life and as a means to salvation.[5] More appropriately, religion systematically constructs power. In other words, religion helps define strategic power relationships (both real and perceived) between different parties.[6] As Peter Brown argues, 'the cultural and religious aspects of the public life' in the towns of the Roman empire were no 'mere trappings which the urban élites could or could not afford...'[7]

Groups that wished to maintain power, encourage believers, or attract adherents, especially those who participated in and benefitted from Rome's 'web of power' (including Roman citizens, freedmen, and even slaves),[8] had to make clear that their movement or group

---

1. P. Brown, *The Making of Late Antiquity* (Cambridge, MA: Harvard University Press, 1978), p. 23.
2. F. Millar, *The Roman Empire and its Neighbors* (New York: Holmes and Meier, 2nd edn, 1981), p. 196. Cf. his 'Empire, Community and Culture in the Roman Near East: Greeks, Syrians, Jews, and Arabs', *Journal of Jewish Studies* 28 (1987), pp. 143-64.
3. Cf. A. Jones, *The Greek City: From Alexander to Justinian* (Oxford: Clarendon Press, 1949), p. 76.
4. Brown, *The Making of Late Antiquity*, p. 36.
5. Price, *Rituals and Power*, p. 247.
6. Price, *Rituals and Power*, pp. 241-42.
7. Brown, *The Making of Late Antiquity*, p. 34.
8. Garnsey and Saller, *The Roman Empire*, pp. 118-25.

operated within the bounds of lawful society. Important also would be the antiquity and the widespread influence of the group's traditions.[1] Thus, according to Tacitus, Ephesus received approval from the Romans for its cult of Artemis to serve as a site for asylum based on ancient myths (*Annals* 3.60–61). It helped also if a movement could exhibit the universal significance of its deity if it wished to appeal to persons who co-operated with the 'web of power'. Allegiance or support came more readily to movements or groups whose religion or deity made sense of a world grown large and under the rule of a distant power.

The Christian author Luke,[2] the Jewish historian Josephus, and the Greek novelist Chariton provide important clues as to how some associated with the elite class in the Greek East incorporated the language of religion and myth to bolster their own sense of power. Several features highlight the respective authors' expression of this process: (1) the antiquity of the worship of the deity;[3] (2) the power and presence of the deity across the οἰκουμένη (the Roman world); (3) the legitimate social customs of the author's group amid the legal system, customs acknowledged (but not always practised) in the narrative by powerful regional and international political figures; and (4) the deity's activity behind the scenes influencing the narrative events. Each author draws on religious and mythic traditions to display for the reader that the major source of power within a more broadly defined all-pervasive 'web of power', comes from the group's (or writer's) deity.

Luke: The Writer and his World

From the birth of Jesus to Paul's final speech in Rome, Luke makes clear that the activities of the Christian movement did not take place in

1. R. MacMullen, *Paganism in the Roman Empire* (New Haven: Yale University Press, 1981), pp. 2-4.
2. Luke serves as a convenient title for the author of the Gospel of Luke and Acts of the Apostles. The use of the name is not meant to suggest any identification with a known historical personage; see R. Maddox, *The Purpose of Luke–Acts* (Edinburgh: T. & T. Clark, 1982), pp. 3-6.
3. E.L. Bowie, 'Greeks and Their Past in the Second Sophistic', *Studies in Ancient Society* (Past and Present Series; ed. M.J. Finley; Boston: Routledge & Kegan Paul, 1974), pp. 166-209; cf. Brown, *The Making of Late Antiquity*, p. 28.

a corner (Acts 26.26).[1] Luke's consummate artistry[2] communicates a
plethora of social, political, economic and religious information perti-
nent for an audience concerned with two sets of issues. First and most
immediate were the individual and community concerns internal to the
group itself. Why should one join? What should one believe? How
should one act? What is one's relation to Jesus, to the early apostles, to
God? Equally significant for Luke was the relation of the movement
to external factors, most particularly the 'web of power' that bound in
varying degrees Roman authority and power with most social, economic, political, and religious facets of life. How were individual
members and the movement as a whole to engage this 'web of power'?

Human Agents, Divine Implications
Luke depicts the constancy and foreknowledge of God who employs
human agents to accomplish his designs. Power terminology perme-
ates Luke's narrative.[3] Jesus in Acts 1.8 clarifies the nature and result
of the movement's power: 'you will receive power [δύναμις] when
the Holy Spirit comes upon you; and you will bear witness for me in
Jerusalem, and all over Judea and Samaria, and away to the ends of
the earth'.

In addition, the narrative has the divine plan revealed to the partici-
pants. As D. Tiede argues, 'Perhaps no New Testament author is more
concerned than Luke to testify to the accomplishment of the will of
God in history or so caught up in the language of the divine plan and
predetermined intention, purpose, and necessity'.[4] Luke's attachment
of προ- prefixes to verbs indicates God's preordained work in the
lives of those involved.[5] The frequent use of δεῖ[6] also becomes the

1. J. Fitzmyer, *The Gospel According to Luke I–IX* (Anchor Bible Series, 28;
Garden City, NY: Doubleday, 1982), pp. 393-94.
2. C.H. Talbert, *Literary Patterns, Theological Themes, and the Genre of Luke–
Acts* (Missoula, MT: Scholars Press, 1974), p. 1.
3. E.g. the use of the term δύναμις at significant junctures of the narrative in
Luke–Acts (Acts 1.8; 6.8; 8.13).
4. D.L. Tiede, *Prophecy and History in Luke–Acts* (Philadelphia: Fortress
Press, 1980), p. 32. Cf. E. Richard, 'The Divine Purpose. The Jews and the
Gentile Mission (Acts 15)', in C.H. Talbert (ed.), *Luke–Acts: New Perspectives
from the Society of Biblical Literature Seminar* (New York: Crossroad, 1984),
p. 192.
5. Most appropriate are the following examples: Acts 3.20; 22.14; 26.16

author's way of stressing God's ever-active role, and functions much as the Greek notion of πρόνοια.[1] Peter's inaugural speech, replete with allusions to God standing behind the action, offers a typical example. Jesus' signs and wonders, Peter claims, exhibit God's activity (Acts 2.22) and even Jesus' death fits the plan and foreknowledge of God (Acts 2.23). God has sworn to David that one of his descendants should be put on his throne (2.30). God has foretold all these events through the prophets (Acts 3.15-26), has raised Jesus from the dead (4.10), and created the universe—'Sovereign Lord, who made the heaven and the earth and the sea and everything in them. . . ' (Acts 4.24). Even Herod Antipas, a member of the local aristocratic class, Pontius Pilate, the Roman procurator, the Gentiles, and the people of Israel did what God had ordained (προώρισεν [Acts 4.28]).

God's power extends over the cosmos and through history. Paul's speech before the people of Lystra, who have just associated him with the god Hermes, makes this clear.

> Men, why are you doing this? We also are men, of like nature with you, and bring you good news, that you should turn from these vain things to a living God who made the heaven and the earth and the sea and all that is in them. In past generations he allowed all the nations to walk in their own ways; yet he did not leave himself without witness, for he did good and gave you from heaven rains and fruitful season, satisfying your hearts with good and gladness (Acts 14.15-18).

The author redefines for his audience the web in which acts of miraculous and political power must be perceived. Nations and the cosmos itself function at the behest of the Christian God.

Travel, which forms a constituent part of the structure of Luke–Acts, emphasizes the universal scope and power of Luke's God who creates and rules over all aspects of society.[2] In the course of their travel across the οἰκουμένη, the promulgators of the religion refer

---

(προχειρίσασθαι); 10.41 (προκεχειροτονημένοις); 4.28 (προώρισεν).

6. Lk. 2.49; 4.23; 9.22; 12.12; 13.14, 16, 33; 15.32; 17.25; 18.1; 19.5; 21.9; 22.7, 37; 24.7, 36, 44; Acts 1.16, 21; 3.21; 4.12; 5.29; 9.6, 16; 14.22; 15.5; 16.30; 19.21; 19.36; 20.35; 23.11; 24.19; 25.10; 27.24.

1. F. Danker has rightly observed that δεῖ operates in the same manner as πρόνοια. See 'The Endangered Benefactor in Luke–Acts', in *SBL Seminar Papers* 20 (ed. Kent H. Richards; Chico, CA: Scholars Press, 1981), pp. 46-47.

2. H. Conzelmann, *The Theology of Luke* (trans. G. Buswell; New York: Harper & Row, 1961), pp. 18-94.

repeatedly to Jewish scriptures and themes, highlighting the movement's ancient roots. Speeches by Peter, James, Stephen, and Paul
make direct links with Christ and the covenant begun with Abraham
and continued through Moses. The constant retelling of the Jesus story
in light of Old Testament prophets and scriptures[1] situates the 'new'
Christian movement amid the ancient and venerable Jewish tradition, a
tradition widely recognized throughout the Roman empire.[2] In addition, the repeated mention of synagogues throughout the journeys of
the major characters stresses the spread of the Jewish faith throughout
the οἰκουμένη, and effectively associates the Christian movement
with an acknowledged ancient religion.[3] The proper interpreters of
the venerable Jewish tradition, however, were followers of Jesus.

Luke shows the importance of his movement within the political and
social fabric of Graeco-Roman society. Unlike Chariton of
Aphrodisias, however, who wrote from a city in the Greek East with
clear legitimate ties to Rome, or Josephus, who struggled with the
aftermath of the Jewish revolt under the patronage of the Flavian
emperors, Luke had to depict the Christian movement as offering no
immediate threat to the political and social fabric of the Roman
empire. Thus, at the end of Luke's gospel, a Roman procurator, a
Jewish king, a thief, and a centurion, persons intimately connected
with Roman justice, in rapid succession absolve Jesus of complicity in
any illegal or subversive activities. Indeed, Luke argues instead that
the Jewish leadership circumvents proper judicial channels and Roman
authority. Pilate 'released the man who had been thrown into prison
for insurrection and murder, whom they asked for; but Jesus he delivered up to their will' (Lk. 23.25). The onus for Jesus' death falls on
certain misguided Jews, not on subversive activity on the part of
Jesus.[4]

Paul's activity in Acts often parallels Jesus' activities in the Gospel

---

1. C.H. Talbert, 'Promise and Fulfillment in Lucan Theology', in *idem* (ed.),
Luke–Acts: New Perspectives from the Society of Biblical Literature Seminar,
pp. 91-103.

2. P.F. Esler, *Community and Gospel in Luke–Acts: The Social and Political
Motivations of Lucan Theology* (SNTSMS, 57; Cambridge: Cambridge University
Press, 1987), pp. 215-19.

3. Esler, *Community and Gospel*, pp. 211-17.

4. Cf. the prediction of Jerusalem's destruction (Lk. 19.41): 'Would that today
you knew the things that make for peace.'

of Luke,[1] including the stress on the innocence of the Christian movement. In a series of confrontations with Jews and Greeks, Paul reiterates the Christian movement's non-subversive character. A tribune rescues Paul from a mob in Jerusalem (Acts 21.31-40). When Paul speaks in Greek, the tribune thinks he may be the Egyptian who stirred up a revolt and led four thousand assassins to the wilderness (Acts 21.38). He takes Paul back to the barracks (Acts 22.24) in order to scourge him, but stops when he finds that Paul is a Roman citizen. The tribune presents Paul to the judicial branch of the Jews, the Sanhedrin, but once again the Jewish leadership circumvents Roman order and justice. The tribune, fearing violence, has to take Paul by force from the Jewish council and return him to the barracks (Acts 23.2-10). Luke contrasts such subversive activities by the Jews and revolutionary acts of the Egyptian with the 'model' citizen Paul. The readership knows the truth: Paul has done nothing to warrant the charges against him.

Paul's hearing before Felix, the Roman procurator, provides an additional opportunity for the Jewish leadership to charge sedition and for Roman officials to find nothing wrong (Acts 24.1-27). The innocence of Paul (and by implication the Christian movement) finds explicit support in Paul's trial before Festus (Acts 25.1–26.30). Paul argues that he has offended neither law, temple, nor Caesar (25.8). Paul's appeal to Caesar (25.11) circumvents a trial by Jewish law and closes the trial by Festus. Festus finds no serious charges against Paul and concludes that the Jews have 'certain points of dispute with him about their own superstition and about one Jesus, who was dead, but whom Paul asserted to be alive' (Acts 25.19). As Haenchen suggests, Luke depicts some Roman officials who plainly do not understand the theological dimensions of the debate.[2] However, Sergius Paulus, senatorial proconsul of Cyprus, and Cornelius, the centurion, remain important exceptions. Certain local elites also come off somewhat better.[3]

1.   Talbert, *Literary Patterns, Theological Themes, and the Genre of Luke–Acts*, pp. 51-66.
2.   E. Haenchen, *The Acts of the Apostles* (Oxford: Basil Blackwell, 1971), pp. 674-75; cf. Gallio, who hears the Jewish attack on Paul but refuses to make a judgment because it is an internal matter (Acts 18.12-17).
3.   Festus declares Paul innocent (Acts 25.18; 25.25; 26.31), Agrippa II, Bernice and 'prominent men of the city' (Caesarea) find no guilt in Paul (Acts 25.23-

From Acts 21.27 through 26.32, Luke charts how the charges by Jewish leaders that Jesus, Paul, and (by implication) the Christian movement of Luke's day disrupted the social order, perverted Roman law, and threatened Rome's political authority, have no foundation. With no exceptions, the Roman authorities find the Christian representatives completely innocent of any activities against the state.[1] Some still view this as Luke's effort to write an apologetic on behalf of the Christian movement to Roman officials. They argue that the effort to incorporate Jewish tradition, mission, and outlook associates Christianity with a legitimate and accepted religion, Judaism, in the Graeco-Roman government, a *religio licita*. Evidence remains sparse for Roman authorities in Jesus' or Luke's day having any interest in Luke's theological argument or in sorting out pro-Roman statements. C.K. Barrett's classic remark still has merit: 'No Roman official would ever have sifted through so much that in his view was theological and ecclesiastical rubbish in order to gain so small a grain of relevant apology'.[2] Nor, as P. Esler astutely points out, would the Christian movement wish to associate itself too closely with Judaism, especially when its members (which included Gentiles) would be expected to pay the Jewish tax to the Roman state.[3] In addition, the kingly titles given to Jesus at birth would hardly appeal to Roman officials. And Luke's directive that church members pay their taxes would have little significance to a Roman official who would not assume that they would do otherwise.[4] Luke does not show the close ties between Christianity and Judaism and the universal significance of the movement in order to plug Christianity into a legally recognized

24), and Paul himself recalls that no guilt was found (Acts 28.18); cf. Haenchen, *The Acts of the Apostles*, pp. 692-93.
    1.   Luke 23; Acts 16.39; 18.15-16; 19.37; 23.29; 25.25; 26.32. See discussion by W.G. Kümmel, in *Introduction to the New Testament* (trans. H.C. Kee; Nashville: Abingdon Press, 1975), p. 162-63.
    2.   C.K. Barrett, *Luke the Historian in Recent Study* (A.S. Peak Memorial Lectures, 6; London, 1960), p. 63; cf. P. Walaskay, *'And so we came to Rome': The political Perspective of St Luke* (SNTSMS, 49; Cambridge: Cambridge University Press, 1983), p. 18.
    3.   Esler, *Community and Gospel*, p. 213.
    4.   See the useful discussion by Walaskay, *'And so we came to Rome': The political Perspective of St Luke*, pp. 35-37.

religion for the sake of Roman officials.[1] Luke makes clear that Pilate, Herod, the people of Israel, and the Gentiles conspired against Jesus and played an active role in his death (Acts 4.27). Roman justice (and the justice of local elites in the Greek East) has its limits. Luke's narrative recognizes, and for the most part remains sympathetic with, Roman power exercised in proper fashion. His audience probably included Roman citizens, as Esler notes.[2] For that reason religion and politics intertwine readily in Acts. Luke portrays an unstoppable, non-subversive religion. Those who disrupt society are the Jewish leadership who have misappropriated Jewish tradition or magistrates or the hoi polloi, who for economic gain, or political expediency, or misguided religious allegiance, circumvent the norms and laws of the empire and of God. Luke reaffirms that Christians from the beginning have been innocent bystanders. Persecutors in Acts consistently go out of the bounds of normal society and proper law.

Luke appears to address Christians and possibly non-Christians who participate and benefit in some fashion from the 'web of power' binding the Roman empire. Such persons could identify with characters like Cornelius the centurion, Lydia the maker of purple dyes, Levi the tax collector, and those wealthy enough to own homes (Jason of Thessalonica; Mnason of Cyprus; Simon the tanner), the type of persons in Graeco-Roman society who sought power and a sense of control.

Yet Luke does not write an *apologia pro imperio*: that is, he does not paint a picture of the Roman empire that plays down Roman culpability in the persecution of Jesus and the early church.[3] Roman leadership, with a few exceptions, has its warts. Pilate declares Jesus innocent three times but nevertheless allows an outside group, the Jewish leaders, to dictate the death sentence. Felix seeks bribes. Festus can only call Paul mad. Magistrates of the Roman colony Philippi beat Paul, a Roman citizen (16.12-39). Such portraits do not make representatives of the Roman power structure look very attractive. Further, even though the Lukan writer has no problem acknowledging legitimate Roman power as practised by Roman leaders such as Sergius

---

1. Kümmel, *Introduction to the New Testament*, p. 163.

2. Esler, *Community and Gospel*, p. 212.

3. Wengst, *Pax Romana*, pp. 89-105; Walaskay, *'And so we came to Rome'*: *The political Perspective of St Luke*, pp. 64-67.

Paulus, the tribune, or Cornelius the Centurion or, on a regional and local level, by the Asiarchs (19.31) and the town clerk (γραμματεύς) of Ephesus (19.35), such power always works within the context of the Christian God's purposes. The power of Roman and local elite groups remains an interim operation from the writer's perspective. Those who join the Christian movement, including apparently members of the Roman apparatus who carry out the wishes of the Roman empire, participate in an ancient and much larger order, the present and future Kingdom of God.

Luke presents a universally significant, morally upright movement with ancient roots that has spread across the οἰκουμένη, a movement that promises its adherents future power as well as present stability. The ultimate power broker within this expanded web of power remains for Luke the Christian ancestral God.[1]

Josephus: The Writer and his World

The Jewish War of Josephus, a first-century aristocrat from Judaea, reflects a man whose world has undergone a radical, if not traumatic, change. Josephus even asks the readers' indulgence as they read his history of momentous events: 'I cannot conceal my private sentiments, nor refuse to give my personal sympathies scope to bewail my country's misfortunes' (*War* 1.9). Josephus, more urgently than either Luke or Chariton, must respond to Roman power. The Jewish Wars were still fresh in Greek, Roman, and Jewish minds. Indeed, Josephus's own benefactors, the Flavians, continued to make political capital of the wars, as is evident from the Judaea Capta coin series and the building of Titus's arch by Domitian in Rome.[2] Josephus had to legitimate the relation of the Jewish people within the Graeco-Roman world, especially in response to what he saw as scurrilous attacks and false histories written by Greek historians (*Ant.* 1.5; *War* 1.7-8).

More to the point, Josephus had to address for himself and the Jewish people how one made sense of the disastrous defeat, which included the destruction of the Jerusalem Temple, a central symbol

---

1. Cf. Esler, *Community and Gospel*, pp. 215-16.
2. For bibliography see C. Vermeule, *Jewish Relations with the Art of Ancient Greece and Rome: 'Judaea Capta Sed non Devicta'* (Art of Antiquity 4.2; Boston: Department of Classical Art, Museum of Fine Arts, 1981).

for many Jews (and especially Josephus). In particular, what role did Rome play in the scenario? How should Jews have responded to Roman power and presence? Josephus's answer to those questions shows some remarkable similarities to Luke, although substantive differences exist as well. Josephus, like Luke, addresses the Jewish relation to Roman power by placing it within the context of Jewish (and, as T. Rajak has shown, Greek) tradition.[1] Josephus stresses the antiquity (and thus the legitimacy) of the Jewish movement, its presence across the οἰκουμένη, and the fact that in many political and historical events impacting on the Jewish nation, the Jewish God stands behind the scenes (including the Roman victory). Like Luke, he also contrasts agents of Rome who govern appropriately (and therefore on behalf of the Jewish deity) with those who govern inappropriately (and therefore against the norms set forth by their own government). In short, both Josephus and Luke reinterpret the Roman web of power drawing on their Jewish tradition and religious symbol system.

Human Agents, Divine Implications
Menachem Stern has persuasively argued that Josephus, in *The Jewish War*, does not dwell on the benefits of the *Pax Romana*.[2] Benefits achieved by the Romans derived largely from Roman virtue and not from Tyche. Josephus, he suggests, portrays Rome's world dominance as the outcome of divine will. The Jewish rebels did not receive help from God because he was on the side of the Roman Empire; Josephus, Stern argues, perceives God moving from nation to nation, 'giving the scepter of empire to each in turn; now He has bestowed it upon Italy'.[3] Feldman argues that Josephus's silence about the benefits of Roman rule in *The Jewish War* was due to his fear that others might label him an assimilationist.[4] Yet Josephus does not simply accept the yoke of Roman rule. Roman power is viewed through the lenses of belief in a powerful and prestigious Jewish God who works through history.

---

1. T. Rajak, *Josephus: The Historian and his Society* (Philadelphia: Fortress Press, 1984), p. 79.
2. Menahem Stern, 'Josephus and the Roman Empire', in L.H. Feldman and G. Hata (eds.), *Josephus, Judaism, and Christianity* (Detroit: Wayne State University Press, 1987), p. 76.
3. Stern, 'Josephus and the Roman Empire', p. 77.
4. L.H. Feldman, 'Introduction', in Feldman and Hata (eds.), *Josephus, Judaism, and Christianity*, p. 25.

Agrippa's famous speech makes it clear that the Jewish movement had spread across the οἰκουμένη. This, of course, reflects a real 'situation', as many have pointed out.[1] Agrippa's point emphasizes the potential destruction facing all Jews if the revolt against Rome takes place (*War* 2.399). His statements also indicate to the reader the extent (and by implication the importance) of the Jewish presence. This becomes a leitmotif in Josephus's *Antiquities*. In short, God works through history, benefitting those who follow the Jewish laws and setting up 'irretrievable disasters' for those who transgress them (*Ant.* 1.14). Josephus goes to great lengths to stress the antiquity of the Jewish movement, its spread across the οἰκουμένη, its recognition as a legitimate movement by Roman officials, and the power of the Jewish God. All this means nothing, however, if the adherents stray from God's purposes. 'Neither its antiquity, nor its ample wealth, nor its people spread over the whole habitable world, nor yet the great glory of its religious rites, could aught avail to avert ruin' (*War* 6.442).

Even the Romans are subject to God's law. Numerous examples show God at the center of Roman victories, primarily due to the wanton disregard of God's wishes by Jewish defenders. Cestius almost wins the city of Jerusalem early on in the campaign, but God 'turned away even from His sanctuary and ordained that the day should not see the end of the war' (*War* 2.539). Titus bolsters his men's courage by arguing that the Jewish God must be angry at the Jerusalem defenders and that 'to betray a divine Ally would be beneath our dignity' (*War* 6.39-41). Indeed, Josephus claims that 'God it is then, God Himself, who with the Romans is bringing the fire to purge His temple and exterminating a city so laden with pollutions' (*War* 6.110). Indeed any attempt by the brigands to hide from the Romans is futile, as they were not destined to escape either God or the Romans (*War* 6.371). When Titus surveys the massive walls of the temple, he exclaims 'God indeed has been with us in the war. God it was who brought down the Jews from these strongholds; for what power have human hands or engines against these towers?' (*War* 6.411).[2] T. Rajak

---

1.   See discussion by L.H. Kant, 'Jewish Inscriptions in Greek and Latin', *ANRW* II.20.2 (1987), pp. 671-713.

2.   Cf. Rajak, *Josephus: The Historian and his Society*, p. 100, who notes that in Josephus Roman generals often mention the role of God in history.

EDWARDS *Surviving the Web of Roman Power* 191

rightly argues that Josephus had to make religious sense of the
destruction of the temple. His presentation concerns 'God's purpose
for the world and his arrangements for the destiny of nations, centered on a scheme of sin and punishment'.[1] Thus, Josephus stresses
στάσις, civil strife, as a major sin against God and the cause of the
destruction.[2] D. Ladouceur adds that in 'granting Rome and her agents power,
God also assigned responsibilities. Those who discharge their responsibilities, like Titus, prosper; those who do not, like Catullus, are
punished, in this case by the time-honored method of an incurable
bowel disease.'[3] Ladouceur overstates the case when he argues that
Josephus did not distinguish between 'rendering unto Caesar what was
Caesar's and rendering unto God what was God's'.[4] Rather, Josephus
has defined Roman power within a new rubric, the power of the
Jewish God. Again, a writer from the Greek East stresses for his
reading audience the ancient roots and universal scope of his movement and the group's powerful deity as a major player in significant
historical events. As Josephus grapples with the import and trauma of
the Jewish War, he has effectively reformulated the rubric under
which one answers why the Romans won. In one sense, Josephus
ironically turns the tables. The Romans did not so much win the war
as the Jews, by disobeying God, lost it. Roman power operates, from
Josephus's perspective, under the aegis of the Jewish God.

Chariton: The Writer and his World

Chariton's novel, *Chaereas and Callirhoe*, represents at first glance an
odd addition to this discussion. Unlike Luke and Josephus, the author
depicts events far removed from his own world. Few disagree that
even though the author uses many devices from the field of historiography, he does not write history, nor does he even mention the
Romans.[5] Nevertheless, his potential readers included those who know
Roman presence and power only too well. The text provides images

1. Rajak, *Josephus: The Historian and his Society*, pp. 78-79.
2. Rajak, *Josephus: The Historian and his Society*, pp. 92-98.
3. D.J. Ladouceur, 'Josephus and Masada', in Feldman and Hata (eds.),
Josephus, Judaism, and Christianity, p. 110.
4. Ladouceur, 'Josephus and Masada', p. 111.
5. Although he does mention Italy (1.1.2; 1.12.8; 3.3.8).

from the perspective of elites in the Greek East as to proper behavior between members in society and between those who are ruled, their rulers, and the divine realm.

Human Agents, Divine Implications

Chariton's narrative in style and structure appears as a history or biography of the daughter of Hermocrates,[1] the naval commander who, according to Chariton, became the leading political figure and war hero in Syracuse after the defeat of the Athenians in the Peloponnesian War (1.1.1, 3).[2] Not surprisingly, the setting of Chariton's romance, the period following the Peloponnesian War, belongs to the classical period of literary and political fame for the Greeks. As E.L. Bowie has shown, Greeks during the imperial period often portray this 'classical' period in heroic terms as a means to interpret their present diminished situation amid the grandeur of their past.[3]

Chariton structures a work replete with power relationships between the divine and human realm, relations familiar to a Greek audience. The narrative begins with a description that compares Callirhoe, the heroine, to the goddess Aphrodite, and ends with her praying at the base of a cult statue of Aphrodite in Syracuse.[4] Throughout the narrative, Callirhoe acts out on the human plane mythic and social

---

1. A recent fragment of the *Metiochus and Parthenope* romance indicates the importance of historiography for the early romances. See H. Maehler, 'Der Metiochus-Parthenope-Roman', *Zeitschrift für Papyrologie und Epigraphik* 23 (1976), pp. 1-20. See also T. Hägg, *The Novel in Antiquity*, (Berkeley and Los Angeles: University of California Press, 1983), pp. 16-17; and B.E. Perry, who remarks 'What Thucydides did for the Peloponnesian War, that Chariton has done for the daughter of Hermocrates!', *The Ancient Romances: A Literary-Historical Account of Their Origins* (Berkeley: University of California Press, 1967), p. 137.

2. This places Callirhoe in the upper strata of Syracusan society. Little is known about the real daughter of Hermocrates. See discussion by Perry, *The Ancient Romances*, p. 353 n. 25; K. Plepelits, *Chariton von Aphrodisias: Kallirhoe* (Stuttgart, 1976).

3. E.L. Bowie, 'Greeks and Their Past in the Second Sophistic', in M.I. Finley (ed.), *Studies in Ancient Society* (Past and Present Series; Boston: Routledge & Kegan Paul, 1974), pp. 166-209.

4. 1.1.1-2; 8.8.15-16. Accurately observed by E.H. Haight, *Essays on the Greek Romances* (Port Washington, NY: Kennikat Press, 1943), p. 32; T. Hägg, *Narrative Techniques in Ancient Romances: Studies of Chariton, Xenophon, Ephesius and Achilles Tatius* (Stockholm: Almqvist & Wiksell, 1971), p. 216.

roles of Aphrodite, roles that include Aphrodite's power to unite cities and nations,[1] her appearance as goddess of love,[2] and her close affiliation with the sea.[3] Callirhoe is cultured (7.6.5), even-tempered (1.2.6), and well bred.[4] Chariton describes Callirhoe as an absolutely amazing young woman,[5] the ἄγαλμα[6] of all Sicily (1.1.1) whose

1. At Aphrodisias this aspect is evident in a series of coin issues that feature the cult statue of Aphrodite of Aphrodisias with those of other cities under the label ὁμονοία; Ephesus (*BMC Caria* 18, no. 161, p. 53, plate 44), Antiochia (*BMC Caria* 18, no. 162, p. 53), Hierapolis (*BMC Phrygia* 25, no. 166, p. 257) and Neapolis (D.J. MacDonald, 'Greek and Roman Coins from Aphrodisias', British Archaeological Reports Supplementary Series 9 [1976], p. 31). The coins also indicate Aphrodisias's close association with the Roman emperors, especially Augustus (MacDonald, 'Greek and Roman Coins', p. 30).

2. Readily available in literary sources such as Homer, which Chariton clearly uses in his work; for Chariton's citations see Warren Blake, 'Index Analyticus', in *Chariton Aphrodisiensis: De Chaerea et Callirhoe Amatoriarum Narrationum* (Oxford: Clarendon Press, 1938), pp. 129-42.

3. At Aphrodisias of Caria, a third century CE *aedicula* of Aphrodite features Aphrodite drying her hair on a half shell held by two tritons; see K. Erim, 'Recent Archaeological Research in Turkey', *Anatolian Studies* 32 (1982), p. 13. Iris Love has shown that nearby Cnidos had an active cult to Aphrodite Euploia, see *AJA* 82 (1978), pp. 324-25. L.R. Farnell provides additional references to this aspect of Aphrodite in *The Cults of the Greek States* (Oxford: Clarendon Press, 1897), II, pp. 636-38.

4. See J. Helms, *Character Portrayal in the Romance of Chariton* (The Hague: Mouton, 1966), pp. 45-66.

5. θαυμαστόν τι χρῆμα παρθένου.

6. Kenneth Scott translates ἄγαλμα as 'cult image' (in 'Ruler Cult and Related Problems in the Greek Romances', *Classical Philology* 33 [1938], p. 384), perhaps too extreme but more plausible than Warren Blake's 'admiration' (*Chariton's Chaereas and Callirhoe* [Ann Arbor: University of Michigan Press, 1939]), Georges Molinié's 'trésor' (*Chariton: Le roman de Chairéas et Callirhoé* [Paris: Budé, 1979]), or K. Plepelits's 'Entzücken' (*Kallirhoe*). Scholars generally consider ἄγαλμα as an object placed in the temple and designed for worship; for references see A. Nock, 'Synnaos Theos', *Essays on Religion and the Ancient World* (ed. Z. Stewart, Cambridge, MA: Harvard mUniversity Press, 1972), I, p. 204 n. 5. Price, however (*Rituals and Power*, p. 178), notes that translating ἄγαλμα as 'cult statue' assumes a cult association that does not always occur. Some private citizens did not receive public cult status during the imperial period even though they had images (ἀγάλματα) placed in sacred locations, one even at Aphrodisias (*Monumenta Asiae Minoris Antiqua*, 8 [ed. W. Calder and J. Cormack; Manchester: Manchester University Press, 1962], pp. 76-77, no. 412). This does not diminish the fact that

beauty compares to that of Aphrodite Parthenos.[1] Callirhoe's human appearance embodies the κάλλος of the goddess Aphrodite (1.1.2).[2] Indeed, Callirhoe's presence and appearance recall Aphrodite's power, but do not replace it.

In the ancient romances, comparisons of the human protagonist (both hero and heroine) with a deity occur with great frequency.[3] Such an attitude reflects a common feature in Graeco-Roman society, especially with regard to political figures in Asia Minor. Such identification with a god or goddess supported the maintenance of the political and social *status quo*. During the Imperial period it was common for women in major political families (most notably those of the emperors) to be associated with deities such as Aphrodite. Caligula's mother, Agrippina, and later his sister Drusilla, for example, were both called the New Aphrodite.[4] At Assos in Turkey a bath was dedicated to Julia Aphrodite (Livia).[5] Such associations had overt political and social as well as religious overtones.

the divine καλλός of Callirhoe shines throughout the narrative. See also the discussion of the term by W. Burker, *Greek Religion* (trans. J. Raffa; Cambridge, MA: Harvard University Press, 1985), pp. 65, 91, 94, 187.

1. Parthenos is an unusual epithet for Aphrodite (although see *Bulletin de Correspondance Hellénique* XXXII [1908], p. 500). Marcel LaPlace plausibly suggests an allusion to Athena Parthenos in 'Les légendes troyennes dans le "roman" de Chariton Chairéas et Callirhoé', *REG* 93 (January–June, 1980), pp. 124-25. For discussions on the role of cult statues in antiquity see Nock, 'Synnaos Theos', *Essays*, I, pp. 202-51; Price, *Rituals and Power*, pp. 170-206.

2. Cf. R. Petri, *Über den Roman des Chariton* (Beitrage zur Klassischen Philologie; Meisenheim an Glan: Verlag Anton Hain, 1963), pp. 11-12; and Helms, *Character Portrayal in the Romance of Chariton*, pp. 42-45, who note the close relationship between Callirhoe and the goddess Aphrodite but who downplay its importance for the narrative. Peter Walsh (*The Roman Novel* [Cambridge: Cambridge University Press, 1970], pp. 55 n. 2; 200) cites the similar role played by Psyche in Apuleius's *Metamorphoses*.

3. E.g. Xenophon's *Ephesiaca*, 1.2.6-8; 1.12.1; 2.2.4; Heliodorus, *Aethiopica* 1.2; 1.7; 2.23; 2.39; 3.4; 10.9.

4. D. Magie, *Roman Rule in Asia Minor* (Princeton, NJ: Princeton University Press, 1950), I, p. 512.

5. C.C. Vermeule III, *Roman Imperial Art in Greece and Asia Minor* (Cambridge, MA: Harvard University Press, 1968), p. 457. See also Nock, 'Synnaos Theos I', *Essays*, I, pp. 226-27; J. Aymard, 'Venus et les imperatrices sous les derniers Antonina', *Mélanges d'archéologie et d'histoire* 51 (1934), pp. 178-96.

Callirhoe's appearance in public forums mixes civic and religious dimensions. As the human vehicle for Aphrodite, Callirhoe's κάλλος overwhelms crowds and undoes the fortitude of political leaders. When kidnapped by pirates, Callirhoe is carried from Syracuse to the country estate of Dionysius, a Greek aristocrat, in Miletus. Her sudden entrance astounds (καταπλήσσειν) all who see her, and the slaves and servants believe that they have seen a goddess, since word (λόγος) had it that Aphrodite appeared (ἐπιφαίνειν) in the countryside (1.14.1). Callirhoe's religious and corporate significance appear in her connection to Sicily and Syracuse.[1] Chariton's comparison of Callirhoe's beauty (κάλλος) with that of Aphrodite Parthenos (1.1.2) may allude to Athena Parthenos, the premier deity for the political and religious life of Athens.[2] Chariton, however, indicates that in certain respects Aphrodite surpasses Athena. The narrator makes this point in a scene set at Miletus, in which the crowds see Callirhoe with her newborn son as she prepares to pray before Aphrodite's cult statue.

> she took the child in her arms, and thus presented a most charming sight, the like of which no painter has ever portrayed, nor sculptor fashioned, nor poet described to the present day; for no one of them has created an Artemis or an Athena holding a child in her arms (3.8.6).

Aphrodite's power, equal on the political plane with that of Athena and Artemis, surpasses theirs in her ability to bear a child, most notably one who serves as the founder of the Roman Empire. Allusions to the significance of Callirhoe's child for Syracuse further Callirhoe's corporate significance in the narrative.

Callirhoe's child may draw on the powerful myth of the child that Aphrodite gave to the world, Aeneas, founder of Rome and ancestor to the Julio-Claudian emperors. When Callirhoe finds she is pregnant, she agrees to marry Dionysius to preserve the image of Chaereas. This is one of the few events that looks beyond the world of the narrative itself.[3] The son, Chariton states, will come in triumph to Syracuse from Ionia when he grows up, surpassing in glory even his grandfather Hermocrates (3.2.13; 8.7.11-12). The child is compared

1. J. Bompaire, 'Le décor sicilien dans le roman grec et dans la littérature comtemporaire (II siècle)', *REG* 90 (1977), pp. 55-68.
2. M. LaPlace, 'Les légendes troyennes dans le "roman" de Chariton', pp. 124-25.
3. Hägg, *Narrative Technique in Ancient Greek Romances*, p. 309.

to Zethos and Amphion (founders of Thebes) and Cyrus (founder of the Persian empire [6.8.7; 2.9.4-5]).

Scholars have puzzled over the unusual inclusion of a son in a romance narrative. Further, it seemed odd that after the reunion of Chaereas and Callirhoe, they left their son in the care of a local aristocrat in the Greek East, Dionysius. Perry suggests that it could only reflect the pressure of popular or historical tradition that forced the author to include it.[1] However, no evidence exists that the real daughter of Hermocrates (mentioned in Diodorus Siculus [13.112] and Plutarch [*Dionysios* 3]) had a child. Marcel LaPlace persuasively argues that the child, like Cyrus, Zethos, and Emphion before him, is also a founder; one who upon his return will surpass the glories of his father and grandfather. Suggestive but difficult to prove is LaPlace's argument that the child alludes to Aeneas, the son of Aphrodite and Anchises, the founder of the Roman empire. To be sure, Chariton may write a symbolic history of the birth of the son of Chaereas and Callirhoe, which shows two Syracusans who after a period of discord, wars, adventures, and the whim of Fate, looking forward to a new time when their son will inaugurate an age of gold. And a reader in Asia Minor may associate the unnamed son of Callirhoe, who comes from the east to inaugurate a new day, with Aeneas, who anticipates the Julian *gens*.[2] Certainly the city of Aphrodisias promoted the connection between Aeneas, Aphrodite, and the Julio-Claudian line.[3] More importantly, the child who unites East and West is Greek (cf. 8.1.15), stressing the future power and prestige of the Greeks.

Chariton ends his work showing Chaereas as a general united with Callirhoe, the reflection of Aphrodite. When Chaereas and Callirhoe advance before the soldiers of Chaereas, Chariton reports that the two combined (ὁμοῦ) 'the sweetest fruits of war and of peace, the triumph and the wedding' (8.1.12). In addition, Chariton implies that marriage and family suggest stability and continuity in society, something Aphrodite could provide. A recurring theme in the ancient Greek romances is the emphasis on lawful marriage. Even in her second

---

1. Perry, *The Ancient Romances*, p. 138.
2. LaPlace, 'Les légendes troyennes dans le "roman" de Chariton', pp. 124-25.
3. K.T. Erim, *Aphrodisias: City of Venus Aphrodite* (New York: Facts on File, 1986), pp. 111, 118.

marriage, Callirhoe remains faithful to the memory of Chaereas. Chariton is at pains to make clear the importance of this element. Marriage was an important part of the maintenance of the society, a factor assumed throughout the narrative. The marriage of Chaereas and Callirhoe represents part of the very fabric of society itself. Disruption of the marriage disrupts society.

The major stops in Callirhoe's journeys across the landscape of the eastern Mediterranean world seldom occur without the appearance of a temple of Aphrodite or worshippers of the godess. The narrative opens with Callirhoe proceeding to the temple of Aphrodite in Syracuse during a public festival of the goddess.[1] Later, when Callirhoe is carried to the estate of the Milesian aristocrat Dionysius, the shrine of Aphrodite becomes a significant center of activity in the narrative. The cult is venerated by aristocrats (Dionysius holds the goddess in special honor [2.2.5]) as well as countryfolk who recognize the importance and viability of the cult. Even Callirhoe's trip to Babylon stresses Aphrodite's power. Stateira, the queen of Babylon herself, holds the goddess in special honor (5.9.1). Artaxerxes, the Persian king, recognizes the power of the goddess and offers sacrifices so that she might intervene on his behalf (6.2.4). The narrative displays Aphrodite's power and presence among all social classes, but most especially the elite throughout the ancient Mediterranean world.

The power of Aphrodite successively affects most major political figures whom Callirhoe meets. The first figure to encounter her power is Chaereas, who has many of the qualities and attributes of the other leaders in the narrative: these include high political connections, heroic appearance, and παιδεία. He is the son of Ariston, the second leading figure of Syracuse. Polycharmus, his friend and companion, describes him as 'once at the very top in Sicily, in reputation, wealth, and handsome appearance' (4.3.1). Chaereas combines heroic features with popular Stoic virtues such as self-control, proper observance of the law, an aristocratic education, and an emphasis on reason.[2] Indeed,

1.   For this essay, it matters little whether a temple to Aphrodite existed or whether such a festival actually occurred at Syracuse. Readers in the Greek East would understand the implications of the festival. See G. Schmeling, *Chariton* (TWAS, 295; New York: Twayne Publishers, 1974), p. 83.

2.   For a brief discussion of the use of popular Stoic thought in the ancient romances, see K. Berger, 'Hellenistische Gattungen im Neuen Testament', *ANRW* II.25.2 (1984): especially pp. 1264-68, 1278-81. Chaereas appears in a bad light

Images of Empire

Chaereas represents the free and educated Greek whose training and bearing stand in marked contrast to the barbarian.[1] Aphrodite, through her agent Eros, causes Chaereas and Callirhoe to meet during the festival of Aphrodite.[2] Divine beauty (κάλλος) meets nobility (εὐγενεία). They fall in love (πάθος ἐρωτικός) (1.1.6) and display characteristics closely linked with death. Chaereas is described as mortally wounded as a hero in battle (1.1.7), suffering from disease (νόσος), withered in appearance, and close to death because of the suffering of his noble soul (διὰ πάθος ψυχῆς εὐφυοῦς [1.1.10]).[3] This power of Aphrodite to overcome the reason and control of a heroic and political figure is repeated as she debilitates the ψυχή of Dionysius, the most powerful man in Miletus, Mithridates, the governor of Caria, and even Artaxerxes, the King of Persia himself.

Chariton wrote during the golden age of Aphrodisias, a city whose fortune prospered under the aegis of Rome. Kenan Erim notes that during the early centuries of this era, Aphrodisias 'reached great fame and prosperity both as a religious site and as a center of art and culture'.[4] A *Sebasteion* found at Aphrodisias indicates how important the cult of Aphrodite was for the city's political and religious identity. According to Erim, the *Sebasteion* proclaims 'the close affiliation of

when he betrays these qualities of proper conduct. The best example occurs when his lack of self-control and unfounded jealousy cause the apparent death of Callirhoe (1.4.12).

   1.   The stress of the free status of the Greek in relation to barbarians during this period is discussed by E. Gruen, *The Hellenistic World and the Coming of Rome*, I, pp. 132-57. The popularity of this motif in the Greek world is exhibited in a fragment of a relief found at Athens by T. Leslie Shear, Jr. Shear notes that the barbarians were portrayed in standard fashion, rugged features, anguished in defeat but still proud with a look of anger: 'his is the portrait of the noble savage whose merciful treatment at his captor's hand serves to ennoble still more the emperor [Trajan] himself'. 'The Athenian Agora: Excavations of 1972', *Hesperia* 42 (1973), p. 404.
   2.   5.1.1 indicates that Aphrodite managed (πολιτεύειν) the marriage.
   3.   Love as a malady represents a popular topos that cuts across genres. See the brief summary of a paper given by Carlos Miralles entitled 'Eros as *nosos* in the Greek novel', in *Proceedings for the Ancient Novel*, p. 20.
   4.   S.v. 'Aphrodisias', in R. Stillwell (ed.), *The Princeton Encyclopedia of Classical Sites*, (Princeton, NJ: Princeton University Press, 1979 [1976]), p. 68. See also Erim, *Aphrodisias: City of Venus Aphrodite*; 'The School of Aphrodisias', *Archaeology* 20 (1967), p. 18.

the city's goddess with the Julio-Claudian house, as well as with Rome. There can be no doubt that the cult of Aphrodite at Aphrodisias was intimately connected with the development of the Imperial cult'.[1] Aphrodite was a central symbol for the political and economic well-being of the city. As with most western Greek cities, Aphrodisias had to define itself in relation to the rising Roman star. For Aphrodisias, group identity and group success—at least among the ruling class[2]—centered on Aphrodite. She was central in treaties (both with Rome and surrounding cities), in new buildings that were dedicated to her,[3] in her maintenance of the social and political fabric of Aphrodisias,[4] and in her role as a goddess whose reputation and power were universal.

Chariton's work, *Chaereas and Callirhoe*, reflects the civic and religious pride that the city of Aphrodisias felt for its cult of Aphrodite. In his fictive history, he depicts Aphrodite's power extending across political and social boundaries, alludes to the promise of a New Age, and stresses the necessary combination of a peaceful and stable society: victory in war and lawful marriage. Chaereas's search for Callirhoe does not merely represent a human quest for meaning in a world grown large, nor is it simply pleasurable reading. Rather, Chariton

1. K. Erim, 'Recent Archaeological Research in Turkey' *Anatolian Studies* 33 (1983), p. 234; cf. R. Smith, 'The Imperial Reliefs from the Sebasteion at Aphrodisias', *JRS* 77 (1987), pp. 88-138; K. Erim, *Aphrodisias: City of Venus Aphrodite*, pp. 106-23; J. Reynolds, 'Further Information on Imperial Cult at Aphrodisias', *Studii Clasice* 24 (1986), pp. 109-17.

2. Price rightly observes that the wealthy and powerful in Greek cities were not the only beneficiaries. Indeed a form of welfare was established in which the whole town participated in games, festivals, and religious observances generally paid for by the wealthy in the city. See *Rituals and Power*, pp. 101-32; cf. R. MacMullen, *Paganism in the Roman Empire* (New Haven: Yale University Press, 1981), especially pp. 18-42.

3. For example, a dedication found on the architrave blocks of the first portico of the Sebesteion read 'To Aphrodite, the deified Augusti, Tiberius Claudius Caesar and the People', K. Erim as quoted by M. Mellink, 'Archaeology in Asia Minor', *AJA* 85 (1981), p. 472; for other examples see J. Reynolds, *Aphrodisias and Rome* (Journal of Roman Studies Monographs, 1; London: Society for the Promotion of Roman Studies, 1982).

4. A. Laumonier (*Les cultes indigènes en carie* [ed. E. de Boccard; Paris: Bibliothéque des Ecoles Françaises D'Athénes et de Rome, 1958], p. 499) also draws attention to Aphrodite as the patroness of the city.

participates in Aphrodisian society's attempt to define itself amid the Roman 'web of power'. Callirhoe, Aphrodite's representative, highlights the power of Aphrodite across the landscape of the οἰκουμένη. Chariton's narrative affirms and confirms the power and significance of Aphrodite over the machinations of fate and social upheaval (represented by pirates, wayward politicians, disruption of proper marriage, separation from family, friends, country, and spouse). In addition, Chariton makes clear the power of Aphrodite before the political order: even the mightiest are susceptible to her power. The latter of course is of particular importance for a Greek city that understands the power of Rome through the lens of Greek tradition and pride.

To whom might Chariton's text appeal? On the one hand it would appeal to Aphrodisians, who looked with pride at their cult of Aphrodite as the one that created and sustained their present prosperity; even the emperors acknowledge, they would argue, the power and significance of Aphrodite. In short, the elites on the periphery of Roman power gained local prestige and civic power by their association with Rome and their promotion of Aphrodite as the deity whose power encompasses even the Roman empire. On the other hand, Chariton's work would also appeal to those outside of Aphrodisias proper who acknowledge the universal power of Aphrodite, especially soldiers and merchants. Each group was well disposed toward a deity, such as Chariton's Aphrodite, who controls cosmic forces and political rulers, had a universal presence throughout the οἰκουμένη, and provided a means with which persons could participate within the 'web of power' of the Roman world with a modicum of power.

Conclusion

Local ruling elites and their immediate subordinates in the Greek East incorporated Roman power within their own frameworks of meaning. Three writers, Chariton of Aphrodisias, Josephus, and the author of Luke–Acts, all provincial writers from the Greek East, use religion to construct a power base that explicitly or implicitly redefines for their audience the 'web of power' existing between Rome and members of the Greek East. Despite diverse backgrounds and concerns unique to their groups, Luke, Josephus, and Chariton acknowledge and affirm the practice and observance of legitimate law and customs.

Nevertheless, each author places political figures and historical events under the aegis and guidance of a deity with whom the writer and the groups that they represent have close ties. Josephus, the Jewish historian, acknowledges Roman power, but presents to his audience a Jewish God who stands behind Roman success and Roman power in the Jewish Wars (and more to the point, the Jewish defeat). The writer of Acts places for his audience the hand of the Christian God in the political decisions and the historical events that take place as the movement expands to the 'ends of the earth'. Chariton, a bit more circumspect than the others, nevertheless shows his readership that political power functions in co-operation with the power of Aphrodite, a point that his city, Aphrodisias in Caria, promotes through its statuary, epigraphy, and buildings.

The writers recognize and to an extent appreciate outside political powers; each writer, however, extols the virtues of his deity in light of those powers. The authors' works indicate how some members of local elites and their affiliates in the Greek East sought to make sense of their groups, their tradition, and their gods amid the ever present web of Roman power.

LUKE–ACTS: A MIXED POPULATION SEEKS A HOME IN THE ROMAN EMPIRE

Vernon K. Robbins

The thesis underlying this paper is that Luke–Acts is a narrative map grounded in an ideology that supported Christians who were building alliances with local leaders throughout the eastern Roman empire. In language that merges social and historical geography, a discipline Robert David Sack calls 'human geography', Luke and Acts present a strategy of territoriality.[1] If we apply insights from the work of Sack and others to Luke–Acts, we see that this two-volume narrative presupposes that the eastern Roman empire is an appropriate workplace for the emissaries of God who are carrying out the project inaugurated by Jesus of Nazareth. The image in the two-volume narrative of the officials who hold the highest positions in the Roman Empire ranges from matter-of-fact to positive. At one end of the spectrum, the narrator describes decrees and edicts of emperors without negative or positive comment, simply accepting them as the framework in which certain events occur. At the other end, Paul, a Pharisee with Roman citizenship who converts to Christianity, successfully claims the right to appear before the emperor as a means to avoid legal judgments in the East. This means that Christianity functions in the domain of the Roman Empire, and this empire is good because it works symbiotically with Christianity. Roman law, correctly applied, grants Christians the right to pursue the project started by Jesus, and the goals of Christianity, rightly understood, work congruently with the goals of the Roman empire.

From the point of view of the proposal in this paper, previous

---

1. The language of 'territoriality' comes from R.D. Sack, *Human Territoriality: Its Theory and History* (Cambridge Studies in Historical Geography, 7; Cambridge: Cambridge University Press, 1986). I am grateful to my colleague Thomas S. Burns for guiding me to this and other books as I was pursuing the thesis in this paper.

approaches have not dealt satisfactorily with the aggressive strategy of the action and speech in Luke and Acts. Beginning with the work of C.A. Heumann in 1721, interpreters regularly have viewed Luke–Acts as a defense of Christianity, an *apologia pro ecclesia*, for Roman officials who consider it a threat to the empire.[1] In 1983, Paul Walaskay proposed that this approach should be 'turned upside down': Luke–Acts is a narrative designed to persuade members of the church that 'the positive benefits of the empire far outweigh the occasional intrusiveness of an errant emperor'. In other words, the author presents 'an *apologia pro imperio* to his church'.[2] Philip Esler, weighing the two alternatives, argues that both sides are better served by viewing the two-volume work as a text of legitimation for Christianity.[3]

These approaches have not addressed the overt strategy of territoriality contained in the two volumes. The approach to Luke–Acts as an *apologia pro ecclesia* mistakes the two-volume work as a defensive narrative in an environment filled with legal and political obstacles rather than as an aggressive narrative in an environment perceived to be teeming with opportunities. Viewing Luke–Acts as an *apologia pro imperio* suggests that the subject matter concerns the Roman Empire rather than Christianity. Viewing Luke–Acts as a narrative of legitimation for Christianity is better, but this approach still does not give adequate attention to the aggressive strategies in the portrayal of Roman, Jewish, and Christian leaders in the narrative. Viewing the two books as a narrative map of territoriality for the development of Christian alliances throughout the eastern Roman Empire provides a better hermeneutical tool than viewing it as an *apologia pro ecclesia*, an *apologia pro imperio*, or a narrative of legitimation.

1. The Implied Author's Mimetic Desire toward Rome

The thesis of this paper builds on the beginning point of René Girard's theory about human culture—namely that mimetic desire is at work

---

1. P.W. Walaskay, *'And so we came to Rome': The Political Perspective of St Luke* (Cambridge: Cambridge University Press, 1983), pp. 5-14.

2. Walaskay, *'And so we came to Rome'*, p. 64. The statement about turning the interpretation 'upside down' is a pun on Acts 17.6.

3. P.F. Esler, *Community and Gospel in Luke–Acts: The Social and Political Motivations of Lucan Theology* (SNTSMS, 57; Cambridge: Cambridge University Press, 1987), pp. 16-21, 93-130.

wherever humans engage in joint activities with one another, form groups with boundaries, and establish rituals and traditions involving speech and action. Mimetic desire functions where there is a subject, an object, and a rival. The proposal is that humans desire certain objects and not others in a particular social context, because one or more other persons in the setting desire those same objects. In other words, a subject knows what to desire by seeing what a rival desires. This means that:

> *the subject desires the object because the rival desires it.* In desiring an object the rival alerts the subject to the desirability of the object. The rival, then, serves as a model for the subject, not only in regard to such secondary matters as style and opinions but also, and more essentially, in regard to desires.[1]

One of the primary focuses of attention in the narrative is on power.[2] The power in the environment, according to the narrative, resides in the military and legal structure of the Roman empire. Thus, the narrative treats the upper levels of this power structure with special deference. The narrator evokes Theophilus, a Roman official whom he addresses as 'most excellent',[3] as a model in the opening verses of Luke and Acts. Very soon, in addition, the narrator refers to Roman emperors who reign over events in Syro-Palestine (Lk. 2.1; 3.1). By the end of the narrative, Paul, as a result of an appeal to Caesar

---

1. R. Girard, *Violence and the Sacred* (trans. P. Gregory; Baltimore and London: Johns Hopkins University Press, 1977; French original, 1972), p. 145. The proposal in this paper is that human territoriality rather than sacrifice is the major framework in which mimetic desire functions in Luke and Acts. This is based on my view that it is not necessary for Girard's insight about mimetic desire to focus on sacrifice, as Girard himself appears to think, in order for it to be instructive for analysis of texts.

2. Another is on wealth: see H. Moxnes, *The Economy of the Kingdom: Social Conflict and Economic Relations in Luke's Gospel* (Philadelphia: Fortress Press, 1988). The implications of the focus on power for the possession and use of wealth must be left for another paper; but see R.L. Rohrbaugh, 'The Pre-Industrial City in Luke–Acts: Urban Social Relations'; and H. Moxnes, 'Patron–Client Relations and the New Community in Luke–Acts', in J.H. Neyrey (ed.), *The Social World of Luke–Acts: Models for Interpretation* (Peabody, MA: Hendrickson Publishers, 1991), pp. 125-49, 241-68.

3. κράτιστε: Lk. 1.3. The apostle Paul and Claudius Lysias use the same title of honor to address governors under Roman appointment in Acts 23.26; 24.3; 26.25.

(Acts 28.31), is in Rome preaching and teaching openly and unhindered. This means that the implied author, whose mimetic desire is focused on Rome's successful establishment of power from Rome to Jerusalem, yokes Christianity to Rome's success by inverting the process: that is, by showing the expansion of Christianity from Jerusalem to Rome.

The aggressiveness of the two-volume narrative appears in criticisms that the narrator feels free to make of members of local families or groups, even if they have been invested with power by Rome. These criticisms may concern a misuse of power based on wealth. In the Gospel of Luke, Pharisees are a major object of attack for their love of money.[1] In Acts, however, the narrator casts a negative light only on Pharisees who want to maintain exclusive religious practices after becoming members of the believing Christian community.[2] Pharisees who remain leaders of the Jews, in contrast, speak out courageously in attempts to be fair with Christian leaders.[3] People invested with power by Rome come under attack as the narrator criticizes Herod Agrippa I as an evil-doer and implicates Felix as a fraudulent governor.[4] Thus, within the framework in which the implied author inverts the Roman success story by displaying Christianity walking and sailing its way from Jerusalem to Rome, the desire of the implied author for power emerges in the aggressiveness the narrative displays with local leaders who have power, whether or not that power has been invested by the Roman military and legal system.

2. *The Power Structure of the Roman Empire and of Christianity*

For Luke–Acts the highest power in the Roman empire is the emperor, and the place of his power is Rome. No emperor appears in a scene in Luke or Acts; at every stage the emperor remains out of sight, wielding his power and protection at a distance. The first reference to an emperor is in Lk. 2.1, where the narrator places the birth

---

1. Moxnes, *The Economy of the Kingdom*, pp. 139-53.
2. Acts 15.5. See D.B. Gowler, *Host, Guest, Enemy and Friend: Portraits of Pharisees in Luke and Acts* (New York: Peter Lang Publishing, 1991), pp. 5-6, 281-82, 300-302, 309, 313.
3. Acts 5.34-39; 23.9.
4. Herod Agrippa I: Acts 12.22-23. Felix: Acts 24.26-27.

of Jesus in the environment of Roman history. From the narrator's point of view, the will of the emperor Caesar Augustus to have a census taken in Syro-Palestine caused Jesus, whose hometown was Nazareth in Galilee, to be born in Bethlehem, the city of King David.[1] According to Acts 5.37, Judas the Galilean resisted the census and attracted a following, but, as Gamaliel puts it, 'he perished and all who followed him were scattered'. In other words, 'unnamed powers' destroyed him, and his followers disappeared. The reader is not told exactly who caused Judas's destruction, but a general scenario can be inferred from the references to Quirinius, the governor of Syria. The emperor's power extends from Rome to Syria, Galilee, and Judaea in such a manner that the emperor never need be present to assure that his will be obeyed.

One chapter later (Lk. 3.1-2), the narrator exhibits the finely-tuned administrative presence of Roman power throughout the eastern region of the Mediterranean where Christianity began. During the fifteenth year (28–29) of the reign of the emperor Tiberius Caesar,[2] Pontius Pilate was governor of Judea, Herod Antipas was tetrarch of Galilee, his brother Philip was tetrarch of Ituraea and Trachonitis, Lysanias was tetrarch of Abilene, and Annas and his son-in-law Caiaphas held the high-priesthood in Jerusalem.[3] The power of the distant emperor extends throughout the region in a detailed jurisdictional manner: men with Roman names having charge of Judea and Abilene; members of the Herodian family who have had a close alliance with Rome since 40 BCE being in charge of Galilee, Ituraea

---

1. A special feature of the reference to Augustus Caesar in Lk. 2.1 is the use of a transliteration of the Latin term *augustus*, rather than a translation of the term into Greek as Σεβαστός: J.A. Fitzmyer, *The Gospel According to Luke I–IX* (New York: Doubleday, 1981), p. 399. In contrast, the translated form Σεβαστός stands on the lips of the prefect Porcius Festus when he addresses King Herod Agrippa II in Acts 25.21, 25 (speaking of a later emperor); and after this the narrator uses the term in reference to the Augustan Cohort, to which the centurion Julius belongs (Acts 27.1). Luke 2.1 is the narrator's initial reference to an emperor as he addresses Theophilus. In other words, at the beginning of the account the narrator adopts a social location in the presence of a Roman official Theophilus, and as the narrator proceeds he places the events in the framework of the jurisdictional power of the Roman emperor over Syro-Palestine.

2. Tiberius reigned 14–37.

3. For details about the rulers and regions, see Fitzmyer, *The Gospel According to Luke I–IX*, pp. 455-58.

and Trachonitis; and Annas, who was appointed high priest by the Roman governor P. Sulpicius Quirinius in 6, and his son-in-law Caiaphas in control of the high priesthood in Jerusalem.[1] Thus, as the emperor Augustus Caesar reigned at a distance over the birth of Jesus, so Tiberius Caesar reigned at a distance over the activity of John. In Acts, Claudius (41–54) is referred to as the emperor during the great famine over the inhabited world (Acts 11.28) and as the emperor whose edict expelled Priscilla and Aquila from Rome (Acts 18.2). Neither positive nor negative statements by the narrator accompany the presentation of this information. Gaius Caligula (37–41) is never mentioned by name, nor is Nero (54–68), since as the narrative progresses toward its conclusion the emperor is referred to simply as Caesar or Sebastos.[2] There is no portrayal of a trial of Paul before the emperor; in fact only Paul and his work receive attention once the centurion Julius successfully escorts him to Rome. The power that brought Paul to Rome is the God of Israel. Thus a major issue is the relation of the power of the emperor to the power of the God of Israel.

From the perspective of Luke and Acts, the power structure of Christianity works symbiotically with the power structure of Rome. The manner in which these power structures work together is exhibited by two stories about centurions that are strategically located at Lk. 7.1-10 and Acts 10. In order to understand these stories, we need to know that a centurion, who is in charge of 100 soldiers in the Roman army, receives a mustering-out pay after serving his duty that is sufficient for him to be a member of the order of decurions.[3] The status of decurion entitled a person to be a member of the council in a city in the eastern Roman empire. In Rome itself, office-bearers were drawn almost entirely from two orders, the senatorial and the equestrian. To qualify for senatorial rank, it was necessary to hold 'property worth 250,000 times the day's wage of a labourer', with somewhat less than half that amount for equestrian rank.[4] Decurions

---

1. Fitzmyer, *The Gospel According to Luke I–IX*, p. 458.
2. Καῖσαρ: Acts 17.7; 25.8, 10, 11, 12, 21; 26.32; 27.24; 28.19. Σεβαστός: Acts 25.21, 25; 27.1.
3. Esler, *Community and Gospel in Luke–Acts* , p. 184.
4. R. MacMullen, *Roman Social Relations, 50 BC to AD 284* (New Haven: Yale University Press, 1974), p. 89.

were expected to possess about one-tenth of the amount required for a senator.[1] In the eastern region of the empire, decurions rather than senators or equestrians were the council members, and magistrates were almost always elected from the decurions.[2] Thus the decurions were the local aristocracy in the eastern empire, and a centurion was either already a decurion or well on his way to becoming one.

In Lk. 7.1-10, a centurion sends people to Jesus to ask him to come and heal his slave. From the information above, we know that the request comes from a person who has recognizable status in the power structure of the eastern Roman empire. From Luke's perspective, people in Capernaum know that Jesus can heal because of his previous activity there (Lk. 4.23, 31-41). When the centurion sends people to Jesus, he is replicating the process by which the emperor transmits his will throughout the region. Just as the emperor remains out of sight at a distance, so the centurion remains out of sight. First the centurion sends 'elders of the Jews' to Jesus, requesting that he come and heal his slave. Neither the Jews nor Jesus hesitate: the Jews come to Jesus and Jesus goes with them. In other words, both the Jews and Jesus readily submit to the will of the Roman centurion. In the process, the Jews indicate to Jesus that the centurion is worthy to receive a benefit, since he loves the Jewish nation and he built the Jews their synagogue in Capernaum. After sending elders of the Jews to Jesus, the centurion sends 'friends'. They address Jesus as 'κύριε' and they tell Jesus that the centurion does not consider himself worthy to have Jesus come under his roof and he would not be so presumptuous as to come to Jesus directly. Then the message of the centurion contains a command: 'Say the word, and let my servant be healed', and the command is succeeded by a rationale:

'For　(a) I am a man set under authority,
　　　(b) with soldiers under me:
　　　　　(1) I say to one, "Go", and he goes;
　　　　　(2) and to another, "Come", and he comes;
　　　　　(3) and to my slave, "Do this", and he does it.'

When Jesus hears this, he marvels and says that not even in Israel has

---

1. MacMullen, *Roman Social Relations*, p. 90; J. Gagé, *Les classes sociales dans l'empire romain* (Paris: Payot, 1964), p. 163.
2. P. Garnsey, *Social Status and Legal Privilege in the Roman Empire* (Oxford: Oxford University Press, 1970), pp. 251-56.

he found such faith. When the people who had been sent return to the house, they find the slave well.

With this story, the narrator presents an interchange that his addressee Theophilus can understand at once. The manner in which power is channeled from the emperor to the people in Syro-Palestine provides the framework in which the centurion communicates with Jesus. But, the reader is led to understand, God's power can be transmitted in a similar manner. The transmission of commands and power from Jesus through a centurion's friends and Jewish elders replicates the centurion's transmission of power to get certain results. Here then, in the territory over which the Roman emperor reigns, a Roman official has needs that the founder of the Christian movement meets. In social terms, the centurion, who is a broker between the emperor and the Jewish people, successfully negotiates with Jesus, who is a broker between God and people who live in the world over which the emperor reigns (Lk. 2.1).[1] At this point in the story, then, a broker within the jurisdictional power structure of the Roman empire becomes the recipient of a broker within the power structure of the God of Israel. Given the dynamics of reciprocity in first-century Mediterranean society, the centurion will now stand in obligation to Jesus much as the Jews stood in obligation to the centurion at the beginning of the episode.[2] In this story, then, God's power begins to flow through Jesus from Syro-Palestine to Rome. From a narrative point of view, God's power reaches Rome only through a sequence of events that present situations virtually as complex as those which brought the power of the emperor from Rome to Syro-Palestine.

With the healing of the slave of the Roman centurion in Luke 7, the centurion initiates the action, and his action provides the social and political framework for the power of God to flow into the domain of Roman leaders and through Roman leaders to Rome itself. According to the narrator's view, the centurion acts in a manner that reveals his acceptance of the power structures with which Jesus is involved. From the centurion's point of view, and therefore from the narrator's point of view, the structures of power in the Roman empire work

1. B.J. Malina, 'Patron and Client: The Analogy Behind the Synoptic Theology', *Foundations & Facets Forum* 4.1 (1988), pp. 2-32.
2. B.J. Malina, *The New Testament World: Insights from Cultural Anthropology* (Atlanta: John Knox Press, 1981), pp. 80-82.

symbiotically with the structures of power in Christianity.

While the story of the healing of the centurion's slave sets the stage for a symbiotic relation between the activity of Jesus and the Roman power structure, the story about Cornelius in Acts 10 exhibits more fully the nature of the symbiotic relation of power structures in the Roman empire and Christianity. In Acts 10.3-4, the God of Israel sends an angel to Cornelius, a devout centurion of the Italian Cohort, telling him that his prayers and alms have ascended as a memorial to God, and that he should send men to Peter to bring him to Cornelius. In this instance, then, the God of Israel takes the initiative by sending commands to a centurion, who in turn sends soldiers with the commands to Peter. The next day, the heavens open before Peter, a great sheet descends, and a voice from heaven dialogues with Peter about killing and eating all kinds of animals, birds, and reptiles (10.9-16). During the time of Peter's perplexity over the meaning of the vision, the emissaries of Cornelius come to fetch him. The language of the men is reminiscent of the language of the elders of the Jews in Lk. 7.4-5 as they refer to Cornelius as 'an upright and God-fearing man, well spoken of by the whole Jewish nation' (Acts 10.22). When Peter goes to Cornelius's house, Cornelius falls down at Peter's feet and worships him, but Peter lifts him up, telling him that he too is a man (Acts 10.25-26).

In other words, Peter's location in the Christian power structure is similar to the centurion's location in the Roman power structure. For this reason, they can communicate face to face without obeisance or other extraordinary formalities.[1] After they exchange information, Peter preaches to Cornelius and his household, the holy spirit falls on all of them, and Peter commands that they be baptized in the name of Jesus Christ (10.28-48). In this instance, then, God initiates the action, and he initiates it both with the centurion and with Peter. According to the narrator's view, both the centurion and Peter respond in a manner that reveals their acceptance of the power structures with which they are involved. In the final analysis, then, God is the one who oversees the symbiotic relationship of the structures of power in the Roman empire and in Christianity.

---

1. See V.K. Robbins, 'The Social Location of the Implied Author of Luke–Acts', in Neyrey (ed.), *The Social World of Luke–Acts*, pp. 305-32, for explication of Paul's relation to Jewish and Roman leaders in Acts.

3. *The Eastern Roman Empire as the Workplace of Christianity*

People who have power exercise that power in particular places. Thus we need to turn to a discussion of the places, that is, the geographical spaces, where power 'takes place' in Luke and Acts.[1] Robert Sack's study, referred to earlier, investigates human territoriality in various kinds of spaces, and this focus will help us in our analysis. For Sack, territoriality in humans is

> a spatial strategy to affect, influence, or control resources and people, by controlling area; and as a strategy, territoriality can be turned on and off. . . Territoriality in humans is socially and geographically rooted. Its use depends on who is influencing and controlling whom and on the geographical contexts of place, space, and time.[2]

Humans can use territoriality for various reasons, and with humans it presumes a form of control over an area or space that humans conceptualize and communicate. Therefore, territoriality can be constituted by all kinds of variations and flexiblity. The workplace is an excellent example. During work hours, workers are limited to certain kinds of spaces. A modern secretary is supposed to be at a work station at a particular time of day and remain in its vicinity until the day ends. At the end of the work day, the work space may invert into a space that is off limits to the worker. If the secretary returns and spends time in that space 'without a well-communicated reason', the time in that space may be considered to be in violation of territorial presuppositions surrounding that workplace. Territoriality is created by humans in highly complex ways for reasons that they conceptualize and communicate, and the workplace exhibits the flexibility and complexity of it especially well.[3]

As indicated above, the thesis of this paper is that Luke–Acts presents the eastern Roman empire as a fully appropriate workplace for Christianity. The presentation is territorial, because other people also are at work in the area. With this approach, we also become aware of another aspect of Luke–Acts. The narrative approaches Christianity

---

1. For the use of this language with religious narrative, see J.Z. Smith, *To Take Place: Toward Theory in Ritual* (Chicago: University of Chicago Press, 1987).
2. Sack, *Human Territoriality*, pp. 1-2.
3. Sack, *Human Territoriality*, pp. 169-215.

from the perspective of work: God's work and people's work. This is undoubtedly one of the reasons why some interpreters find it difficult to compare Acts with erotic novels that appear to be designed for entertainment. Since there are many aspects in common among Acts and erotic novels,[1] perhaps the difference in tone is primarily the result of the perception of Christian activity as a kind of work.

In order to approach this appropriately, we need some insight into the perception of work in Mediterranean antiquity. Without going into detail, two aspects of work in antiquity are important for this paper. First, people in modern life often identify work with some specialized activity they perform during specific hours of certain days in a week, month, and year. Also, a person in the modern world often distinguishes sharply between 'religious' work and 'secular' work. Anyone who lives or has lived in a traditional rural setting, or perhaps an ethnic environment, may know how kinds of work flow into one another. In the not too distant past, it was common for farmers in the USA to do everything from keeping their own accounts to repairing their cars, tractors, and machinery, as well as butchering livestock and vaccinating their own pigs and cattle. Thus, work was embedded in a person's life in such a manner that a wide range of work activities could flow into one another during any part of any day or night. In fact, often what we call recreation was very close to work, as a person used a horse or a tractor to pull a sled, or rode a horse to drive the cattle from the pasture to the barn for milking. Also, religious work was often embedded in one's regular work. Helping a neighbor with work when he was sick could be a religious and secular activity at the same time. Thus, work in antiquity, as well as in traditional settings even now, may be a 'way of life' that covers a wide range of activities and intermingles what we would call religious and secular work.

It was the case, however, that people distinguished in antiquity between simple 'working with one's hands' (or with 'one's body', as the Greeks put it) and working as an independent artisan (βάναυσος or τεχνίτης), since the artisan is further removed from his employer and subject only to a limited servitude. In fact, by the exercise of his skill and wise use of slaves or laborers, an independent artisan may

---

1. R. Pervo, *Profit with Delight: The Literary Genre of the Acts of the Apostles* (Philadelphia: Fortress Press, 1987): compare the article by Douglas Edwards in this volume.

even gain enough property to enter the wealthy class.[1] The proposal in this paper is that Luke and Acts present Christian activity as a kind of work embedded in a way of life in the eastern Roman empire. Jesus inaugurates the program which God gives to him, and various kinds of people carry out the work at various levels. By the time the reader gets to the last half of Acts, Christian activity occurs at the level of the independent artisan or above.

The proposal that Luke–Acts views Christian activity as a kind of work in the eastern Roman empire is supported, first of all, by Loveday Alexander's exceptional study of the preface to Luke. Her investigation shows that the author has penned the preface to Luke with technical or professional prose characteristic of school texts of various kinds, including perhaps manuals for artisans.[2] As we pursue this insight throughout Luke and Acts, we discover that the leaders within early Christianity function at the level of independent artisans or above, and, as a result, there is close association with people of artisan status throughout the eastern Mediterranean. The territorial nature of the work becomes clear as local artisans complain about the effect of the work of Christians in their locale.

Secondly, one of the effects of Luke–Acts is to change the center of the holy work of a devout person from work in the temple to a kind of cottage industry that operates in the domain of synagogues and households. God begins this transformation by sending an angel to Zechariah, a priest, while he is at work in the temple (Lk. 1.5-23). The end result of this visit is the birth of John the Baptist, who functions outside the temple among all kinds of people. When asked for specific advice, John functions like an overseer of distribution of clothing and food, of fair collection of taxes, and of restrained action by soldiers (Lk. 3.10-14). In other words, the Baptist's holy work is like that of a public officer who directs the use and exchange of goods, money and power among the people. By God's command a priest's son has taken God's holy work out of the temple into the region around the Jordan where he works as God's officer among the people.

1. G.E.M. de Ste. Croix, *The Class Struggle in the Ancient Greek World from the Archaic Age to the Arab Conquests* (London: Gerald Duckworth, 1981), pp. 181-85.

2. L.C.A. Alexander, 'Luke's Preface in the Context of Greek Preface-Writing', *Novum Testamentum* 28 (1986), pp. 48-74.

As Jesus begins his work, he goes to a synagogue on the sabbath. In the synagogue he announces the program of work God has given to him: (a) preaching good news to the poor; (b) releasing captives; (c) recovering of sight to the blind; (d) setting at liberty those who are oppressed; and (e) proclaiming the acceptable year of the Lord (Lk. 4.18-19). This program of work is significantly different from the type of work people regularly perform in the temple, and the response of the people shows that it also is not the kind of work people regularly performed in the synagogue.[1] The basic model for this kind of work for God comes from the traveling prophets, Elijah and Elisha, who did things like helping a poor widow and cleansing a leper (Lk. 4.25-27). Jesus' announcement of the work causes great furor in the synagogue and leads to an attempt to kill him (4.29-30). Therefore, Jesus goes away from the synagogue in Nazareth to the synagogue in Capernaum, and there on the sabbath he begins his work (4.31-37). After teaching with authority and casting an unclean spirit out of a man in the synagogue, Jesus goes to Simon's house, and there he heals Simon's mother-in-law of a fever (4.38-39). Then people who are sick with various diseases are brought to Jesus at the house, and Jesus heals them (4.40-41). When Jesus leaves the house the next day and goes to a lonely place, people come to him there, then he continues on to synagogues throughout Judaea (4.42-44). Jesus' activity, then, defines the central workplaces of Christianity to be in synagogues and houses.

The sequence of events at the beginning of Luke establishes the workplaces for Christ's followers throughout Luke and Acts. The beginning of Acts replicates the movement from Jerusalem temple to synagogues and houses. As the mission moves into the Diaspora, the work begins in synagogues, but when rejection becomes too great there, the work is taken into houses and people come to the houses to get the services of Christ's followers. Even when Christ's followers go outside a house or synagogue, however, they encounter people with whom they carry on the work. According to God's will and plan, then, synagogues are the appropriate workplaces for Christ's

---

1. For the social significance of transference of God's work from the temple to the household, see J.H. Elliot, 'Temple versus Household in Luke–Acts: A Contrast in Social Institutions', in Neyrey (ed.), *The Social World of Luke–Acts*, pp. 211-40.

followers to begin their work in a region, especially on a sabbath. In addition to synagogues are houses, where the followers receive hospitality and offer their services.[1] This house will become a place where visitors come for their services. But even when Christ's followers go outside the house, they see people to whom they offer their services, and many people will come to them for this purpose when they hear they are in the vicinity.

The work pattern for Christ and his followers is a strategy of territoriality that begins through God's empowering of leaders in the Jerusalem temple and continues in synagogues, houses, and public areas from Galilee and Judaea to Rome. Christ's followers, in the narrator's view, have no choice but to do this work, just as people in the Roman military and legal system have no choice but to do their work. Commands come down from the top which they obey.

4. *Levels of Workers in the Workplace*

Just as God and the emperor create tasks for people by their commands, so Jesus, Christian leaders, and people in the Roman military and legal system work through people who are their subordinates. To fulfill the tasks that have been given him by God, Jesus enlists a group of twelve and sends them out (Lk. 6.12-16; 9.1-6) and then appoints seventy(-two)[2] to go out as 'laborers into the harvest' (10.1-12). We should not miss the image of the laborers in the field. Luke 4–10 allows the images of the work of an itinerant prophet, the work of an overseer or landowner, and the work of a centurion to flow into one another. In fact, the narrator perceives the work roles of each to have much of the same status in Mediterranean society. The prophet, the overseer, and the centurion are set under authority, but in turn they have people under their authority.

When we come to Acts, Peter and John continue the basic work program of preaching and healing that Jesus introduced in Luke 4. But this work broadens in the context of the dramatic experiences of

---

1. For the basic pattern, see the sequence in Philippi: (a) on the sabbath day . . . to . . . a place of prayer (Acts 16.13); (b) when she [Lydia] was baptized with her household. . . ' . . . come to my house and stay' (Acts 16.15).

2. For the textual variation in the number, see J.A. Fitzmyer, *The Gospel According to Luke X–XXIV* (New York: Doubleday, 1985), pp. 845-46.

Peter and Paul. In Acts 9 Saul, who carries from the high priest to synagogues letters that give him the right to bring Christians bound to Jerusalem (9.1-2, 14), is made into a 'chosen vessel' (σκεῦος ἐκλογῆς) to carry Jesus' name before Gentiles, kings, and sons of Israel (9.15). Dramatically, then, a kind of work associated with the priesthood at Jerusalem is changed into work for which the metaphor is the distribution of a certain kind of goods (the name of Jesus), like oil, carried in a vessel. The work is to be carried out wherever there are Gentiles, kings, and sons of Israel. The initial power of Paul, then, comes from the Jerusalem Temple, but this power, which remains in the control of the high priest, is subverted by Jesus, who appears to Paul from heaven.

In Acts 10 (the chapter concerning the centurion Cornelius discussed above) Peter's experience with the sheet that comes down from heaven, and the conversion of Cornelius's household, transform the work of the devout from concern with clean and unclean food—that keeps a person away from Gentile households—to one which goes into that household and makes it a Christian space. Peter is lodging in the house of Simon the tanner at Joppa when Cornelius sends for him (10.32). Thus, Christian work occurs in spaces where independent artisans lodge, and when Peter goes to Cornelius's house the work is undertaken in places where military personnel ranking above the regular soldier dwell.

In Acts 13, when Paul and Barnabas go to Cyprus, they are summoned by the proconsul Sergius Paulus, who becomes a believer in the Christian way of life (13.7-12). With this event, then, Cyprus becomes a certified workplace for Christians with a member of the senatorial order sanctioning the place of work.[1] When the reader comes to Acts 16, the narrative begins to exhibit Christianity as an activity that challenges the moneymaking activities of various people and refers to the means by which Paul makes money. In 16.19, Paul destroys the moneymaking of owners of a slavegirl by casting out the spirit of divination within her. In 18.2-3, Aquila and Priscilla reside with Paul because they all share the same tent-making trade. In 19.19, people who practice magic arts burn books valued at 50,000 pieces of silver. And finally, in 19.23-41, the narrator presents a lengthy scene

---

1. As proconsul Sergius Paulus must have been a member of the senatorial order.

in Ephesus where the silversmiths bitterly complain that Christianity is ruining their business. This series of events reveals that, from the narrator's perspective, the activity of Christian leaders is an occupation that occurs in an arena that affects other people's work. When Christians work in the environments to which they have been sent, regularly there are objections similar to those of local populations toward people doing the work of Roman government.[1] These dynamics are a natural part of introducing new, important activities into new areas, and they often require negotiation between people whose work may be dislocated by someone else's work. But the genius of the Roman empire resided in its widespread achievement of 'compulsory co-operation'.[2]

When Paul is asked to defend his activities in the succeeding chapters, he emphasizes that he has no choice. He was engaged in very different activities before 'the God of our fathers' appointed him to his new work (Acts 22.14-15). He explains that he went to Jerusalem to bring his nation alms and offerings, which was part of his work (24.17). And Paul stresses that he was not disobedient to his heavenly vision (26.19). Just as responsible people in the Roman military and legal system obey the commands that come to them, so Paul is a responsible Christian who obeys the commands that come to him. The narrator supports Paul's claims by presenting a scene where Jesus stands before Paul giving him instructions (23.11), and Paul explains the necessity that has been laid upon him, with the implication that they understand such necessities (26.16-18).

Christians, then, have nothing against the law of Jews, against the temple, or against Caesar (Acts 25.8). They simply do the work they are commanded to do. Christians function much like people who receive commands from officials in positions of higher authority in the Roman military and legal system. Christians, like people who are part of the Roman system, are set under authority and often have people under them who help with the work.

1. R. MacMullen, *Enemies of the Roman Order: Treason, Unrest, and Alienation in the Empire* (Cambridge, MA: Harvard University Press, 1966), esp. pp. 163-241.
2. M. Mann, *The Sources of Social Power*. I. *A History of Power from the Beginning to AD 1760* (Cambridge: Cambridge University Press, 1986), pp. 262-98.

5. *Building Alliances among a Mixed Population*

In order for a strategy of territoriality to be successful, it must employ tactics that produce good results over a period of time. The practitioners of the Roman empire, by all accounts, had such tactics at their disposal. One of the tactics was to negotiate with the people both inside and outside the boundaries of the empire rather than to concentrate on 'boundary defense'.[1] When the Parthians under the rule of the Arsacids defeated the Roman army in a battle, the Roman response was to negotiate with the Parthians about rule over Armenia: Rome invested an Arsacid as king over Armenia, keeping Armenia under Roman jurisdiction and Parthia in conversation with Rome.[2]

Another tactic, which was a corollary of the absence of 'boundary defense', was to deploy legionary and auxiliary forces locally wherever they were needed. This tactic created a psychological image of 'presence everywhere'. People often did not resist the will of the Roman empire because they had a fear that they simply could not escape the power of Rome.[3]

Another tactic was the granting of citizenship to the populations of entire cities that had done something beneficial for the Roman empire. Citizenship brought privileges to the members of such cities, like grain rations during a famine and protection of various kinds when needed.[4]

The proposal in this paper is that Luke–Acts portrays Christians using tactics similar to those that brought success to Rome. First, instead of focusing on boundary defense, Christians continually negotiate with outsiders and insiders to pursue their goals. Whenever Peter or Paul are brought before Jewish or Roman authorities, they explain what they are doing and try to get an agreement that they should be allowed to do it. But more than this, the commands of God and the Lord Jesus require that they negotiate with people outside the boundaries. Peter has no choice but to go to Cornelius's house and work out his relationship with Gentiles in their own house (Acts 10).

1. E.N. Luttwak, *The Grand Strategy of the Roman Empire: From the First Century AD to the Third* (Baltimore: Johns Hopkins University Press, 1976), p. 19.

2. Luttwak, *The Grand Strategy of the Roman Empire*, p. 9.

3. Luttwak, *The Grand Strategy of the Roman Empire*, pp. 33-35, 13-18.

4. J.P.V.D. Balsdon, *Romans and Aliens* (Chapel Hill: University of North Carolina Press, 1979), pp. 82-96.

Then, after this happens, he has to negotiate with people inside the boundaries. Going up to Jerusalem, Peter tells how he was required by the Spirit to accept Cornelius and his household (11.1-18). Paul, in turn, uses a tactic similar to that used by Rome with Parthia when he is taken before the Jewish council in Acts 23. When Paul violates Jewish law by reviling the high priest after the high priest commanded people to strike him on the mouth (23.1-5), he diverts attention from his guilt by asserting that he did not know he was the high priest, by showing his knowledge of Torah, and by changing the subject to resurrection of the dead. With these tactics, Paul negotiates with Pharisees in such a manner that they turn against Sadducees and find no guilt in Paul. The key to this strategy, when it is compared to Roman strategies of negotiation, lies in Paul's offering Pharisees a way to exercise power over Sadducees. In other words, much as Rome helps Parthians establish dominance over Armenia, so Paul helps Pharisees establish dominance over Sadducees. The side benefits of the negotiations, of course, go respectively to Rome and to Paul.

Another tactic was the use of legions and auxiliary forces wherever they were needed to create the image of 'presence everywhere'. This approach begins in Luke when Jesus sends out not only the twelve (Lk. 9.1-6), but the seventy(-two) who go to 'every town and place' to which Jesus himself is about to travel (10.1-11). Then in Acts 8.5-25 the Hellenist deacon Philip goes to Samaria, and two members of the twelve, Peter and John, go out and certify what Philip has done. Then, wherever Peter and Paul go, they win auxiliaries who maintain a local presence for Christianity as the Christian legionary forces go on their way to another city or region.

Another tactic concerns the granting of citizenship. According to Acts Christians, like Romans, grant full citizenship to people who show their allegiance to Christian belief. They do not maintain the strictures of the Greeks, who require an identity associated with activity in the gymnasium, or those of the Jews, who require circumcision for males and exclusionary eating practices. People of any kind—Ethiopian, Parthian, Greek, Roman, slavewoman—can become full members of the believing community.[1] In other words, the

---

1. See a discussion of the mixed population in the Christian community in Robbins, 'The Social Location of the Implied Author of Luke–Acts', in Neyrey (ed.), *The Social World of Luke–Acts*, pp. 315-18.

Christian tactics of territoriality appear to be driven by Roman ideology for running the empire, rather than by Greek or Jewish ideology that focuses much more on defending boundaries, establishing physical dominance, and maintaining strict rules for citizenship rather than opening citizenship to people who show some form of allegiance. Finally, the narrator grounds the tactics of Christianity in the basic interests of God that are similar to the interests of the Roman empire. Both are interested in salvation and peace. The terms savior (σωτήρ) and salvation (σωτηρία) never occur in Mark or Matthew, but they are very significant in Luke and Acts.[1] Likewise, peace (εἰρήνη) is a major concept throughout both volumes.[2] The importance of these terms is indicated by the Priene inscription, which reads in part:

> Providence that orders all our lives has in her display of concern and generosity in our behalf adorned our lives with the highest good: Augustus, whom she has filled with *arete* for the benefit of humanity, and has in her beneficence granted us and those who will come after us [a Savior] who has made war to cease and who shall put everything [in peaceful] order; and whereas Caesar, [when he was manifest], transcended the expectations of [all who had anticipated the good news], not only by surpassing the benefits conferred by his predecessors but by leaving no expectation of surpassing him to those who would come after him, with the result that the birthday of our God signalled the beginning of Good News for the world because of him. . .[3]

The major interests of Augustus, which are salvation and peace, are the major interests of God, according to Luke and Acts. One passage in Luke and two in Acts will make this final point:

> And you, child, will be called the prophet of the Most High;
> for you will go before the Lord to prepare his ways,
> to give knowledge of *salvation* to his people in the forgiveness of their sins,
> through the tender mercy of our God,
> when the day shall dawn upon us from on high
> to give light to those who sit in the darkness and in the shadow of death,
> to guide our feet into the way of *peace* (Lk. 1.76-79).

---

1. Σωτήρ: Lk. 1.47; 2.11; Acts 5.31; 13.23. Σωτηρία: Lk. 1.69, 71, 77; 19.9; Acts 4.12; 7.25; 13.26, 47; 16.17; 27.34.
    2. Lk. 1.79; 2.14, 29; 7.50; 8.48; 10.5, 6; 11.21; 12.51; 14.32; 19.38, 42; 24.36. Acts 7.26; 9.31; 10.36; 12.20; 15.33; 16.36; 24.2.
    3. F.W. Danker, *Benefactor: Epigraphic Study of a Graeco-Roman and New Testament Semantic Field* (St Louis: Clayton Publishing House, 1982), p. 217.

So the church throughout all Judaea and Samaria had *peace* and was built up; and walking in the fear of the Lord and in the comfort of the Holy Spirit it multiplied (Acts 9.31).

Let it be known to you then that this *salvation* of God has been sent to the nations; they will listen (Acts 28.28).

God has given commands for people to work throughout the eastern Roman empire to bring salvation and peace. Followers of Christ carried the work first into the regions surrounding Judaea, bringing peace wherever the church was built up. They have continued to work, often under difficult circumstances, until this salvation has reached Rome, the very center of proclamation of peace to the world.

Conclusion

The proposal in this paper has come full circle. The suggestion is that Luke–Acts is a narrative map of territoriality for the eastern Roman empire. The narrative map presupposes a compatible, symbiotic relation between Christianity and Rome. The key to the strategy is the perception of synagogues, houses, and public places in the eastern empire as workplaces God has selected for Christians to work programmatically from Jerusalem to Rome. The people with tasks in these workplaces function at different levels. Beginning with Jesus, those whom God appoints function at the level of independent artisans or above. These people receive commands from God, and these people regularly give commands to people who work under them. As Christians do their work, they use tactics analogous to those of Roman leaders as they focus on negotiation rather than defense of boundaries, as they use legions and auxiliary forces to create an image of presence everywhere, and as they grant full citizenship to those who show allegiance to them. Mimetic desire within the implied author of Luke–Acts, therefore, focuses on power in the Roman empire. Just as the emperor guarantees that the Roman empire works programmatically toward its goals, so God makes sure that his will is communicated again and again through angels who transmit special messages, through the Lord Jesus who appears at crucial moments, through the Spirit who comes upon people as a sign of God's presence and approval, and through faithful Christian leaders who obediently persist in the tasks they are commanded by God to do.

OPPONENTS OF ROME: JEWS AND OTHERS

Martin Goodman

How exceptional was Jewish hostility to Roman rule? Did other provincials in the early empire feel similar hatred, or was there something about Jews, or Jewish social structures, or Judaism, that stimulated extraordinary antagonism to imperial power? I hope in this paper to suggest ways of approaching this rather basic but contentious question. I do not expect to answer it, but I shall be satisfied if readers are left with slightly more doubts when confronted with the confident views on the matter often expressed by historians in modern times. For such authors it is obvious that, since Judaism was a unique religion and Jewish rebelliousness was exceptional, the former must have caused the latter.[1] I am not convinced by the logic of this assertion, and I hope in the following pages to infect a wider audience with my uncertainty.

The question posed raises a larger issue of the methods a historian can use to discover what people thought in the past about the political system under which they lived. It seems to me that there is a limit to the insight to be achieved by simply collecting quotes from the extant literature, unless some evidence survives of the way such literature was read. Thus Christians who read Revelation as sacred scripture could still address apologies to the emperor to assert their loyalty to Rome, and Tacitus's sympathy for Calgacus did not prevent him treating the compulsive militarism of Agricola as the acme of virtuous

---

1. This argument is found, more or less explicitly, in reviews of my book (M. Goodman, *The Ruling Class of Judaea: The Origins of the Jewish revolt against Rome AD 66–70* [Cambridge: Cambridge University Press, 1987]), by B.D. Shaw, *JRS* 70 (1989), pp. 246-47; J. Geiger, *Journal of Roman Archaeology* 3 (1989), pp. 291-93; E. Bammel, *JTS* 40 (1989), pp. 213-17; and in the discussion of the same book by P.A. Brunt, *Roman Imperial Themes* (Oxford: Oxford University Press, 1990), pp. 517-31 (527-30).

behaviour for a senatorial Roman. It is not impossible that much of the vituperation against Rome in Christian or Rabbinic writings had more to do with the self-image of the writers than their attitude to the empire, and that anti-imperial invective should be treated as a rhetorical device rather than a statement of political attitudes. After all, recent authors and readers of tracts that attack the establishment have not infrequently been content to live within normal social and political conventions, and it is hazardous to gauge an acquaintance's political attitudes from the books on his or her shelves. It is even more difficult to make a valid judgment when the great majority of the book collection has by chance been destroyed and only a small proportion remains for inspection. How many texts attesting a particular attitude in antiquity must survive for that attitude to be considered normal?

From these remarks, it may be surmised that I can see little value in prolonged dispute over the extent to which Jews' behaviour in first-century Palestine was *conditioned* by the messianic or other anti-Roman notions to be found in a (limited) number of texts surviving from that period. The view that all evidence that could conceivably point towards such an attitude should be conflated to produce a picture of a general atmosphere of 'Zealotism', containing diverse strands, to which all or most rebellious actions by first-century Jews should be attributed, is perfectly coherent and possible,[1] but so, too, is the alternative view that no disparate evidence should be conflated in the absence of overwhelming reason, and that therefore the failure of Josephus in his detailed narrative of first-century Palestine to ascribe any clear-cut blame to the religious ideologues of whom he disapproved should be taken as evidence that such ideologues were not responsible for most of the unrest.[2] Prophecies from sacred scripture about Israel's eventual victory over the nations, or the contemporary oracle that a ruler would come forth from Judaea (Josephus, *War* 6.312-13), could provide an incentive for some to hate Rome, but other pious Jews could believe in the same texts and oracles without

---

1. M. Hengel, *The Zealots: Investigations into the Jewish freedom movement in the period from Herod I until 70 AD* (trans. D. Smith; Edinburgh: T. and T. Clark, 1989).
2. J. Neusner, W.S. Green and E.S. Frerichs (eds.), *Judaisms and their Messiahs at the turn of the Christian Era* (Cambridge: Cambridge University Press, 1987); R.A. Horsley, *Jesus and the Spiral of Violence: Popular Jewish Resistance in Roman Palestine* (San Francisco: Harper & Row, 1987), esp. pp. 77-78.

any such reaction. After all, two of the Jews best known to us from the first century CE, Josephus and Philo, were both ostentatiously pious and knowledgeable about their ancestral religion, but both were philo-Roman. Josephus accommodated the so-called 'messianic oracle' mentioned above by asserting that it referred to the emperor Vespasian, just as Isaiah had referred to the Persian King Cyrus as an anointed one chosen by God (Isa. 45.1). Other Jews might have disagreed, but we have no evidence that they would have thought Josephus wholly maverick, since we do not know what the standard view of the oracle was by the late first century. I have already referred to the dangers involved in trying to discover what was normal by counting attestations to any one idea.

If staring at texts can only have limited value, it seems to me that real opposition can only be asserted with any certainty when it appears to have provoked action rather than just words, whether such action was taken by the malcontents themselves or by the state in anticipation of their disaffection. If it can be shown that many subjects of Rome in the early empire, and not just Jews, either rebelled or wanted to rebel, or, more cautiously, may have wanted to rebel, it will become less plausible to assert that the unruliness of the Jews was exceptional.

To show the existence of such widespread disaffection will not prove easy. It is not reasonable to expect that either state or subject will have written much about so distasteful and dangerous a topic, nor that much that was written will have survived. Nonetheless, something can be said. The argument is best presented in two stages: first, the evidence that provincial revolts took place, and second, possible reasons why other regions whose inhabitants may have been no less disgruntled chose not to rebel.

The positive evidence will be considered first. Most of this has to be found in incidental remarks within the more general political narratives of Greek and Roman historians. Fortunately, and despite a general tendency to ignore both urban riots and rural violence, both of which were endemic in parts of the empire, such authors found it harder to pass over in silence those national revolts that required full-scale military action for suppression. Nonetheless, Roman writers rarely expatiated on such rebellions by peoples already regarded as conquered. Unless an emperor was directly involved, reconquest was often treated as a policing matter that brought little glory: thus, Augustus's propaganda was silent about operations in Spain after 26

BCE, either because the pacification of the province had been celebrated just before, or because Augustus was no longer involved in the fighting.[1]

Spotting a provincial revolt is thus not always easy. It is not always possible to tell whether an apparently national rebellion was in fact an action by a Roman aristocrat whose provincial origin was held against him by his enemies (as may have been the case with the uprising led by Vindex in 68 CE).[2] The boundaries may be unclear in the sources between a peasant protest at the extortion of taxes (when the main aim may simply have been pillage), a campaign of violent rampage by a group of brigands, and a full-scale war aimed at the recovery of liberty from Roman rule. An inscription referring to military action against provincials, or archaeological evidence of widespread urban destruction, or a regional programme of reconstruction, could refer to any or all of these phenomena. Provincial unrest might be not so much anti-Roman as fomented by an outside power, most obviously in the backing given to the false Neros by Parthia in the late first century, or, more often, by a deviant Roman official seeking power for himself through civil war.[3] Any combination of such factors may indeed have contributed to any one particular episode.

Nonetheless, despite such problems in analysing the evidence, good grounds remain to suppose that revolts against Rome by inhabitants of areas considered by the state as lying within the *imperium Romanum* were a frequent threat in the first century of the principate, and a continuing if rare problem thereafter. Revolts were mostly sudden and seem often to have taken the Romans by surprise. Those concerned were evidently regarded as basically conquered or tamed by the awe of Rome and no longer a threat, even in those areas where rebellion broke out soon after the initial conquest, as in Pannonia and

1. A. Brancati, 'Augusto e la guerra in Spagna', *Studi urbinati de storia* 26 (1963), pp. 87-151 (106-50).

2. Contrast P.A. Brunt, 'The revolt of Vindex and the fall of Nero', *Latomus* 18 (1959), pp. 531-59 (reprinted in Brunt, *Roman Imperial Themes*, pp. 9-32) to S.L. Dyson, 'Native revolt patterns in the Roman Empire', *ANRW* II.3 (1975), pp. 138-75 (158-61).

3. On the false Neros, see G.W. Bowersock, 'The mechanics of subversion in the Roman provinces', in A. Giovannini (ed.) *Opposition et résistances à l'empire d'Auguste à Trajan* (Entretiens sur l'antiquité classique, 33 [1986]; Geneva: Fondation Hardt, 1987), pp. 291-320 (309-11).

Dalmatia in 10 BCE, in Britain under Boudicca or in Germany under Arminius.[1]

In some regions revolts continued sporadically for years. In Africa the Gaetulians and their allies rebelled in 6 CE and a heterogeneous group joined the charismatic Tacfarinas in 24 CE. Mauretania rebelled under Aedemon, a freedman of the Numidian king Ptolemy, in the fortics CE and again under Vespasian and Domitian; under Domitian the Nasamones also rose up and defeated the governor of Numidia. It is hard to distinguish frontier disturbances in Africa under Antoninus Pius and M. Aurelius from the activities of bandits, but the rebellion against Pertinax in the late second century was a major military uprising.[2] In Gaul, revolt was not infrequent from the conquest by Caesar to the early Flavian period, apart from a short period of peace in the later years of Augustus; though it is debated whether the major rebellions of the first century CE, in 21 CE and 68 CE, genuinely possessed or were only ascribed a nationalistic character.[3] In the Balkans, massive revolts in 6–9 CE in Pannonia and Dalmatia were subdued with great effort but sufficient success for no more unrest to be recorded,[4] and in Spain the rebellions of 26, 19 and 16 BCE that followed Augustus's proud boast that the province was pacified were genuinely the last flickers of resistance.[5]

In other areas revolt was endemic. The German tribes east of the Rhine that freed themselves from Roman rule under Arminius in 9 CE were followed successfully by the Frisii in 28 CE; and the revolt of the Batavi under Civilis in 69 CE seems to have been defused eventually only by the grant of concessions. Even regions that had endured Roman rule in peace for decades or even centuries could erupt unexpectedly, as in the insurrection in Alexandria in 152–53 CE which cost the life of the prefect of Egypt.[6]

---

1. S.L. Dyson, 'Native revolts in the Roman Empire', *Historia* 20 (1971), pp. 239-74.
2. Dyson, 'Native revolt patterns', pp. 162-67.
3. S. Lewuillon, 'Histoire, société et lutte des classes en Gaule: une féodalité à la fin de la république et au début de l'empire', *ANRW* II.4 (1975), pp. 425-583 (486-535); Dyson, 'Native revolt patterns', pp. 152-61.
4. Dyson, 'Native revolts', pp. 250-54.
5. Dyson, 'Native revolt patterns', pp. 146-52.
6. Dyson, 'Native revolts', pp. 253-58, 264-67; N. Lewis, *Life in Egypt under Roman Rule* (Oxford: Oxford University Press, 1983), p. 205.

There is no good reason to think of all such revolts as lost causes. It seems likely that the greater tendency of frontier zones to rebel was due to a (correct) belief that Roman forces might be more willing to leave them free. In the East, neither Armenia nor Mesopotamia remained under Roman control for long, and the ability of tribes in Scotland to repel the legions may have given other northern Britons hope, as did the free state of Maroboduus, which the people of Dalmatia and Pannonia tried to emulate in the early first century.[1] Undoubtedly some revolts that occurred soon after conquest by Rome can best be seen as a final desperate attempt to reverse the political trend by those native leaders who were in the forefront of the changes coming over their society, and thus were in a particularly good position to appreciate the incipient danger that such change would prove irreversible. Many such flare-ups may have lacked calculation of the feasibility of success, constituting little more than demonstrations of hostility towards the existing order rather than attempts to replace it.[2] But other provincials were apparently sufficiently attuned to take advantage of periods of Roman weakness. During the civil war of 69 CE, rebellions were in progress in northeast Anatolia (Tacitus, *Hist.* 3.47), in Britain against Rome's puppet monarch Cartimandua (3.45), and in Germany among the Batavi (Tacitus, *Hist.* 4 *passim*; 5.14-26) as well as in Judaea. In all such cases, any expectation that Rome would leave such small pockets untouched if they were perceived as hostile to the empire was undoubtedly foolish, but a hope that the natives would be allowed to rule themselves in alliance with Rome was not at all unreasonable. After all, Rome was quite happy to control much of the area within her *imperium* in the first century C E by friendship treaties with local rulers rather than by direct rule (cf. Strabo. 6.4.2 [288]).[3]

It is not always possible to discover what caused such rebellions and, therefore, how much they differed from that in Judaea. Roman authors who referred to them undertook little analysis. The personal

1. For Maroboduus as a model, see Dyson, 'Native revolts', p. 252.
2. This is the main thesis of Dyson, 'Native revolt patterns'.
3. Some of these alliances are discussed in D. Braund, *Rome and the Friendly King: The Character of the Client Kingship* (New York: Croom and Helm, 1984). On the lack of distinction in Roman eyes between direct rule and rule through puppet vassals, see B. Isaac, *The Limits of Empire: The Roman Army in the East* (Oxford: Oxford University Press, 1990), p. 119.

grudges of revolt leaders were often blamed—the disgruntled Boudicca; the deserter Tacfarinas; the ambitious Classicus in Gaul in 68 CE; the Batavan auxiliary commander Civilis, frightened for his safety under Vitellius in the same year. It is hard to know whether the Roman tendency to name wars after the enemy commander (for example, the revolt in Pannonia and Dalmatia in 6 CE was known as the *bellum Batonianium* [*CIL* 5.3346] in memory of Bato) reflects the actual role of such men as instigators of unrest or only the Roman perceptions of them. It was taken for granted by Tacitus that foreign nations, like Roman senators, would share a love for *libertas* (Tacitus, *Agricola* 30-32).

But the immediate cause was usually perceived to be the imposition or extortion of taxation. The provincial census was said to have provoked an uprising in Pannonia in 10 BCE (Dio 54.36.2-3). The German revolt which destroyed Varus in 9 CE may have been caused by his decision to start taxing the region, which had been occupied since 9 BCE (Dio 56.18.4). Gallic revolts in 12 BCE and 21 CE were both sparked off by opposition to extortionate officials.[1] Bato in Dalmatia in 6 CE is said to have complained about the financial officers as wolves preying on the province (Dio 56.16.3).

However it would be rash to depend too heavily on the imperial power for any analysis of reasons for disaffection. It is strange that Roman governors so often failed to realize how discontent was growing if they regularly believed revolt for liberty to be natural and obvious, and if they therefore expected violent opposition to taxation. The freedman Licinius, blamed for extortion in Gaul, is alleged to have argued that bleeding the provincials would be a positive disincentive to rebellion (Dio 54.21.8). A better understanding of the motives of rebels can only be found by looking at the views of the provincials themselves, but, except in the case of the Jews, such a task is not easy.

We have no direct evidence what Thracians or Gauls thought about the empire, and the material that does survive to give an insight on provincial attitudes to Rome is highly partisan and unrepresentative. In Egypt, a mass of papyri gives occasional clues, but the Egyptian peasantry was much more closely monitored by Roman officials than were inhabitants of other parts of the empire and therefore less likely

---

1. Dyson, 'Native revolt patterns', pp. 155, 157.

to strike out for independence—the revolts of the mid-second century were exceptional. Preservation of papyrus copies of the martyrdom narratives of Alexandrian Greeks, even up country in Egypt, shows a dislike of Rome among Greeks in Egypt in general; in the Martyr Acts, Roman emperors from Augustus to Commodus or Caracalla are accused of tyranny and immorality in their refusal to give Greeks their due rights and privileges in the city; some emperors were even claimed as crypto-Jews to explain their injustice and avarice.[1] But although Alexandria was the site of communal battles against the Jews in the first century and of frequent demonstrations against the Roman prefect whose headquarters lay in the heart of the city, and although the city rashly supported the pretender Avidius Cassius in 175 CE and incurred the wrath of Caracalla in 215 by mocking him (Dio 78.22-23), Alexandrian Greeks never rebelled on their own account. Nor is the evidence from elsewhere in the eastern Mediterranean much more helpful. There does indeed survive a great mass of pagan Greek literature from the first two centuries CE, which reveals in its harking back to the classical era a certain ideological opposition to Rome, but the areas from which such authors came—Greece, the coastal cities of Asia Minor, the big cities of Syria—were, with rare exceptions, not among those that tried to rebel.[2]

When the evidence is so limited, it would be rash to assert categorically that none of the provincial unrest apart from that of the Jews was stimulated by religious beliefs and emotions. It is at any rate not to be doubted that anti-Roman sentiment *could* be expressed throughout the empire in religious terms. In more than one Alexandrian pagan martyr-act, the heroes are portrayed as appealing to Serapis against Rome.[3] Oracles who could foretell an emperor's glory could as easily predict disaster, although charges of *maiestas* might discourage wide publication of such prophecies, and temple authorities reserved anti-Roman miracles for the protection of their own rights, as when the statue of Zeus at Olympia laughed when Caligula tried to

---

1. H.A. Musurillo, *The Acts of the Pagan Martyrs: Acta Alexandrinorum* (Oxford: Clarendon Press, 1954); Lewis, *Life in Egypt*, pp. 196-207.
2. On the ideology of the so-called Second Sophistic, see E.L. Bowie, 'Greeks and their past in the Second Sophistic', *P&P* 46 (1970), pp. 3-41. On near-rebellion in Sardis, see Plutarch, *Praecepta gerendae reipublicae* 32 (*Mor.* 825 d).
3. Musurillo, *Acts*, pp. 4-5, 45.

transport it to Rome (Suetonius, *Cal.* 57.1). In Egypt, the Potter's Oracle and Lamb's Oracle, and the Asclepius apocalypse preserved in the Hermetic corpus, were all copied in the early imperial period, and their predictions of the victory of Egypt and her gods over foreigners may have comforted the oppressed.[1]

On the other hand, as has been often pointed out, those narrative accounts of revolt that survive suggest that religious emotion functioned not as a cause of war but only as comfort and encouragement once war was under way. A priest led the Egyptian revolt of 172–73 CE (Dio 72.4). Julius Civilis in 69 CE gathered his Batavan followers to feast in a sacred grove and signified a religious vow by neglecting to cut his hair (Tac. *Hist.* 4.61). The support of the prophetess Veleda for his cause was of such importance that her services may have been taken over by the Romans themselves in later years.[2] More sinister were the human sacrifices practised by Arminius in the Teutoburger Wald and the wild posturings of druids at Anglesey (in support probably of resistance to Rome in Wales, not by Boudicca and Iceni, who were too far distant). Druids were also active in Gaul, where their prophecy that the burning of the Capitol signified the demise of Rome encouraged Gauls to think of joining the Germans in revolt (Tac. *Hist.* 4.54); it is likely that the anti-Roman prophecy of the self-proclaimed god Mariccus in the same year was made in concert with them (Tac. *Hist.* 2.61), and the Romans seem to have believed, albeit probably wrongly, that druids were responsible for stimulating opposition to their hegemony in both Gaul and Britain.[3] The revolt of the Bessi in the Macedonian area in 11 BCE was whipped up by a priest of Dionysus who used divination to encourage unrest (Dio 54.34, 5-7). It is hard to see how the Jewish rebels' devotion to the Jerusalem Temple cult, and their hopes for divine intervention once the revolt had started, differed from any of this.

1. On such oracles, see H. Fuchs, *Die geistige Widerstand gegen Rom in der antiken Welt* (Berlin: de Gruyter, 1938); A. Momigliano, 'Some preliminary remarks on the "Religious Opposition" to the Roman empire', in A. Giovannini (ed.), *Opposition et résistances à l'empire d'Auguste à Trajan*, pp. 103-33.

2. On Veleda, see Dyson, 'Native revolts', pp. 265-67; Momigliano, 'Preliminary remarks', p. 109.

3. On druids, see Dyson, 'Native revolts', p. 260; 'Native revolt patterns', pp. 157-59.

The sceptical reader may retort at this stage that such stories of sporadic outbursts, in diverse areas of the Mediterranean world and Northern Europe over two centuries, pale into insignificance when compared to the concentrated fury of the three Jewish revolts between 66 and 135 CE. Such sceptics may indeed be right (though it is worth recalling in how many generations Jews did *not* rebel). But in the second part of my argument, I shall try to respond to this objection by offering a possible explanation why many disaffected regions, however disgruntled their inhabitants, may have chosen not to oppose Rome.

In those regions where no unrest is attested over long periods, any one of three explanations of such non-attestation can be assumed. Either trouble occurred but was not reported, or the provincials concerned were essentially happy with their lot, or they were unhappy but did not dare to revolt. According to the standard accounts of the Roman empire, the middle explanation, that of contentment, is usually attributed to those subjects of Rome in provinces such as Asia, where no Roman troops were to be found quartered in any concentration. In contrast, so it is generally assumed, regions like Britain that were accorded a large permanent legionary garrison were reckoned 'troublesome'. On such an analysis, the Jews of Judaea will not have been considered a major political threat in 6 CE, since the province was allocated little more than three thousand men at the most, all auxiliaries, but the stationing of one legion in Jerusalem after 70 CE and a second in Northern Palestine in the second century demonstrated increased Roman concern about this rebellious people.[1]

Now, it seems to me that the positive elements of this argument make quite good sense—increased military presence implied concern about the natives' loyalty—but I am less sure that lack of troops implied actual quiescence or even a belief among Roman officials that the provincials in that area were happy to be ruled by Rome. Much depends on how the early imperial army is believed to have functioned. This is not a question to be answered as easily as is often supposed.

I will begin at the beginning of the Principate, after Octavian's

---

1. On the Roman army in Judaea, see E. Schürer, *The History of the Jewish People in the Age of Jesus Christ* (rev. and ed. G. Vermes and F. Millar; Edinburgh: T. & T. Clark, 1973), I, pp. 362-67; Isaac, *Limits of Empire*, pp. 104-107.

victory over Marcus Antonius at Actium in 31 BCE. When Octavian disbanded some of the enormous number of legions left in the field at the end of the civil wars that had raged fairly continuously for the previous eighteen years, why did he retain so many under arms and begin the tradition of the maintenance of a standing army in peacetime? What was the point of keeping perhaps twenty-six (and, after 25 BCE, twenty-eight) legions in the field, not to mention the innovation of keeping some auxiliary units permanently available?[1] Modern scholars have tended to turn to Cassius Dio for an answer. According to Dio (52.27), Agrippa in 29 BCE argued for a return to the old ways of levying troops only when needed, but Maecenas successfully urged Augustus that permanently armed and trained soldiers were needed, 'for we can no longer rely upon forces called out for the occasion, owing to the distance which separates us from the borders of our empire and the enemies which we have upon every side'. It seems to me that this picture was accurate enough for Dio's day, but less obviously so for the first century BCE.[2]

The main anachronism in Dio's picture lies in his assumption that the Roman state was at risk of concentrated attack on the frontiers. In the early empire, candidates for such hostile behaviour by peoples adjacent to the *limes* were not always readily discernible: only the Parthian state might be considered both sufficiently organized and expansionary to be a threat. In practice many soldiers of the imperial army never had to see active service at all, not just because deterrence worked, but because there was no enemy. Not even the much less

---

1.   H.M.D. Parker, *The Roman Legions* (Oxford: Clarendon Press, 1928); G.L. Cheesman, *The Auxilia of the Roman Imperial Army* (Oxford: Clarendon Press, 1914); D.B. Saddington, 'The development of the Roman auxiliary forces from Augustus to Trajan', *ANRW* II.3 (1975), pp. 176-201. See L. Keppie, *The Making of the Roman Army, from Republic to Empire* (London: Batsford, 1984), pp. 145-71.

2.   On anachronisms in Dio, see F. Millar, *A Study of Cassius Dio* (Oxford: Oxford University Press, 1964), pp. 102-18. For a recent discussion of the role of the Roman army, see the analysis by Isaac, *Limits of Empire*. I agree with almost all his perceptive criticism of older scholarship and his emphasis on the role of the army as internal security force, but am inclined, perhaps rashly, to push scepticism even further than he does; particularly with regard to Judaea, about which his view is conventional (pp. 55, 77-89). See my forthcoming review in *Journal for the Study of Judaism*.

serious danger of barbarians making small-scale incursions across the
frontiers for booty was often plausible in the early empire, when it is
unlikely that the material culture of the areas adjacent to the *limes* on
the Roman side differed greatly from its counterpart on the barbarian
side.[1]

On the other hand, even if attack threatened, a large standing army
was not the obvious way to counter it. During the Republic, over
centuries of expanding Roman power, wars had usually been fought
by Rome in concentrated campaigns with specially levied legions.
Peace and the retention of conquests was ensured by the threat of
retaliation against opponents. Instant, or even rapid, retaliation was
never possible or expected outside Italy. So the extra distance to be
covered by armies defending the greatly expanded territory controlled
by Rome by the first century BCE did not require alteration to the
principle that legions should be levied only for particular campaigns.
It was only necessary that the enemies of Rome should know that
Rome would always retaliate—in time.[2]

The number of legions required by the state in the late Republic for
this defensive purpose was not great. In the previous century and a
half before 31 BCE, the total number of legions needed for external
wars in any one year had been as few as three in the years 127, 120,
118, and 100 BCE, and the average number of legions in the field
between 167 and 91 BCE was less than seven, while throughout the 90s
BCE the figure never rose above that number. As recently as 59 BCE
fifteen legions had sufficed.[3] The massive increases in legionary and
auxiliary enrolment that took place in the late Republic were stimulated by the ambitions not of non-Romans, but of senatorial politicians
seeking power in civil wars. With the cessation of those civil wars, a
standing army of the size that was in fact retained by the Julio-
Claudians was, on the face of it, unnecessary.

Not only was it unnecessary, but it created its own problems. What

1. On the cultural unity of the Rhine area in the first century BCE, see M. Todd,
The Northern Barbarians 100 BC–AD 300 (rev. edn; Oxford: Basil Blackwell, 1987),
pp. 32-34.
2. On Roman use of public ferocity to instil terror in the Republic, see
W.V. Harris, *War and Imperialism in Republican Rome, 327–70 BC* (New York:
Oxford University Press, 1979), pp. 50-53, 263-64.
3. For these figures, see P.A. Brunt, *Italian Manpower, 225 BC–AD 14*
(Oxford: Oxford University Press, 1971), pp. 432-33, 449.

was to be done with this vast army? Only foreign conquest could justify the retention of so many legions in the eyes of the Roman public, but foreign wars were risky: grand campaigns could fail, and failure might alienate both soldiers and people. Nonetheless, from 16 BCE a proportion of the troops was set to work in the extension of the northern frontier, and by the end of Augustus's principate he could point to an extraordinary achievement of conquest.[1] But such aggressive wars did not constitute the reason for retaining so many soldiers. For the first fifteen years of Augustus's domination, most of the legions were idle. Even when the army was at its busiest, in 29 BCE, at least fourteen legions remained unused; it is, of course, in any case not clear that the campaign of M. Licinius Crassus against the Getae and Bastarnae had Octavian's blessing. No fighting was done by any legion in 18 and 17 BCE. On average, twenty legions were inactive every year. Indeed, so little was done by the legions in these years that Mommsen argued (wrongly) that the full complement of Augustan legions was not created until later in his rule.[2]

In sum, most of this great force had nothing to do. Wars continued to be fought by taking soldiers to the campaign area from bases far away. When Tiberius threatened aggression against Parthia in 20 BCE, he brought troops from the west, and the three legions based in Syria formed only part of his complement; Tiberius's army could easily have been levied *ad hoc*.[3] Velleius Paterculus (2.113) expatiated on the huge force gathered in 7 CE against the rebels in Pannonia and Dalmatia. It was of exceptional size—but it included only ten legions; eighteen remained in reserve.

Not only was this huge force mostly idle, but much of the activity in which it was involved was of its own making. The upkeep of so many soldiers cost a great deal of money—according to Luttwak's calculations, 'only' about half the income of the state.[4] It seems likely that the

---

1. P.A. Brunt, 'Review of H.D. Meyer, *Die Aussenpolitik des Augustus*', *JRS* 53 (1963), pp. 170-76.
2. Keppie, *Making of the Roman Army*, pp. 154-63. On the foundation of the imperial legions, T. Mommsen, *Res Gestae Divi Augusti* (Berlin, 1883), p. 70; Parker, *Roman Legions*, pp. 72-92; Keppie, *Making of the Roman Army*, pp. 132-44.
3. For the legions used, see Parker, *Roman Legions*, p. 91.
4. E.N. Luttwak, *The Grand Strategy of the Roman Empire from the First Century AD to the Third* (London: Johns Hopkins University Press, 1976), p. 16.

regularization of the provincial census under Augustus was rendered necessary by the need to raise more money regularly.[1] It was the census, as has been seen above, that often sparked off revolt. In the case of the Batavi in 69 CE, enlistment of men to fight rather than exaction of money to pay others had the same effect (Tac. *Hist.* 4.12-14). I suspect that it is futile to hope that any ancient source will explain this shift in Roman politics from use of *ad hoc* armies in the Republic to a standing army under the principate. Modern scholars may speculate as to its cause. It is possible that Octavian in 31 BCE held on to legions for intended campaigns that never came to fruition, and that the failure of the regime in later years to rid itself of the burden of permanent military forces was due simply to conservatism—in particular, no later emperor liked publicly to undo what Augustus had done.[2]

It is also possible that Octavian and his successors hung on to a large force primarily to deter rivals within the senatorial elite. Octavian's own early career had demonstrated the ease with which legions could be raised on private initiative by the ambitious, and it was characteristic of Augustus that he viewed Roman politics in the light of his own success—hence, for instance, his concern to find a private heir to inherit public power. Thus, after Actium, Octavian kept his military force large enough not just to win any possible civil war but also to preclude any such challenge in the first place.[3]

I believe this to be quite a likely explanation for the retention of a standing army by emperors, but it would be naïve to expect any ancient writer to state such a fact openly, and the hypothesis is therefore bound to remain unproven. Since the legions were themselves commanded by senators even when under the emperor's

1.   Brunt, *Roman Imperial Themes*, pp. 329-35, 345-46, 531-40.
2.   R.E. Smith, *Service in the Post-Marian Roman Army* (Manchester: University of Manchester Press, 1958), emphasizes the long service of some legions in particular provinces in the Late Republic as a precursor of the Augustan standing army. But on the differences, see Keppie, *Making of the Roman Army*, pp. 76-78, 146.
3.   On Octavian's private army in 44 BCE, see e.g. A.H.M. Jones, *Augustus* (London: Chatto and Windus, 1970), pp. 16-17; on his search for an heir, Jones, *Augustus*, pp. 79-80. On the maintenance of the emperor's power an an 'essential function' of the army, see Isaac, *Limits of Empire*, p. 2.

auspices, a military dictatorship of this kind could only operate if the self-image of such senatorial generals was carefully massaged. It was perhaps for this reason that Augustus, in his public restoration of the Republic and insistence on senatorial dignity, tried to maintain the prestige of the ruling elite. No Roman could be compelled to enter public life, and a constant stream of generals prepared to lead the emperor's troops could only be ensured if they were rewarded sufficiently. An important part of their reward was that they were enabled to retain their self-esteem.[1]

For present purposes it does not greatly matter which, if either, reason for Octavian's failure to disband more troops is correct, provided that it is recognized that there is no evidence that the creation in the principate of a standing army signified a new Roman strategy that involved stationing troops wherever trouble might be expected. There is no reason to suppose that Romans became any more interested than they had been during the Republic in *rapid* response to unrest. I do not know of any evidence that Roman military roads outside Italy were built for speedy rather than just safe transport for troops and their baggage trains.[2] In the early empire, the Romans, not their enemies, generally chose the time for campaigns to start. When revolt broke out in Judaea in 66 CE, Cestius Gallus and his troops only marched on Jerusalem some considerable time after the outbreak of war, when it was clear that the internecine strife would not come to an end of its own accord (Josephus, *War* 2.499). He was in no hurry to stamp out the insurrection despite the fact that he had four legions on permanent stand-by in Antioch, which was linked to Judaea by a fine new road constructed by Claudius.[3]

Gallus was in no hurry, because Roman control of the empire continued to be achieved in the imperial period, as in the Republic,

1. I hope to develop more fully elsewhere this general argument about the workings of the early Principate. On emperors' relations with the Senate, see F. Millar, *The Emperor in the Roman World (31 BC–AD 337)* (London: Gerald Duckworth, 1977), pp. 341-55.

2. R. Chevallier, *Roman Roads* (trans. N.H. Field; London: Batsford, 1976), p. 203, assumes that speed in transport was an important reason for road building but provides no evidence for such a view in antiquity. On the need for *secure* communications, see now Isaac, *Limits of Empire*, pp. 102-103, 113.

3. R.G. Goodchild, 'The coast road of Phoenicia and its Roman milestones', *Berytus* 9 (1948), pp. 91-127.

primarily by instilling fear of retaliation into prospective and actual rebels, rather than by preventing outbreaks through physical force on the spot. That retaliation remained a major weapon can be seen by looking at the state's treatment of rebels in the early principate. Roman actions against foreign peoples were often vicious, even on initial conquest—thus many of those who fought against Rome in Pannonia and Dalmatia in 13 and 12 BCE were sold into slavery (Dio 54.32.3-4). But punishment could be even more horrific after rebellion. Hundreds of thousands of Jewish captives were killed in public shows in Caesarea in the autumn of 70 (Josephus, *War* 7.37-40). Those Spanish rebels in 19 BCE who were not slaughtered were forcibly resettled in a different region where geography would be less favourable to dissent (Dio 54.11.5-6). The Jews of Cyprus were forbidden to set foot on the island after 117 CE (Dio 68.32-33). More drastically still, Judaean Jews were entirely excluded from the region around the holy city of Jerusalem after the defeat of Bar Kochba in 135 CE (Justin Martyr, *I Apol.* 47). It was important for this policy of deterrence that suppression should be seen to be thorough, hence the extraordinary efforts made to subdue the last remnants of Judaean resistance: witness the operations at Masada in 73–74 CE, as revealed by the huge ramp erected in the middle of the desert.[1]

Deterrence by terror often involved advertisement of punishments meted out: hence, for instance, the distribution under Vespasian of the coins proclaiming *Judaea Capta*, with their image of a Jewess weeping (*BMCRE* II, 115-18). Who can know whether inhabitants of Syria or Cilicia or Greece chose not to rebel because they were happy with their lot or because, after rational consideration of what had happened to people like the Jews, they elected (most of the time) to suffer in silence?

What should be concluded from all this about Jewish history is, I suggest, negative but not necessarily therefore negligible. Parallels can be found to the Jews' reaction to the census in 6 CE and to the use of native religious beliefs in the encouragement of the rebels. Other parts of the empire besides Judaea witnessed rumblings of discontent over long periods. It was not only the Jews who evoked horrific retaliation

---

1. Y. Yadin, *Masada: Herod's fortress and the Zealots' last stand* (trans. M. Pearlman; London: Weidenfeld & Nicholson, 1966); Luttwak, *Grand Strategy*, pp. 3-4.

by the imperial state, suffering the deaths of thousands of captives and forcible resettlement. Most important of all, the fact that most provincials at most times (including most Jews) did not rebel may have been a result of fear, not contentment.

If all this is correct, it is at least possible that the picture in modern scholarship of Jews as more committed to revolt than any other provincials under Roman rule should be rejected on the grounds that it has been concocted from systematically biased evidence. The traditional view relies heavily on Roman, and specifically Flavian, propaganda.[1] It is necessarily coloured by the chance survival, mostly through the Christian tradition, of those (not very numerous) Jewish texts that preached the eventual victory of Israel over the nations. If students of the Roman empire begin to treat with greater suspicion the argument from silence that lack of evidence for revolts by most non-Jewish provincials proves their lack of desire to rebel, Jewish resistance may come to seem less *sui generis* after all.

---

1. On Flavian propaganda, see Goodman, *Ruling Class*, pp. 235-39.

JEROME'S CONCEPTS OF EMPIRE

Steven Fanning

A study of almost any area of intellectual activity in late Antiquity and the early Middle Ages must take serious consideration of the many and significant works of St Jerome. For the Latin West, certainly, his translation of the Bible would have been read by absolutely everyone who aspired to any education.[1] His translation of the *Chronicle* of Eusebius was one of the foundations of Latin Christian history and the point of departure for subsequent chroniclers for centuries afterwards,[2] who worked to bring Jerome's work up to date with their own material. Serious biblical scholars drew on his many commentaries and homilies not only for the learning that they displayed, but also for the store of Greek and Hebrew knowledge that the self-proclaimed trilinguist passed on. In his polemic works, Jerome defended his brand of orthodoxy and spilled out his bile on those who dared to quarrel with him. Thus the concepts and language employed by Jerome either directly or subtly influenced the intellectual outlook of the Middle Ages more than any other single figure.

Despite his incontestable intelligence and outstanding linguistic abilities, Jerome was certainly no great original thinker. He was a scholar, but not a philosopher or theologian. Proud of his good Roman education and being a good Latinist, Jerome was not given to speculation. Therefore his thoughts can be seen as essentially conservative, and the concepts that he expressed and the language he used for that expression can be considered to be 'typical' for the Latin

---

1. B. Smalley, *The Study of the Bible in the Middle Ages* (Notre Dame, IN: University of Notre Dame Press, 1970 [repr.]), pp. xi-xxii.

2. B. Croke and A.M. Emmett, 'Historiography in Late Antiquity: An Overview', in B. Croke and A.M. Emmett (eds.), *History and Historiography in Late Antiquity* (New York: Pergamon Press, 1983), pp. 3-4.

Christian world of the late fourth and early fifth centuries.

In many ways, it is especially useful to examine Jerome's works for insight into political concepts, because he was not intending to write on that particular subject. His political thought is largely unconscious and ancillary to the subjects with which he was expressly concerned. For the most part, he was not trying to tell us what ideal governments or rulers should be like. His descriptions were based on what was, not on what ought to be. In this respect, Jerome is far more useful than Augustine for a view of actual Roman political thought, as opposed to theory, around the turn of the fifth century.

Jerome's translation of the Bible is especially valuable for this purpose. The Bible is filled with political thought and terminology, concerning kings, princes, prophets, chieftains and, of course, God. Additionally, we have Greek and Hebrew texts against which to check the Vulgate translation. With certain choices of Greek and Hebrew words before him, Jerome selected particular Latin words as their equivalents, which must tell us something of what those words meant in the Latin world of his time. Recently Herwig Wolfram[1] used the Gothic translation of the Bible in just this manner to uncover the essential political framework of the Visigoths before their entry into the Roman Empire, at about the time of Jerome's early career.

The Vulgate ought to be ideal for this sort of information, for Jerome made very clear his theory of translation. In general, the translator ought to try to convey the sense of his original text, for the differences between languages makes word for word equivalency impossible and the result would be unintelligible. However, for the holy scriptures, meaning and significance reside in the very words themselves, and the translations ought to be as literal as possible.[2] Moreover, Jerome repeatedly affirmed that his translation was of the Hebrew text.[3] Thus we ought to expect the Vulgate to be an extremely literal translation of the Hebrew text as it stood in his day. In this, of course, as in so many other aspects of his life, Jerome engages in

1.   H. Wolfram, *History of the Goths* (trans. T.J. Dunlap; Berkeley: University of California Press, 1988), pp. 94-114.

2.   Jerome, *Lettres* (trans. J. Labourt; Paris: Société d' Edition 'Les Belles Lettres', 1949–1963), *ep.* 57.

3.   J.N.D. Kelly, *Jerome: His Life, Writings and Controversies* (London: Gerald Duckworth, 1975), pp. 159-63.

deception and hyperbole. Jerome's translation, in fact, is extremely inconsistent. It is based on the Hebrew text, the Septuagint translation as well as other Greek translations, the Old Latin text (or texts) as well as apparently on whim. Some parts are very literal, others convey the sense of his sources, while others are virtual paraphrases.

The direct aim of this research is to investigate a very narrow range of political terminology as used by Jerome: imperial terminology, the usage of *imperium* and *imperare*. An understanding of the concepts associated with these words will contribute to a proper appreciation of the inherent meaning of the most elevated political terminology available in Latin. It will also give clues to the understanding of the Roman Empire in Jerome's time—was it unique, was it universal, and what, exactly, was an empire?

One of the most basic questions concerns the meaning of the word *imperium* itself. There are obviously many nuances attached to it— such as command, power, strength, honour. But what of its more political connotations? Does the term *imperium Romanum*, or *imperium Romanorum*, have any specific and unique meaning? Throughout Jerome's *Commentary on Daniel*, the Roman Empire is identified as the fourth *regnum*, that of iron (2.40; 7.7). This free usage of *regnum* for the Roman Empire seems to be equalled by his usage of both *regnum* and *imperium* for the great world empires that preceded the Roman—those of the Babylonians, Chaldeans, Persians, and Macedonians (2.31, 39; 5.1; 6.1, 25-27; 8.5). This same sort of usage can be found in the works of other Latin writers around the same time as Jerome—Augustine, Orosius, Sulpicius Severus and, a bit later, Jordanes.[1] This has led to the interpretation that *imperium* lost any special meaning and was simply a synonym for 'rule'.[2]

However, when viewed at closer range, this apparent synonymity is

---

1. S. Fanning, 'Emperors and Empires in Fifth-Century Gaul', in J. Drinkwater and H. Elton (eds.), *Fifth-Century Gaul: A Crisis of Identity?* (Cambridge: Cambridge University Press, 1991).

2. J. McClure, 'Bede's Old Testament Kings', in P. Wormald, D. Bullough and R. Collins (eds), *Ideal and Reality in Frankish and Anglo-Saxon Society: Studies Presented to J.M. Wallace-Hadrill* (Oxford: Basil Blackwell, 1983), pp. 97-98; J. Campbell, *Bede's 'Reges' and 'Principes'* (Jarrow Lecture 1979; Jarrow: The Parish of Jarrow, 1979), p. 3; H. Vollrath-Reichelt, 'Königsherrschaft bei den Angelsachsen', in her *Königsgedanke und Königtum bis zur Mitte des 9. Jahrhunderts* (Vienna: Böhlau Verlag, 1971), pp. 79-80.

not as clear as it has seemed. If *imperium* and *regnum* are essentially the same, then we should expect to find one term used about as frequently as the other, without any obvious distinctions. However, an examination of Jerome's use of *imperium* and its associated verb *imperare* in the Vulgate, used in a political sense, reveals that the word is used rarely and is applied to very few states or rulers. It is applied to the *duces* of Edom (Gen. 36.43), Eglon king of Moab (Judg. 3.19), and the Philistines when they dominated Israel (Judg. 15.11). It is also used for Israel and its early leaders and judges, such as Joshua and Jephthah (Josh. 1.10; Judg. 11.14), the prophet Samuel, its great kings Saul, David and Solomon (1 Sam. 22.4; 1 Chron. 18.3; 21.6; 2 Sam. 2.11; 3.21; 1 Kgs 12.4; Sir. 45.15, 23), as well as for the first several kings of Judah after the split of the kingdom following Solomon's death (2 Chron. 10.14; 13.21; 15.16; 24.21; 25.3; 31.13; 35.10). Jerome also used these two imperial words for non-Israelite states and rulers. Arphaxad, king of the Medes, had an *imperium* (Jdt. 1.1), as did Ahasuerus or Artaxerxes (Est. 1.3, 12, 15, 18, 20; 2.8; 3.15), as well as the Persian kings Cyrus and Darius. In addition, Nebuchadnezzar, king of the Babylonians, had an *imperium*. At this point, the list of holders of *imperium* does not seem to be very exclusive.

If one turns to the Hebrew and Septuagint texts to see what Jerome might have been looking at that could have led him to use *imperium* or *imperare* on these occasions, absolutely no clue emerges. On some occasions, there is no word at all in the Greek or Hebrew texts that implies rule or power in any form (Gen. 36.43, 41.14). There are sixteen different Hebrew words that appear where Jerome has *imperium* (for example: ממלכה, יד, מצות, צוה, עז, פה, גבורה, דבר, צוה, מאמר, חקף, משרה) and about the same number of different Greek words in the Septuagint text (for example: ῥῆμα, πρόσταγμα, φωνή, στόμα, ἰσχύς, τιμή, δόξα, κράτος, χείρ, λόγος, βασιλεία). Sometimes these words are nouns, sometimes verbs. The same general situation exists for Jerome's use of *imperare*. Thus the Septuagint and Masoretic texts provide no guidance in their vocabulary to Jerome's imperial usage in the Vulgate. There are no specifically 'imperial' words in Greek or Hebrew, and Jerome's use of these Latin words is based on their contexts and not on the vocabulary of his sources.

However, if one turns to another of the imperial words, *imperator*, a startling find emerges. Despite the great numbers of holders of *imperium* in the Vulgate, as well as subjects of the verb *imperare*, there is only one *imperator* to be found, Ahasuerus, in Est. 3.2. Since the Hebrew word appearing there, מלך, and the Greek word, βασιλεύς, occur about 2800 times each in the Old Testament, something about Ahasuerus obviously seemed especially imperial to Jerome. This impression is strengthened when it is noticed that, in Est. 1.20, *imperium* is attributed to this same Ahasuerus. The Hebrew word here is מלכות (the Greek is βασιλεία). It appears about 100 times in the Old Testament, and nearly always it is rendered *regnum* or *regna* in the Vulgate. Only this one time, associated with Ahasuerus, is it rendered *imperium*.

Thus Ahasuerus is the only מלך (or βασιλεύς,) who is an *imperator*, and only his מלכות (or βασιλεία) is an *imperium*. The description of Ahasuerus in the book of Esther is likewise very striking. He stands as the most powerful ruler described in the Old Testament. He is *rex maximus* (Est. 13.1). His *imperium* is very broad, *latissimum* (Est. 1.20), stretching from India to Ethiopia, comprising 127 provinces (Est. 1.1), which include many lands and peoples (Est. 8.13). Moreover, with the exception of God, Ahasuerus has *imperium* and *imperare* applied to him more frequently by far than anyone else in the Old Testament (eleven times for *imperium* and twice for *imperare*; next after Ahasuerus, David was associated with *imperium* twice and *imperare* twice, while Solomon was associated with *imperium* once and *imperare* three times). One might then postulate that *imperium* is closely associated with a great king, with jurisdiction over a large area, with domination over many lands and peoples, or with a less magnificent version of the rule and authority of Ahasuerus. With this in mind, a review of Jerome's use of *imperium* in a political sense reveals that this is not as much of a hodge-podge affair as it seemed at first. Israel had *imperium* (1 Sam. 2.10; 8.11; 12.4, 12), and its rule over many peoples and the great extent of its territory was emphasized from the time of the Israelites' first entry into Canaan. God told them that their land would stretch from the desert to Lebanon and the Euphrates, including all the land of the Hittites, and as far as the Great Sea (Josh. 1.4). Then Israel conquered thirty-one kings, whose lands were taken over (Josh. 12.1), and the Canaanites were made tributaries of Israel (Judg. 1.30, 33), as they still were at the time of the writings of the books of Kings and Chronicles, or so it was said (1 Kgs 9.21). This Israelite conquest of Canaan and subjugation of many peoples left a lasting memory among the Jews, and was recounted by both Josephus (*Ant.* 5.88–89) and the author of the Acts of the Apostles (13.19). Imperial language was used for Edom, Moab and the Philistines, and in such cases, the Israelites were subject to those peoples (Josh. 3.8; 3.12-14; Judg. 3.19; 15.11; 10.7, 8; 13.11). Thus Israel conquered many other nations and kings and had *imperium*. Then it was conquered by other peoples and fell under their *imperia*.

Samuel, however, renewed the *imperium* of the Israelites (Sir. 46.14). Israel's rule over other peoples returned and Saul had an *imperium* (1 Sam. 22.4). He fought against enemies on all sides and defeated many of them (1 Sam. 14.47-48; 15.7). King David also had an *imperium* (1 Chron. 18.3; 21.6; 2 Sam. 2.11; 3.21) and ruled over all Israel and Judah (2 Sam. 2.9; 3.12; 8.15; 10.17; 5.5), conquered many *gentes* (2 Sam. 8.11), and was over many *reges* (2 Sam. 10.19). It was said that he extended his *imperium* as far as the Euphrates (1 Chron. 18.3) and was over many *gentes* (1 Chron. 18.11). Jerome elsewhere wrote that David subjugated all surrounding peoples to his rule and was the conqueror of all nations (*Hom.* 24). Solomon also held an *imperium* (1 Kgs 12.4; Sir. 47.15, 23). He was over *omnia regna* from the Euphrates to the territory of the Philistines and the border of Egypt (1 Kgs 4.21). He had power over all the kings in that area and made tributaries of many peoples (2 Chron. 9.26). Under Kings David, Solomon and Rehoboam, there were established officers in charge of collecting the tribute that came in from the many subject peoples (2 Sam. 20.29; 1 Kgs 4.6; 12.18; 2 Chron. 10.18). In one of his letters, Jerome referred to David and Solomon as *reges potentissimi*.[1]

Following the death of Solomon and the division of his kingdom, the great world empires arose and dominated Samaria and Judah. Arphaxad, king of the Medes, subjugated *multae gentes* to his *imperium* (Jdt. 1.1). Nebuchadnezzar was king of kings (Dan. 2.37) and wanted every land subjugated to his *imperium* (Jdt. 2.3), and many *regna* were under his hand (Jer. 34.1). After Ahasuerus, already discussed, King Cyrus had an *imperium* (Isa. 45.24), and God gave him *omnia regna terrae* (2 Chron. 36.23). King Darius had an *imperium* and *imperavit super regnum Chaldeorum* (Dan. 9.1). The

---

1.   Jerome, *Lettres*, *ep.* 129.4.

Persian kings Artaxerxes and Darius also took tribute from the Jews as well as others (Ezra 4.13, 20; 6.8; 7.24; Neh. 5.4). Jerome's other writings also apply superlative language to these rulers. Darius was *rex potentissimus* (*Comm. Dan.* 8.4), and the Babylonians had a *regnum potentissimum* (*Comm. Dan.* 7.4). In the prophecy of Daniel, the bronze *regnum* would *imperabit universae terrae* (Dan. 2.39). The verb applied to the *rex universae terrae* was *imperare* (Eccl. 5.8). The rule over many peoples that is inherent in *imperium* is also seen in Ezekiel, where it was foretold that the divisions of the Israelites would come to an end. No more would there be two *gentes* divided into two *regna*. There would be one *gens* and one *rex* would be *omnibus imperans* (Ezek. 37.22).

When Jerome discussed the nature of the Roman empire, these same implications of rule over many nations, kingdoms or peoples are evident. All *nationes* have been killed or subjected to tribute and servitude by the Romans (*Comm. Dan.* 7.7). In the Roman empire, all peoples are gathered together,[1] it holds all *gentes*,[2] former *regna* are in the empire, and the Roman army was the conqueror and lord of the world.[3] Jerome wrote that before the coming of Christ, each *gens* had been under its own king, and no one could go from one *natio* to another. But all were made into one in the Roman *imperium* (*Comm. in Esaiam* 5.19, 23).

It is especially interesting to note the ease with which Jerome identified the Roman empire as the fourth *regnum* in Daniel's prophecy. Rome took its place as a *regnum* along with the previous great *regna*, and Jerome never attempted to explain away Rome's lowly position (literally and figuratively) as the kingdom of iron, below those of gold, silver and bronze. Rome was certainly a great empire, it *domat omnia* (*Comm. Dan.* 2.40) and comprised *orbis terrarum* (*Comm. Dan.* 7.7), yet Jerome never attempted to elevate Rome to a greater position than that of the *regnum ferreum*, as the last of a sequence of great empires.

From this survey, it is clear that Jerome did not employ *regnum* and *imperium* as synonyms. In a political sense, *imperium* has a definite significance. It is the dominance over a plurality of other

---

1. Jerome, *Lettres, ep.* 77.11.
2. Jerome, *Lettres, ep.* 60.16.
3. Jerome, *Lettres, ep.* 60.17.

peoples—*gentes, populi, nationes.* A *regnum* with such dominance is an *imperium*, though it was not necessary always to use the word *imperium* for such a state or to describe the rule of one who held such an authority. Thus every *imperium*, including the *imperium Romanorum*, was also a *regnum*, but not every *regnum* was an *imperium*. *Imperium* is 'imperial' rule, not merely rule. The key concepts associated with political *imperium* are the dominance over many peoples, the taking of tribute from them, and a superlative title for the holder of such rule, such as *rex maximums, rex regum,* or *rex potentissimus*, which ought to be considered as rough equivalents of *imperator*.

It is really not surprising that Jerome was so cautious in his use of the term *imperator* in the Vulgate, applying it only to Ahasuerus. In general, Jerome did not often apply that word to the *imperatores par excellence*, the Roman emperors. In his letters, the usual term for them is *principes*. It is interesting to observe that Jerome also used the word *rex* for Roman emperors,[1] although this can hardly be seen as necessarily derogatory, for Christ was *rex coeli* (*Comm. Dan.* 4.34), *rex omnium* (*Comm. Dan.* 7.2, 3), and *rex gloriae* (*Comm. Dan.* 8.16-17). Thus there is a linkage in terminology. An *imperium* is in fact a *regnum*, thus an *imperator* is also a *rex*, though again not every *rex* was an *imperator*.

In every usage discussed, Jerome broke no new ground, expanded no terminology, extended no theory. The Roman empire was styled a *regnum* by Sulpicius Severus, Augustine, Orosius, Claudian, Ennodius, Jordanes, Gildas, and Paul the Deacon. Non-Roman states that wielded authority over a multiplicity of peoples were styled *imperia* by Ammianus Marcellinus, Augustine, Orosius, Sulpicius Severus, Jordanes, and many others. The concept of the Roman Empire as a gathering together of many peoples is to be found in Origen, Tertullian, Augustine, Rutilius Namatianus, and Claudian. Roman emperors were styled *reges* by Statius, the *Scriptores Historiae Augustae*, Ammianus Marcellinus, Hilary of Poitiers, Lucifer of Cagliari, Augustine, Orosius, Venantius Fortunatus, Sulpicius Severus, Ennodius, and many others.[2]

If one turns to the non-political use of imperial language in the Vulgate, yet another pattern emerges. One-third of the instances refer

---

1. *Comm. Dan.* 11.31; *Lettres, ep.* 60.15, 82.3; 123.16; *Hom.* 49.
2. On all these points, S. Fanning, 'Emperors and Empires'.

to God or Jesus in particular (56 out of 148), with the most common expression being *imperium Domini*. The others enjoying this attribute are not nearly as lofty—Joseph, Reuben, Moses, Aaron, one's parents, Naomi, *duces* and *principes*, elders, military commanders, the 'kings' among the plants (olive trees, vines, brambles) and so on. However, this *mélange* of imperial figures does exhibit one common characteristic—its members are authorities that must be listened to, must be obeyed. One is reminded of John Mortimer's colourful 'Rumpole of the Bailey', who reflected on his wife Hilda as 'she who must be obeyed'. God and the incarnate person of the Godhead obviously stand in this category. The Hebrew phrase that Jerome read here and rendered *imperium domini* is פּ׳ יהוה, which Jerome also translated by such expressions as *sermo Dei* (Num. 4.37), *praeceptum Domini* (Num. 3.16), *verbum Domini* (Num. 4.41) and *os Domini* (Deut. 8.3). All of these can be taken to be as authoritative and ineluctable as *imperium domini*. Certainly, Jerome's imperial language for God, in comparison with the Greek and Hebrew readings, heightens the sense of the majesty of God, a special sense unobtainable in Greek and Hebrew.

This connotation of a command that must be obeyed is most clearly seen in the instance of the verb *imperare* when applied to Jesus, when he walked on the Sea of Galilee and when he commanded the wind and the sea, and they obeyed (Mt. 8.26; Lk. 8.25); when he cast out unclean spirits and devils (Mt. 1.27; Lk. 8.31); when he rebuked a fever and it went away (Lk. 4.39). Most telling is the amazement expressed when he commanded an unclean spirit to depart, and it went (Lk. 14.22; 17.9). The verb is also used for masters who ordered their servants to do something, and it was done. This voice of authority is therefore appropriate in royal officers, army commanders, Moses and Aaron, parents, an elder brother, a mother-in-law towards her daughter-in-law, and a priest.

Thus there are two distinct concepts surrounding *imperium* and *imperare* in the body of Jerome's writings and translations. There is political imperial usage, which concerns states or rulers over a multiplicity of peoples or *regna*, closely linked to taking tribute from them. In this respect, the Roman empire no doubt is the greatest of the *imperia*, but it is not inherently different from any other *imperia*. The Roman empire is outstanding in its size, but not in its essence. It is not unique, for other *imperia* are held by the Persians and, later, by the

Huns, as is seen in the writings of Ammianus Marcellinus, Gregory of Tours, Gregory the Great, Fredegar, and John of Biclarum, among others.[1] Nor is it genuinely universal, despite the universal language employed by Jerome and other writers. It is also clear from Jerome's writings that the concept of an *imperium* as a conflation of *regna* is not a medieval concept,[2] but it was flourishing in the fourth century. It is obvious that any state or ruler that exercised authority over other peoples, nations, or *regna* could legitimately be styled, or self-styled, an *imperium*, without any element of hubris or arrogance being necessarily involved.[3] Such a claim would not entail a claim that any particular *imperium* was the exact equal of the Roman empire, except in also enjoying such a domination over foreigners.

This use of *imperium* is obviously linked to the root concept of *imperare*, at least as it was understood in the fourth century. Jerome's second concept of 'empire' is as a *commanding authority* (a difficult concept to express simply in English) that must be obeyed, as surely as waves, wind, and demons obeyed Jesus. This sort of authority could easily be applied to those who clearly were not emperors, without political connotations.

Jerome did not create or expand either of these usages, but his principal importance was to embed them in his translations of the Bible, and in his exegetical, polemic and homiletic works that were to hold such a sway over the minds of all educated persons for centuries to come. The Latin Bible, with its rich store of political vocabulary and concepts, would have been the single most important and influential work in the education of all who were likely to think of or write on government in the Middle Ages.

An awareness of the whole ensemble of Jerome's political vocabulary can also be quite useful in grasping the meaning implicit in the entire range of imperial language. Taking an example from Yorkshire, my most recent research has focused on Bede, who was deeply influenced by Jerome's writings, and his use of imperial

---

1. Fanning, 'Emperors and Empires'.
2. As it is supposed in H. Wolfram, 'The Shaping of the Early Medieval Kingdom', *Viator* 1 (1970), p. 16.
3. But see R. Folz, *The Concept of Empire in Western Europe from the Fifth to the Fourteenth Century* (trans. S.A. Ogilvie; Westport, CT: Edward Arnold, 1969), p. 14.

vocabulary, and what that might mean for the idea of the Anglo-Saxon bretwaldaship. In that research, I inevitably noticed the six Anglo-Saxon kings who were said to have held an *imperium* like that of Aethelberth of Kent (*Eccles. Hist.* 2.5), who supposedly was the first of the seven bretwaldas (or eight, if one also counts Egbert of Wessex), and I then studied Bede's application of *imperium* and *imperare* to other kings in the *Ecclesiastical History*. I then went on to examine kings who were described as conquerors in that same work. I found that in every case but one, conquerors had *imperium* or *imperare* applied to them by Bede. The single exception was Aethelfrith of Northumbria, who certainly was presented as a great conqueror. He is reported to have subjected more land to the *gens Anglorum* than any other ruler (*Eccles. Hist.* 1.34). After this study of Jerome's imperial usage, it is clear that Bede's styling of Aethelfrith as *rex fortissimus* (*Eccles. Hist.* 1.34), recalling that Jerome referred to leaders of great *imperia* by such titles as *rex potentissimus* and *rex maximus*, is in fact an example of imperial terminology. All of the conquerors in the *Ecclesiastical History* are enmeshed in imperial concepts, as victors who extended their own boundaries by subjugating neighboring kingdoms and *gentes* and by taking tribute from the conquered. And in a like manner Bede described Aethelfrith. Bede indeed used imperial concepts for Aethelfrith, though not with the words *imperium* and *imperare*.[1]

Thus a clear understanding of Jerome's imperial language will illuminate many dark corners of the history of the political world of late Antiquity and the Middle Ages, even in a source such as Bede, who was writing over 300 years after Jerome's own time in the farthest outpost of the Latin world as it was known to the great Christian exegete and translator. Jerome's influence is certainly not as an innovator or as philosopher, but is in those areas in which he himself sought to excel—his translation of the Bible, in his biblical exegesis, and in his lengthy correspondence with those who sought out his advice or received it without asking for it. It is interesting to see that many of the ideas concerning empire that have long been considered to have been distinctly medieval can actually be observed clearly in Jerome's writings. An empire is the domination of many peoples and

---

1. On these points, see S. Fanning, 'Bede, *Imperium* and the Bretwaldas', *Speculum* 66 (1991), pp. 1-26.

nations; many different *imperia* can coexist; the Roman Empire, while certainly a great empire, is not a unique state. Thus the use of imperial language by non-Roman states and rulers is not an example of hubris or arrogance, but is rather a reflection of political fact. One thing is certain. Had Jerome gained an awareness of how influential his writings were to be in the Latin West, his only disappointment might have been that a time would come when his words were no longer a part of the studies of anyone who aspired to the distinction of being learned.

LET EVERY SOUL BE SUBJECT:
THE FATHERS AND THE EMPIRE*

Gillian Clark

Patristics is an interdisciplinary subject. It stretches between the classical and mediaeval worlds and the Graeco-Roman and Near Eastern
traditions. In the narrower range of Graeco-Roman antiquity, Church
History and Ancient History are acknowledging common interests.
There have been times when church historians were chiefly interested
in the development of doctrines that are central to Christian teaching.
But theological scholarship of the 1970s and 1980s has avoided, or
openly rejected, any claim that patristic teaching is normative for
twentieth-century theology, and has shown increasing concern for the
Fathers as voices from a particular social and intellectual context.[1] At
the same time, historians of the Graeco-Roman world have shown
increasing willingness to use patristic evidence. For our present
purpose the witness of the Fathers is of great importance, because they
lived under the *Pax Romana* and had to work out a theological
response to problems of obedience to power, and exercise of power,
first as subjects and later as agents. They also provide a useful control
on twentieth century methods and assumptions.

This paper makes no claim to be exhaustive, and attempts only to
offer some examples of the way patristic writers respond to Roman
imperial powers.[2] If anyone who says he has read all of Augustine is

*   I am most grateful to Professor Robert Markus for his benevolent and
incisive comments on an earlier version; to Loveday Alexander for discussions over
many years, and particularly of this paper; and to the members of the *Images of
Empire* colloquium.
    1.   E.A. Clark, *Ascetic Piety and Women's Faith* (New York: Edwin Mellen
Press, 1986), p. 4.
    2.   Wide-ranging and relevant studies include C.J. Cadoux, *The Early Church
and the World* (Edinburgh: T. & T. Clark, 1925); S.L. Greenslade, *Church and State*

(probably) a liar, anyone who says she has read all the Patrologia is (almost certainly) a fantasist—though it was delightful to hear from a member of the colloquium that Dr. Darwell Stone, Principal of Pusey House, claimed to have done so: twice!

1. *The Patristic Authors*

Patristic writing is closely linked with the *Pax Romana*. By convention, patristics ends somewhere between the seventh and ninth centuries: its boundary is as hard to define as that between late antiquity and the mediaeval world, but continuity with Graeco-Roman culture is of great importance. In the West, the watershed is the work of Isidore of Seville, patiently assembling ancient learning that he did not always understand. Perhaps there was a comparable break, political if not cultural, in the east under the pressure of the Arab invasions;[1] but however that debate goes, the convention remains. It follows that the men we count as Fathers of the church belonged to the intellectual elite of the Roman empire.

A church Father is an authoritative defender of the faith in the early centuries of the church. His authority comes partly from the extent and quality of his writing, partly from his status within the Christian community. A few Fathers (notably Origen and Jerome) owed their status to spirituality and scholarship, but almost all were bishops, acknowledged leaders of the church. That is why there are no Mothers

from Constantine to Theodosius (London: SCM Press, 1954); E. A. Isichei, *Political Thinking and Social Experience: Some Christian Interpretations of the Roman Empire* (University of Christchurch publications, 6; Christchurch, NZ: University of Christchurch, 1964); F. Paschoud, *Roma aeterna: études sur le patriotisme romain dans l'occident latin à l'époque des grandes invasions* (Rome: Institut Suisse de Rome, 1967); R.A. Markus, *Saeculum: History and Society in the Thought of St Augustine* (Cambridge: Cambridge University Press, 2nd edn, 1988 [1970]), and 'Introduction: The West' and 'The Latin Fathers', in J.H. Burns (ed), *Cambridge History of Mediaeval Political Thought* (Cambridge: Cambridge University Press, 1988), pp. 83-122; W.H.C. Frend, *Religion Popular and Unpopular*, (Variorum Reprints, 9, 10; London, 1976); G.E.M. de Sainte Croix, *The Class Struggle in the Ancient Greek World* (London: Gerald Duckworth, 1981), pp. 394-405.

1.   A. Cameron, 'The Construction of Court Ritual: The Byzantine Book of Ceremonies', in D. Cannadine and S. Price (eds.), *Rituals of Royalty: Power and Ceremonial in Traditional Societies* (Cambridge: Cambridge University Press, 1987), pp. 106-36.

of the church, though there were spiritual and scholarly women, a few of whom have left writings.[1] The churches chose as bishops men who had the intellectual and rhetorical skills to be good preachers, and the administrative skills to be effective leaders. The same abilities that made them leaders and teachers of the church qualified them also for civic administration and public speaking. Even before Constantine we find complaints that the church is taking away people needed for the service of the empire: after Constantine, the church's recruitment of the ruling class was so extensive that it has been blamed for the downfall of the empire in the West.[2] The other side of the coin is complaints from the church—made formally at Nicaea, but occurring even earlier—that men are being made bishops precisely because of their civic status, not because they are mature Christians.

Several of the Fathers—familiar examples are Cyprian, Basil and Ambrose—had inherited or trained for the duties of public life, and had exercised their skills in city government or the imperial civil and military service, the *militia*. When they became bishops they often found that life had not changed that much: they needed all their secular contacts and skills to protect their people.[3] Bishops, in the words of Gregory the Great,[4] scarcely knew whether they were doing the job of pastor or of secular leader. They kept track of finance, investment and property, settled lawsuits, lobbied the imperial court and local officials, and tried to advance or avoid legislation. These were men who not only lived under the *Pax Romana* but knew its workings, and shared in the task of maintaining it.

But the Fathers could not wholly identify with the perspective of a ruling class. They had all in some sense rejected the service of the

1. P. Wilson-Kastner, *A Lost Tradition: Women Writers of the Early Church* (Lanham, MD: University Press of America, 1981).

2. A. Momigliano, Introduction to *The Conflict of Paganism and Christianity in the Fourth Century* (ed. A. Momigliano; Oxford: Clarendon Press, 1963), pp. 1-16; W.H.C. Frend, 'Paulinus of Nola and the Last Century of the Western Empire', *JRS* 59 (1969), pp. 1-11; J.H.W.G. Liebeschuetz, *Barbarians and Bishops: Army, Church and State in the Age of Arcadius and Chrysostom* (Oxford: Clarendon Press, 1990).

3. H. Chadwick, *The Role of the Christian Bishop in Ancient Society* (ed. E.C. Hobbs and W. Wuellner; Protocol of the 35th Colloquy; Berkeley: Center for Hermeneutical Studies, 1983).

4. Gregory, *Letter* 1.24.

empire, by leaving the *militia* or by refusing to enter it. Even when the danger of persecution had passed, they could not ignore Christian experience of the Roman empire as the agent of persecution; even if they acknowledged the need for Christians to serve in government, they could not ignore the Christian tradition of refusal to take life as a soldier or an enforcer of law. Nor could they close their eyes to the victims of the system. Bishops administered church funds: they knew how many were on the welfare rolls and what kinds of need were being forced on the church's attention; it was part of their job to point out to congregations that there were people starving in the streets of wealthy Antioch, or slaves and peasant farmers neglected on country estates. Finally, they interpreted and judged political events and power-structures by the light of non-Roman sacred texts, the Judaeo-Christian scriptures.

2. *Patristic Exegesis*

Patristic exegesis of the Bible is often disconcerting. Many biblical scholars in the late twentieth century are fairly liberal, modestly prosperous, generally powerless academics, whose natural sympathies are with the Jewish people confronting a Roman army of occupation, and who feel bound to learn all they can about first-century Palestine in the effort to hear aright what was said there. Patristic authors are more likely to be reading out guidance for what armies, commanders and governors may do, or expounding the duties of ordinary citizens: they see the NT world as continuous with their own, and the Romans in it are not 'they'; their anxiety about mishearing is that they may fail to bring out the full spiritual sense of a text, or fail to read it as part of a complex of scriptural teaching.

But the most obvious difference is that patristic authors do not contrast one strand of biblical tradition with another, or characterize the approach of a particular author as, for instance, Professors Edwards and Robbins (in this volume, above) characterize Luke–Acts. What they do is best illustrated by example. I take one of the most famous pieces of patristic exegesis, Clement of Alexandria's *On the Rich Man's Salvation*, which is concerned with the interrelated problems of wealth and power.

In the context of a Graeco-Roman city, wealth confers civic power and civic obligation; renouncing wealth, or redistributing it not by benefactions to the city but through the bishop's welfare fund or private charity, means loss of power.[1] Clement's congregation, in mid-second-century Alexandria, includes rich people who are made anxious by the story of the man who asked Jesus what he should do to inherit eternal life, and was told to sell all he had and give to the poor. Clement wants his audience to move on from taking Gospel texts literally; many teachers of first-year theology classes use the same example now, for the same purpose. But the standard tactic now is to juxtapose the different versions from a Gospel synopsis. Clement simply narrates, then says (ch. 5), 'This is what is written in the gospel according to Mark. In all the other acknowledged gospels the wording perhaps differs slightly in some places, but all display the same agreement in overall sense'.[2] These minimised differences include the crucial phrase 'if you would be perfect', which occurs at Mt. 19.21 but not at Lk. 10.21. Clement makes some use of this phrase (ch. 10), but not to show a difference between Matthew and Mark. It is clear to him that the story does not literally require the ruling classes to sell all they have and give to the poor, for—as his audience knows—poverty is no guarantee of sanctity, and there is no point in adding more destitute Christians to the welfare rolls. So Matthew must be stating more fully what Mark means. Clement notes (ch. 17) that Matthew similarly brings out the implicit meaning of the Beatitudes, adding 'in spirit' to 'blessed are the poor' and 'after righteousness' to 'blessed are those who hunger and thirst'. He does not say that the text without the additions is from Luke; still less does he contrast Luke's approach with Matthew's.

This is, I think, characteristic of patristic exegesis. There is willing attention to details of vocabulary and expression, and to the particular emphasis a NT author wants to give. There are arguments from common sense—'he cannot mean X, so he must mean Y'—especially where one text contradicts another. This technique is often combined with heavy allegorizing: it is splendidly displayed by Augustine[3] trying to get Paul off the hook of having said that only men are in the image of God. But what patristic authors will not do is to declare

---

1. L.W. Countryman, *The Rich Christian in the Church of the Early Empire* (New York: Edwin Mellen Press, 1980).
2. Clement of Alexandria, *On the Rich Man's Salvation* 5.
3. Augustine, *On the Trinity* 12.7.

Paul, or any other NT author, tendentious or simply wrong, or to confront readers with conflicts and uncertainties. If contrasts are offered, it is so that they may be resolved. This is not a peculiarly Christian refusal to challenge authority. The same is true of late Platonist exegesis of Homer, and generally of late antique philosophers discussing texts which are central to their school.[1] A.H. Armstrong puts it admirably:

> It is assumed with complete confidence that whatever is found in the documents of traditional authority will, if properly investigated, turn out to be reasonable, and, in all essentials, consistent. There can therefore be no question of a clash between reason and traditional authority: the two cannot be opposed.[2]

1. On patristic exegesis, see further R.P.C. Hanson, *Allegory and Event: A study of the Sources and Significance of Origen's Interpretation of Scripture* (London: SCM Press, 1959), and 'Biblical Exegesis in the Early Church', in P. Ackroyd and C.F. Evans (eds.), *Cambridge History of the Bible. I. From the Beginnings to Jerome* (Cambridge: Cambridge University Press, 1970), pp. 412-53; M. Wiles, *The Divine Apostle: The Interpretation of St. Paul's Epistles in the Early Church* (Cambridge: Cambridge University Press, 1967); G.W.H. Lampe, 'The Exposition and Exegesis of Scripture. I: to Gregory the Great', in G.W.H. Lampe (ed.), *Cambridge History of the Bible. II. The West from the Fathers to the Reformation* (Cambridge: Cambridge University Press, 1969), pp. 155-82; A. Louth, *Discerning the Mystery: An Essay on the Nature of Theology* (Oxford: Clarendon Press, 1983); P. Gorday, *Principles of Patristic Exegesis: Romans 9–11 in Origen, John Chrysostom and Augustine* (New York: Edwin Mellen Press, 1983). For philosophical exegesis, see R. Lamberton, *Homer the Theologian* (Berkeley: University of California Press, 1986); D. Sedley, 'Philosophical Allegiance in the Graeco-Roman World', in M. Griffin and J. Barnes (eds.), *Philosophia Togata: Essays on Philosophy and Roman Society* (Oxford: Clarendon Press, 1989); and for rabbinic exegesis compared with other traditions, P.S. Alexander, 'Quid Athenis et Hierosolymis? Rabbinic Midrash and Hermeneutics in the Graeco-Roman World', in P.R. Davies and R.I. White (eds.), *A Tribute to Geza Vermes: Essays on Jewish and Christian Literature and History* (JSOTSup, 100; Sheffield: JSOT Press, 1990), pp. 101-24. G.E.M. de Sainte Croix ('The Early Christian Attitude to Property and Slavery', in D. Baker [ed.], *Studies in Church History*, XII [Oxford: Basil Blackwell, 1975], pp. 1-38) takes further the exegesis of 'sell all you have'.

2. A.H. Armstrong, 'Pagan and Christian Tradition', *Studia Patristica* 18 (1984), p. 430.

3. *Irenaeus*

After this much preface, my first example comes from the first Father—that is, the first Christian known to have left a corpus of theological writing—Irenaeus of Lyons. He wrote during the reign of Antoninus Pius (138–61 CE) who, according to Gibbon, 'diffused order and tranquillity over the greatest part of the earth',[1] and whose high-minded successor, M. Aurelius, authorized a particularly nasty set of martyrdoms at Lyons in 177. What Irenaeus has to say about government is not the main focus of his argument, and perhaps the more interesting for that: he can move rapidly through arguments he thinks will be acceptable.

Irenaeus wants to refute those heretics who claim that the OT is not a revelation of the true God, and has nothing to do with the NT. He argues that Christ 'recapitulates', or as it were replays, the experience of Adam. So there are correspondences everywhere between OT and NT, and one of these is in the devil's lies. The devil told a great lie to Adam and Eve: 'if you eat the fruit of the tree, you shall not die'. Correspondingly he told a great lie to Christ: 'all this [the kingdoms of the world] was given to me, and I give it to whom I will'.[2] Irenaeus cites Prov. 21.1 and 8.15-16, but above all Romans 13, to prove that power on earth comes from God.

Romans 13 is the key text for patristic authors reflecting on the exercise and acknowledgement of power. It is usually accompanied by 'render unto Caesar' (Mt. 22.21); and it is not contrasted with the very different perspective of Revelation 13, partly for the general reasons discussed in section 2 above, and partly because Revelation was a text used with hesitation, if at all.[3] Irenaeus cites Rom. 13.1: 'Let every soul be subject to the authorities set above; for there is no authority except under God, and those there are were ordained by God'. Some people, he says, have the nerve to say Paul is talking

1. Gibbon, *Decline and Fall of the Roman Empire*, ch. 3.
2. Lk. 4.6; Irenaeus, *Against Heresies* 5.24.1. I. de Lyon, *Contre les Hérésies* (ed. A. Rousseau and L. Doutreleau; Sources Chrétiennes, 263-64; Paris: Cerf. 1969).
3. D. Kyrtatas, 'The Transformation of the Text: The Reception of John's Revelation', in A. Cameron (ed.), *History as Text* (London: Gerald Duckworth, 1989), pp. 144-62.

about angelic powers and invisible rulers: that cannot be right, for Paul goes on to tell us to pay taxes, an instruction confirmed by Jesus when he ordered tax to be paid for himself and Peter (Mt. 17.27). God invented earthly rule because fallen humanity behaved so savagely: if people would not fear God, let them at least fear 'the sword set in full view'. This is why Paul says 'he does not carry the sword for nothing, for he is God's servant, who takes vengeance on the evildoer'. So Irenaeus concludes (5.24.2), 'earthly rule was established by God for the benefit of the gentiles—not by the devil, who is never peaceful and does not wish to see the peoples live in peace—so that people, fearing this rule, should not devour one another like fish, but by the establishment of the laws should restrain the manifold injustice of the gentiles'.

But Irenaeus does not offer a blanket authorization of all earthly government as a peace enforcement agency. Magistrates will be punished, not for what they have done justly and lawfully, but 'for what they have done to subvert justice unfairly, impiously, against the law and tyrannically'. Irenaeus does not discuss the question whether human law might itself conflict with divine law. Nor are rulers necessarily good because God has given them power. God creates human beings and the rulers appropriate to them: 'some (kings) are given for the amendment and benefit of their subjects and the preservation of justice, some for fear and punishment and reproach, some for mockery and insolence and arrogance'.[1]

Irenaeus makes no direct comment on the rule of Rome: what he says could apply to the kings of Israel and Judah as much as to the Roman emperor. What interests him is the fundamental question of one human being's rule over others. He does not envisage Christians as agents of government, only as its subjects: yet what he says about power proves to be a very flexible response.

4. Origen

My second example is Origen, writing a century later than Irenaeus, but partly in response to an argument mid-way between the two. The philosopher Celsus, probably in the early third century,[2] had accused

---

1. Irenaeus, *Against Heresies*, 5.24.
2. H. Chadwick, *Origen: Contra Celsum* (Cambridge: Cambridge University

Christians of failing to support the emperor. In the second and third centuries Christianity had been climbing the social scale:[1] Origen's fellow-Christians in Alexandria and Palestine included many people who could have taken on civic duties or served in the *militia*. But they refused—even, Celsus charged, if it meant letting the barbarians invade and wipe out both Rome and Christianity. We need to remember here the very strong traditional connection between citizenship and fighting for one's city—the basic reason for refusing citizenship to women and slaves. Christian peacefulness, a selling-point for the Apologists, was a mixed blessing.

Origen accepts that Christianity could not have spread unless the world had been at peace.[2] He held that Christians are forbidden all use of force, even in defence of themselves or others.[3] It follows that Christians cannot engage in defence or law enforcement: again, we need to remember that the whole point of holding *imperium* was authority to order the taking of life in war or punishment. Origen acknowledges that an independent Christian state could not survive, because Christianity does not operate through political power. God allowed Rome to end the existence of the independent Jewish state to show that the old dispensation had ended. The Roman empire now performed the necessary tasks of defence and law enforcement; Jesus was born under Augustus because the warring kingdoms were then united under one empire, so men were not forced to fight.

But, Origen argues, Christians do defend the empire by their prayers, like those Graeco-Roman priests who abstain from fighting; and if the whole empire were to be converted to Christianity it would not, as Celsus claimed, succumb as the Jewish state had done: it would be defended by God, just as God has ensured that very few Christians have fallen victim to persecution.[4] He thinks this an unlikely outcome. Origen himself was a victim of persecution, dying of the delayed effects of torture and imprisonment. He had to answer the question[5]

Press, 1953); J. Hoffmann, *Celsus on the True Doctrine* (Oxford: Clarendon Press, 1987).

1.   D.E. Groh, 'Upper-class Christians in Tertullian's Africa: Some Observations', *Studia Patristica* 14 (1976), pp. 41-47.

2.   Origen, *Against Celsus* 2.30.

3.   Origen, *Commentary on Matthew* 26.52.

4.   Origen, *Against Celsus* 8.69-70, 73-75.

5.   Origen, *Commentary on Romans* 9.29.

how we can believe that God gave the power that wars upon the faith. There is a short answer: God gives us many powers—for instance, those of the body—which we can abuse. Do Christians owe obedience to this power? Paul will tell us: Romans 13.1 again.

Origen, characteristically, finds it important that Paul says every soul must be subject, not every spirit. He sees a hierarchy of body, animating soul, and spirit which is in contact with God. Those who have the image and superscription of Caesar in themselves, who have money and possessions and worldly concerns, must render to Caesar. And Caesar has his uses. The powers that be are ministers of God in that they require obedience to the moral law: the Apostolic Council[1] needed to legislate only on those matters not covered by human law. Nevertheless, human law—for instance, the law forbidding Christian assemblies—may be tyrannical, inspired by the devil.[2] If so, the powers are not acting as God's ministers, and Christians must not obey the unjust law. To do so would, presumably, be a clear case of subjecting the spirit. But this disobedience does not license active resistance, returning evil for evil: it requires endurance of punishment.[3]

5. *Hippolytus and Lactantius*

The duty of obedience—this side idolatry—was affirmed even by those who saw far more than specific laws as Satanic.[4] Resistance literature (such as the *Sibylline Oracles*), Roman self-criticism, and the

---

1. Acts 15.29.
2. Origen, *Against Celsus* 1.1.
3. For a more extended discussion of Origen on politics and law, see W. Banner, 'Origen and Natural Law Concepts', *Dumbarton Oaks Papers* (1954), 8.52-82; and G.E. Caspary, *Politics and Exegesis: Origen and the Two Swords* (Berkeley: University of California Press, 1979).
4. For this tradition, see Cadoux, *The Early Church*, pp. 344-48; Paschoud, *Roma Aeterna*, pp. 169-77; Frend, *Religion*; E. Pagels, 'The Fall of the Angels: An Attack on Roman Imperial Power?', *HTR* 78 (1985), pp. 301-25, and *Adam, Eve and the Serpent* (New York: Random House, 1988). For 'resistance literature', see H. Fuchs, *Die geistige Widerstand gegen Rom* (Berlin: de Gruyter, 1938); J.W. Swain, 'The Theory of the Four Monarchies: Opposition History under the Roman Empire', *Classical Philology* 35 (1940), pp. 1-21; and W. Goez, *Translatio Imperii* (Tübingen: Mohr, 1958).

long-standing philosophical critique of imperialism, all nourished Christian hostility to the empire. Melito of Sardis, urging Marcus Aurelius to be sympathetic to Christians, argued that Christianity 'began with Augustus and has grown to full stature along with the Empire',[1] which has flourished accordingly. Hippolytus, a militant and finally schismatic leader of the Roman church in the late second and early third centuries, gave this synchronism a sinister meaning. Christ summons the faithful from all nations:

> the kingdom which now, by the activity of Satan, rules, has imitated this, and it too collects the noblest from all nations and prepares them for war, calling them Romans. That is why the first census took place under Augustus, when the Lord was born in Bethlehem, so that the people of this world could be enrolled by an earthly king and called Romans, and those who trust in the heavenly king should be named Christians.[2]

Hippolytus identified Rome with the fourth beast of Daniel, permitted to rampage, yet doomed to destruction by the fifth empire of Christ and his church. But, in the same Daniel commentary,[3] he expounds Romans 13 and urges obedience. Like Rastafarians living in 'Babylon' now, those who awaited the downfall of the evil empire continued to live in it, subsidize it by their taxes and obey its laws and magistrates unless there was direct conflict with obedience to God. Ideological resistance does not move into political resistance.

The most thoroughgoing challenge to the Roman empire comes from Lactantius, in the *Divine Institutes*.[4] He held the chair of rhetoric at Diocletian's court at Nicomedia, and may well have written some of the *Institutes* while in the emperor's service: we do not know how much. Diocletian's court was the setting for a philosophical onslaught on Christianity, which appears to have been a trigger of the

1. Eusebius, *History of the Church* 26.7.
2. Hippolytus, *Commentary on Daniel* 4.9.2; cited by Cadoux, *The Early Church*, pp. 344, 405.
3. *Commentary on Daniel* 3.23; cited by Cadoux, *The Early Church*, pp. 352-53.
4. N.H. Baynes, review of K.M. Setton, *Christian Attitude towards the Emperor in the Fourth Century Especially as Shown in Addresses to the Emperor* (Studies in History, Economics and Public Law, 482; New York: Columbia University Press, 1941) in *JRS* 34 (1944), pp. 135-40; E. A. Isichei, *Political Thinking*; T.D. Barnes, 'Lactantius and Constantine', *JRS* 63 (1973), pp. 29-46; J.L. Creed, *Lactantius de mortibus persecutorum* (Oxford: Clarendon Press, 1984).

Great Persecution; Lactantius's main purpose is to show that only a Christian commonwealth can meet the philosophic requirement for justice. Society as it is now organized is, he says, fundamentally unjust, because of its huge disparities of wealth and power (5.15): it can be transformed only by adherence to Christian precepts and by the spirit of brotherhood. The success of one nation entails the downfall and suffering of others. To claim that power is legal is no defence, for human laws permit conduct which God's law forbids, notably the taking of life in war or punishment. Human laws vary because they are motivated by self-interest.

> The Romans themselves demonstrate how far distant is profit from justice: by declaring war through the *fetiales*, and doing injuries in proper legal form, and always taking other people's property, they have acquired the whole world (6.9.2-7).

Power is not a necessary remedy in a fallen world, but a manifestation of our fallen condition. God created us as social beings (6.10), but the avarice and ambition of some has led them to seize power and defend their interests by legislation. The devil inspires their wish to rule by the sword (6.4.21).

6. *Eusebius*

After a flight in time of persecution, Lactantius is found in the service of Constantine, whom he lavishly praises in prefaces to books 1 and 7 of the *Institutes*. God, he says, is guiding Constantine to restore justice. It is not clear how much of the Roman empire was then under Constantine's control: for a first response to the Christian empire we turn to Eusebius. Eusebius was a follower of Origen, who had thought it unlikely that the empire would become Christian; and indeed, by Origen's standards, it did not, since it continued to rely on military strength. But in Eusebius's starry-eyed report of the Council of Nicaea, we need not see only the courtier. European history in 1989–90 has reminded us of the astonished gratitude which can be felt when a seemingly indestructible tyranny changes for the better. There had to be a theological response to a Christian emperor—or at least to an emperor who affirmed allegiance to Christ.

Eusebius too draws on philosophical tradition, integrating salvation history with Stoic teaching on the good ruler and with a Platonist vision of the ordered universe. Monarchy and monotheism, he says, go together. Monarchy under Augustus replaced warring polyarchy, just at the time when Christ put an end to polytheism. Peace under a Christian emperor fulfills the OT prophecies of the peaceable kingdom. Constantine himself ranks just below Christ, inspired by the *Logos* to lead his subjects to the truth, his gaze fixed on the heavenly kingdom which is the archetype of that he rules below. The empire will expand to convert the entire human race, and Constantine, fighting at God's command, will offer to God the souls of its people. Church leaders are ministers of the sacraments, and provide a theological *consilium*.[1]

From the perspective of the late twentieth century this is scandalous, a negation of Christ's teaching on power, perhaps the moment at which the church abandoned any pretext of following Christ.[2] From the perspective of the early fourth century it is a reinterpretation of standard philosophical teaching about the good king and his relationship to the One God, so uncontroversial and so convenient that it provided Byzantium with a political theory which lasted for centuries, undisturbed by the theological conflicts that provoked sudden and violent replacements of God's viceroy.[3] Yet it survived only with an important modification.

Constantius II, son of Constantine, re-established monarchy by eliminating his brothers, and tried to establish true monotheism: in other words he was an Arian sympathizer, to many of his subjects a heretic and, to Lucifer of Cagliari and Hilary of Poitiers, Antichrist in person. 'Render unto Caesar' was duly reinterpreted for Christian

---

1. For extended discussions of Eusebius's political theology, see W.E. Seston, 'Constantine as a Bishop', *JRS* 37 (1947), pp. 127-31; F.E. Cranz, 'Kingdom and Polity in Eusebius of Caesarea', *HTR* 45 (1952), pp. 47-66; N.H. Baynes, 'Eusebius and the Christian Empire', in *Byzantine Studies and Other Essays* (London: Athlone Press, 1955); E.A. Isichei, *Political Thinking*; T.D. Barnes, *Constantine and Eusebius* (Cambridge, MA: Harvard University Press, 1981); R. Lane Fox, *Pagans and Christians* (London: Viking, 1986); D.M. Nicol, 'Byzantium', in J.M. Burns (ed.), *Cambridge History of Mediaeval Political Thought* (Cambridge: Cambridge University Press, 1988), pp. 51-79.

2. A. Kee, *Constantine versus Christ: The Triumph of Ideology* (London: SCM Press, 1982); A. Cameron, 'Constantinus Christianus', *JRS* 73 (1983), pp. 184-90.

3. Cameron, 'The Construction of Court Ritual'; Nicol, 'Byzantium'.

Caesars, by none other than Hosius of Cordoba, Constantine's first ecclesiastical adviser:

> God has put the kingdom into your hands, to us he has entrusted the concerns of the church. Just as one who steals your power opposes God who ordains it, so you too should fear to become guilty of a great crime if you draw church concerns to yourself. It is written, Render to Caesar what is Caesar's, and to God what is God's. So we are not allowed to rule the earth, nor are you, O king, allowed to offer sacrifice.[1]

This is the doctrine known as 'separate spheres', beloved of more recent politicians, and it generated new problems, for of course the spheres were not separate. Patristic writers before Constantine had taken the line that government was Caesar's business, not to be undertaken by Christians, though there were probably Christians who did so. After Constantine's conversion, the ruling classes were likely to see the light, especially when they had the option (later withdrawn) of avoiding curial duties by hasty ordination. Christians in government then had the problem of obeying the church's teaching on mercy and peace without (just as Celsus had said) causing a rocketing crime-rate and barbarian invasion. Nor could the church authorities stay clear of Caesar's business, for doctrine had become part of politics. Successive church councils, including Nicaea, tried to restrict lobbying to charitable purposes, but church leaders were often fighting to survive a mix of theological and political charges, and it mattered who got the leading bishoprics. Heresy meant exile for individuals; where its support was strong, it meant riots and eventually war. By the time of Justinian, an emperor could lose his throne, or much of his territory, for taking the wrong line on Chalcedon, or even by an attempt to reconcile.

Peace and public order were undoubtedly Caesar's business; and the other side of Caesar's coin was that the church had, thanks to Constantine, far more property and power to dispute. The *Liber Pontificalis*[2] displays the spectacular difference made to the Roman church by Constantine's endowments. Ammianus, who disapproves of Christians unless they are modest country bishops, records with

---

1. Athanasius, *History of the Arian Controversy* 44; PG 25.745.
2. R. Davis, *The Book of Pontiffs (Liber Pontificalis)* (Translated Texts for Historians; Liverpool: Liverpool University Press, 1989), pp. 16-26.

quiet glee[1] the election of 366, which left 137 dead and Damasus bishop Rome. But good may come out of riots: a similar problem in Milan, in 373, led to the election of Ambrose.

7. *Ambrose*

Ambrose, son and grandson of praetorian prefects of Gaul and himself governor of Aemilia, knew all about exercising power.[2] By the time he had finished, 'render unto Caesar' covered much less than it had. For a start, 'It is written, God's things to God and Caesar's to Caesar: palaces belong to the emperor, churches to the bishop'.[3] Ambrose made this claim because he did not want to concede a church to an Arian congregation, but he was not one to underestimate real estate. He consolidated the Christian presence in Milan, as Damasus did in Rome, with a programme of building churches and martyr shrines.[4] Church funds—the treasury of the poor—also belong to God: this meant that major fortunes could pass out of the control of leading families and the service of the state, a particular annoyance when they were donated by heiresses.[5]

But the most important claim is, 'The emperor is a son of the church...he is within the church, not above the church'.[6] This is not just a western assertion: it is made by Ambrose's contemporary John Chrysostom. Reassuring the people of Antioch,[7] he tells them that their bishop, who has gone to ask pardon from the emperor, is himself a ruler of even higher rank than the emperor: even kings

1. Ammianus 27.3.12-15.
2. J-R. Palanque, *Saint Ambroise et l'empire romain* (Paris: de Beccard, 1933).
3. Ambrose, *Letter* 20.19.
4. R. Krautheimer, *Three Christian Capitals: Topography and Politics* (Berkeley: University of California Press, 1983); B. Ward-Perkins, *From Classical Antiquity to the Middle Ages: Urban Public Building in North and Central Italy. AD 300–850* (Oxford: Clarendon Press, 1984).
5. A. Yarbrough, 'Christianisation in the Fourth Century: The Example of Roman Women', *Church History* 45 (1976), pp. 149-63; E.A. Clark, *Jerome, John Chrysostom and Friends* (New York: Edwin Mellen Press, 1979), and *The Life of Melania the Younger* (New York: Edwin Mellen Press, 1984); J. Drijvers, 'Virginity and Asceticism in Late Roman Elites', in J. Blok and P. Mason (eds.), *Sexual Asymmetry* (Amsterdam: Gieben, 1987), pp. 241-73.
6. Ambrose, *Letter* 21.36.
7. John Chrysostom, *Homily on the Statues* 3.6.

are subject to his judgment. Perhaps only the consciously orthodox Theodosius I would have acknowledged this claim to the point of accepting prophetic rebuke, and even temporary excommunication, for political decisions that others have seen as forgivable or even right, and perhaps only Ambrose would have dared to do it to him. (Not even Ambrose turned the emperor away from the church door, a very influential improvement on the story which appears twenty years later).[1] But the basic position was restated a century later, by Pope Gelasius in his letter of 494 to Anastasius:[2]

> There are two [powers], august emperor, by which this world is chiefly ruled: the sacred authority of the priests, and the kingly power. Of these the influence of the priests is greater inasmuch as they must render account, in the last judgment, for the kings of men. You are aware, most clement son, that although you surpass the human race in rank, yet you bow the neck devoutly to those who preside over divine matters.[3]

It has been pointed out[4] that the distinction between 'authority' and 'power' cannot be conveyed in Greek. But the distinction between imperial and priestly power was clearly seen in the Greek-speaking empire, and was reaffirmed when an emperor's intervention in matters of church government or doctrine was less than welcome.[5] Even a Byzantine emperor, crowned by the Patriarch, enthroned beneath an icon of Christ, allowed to take communion in the sanctuary, had no authority to preach the word of God.

Many scholars have seen a difference between the eastern and western empires on the question of church and state. They point to Constantius II, who (allegedly) told recalcitrant western bishops that

---

1. Theodoret, *HE* 5.18.
2. J. Nelson, 'Gelasius I's Doctrine of Responsibility', *JTS* ns 18 (1967), pp. 154-62.
3. Gelasius, *Letter* 12.2. The first two sentences read in the original: 'duo quippe sunt, imperator auguste, quibus principaliter mundus hic regitur: auctoritas sacrata pontificum et regalis potestas. In quibus tanto gravius est pondus sacerdotum quanto etiam pro ipsis regibus hominum in divino reddituri sunt examine rationem.' (A. Thiel, *Epistulae pontificum Romanorum genuinae* [Braunsberg, 1868], 12.2).
4. J. Nelson, 'Symbols in Context: Rulers' Inauguration Rituals in Byzantium and the West in the Early Middle Ages', in D. Baker (ed.), *Studies in Church History*, 13 (Oxford: Basil Blackwell, 1976), XIII, pp. 97-120.
5. E. Barker, *Social and Political Thought in Byzantium* (Oxford: Clarendon Press, 1957), pp. 86-88.

the bishops in Syria accepted his pronouncements as canons of the church.[1] They sense a greater western wariness about 'the world' and its unchristian culture,[2] or a different perception of holiness in relation to church hierarchies and social structures,[3] or a simple practical distinction between Old Rome, which the emperor had left to the Pope, and New Rome, where emperor and patriarch lived side by side.[4] But I do not think this results in a greater eastern willingness to accept that the emperor is right on matters of theology.

8. The Dilemma of Imperium

How, then, did the Fathers judge those who exercised *imperium*, ordering torture and death in the course of their duties? Cautious approaches can be seen in the church councils under Constantine: magistrates should abstain from communion for the year they hold office, or should report to the bishop on arrival and follow his advice.[5] Eusebius distinguishes two ways of Christian perfection: there are those who do not involve themselves with marriage and property, and those in a secondary state of perfection (an odd concept) who marry and engage in civic life. For them there are 'practical rules for fighting in a just war'.[6] Basil, asking for advice in the 370s, says: 'Our fathers did not count killing in battle as murder, I think so as to pardon those who defended purity and piety. But it may be right to advise those with unclean hands to abstain from communion only, for three years'.[7] Basil's historical claim is dubious: several church orders[8] deny baptism to serving soldiers, and both Siricius and Innocent of Rome, in the late fourth and early fifth centuries, forbade ordination of those in the imperial service (civil or military) and

---

1. Greenslade, *Church and State*.
2. Frend, *Religion*; Markus, *Saeculum*.
3. P. Brown, 'Eastern and Western Christendom in Late Antiquity: A Parting of the Ways', in *Studies in Church History*, XIII, pp. 1-24.
4. E. Patlagean, *Structures sociales, famille, chrétienté à Byzance* (London: Variorum Reprints, 1981).
5. Elvira canon 56, with Lane Fox, *Pagans and Christians*, pp. 664-65; Arles canon 7.
6. Eusebius, *Demonstration of the Gospel* 1.8.
7. Basil, *Letter* 188.13.
8. Cadoux, *The Early Church*, pp. 432-33.

excommunicated those who had done penance for service but returned
to it. But this is not an outright condemnation of the taking of life, for
baptism and ordination entail receiving communion. Many Christians
of this period (like Constantine himself) postponed baptism until they
thought they could live up to Christian standards.

The most interesting response again comes from Ambrose, who had
in his time ordered soldiers to kill, and executioners to kill or to torture. His biographer says that he did not usually employ torture, but
did so when trying to convince the people of Milan that he was the
wrong choice as bishop. But there is an ominous comment in *On Cain
and Abel*: 'Confession saves punishment. In secular justice, those who
deny are tortured on the rack, and the judge experiences some pity for
those who confess' (2.27). Ambrose was consulted by a troubled
magistrate, Studius: if he had to use the death penalty, was he excommunicated? Ambrose replies that Studius has the authority of Paul to
carry the sword as God's agent of retribution. The church cannot ex-
communicate him, though there are Christian groups (presumably
Novatians) who would. He should aim for mercy in the hope of the
criminal's amendment; if after execution he feels bound to abstain
from communion for a while, that is admirable, but the choice is his.

> Our elders preferred to show indulgence to judges, so that while their
> sword was feared, the fury of crime should be repressed, not aroused. If
> communion is denied, the punishment of criminals will seem to be
> avenged (*Letter* 25).

This might well seem the only possible solution in a fallen world
governed by Christians—and Theodosius required[1] that all those in
the imperial service should be sons of the church. But a few decades
later we find a cry of outrage in a pamphlet ascribed to Pelagius:[2]

> Christ stood in humility before the judgment seat: you sit there, propped
> up by pride and arrogance, to judge those who stand before you...In
> your sight the bodies of men, human beings like you, are beaten with
> leaden whips, broken with cudgels, torn with metal claws, burned in the
> flames. Christian compassion can witness this, Christian eyes can bear to
> see it, and not only to see it but to give the order to torture, in the pride of

---

1. Theodosius, *Theodosian Code*, 16.10.21.
2. J. Morris, 'Pelagian Literature', *JTS* ns 16 (1965), pp. 26-60; J.H.W.G.
Liebeschuetz, 'Did the Pelagian Movement have Social Aims?', *Historia* 12 (1963),
pp. 227-41.

power!. . . You entertain your guests with the story, telling them how each man died and after what tortures, and how you flung the corpse on the ground before the people. But you don't want your guests to have the horrors at dinner: you say you are bound by the laws. A moment ago you were vaunting yourself as a hearer of the Gospel—or as a barrister disputing the law of Christ? (*On Riches* 6; *PL* suppl. 1.1385-86).

9. *Augustine*

So there were still voices of protest challenging the acceptance of power. The pamphlet I have just quoted comes out of the distress and recrimination which followed the Gothic sack of Rome in 411. South Italy, Sicily, and North Africa filled with refugees. Among them were radical Christians, arguing as Pelagius did that the church had sold out to the world: coventional politeness and social obligation had simply been renamed 'Christian humility' and 'Christian charity'; the church had identified with the rich and powerful denounced in the Gospels; and yes, you do have to sell all you have. Julian, bishop of Eclanum, did sell his estates for the relief of refugees. On the other hand, non-Christians argued that Christians had brought about the fall of Rome on the spiritual level, by violating the *pax deorum* which had made Rome great, and on the practical level by diverting the resources which could have bought off the Goths once more. One who spoke with particular feeling was Volusianus, uncle of Melania, who had been struggling to sell all she had (equivalent to the holdings of a multi-national corporation) while the Goths were at the gate. Conventional Christians, out of their depth, referred both parties to Augustine, bishop of Hippo. The eventual result was the greatest work of Christian political philosophy, the *City of God*.[1]

Augustine's career brings together the themes of this paper. He was a local boy who made good by the rhetorical talent which took him from Thagaste in North Africa to Carthage, Rome, Milan; when he renounced a secular career, it was the same talent that made the church at Hippo force him into ordination, and his letters show

---

1.   See P. Brown, *Augustine of Hippo: A Biography* (London: Faber & Faber, 1967), chapter 26, and *Religion and Society in the Age of Augustine* (London: Faber & Faber, 1972), part 2, and 'Political Society', in R.A. Markus (ed.), *Augustine: A Collection of Critical Essays* (New York: Doubleday, 1972), pp. 311-35; and above all, Markus, *Saeculum*.

him using all his acquired skills of persuasion and lobbying. Ambrose converted him, at Milan, by demonstrating that the Christian scriptures were not inferior in thought and style, but could be interpreted in accordance with philosophical tradition. Augustine's earliest Christian perspective on the exercise of power[1] shows confidence that human law has a necessary role in preserving peace and justice: it is imperfect in relation to divine law, but that is inevitable, and Christians who aspire to perfection are not forced to do what human law concedes, i.e., to take life in some circumstances.

In the 390s, like many of his contemporaries, he saw salvation history unrolling before his eyes: the victories—military and political—of Theodosius over paganism seemed the fulfilment of prophecy, and Christian Rome the enduring kingdom.[2] But this confidence could not last. Augustine's reading of Paul convinced him that this world is not even an imperfect copy of the divine order: such order as survives is fragmented and distorted by sin, and God's grace is needed for us to achieve anything in the way of peace. Political history taught the same lesson. Augustine remarks, even as he defends the concept of a just war, that unless you actually are an OT king, it is very difficult to be sure you are fighting at God's command. The peaceable kingdom has not come, and we shall not see it on this earth. Augustine comments on Ps. 45.10, 'taking away war even to the ends of the earth':

> We do not yet see this fulfilled. There are wars still, between the nations for kingdom, between sects, between Jews, pagans, Christians, heretics; there are wars and wars will abound, some contending for truth and others for falsehood.[3]

Nor is it the case that God's promises to the seed of Abraham are restricted to citizens of the Roman empire.[4]

So when Augustine had to respond to the Gothic sack of Rome in 410, he was not inclined to see it as an event of eschatological significance. His sermon entitled *On the Destruction of the City*[5] in

---

1.   Augustine, *On Free Will* 1.32-51 (CSEL, 74).
2.   Paschoud, *Roma Aeterna*, pp. 222-33; Markus, *Saeculum*, chapter 2; A.-M. Palmer, *Prudentius on the Martyrs* (Oxford: Clarendon Press, 1989), pp. 21-39.
3.   Augustine, *Enarrationes in Psalmos* 45.13 (CChr Ser. Lat. 38.527).
4.   Augustine, *Letters* 93.22, 199. 46-8.
5.   CChr Ser. Lat. 46.249-62.

fact argues that the city was not destroyed. By comparison with Sodom, whose people went to perdition and which vanished from the face of the earth, Rome has endured only the usual horrors of war, and even those were mitigated because the barbarians respected churches. Many escaped by flight, or by death which took them to God. Nor was Rome condemned for sinfulness: many good people— good by human standards—lived there, but if Daniel could confess his sins to the Lord, how much more should any of us!

In his correspondence, and in *City of God*, Augustine refuses to see the sack of Rome as fulfilment of prophecy. Those who thought the fourth empire had now fallen, and the end of the world was at hand, were referred to Jerome's commentary on Daniel; Augustine does not commit himself on that, or Antichrist, or the Restrainer of 2 Thessalonians.[1] But how was he to answer the challenge that Christianity had destroyed Rome, or that Rome had corrupted Christianity?

Augustine does not have much trouble with the claim that Christianity has ended an empire uniquely approved by the gods—not even when he is addressing Romans who do not interpret history by the light of the OT. He knew the persistent Roman belief that the nation was degenerate and the rot had set in (at any moment from the Punic Wars to the speaker's own time)[2] and the Roman tradition of 'disasters survived' (as much a part of Roman national myth as 'the British muddle through'). He set Orosius to research past calamities in detail to prove that Christianity had not caused worse ones. Orosius was evidently the sort of graduate student that every supervisor dreads, but he does say something of his own—notably that Christ was at birth registered in a Roman census[3]. His pride in his own Roman identity, combined with willingness to debunk Roman claims to special greatness, shows the way for western Christians to adapt to non-Roman rulers.[4]

Is Rome, then, Babylon, the great whore of Revelation, a corrupt and deluded city that worships false gods and persecutes the righteous

---

1. *City of God* 20.19, 23; Augustine, *Letters* 198-99.
2. R. MacMullen, *Corruption and the Decline of Rome* (New Haven: Yale University Press, 1988).
3. Orosius, *History against the Pagans* 6.22.5
4. E.A. Isichei, *Political Thinking*, chapter 7; R.A. Markus, *From Augustine to Gregory the Great* (Paper IV; London: Variorum Reprints, 1983).

with its imperial power? That would be too simple an equation. Augustine saw a straightforward historical link between the two: armed with Jerome's translation of Eusebius's *Chronicle*, he knew that Rome was founded when Babylon fell. The western empire of Rome was equalled only by the eastern empire of Babylon; Babylon is the first Rome, Rome the second Babylon; 'through her it pleased God to reduce the world by War, and to pacify it far and wide, drawing it into one association of state and law'.[1] Augustine does not underestimate the value or the cost of empire. Peace, even imperfect human peace, is a blessing: that is why Jeremiah tells Israel to pray for the peace of Babylon. But there is never any real security; the 'great western Babylon' achieved unity of language at massive human cost. Empires depend on the *libido dominandi*, the lust to dominate, which is the distortion of human relationships resulting from the Fall. Both Israel and Rome were founded by fratricides, Israel by Cain and Rome by Romulus.

In the fallen world, power relationships have replaced the natural hierarchies and willing co-operation that were God's original plan. The *de facto* hierarchy of master over slave and ruler over subject is both an expression of sin and a remedy for the crimes which result from sin. All of us, not just the gentiles, need the fear of the sword to help us in the struggle against sin: many of Augustine's contemporaries thought he departed from tradition by his lack of confidence in the baptized Christian's ability to withstand sin.[2] Earthly power is given by God, though God alone knows why some power-holders are permitted to survive, and piety is no guarantee of success (5.21). Christians who are not in power must not be too proud to submit—as regards this life—to those whom God has allowed to govern; as Paul promises, those in power will confer praise on Christians, either by acknowledging their good conduct or by offering them martyrdom.[3] The best possible outcome is that the truly good, who desire to do God's will, should also possess the skill of governing; the next best is government by those of earthly virtue, whose desire is for the

---

1. *City of God* 18.22.
2. E. Pagels, 'The Politics of Paradise: Augustine's Exegesis of Genesis 1–3 Versus that of John Chrysostom', *HTR* 78 (1985), pp. 67-95, and *Adam, Eve and the Serpent*.
3. Augustine, *On Romans* 72–73 (CSEL, 84.44-46).

wellbeing of the human community. But 'what does it matter under whose rule a dying man lives, so long as those who rule do not compel him to commit impiety or injustice?' (5.17.11).

Again, there is a structural parallel between Rome and Babylon. Abraham came out of Babylon, the Church comes out of Rome. In that sense Rome may stand for Babylon:

> There is a city which is called Babylon. That city is the association of all the lost, from east to west; she holds the earthly kingdom. In conformity with that city there is a state which we now see aging and declining. She was our first mother, in her we were born. We have acknowledged another father, God; we have acknowledged another mother, the heavenly Jerusalem, who is the holy church; her portion on earth is as a stranger. (*Exposition of the Psalms* 26.2.18.)

Augustine accepted that Rome had shown striking examples of human virtue, which had received their reward already in the form of earthly power. But he no longer thought that unique Roman virtue, transmuted by Christianity, had produced the fifth and eternal empire of Christian Rome. Empires come and go, and none enjoys special divine favour or disfavour. What matters is the people who live in them: not a Christian empire, but an empire that contains Christians.

Those whose desire is for God are citizens of God's city, the heavenly Jerusalem; those whose desire is for the things of this world are citizens of the earthly city, Babylon, which also cannot be equated with any existing political order. Only God knows who belongs to which city: we cannot assume that those who are 'about God's business' belong to the heavenly city or that those engaged in government belong to the earthly one. Augustine was several times consulted by men who thought of resigning their power: he urged them to stay in the job for the sake of peace and order.[1] God, he argues, allows exceptions to the rule 'Thou shalt not kill'. It is permissible on God's orders (though no one outside the OT can be certain of having them) or in obedience to properly constituted authority, as an instrument, 'representing the power of the state in accordance with its laws' (*City of God* 1.21). This, we can hardly forget, is the Nuremberg defence.

But the power-holder cannot expect to be happy: the judge cries 'Deliver me from my necessities' (*City of God* 19.6). He must not cut himself off from human society; it is not a sin to do the job that

---

1. Augustine, *Letters* 138, 185.

society requires of him, though he knows he may wrongly convict by torturing the innocent into false confession, or acquit the guilty who can stand pain better. The vital point is that he has no wish to harm, any more than the soldier who does his duty.[1] It is a solution to the needs of a crumbling western empire, then as now. No one can expect to be free of sin, someone must keep the peace, so do your job within the existing laws and try to serve God. Thus it becomes possible for Forces chaplains to bless new weapons of destruction, in the attempt to preserve imperfect and fragmented human peace.

> So, since the two cities are mixed together, we too make use of the peace of Babylon. God's people is so freed from her, by faith, that they make the journey to this [heavenly] city. For that reason the Apostle exhorts the church to pray for her kings and those in power. . . (*City of God* 19.26).

Augustine experienced some of the tensions himself, as he worked for his people in Hippo, trying (for instance) to rescue victims of unlawful slave-trading by threatening the traders with the horrific penalties he hoped they would not in fact suffer.[2] Many bishops had to go further, organizing their cities' defences against Visigoths, Alans and Vandals, using all the skills they had learnt in secular politics. Sidonius Apollinaris, like Ambrose son and grandson of praetorian prefects of Gaul, son-in-law of a short-lived emperor, was praetor of Rome in 468. Four years later, as bishop of Clermont-Ferrand, he was trying to prevent the cession of Auvergne to the Visigoths. Gregory the Great was prefect of Rome in the early 570s; he became a monk, but was sent as papal spokesman to the court at Constantinople, lobbying for support against the Lombards. As Pope he had to organize the defence and supply of Italy, from the papal resources. He acknowledged that he was the emperor's subject, but it must have been peculiarly hard to decide what was Caesar's.[3]

1. Augustine, *Against Faustus* 22.74.

2. Augustine, *Letter* 10* (CSEL, 88).

3. C.E. Stevens, *Sidonius Apollinaris and his Age* (Oxford: Clarendon Press, 1933); J. Richards, *Consul of God: The Life and Times of Gregory the Great* (London: Routledge, 1980); R. Van Dam, *Leadership and Community in Late Antique Gaul* (Berkeley: University of California Press, 1985), chapter 8; J. Herrin, *The Formation of Christendom* (Oxford: Basil Blackwell, 1987), II, p. 4.

10. *Conclusion*

Christians in the first century were almost wholly powerless unless they had an influential contact. Christian emperor and Christian pope in the sixth century held the greatest earthly power. Yet there is a continuity of teaching. The church in a non-Christian empire taught submission to the powers that God allows to rule, provided that they do not require Christians to disobey God's law by worshipping idols or taking life. Refusal to obey human law entailed acceptance of its appalling penalties. Christians could not themselves exercise power because they could not take life: those people who did so could be seen as agents of God, keeping the evil-doer in fear and maintaining a peace which allowed Christianity to flourish, or as agents of a Satanic power which would eventually fall. Either way, they were to be obeyed and subsidized. God, not Christians, would avenge their breaches of their own law.

The church in a Christian empire concluded that God must authorize Christian magistrates also to carry the sword, since government is a necessity in a fallen world. These magistrates must obey the imperfect law of the state and are subject to the moral judgment of the church. No human being, no government, can claim to be God's chosen, vindicated in all its actions and sure of success; Christian Rome endured as a spiritual, not a temporal, power. Empires, however splendid, do not finally matter.

THE FAMILY OF CAESAR AND THE FAMILY OF GOD:
THE IMAGE OF THE EMPEROR IN THE HEIKHALOT LITERATURE

Philip S. Alexander

Rabbi Hosha'yah said: When the Holy One created the first man, the
ministering angels mistook him and wished to say 'Holy' before him. To
what may this be compared? To a king and a governor (ἔπαρχος) who
were in a state coach (*carrucha*). The people of the province wished to say
'Domine!' to the king but they did not know which of the two he was.
What did the king do? He pushed the governor out of the coach so that all
should know that *he* was the governor. So when the Holy One created
the first man, the ministering angels, mistaking him, wished to say 'Holy'
before him. What did the Holy One do? He caused a deep sleep to fall on
him, so that all should know that he was but a man. Thus it is written:
'Cease from man, in whose nostrils is a breath; for how little is he to be
accounted!' (Isa. 2.22) (*Gen. R.* 8.10).

1. *Heikhalot Literature*

It is now widely recognized that the so-called Heikhalot literature has
much to contribute to our understanding of Judaism in late antiquity.
The substantial but amorphous Hebrew and Aramaic writings which
constitute the Heikhalot corpus are very hard to date. They clearly
draw on Palestinian apocalyptic and some of their motifs can be traced
back to second temple times. However, it is unlikely that full-blown
Heikhalot mysticism emerged until the late Talmudic period (i.e.
fourth–fifth centuries CE). Heikhalot mysticism, which flourished in
Palestine and Babylonia, was an esoteric tradition and groups of
adepts met in conventicles to pass on and study its secret lore. They
were much exercised by the Chapter of the Chariot—the vision of
God's throne recorded at the beginning of the book of Ezekiel (Ezek.
1.4-28). But they were not content simply to study Ezekiel's vision in
a passive way: they attempted to replicate the prophet's experience, to

ascend to heaven, to view the throne of glory and to join the angels in the heavenly liturgy. The texts contain detailed instructions as to how to make the ascent and they imply that their elaborate descriptions of the heavenly world are to be regarded as first-hand reports brought back by the adepts from such excursions.[1]

Heinrich Graetz, one of the earliest scholars to take this literature seriously, aptly described its vision of God as 'basileomorphic'.[2] God is overwhelmingly depicted using the imagery of kingship. God's throne is said to be located in the innermost of seven concentric heavenly palaces (*heikhalot*.) The adept who wishes to enter the throne room to see the glory of God has to pass through the seven doors of the seven palaces, each of which is guarded by fierce and haughty angels whose business it is to keep intruders at bay. The door-keepers will only let him through if he has the right passwords consisting of magical names called 'seals', or if he is sponsored by a 'friend at court', such as the archangel Suryah. Much space is devoted in the texts to describing God's throne and the insignia of his office such as his crown and his robe. God is served by a vast angelic retinue, organized into complex, rigid hierarchies. These angels perform a variety of functions: some constitute the celestial law court; others make up the choirs which chant the celestial Sanctus; others still are in charge of the celestial storehouses and carry out tasks associated with the governance of the world and the ordering of nature. All the relations between the 'denizens of the heights' are regulated by strict courtly etiquette and protocol. Three times each day the celestial king formally takes his seat upon his throne and on these occasions the

---

1. The classic introduction to Heikhalot mysticism is G.G. Scholem, *Major Trends in Jewish Mysticism* (New York; Schocken, 3rd edn, 1961), pp. 40-79. See further: I. Gruenwald, *Apocalyptic and Merkabah Mysticism* (Leiden: Brill, 1980); P.S. Alexander, '3 Enoch', in J.H. Charlesworth (ed.), *The Old Testament Pseudepigrapha* (New York: Doubleday, 1983), I, pp. 223-315; D.J. Halperin, *The Faces of the Chariot* (Tübingen: Siebeck–Mohr, 1988). I cite the texts from the magnificent editions of P. Schäfer, *Synopse zur Hekhalot-Literatur* (Tübingen: Siebeck–Mohr, 1981) and *Geniza-Fragmente zur Hekhalot-Literatur* (Tübingen: Siebeck–Mohr, 1984).

2. See Scholem, *Major Trends*, p. 55. Scholem, unfortunately, does not quote the precise reference where Graetz talks of 'basileomorphism'. Graetz's major study of the Heikhalot texts is: 'Die mystische Literatur in der gaonäischen Epoche', *MGWJ* 8 (1859), pp. 67-78, 103-18, 140-53.

angels perform elaborate acts of obeisance and adoration. God himself is not seen by the majority of the angels, who could not withstand the unveiled radiance of his countenance. A curtain shields them from his gaze and only certain archangels, called 'Princes of the Face' (*Sarei Panim*) are permitted to go behind the curtain.

2. *The* Familia Caelestis

The idea that God is a heavenly king or emperor is almost as old as literature itself. It is well represented in the Hebrew Bible, notably in the Psalms. But the highly distinctive Heikhalot treatment of the theme contains numerous details which cannot be derived from the biblical sources. Where do these non-biblical elements come from? What earthly royal court do the Heikhalot texts have in view? There are certain indications that, whatever ultimately are the origins of the various motifs, the Heikhalot writers are thinking of Rome. The most compelling of these indications is their use of the expression 'the family above' (*familia shel ma'alah*).

The expression *familia shel ma'alah* in the Heikhalot texts denotes the angels in general, or more narrowly the heavenly law court—the *bet din shel ma'alah* or *yeshivah shel ma'alah*. It is contrasted on a number of occasions with 'the family below' (*familia shel mattah*). The Heikhalot texts themselves do not explain the latter term, but it is clear from other rabbinic texts that it refers to Israel on earth, or more precisely to the collectivity of the rabbinic Sages (see e.g. *b. Ber.* 16b–17a discussed below). A few examples will serve to illustrate the Heikhalot use of *familia shel ma'alah*.

In *3 Enoch* 12.3-5 (*Synopse* §15) the archangel Meṭaṭron, describing to Rabbi Ishmael his investiture as God's viceregent, says:

> God fashioned for me a kingly crown in which forty-nine refulgent stones were placed, each like the sun's orb, and its brilliance shone into the four corners of the heaven of 'Aravot, into the seven heavens, and into the four quarters of the world. He set it upon my head and he called me 'The Lesser Lord' in the presence of his whole *familia* in the height.

Here one naturally takes *familia* in its broadest sense as a designation for *all* the angels. Again in *3 Enoch* 16.1 (*Synopse* §20) Meṭaṭron tells Ishmael:

At first I sat upon a great throne at the door of the seventh palace, and I judged all the denizens of the heights, the *familia* above, on the authority of the Holy One, blessed be he. I assigned greatness, royalty, rank, sovereignty, glory, praise, diadem, crown and honour to all the princes of kingdoms, when I sat in the court above (*yeshivah shel ma'alah*).

The apposition of *familia shel ma'alah* to 'denizens of the heights' at first sight suggests that here too the meaning is general, but the later reference to the *yeshivah shel ma'alah* perhaps points to the more restricted sense.

In one of the short accounts of the elevation of Meṭaṭron (*Synopse* §§295, 405) God says:

I made for him [Meṭaṭron] a throne corresponding to my throne. . . and I gave into his charge seventy angels corresponding to the seventy nations, and I gave him authority over all the *familia* above and the *familia* below.

The '*familia* above' here might be used generally, but it is more likely to stand in parallelism to the 'seventy angels' who make up the celestial law court. The idea probably is that God gave Meṭaṭron authority over the heavenly law court *and* over Israel on earth. Meṭaṭron is sometimes identified with Michael, the Prince of Israel. He therefore functions not only as Prince of the World and President of the heavenly law court, but as Israel's representative in that court.

At a number of places the Heikhalot texts speak of 'families' (*familiyyot*) of angels. For example, in *Heik. R.* 14.2 (*Synopse* §192) , 'families upon families' (*familiyyot familiyyot*) are said to issue from beneath the throne of glory blowing horns and trumpets. And Geniza Fragment 8, 2a/37 (ed. Schäfer, p. 103) refers to 'myriads upon myriads, camps upon camps and families upon families' streaming from the door of the sixth heavenly palace. This second reference gives a clue to this developed use of the term. The Heikhalot mystics divided the angels up into groups, often called 'camps' in allusion to the organization of the tribes in the wilderness encamped around the tabernacle. Each camp was thought of as being under the command of an archangel. It is quite natural to see each archangel's camp as his *familia*. There is at least one possible allusion to the idea that Meṭaṭron, like God himself, has a *familia*. Towards the end of the David Apocalypse (*Heik. R.* 7.2, *Synopse* §126 [B238]) we read:

At once David arose and recited songs and praises such as ear had not heard. When David opened his mouth and said, 'The Lord shall reign for ever', Meṭaṭron and his [? Meṭaṭron's *not* God's] *familia* began to say, 'Holy, holy holy is the Lord of hosts'.

Two final references to the *familia caelestis* call for brief mention, in order to complete the linguistic picture for the Heikhalot texts. First, in *Synopse* §313 (V228), Rabbi Ishmael tells how at the age of thirteen he manages to elicit from Neḥunyah ben Haqqanah the name of the Prince of the Torah, and he calls him down to earth:

> He [the Prince of Torah] descended in a sheet of flame, his face like the appearance of lightning. When I saw him I was alarmed; I trembled and sank back. He said to me: Son of man, what business have you to disturb the great *familia* (*familia gedolah*)?

Here *familia gedolah* has been formed on the analogy of *sanhedrin gedolah*, and the allusion is once again to the heavenly law court of which the Prince of Torah is a distinguished member. Second, *Synopse* §638 says, 'All the members of the inner *familia* [*familia penimit*] were afraid and trembled. The reference may be to an inner group of angels—the *Sarei panim*—who were admitted to the immediate presence of God. Or, we may have the substitution of an 'inner–outer' dichotomy for the more usual 'upper–lower' dichotomy of the Heikhalot texts. If this is the case, then 'the inner *familia*' may simply be equivalent to 'the *familia* above'.[1]

The *familia* terminology is so characteristic of the recherché style of Heikhalot literature that one is tempted to suppose that it was coined in Heikhalot circles. *Familia* does indeed occur in rabbinic literature in the general sense of the retinue of a king or a military commander. It designates the body of retainers who would accompany such an important person when he made a journey:

> This may be illustrated by a king who was passing from place to place when a pearl fell from his head. The king halted and ordered his *familia* to halt there. He collected the sand into piles and brought sieves. He sifted the first pile and did not find it; the second and did not find it. But in the third he found it. They said: The king has found his pearl (*Gen. R.* 39.10).

---

1. Note the variation of up–down and in–out language in the versions and manuscripts of the story of the Four who entered Pardes: *t. Ḥag.* 2.3-4; *j. Ḥag.* 77b.8-23; *b. Ḥag.* 14b; *Cant. R.* 1.4.1. For discussion see D.J. Halperin, *The Merkabah in Rabbinic Literature* (New Haven: American Oriental Society, 1980), pp. 86-92. *b. Ḥag.* 5b contrasts the inner and outer chambers (*batei gavva'ei. . .batei bara'ei*) of God's heavenly dwelling.

Following supplication, the Angel of the Torah comes down in a sheet of flame to give instruction

We read of the *familia* of Pharaoh (*ARN* A 27, ed. Schechter 42a; *j. Soṭ.* 5.8 [20c.74]); and according to *Gen. R.* 35.3:

> The tribes of Reuben and Gad formed the *familia* of Joshua, and he escorted them to the Jordan [on their return home]. But when they saw that his *familia* was diminished they turned back and escorted him to his home.

However, the majority of the non-Heikhalot references are, as in the Heikhalot texts, to God's heavenly and earthly households,[1] and it is reasonable, I believe, to see the influence of Heikhalot mysticism on this distinctive usage.

An interesting Talmudic occurrence of *familia* in its Heikhalot sense is found in *b. Ber.* 16b–17a:

> Rav Safra on concluding his prayer added the following:[2] May it be your will, O Lord our God, to establish peace in the *familia* above and in the *familia* below, and among the disciples who occupy themselves with your Torah, whether for its own sake or for other motives, and may it please you that all who do so for other motives may come to study it for its own sake!

Rashi takes the *familia* above here as referring specifically to the angelic 'Princes of the Nations' (*Sarei ha-'ummot*), who represent the nations of the world in the celestial realm. On the basis of Dan. 10.20, he claims that 'when there is a dispute among the Princes above, at once quarrelling breaks out among the nations below'. Hence the need for a prayer for peace in heaven. He takes the '*familia* below' as referring specifically to the Sages, doubtless influenced by the subsequent mention of 'the disciples who occupy themselves with Torah'. In other words, he sees here essentially two independent statements: Rav Safra is praying for an end to strife among the angels (and so, by implication, among the nations whom those angels represent), and for peace and harmony in the schools.

This interpretation certainly satisfies the strict grammar of the passage and gives the preposition *be-* ('in') its natural sense, but it leaves the parallelism between *familia shel ma'alah* and *familia shel*

---

1. See e.g. *b. Ḥag.* 13b; *Lev. R.* 31.6; *Sifre Num.* §42, ed. Horovitz 47; *b. Sanh.* 99b; *b. Ber.* 16b–17a; *b. Sanh.* 67b; *Exod. R.* 28.1; *Num. R.* 4.1; *Deut. R.* 11.10; *Midr. Ps.* 11.6, ed. Buber 51a; *Pes. R.* 35.2, ed. Friedmann 160b; *Cant. Targ.* 1.15 (*be-familia be-mal'akhayya qaddishayya!*).

2. This was probably an 'extempore' or 'private' prayer added by Rav Safra after he had completed the statutory public prayer, the Amidah. *b. Ber.* 16b–17a contains a number of examples of these private prayers.

maṭṭah rather weak and redundant. Perhaps what Rav Safra was praying for was peace between the upper and lower households.[1] Such a petition could be interpreted in two ways. Assuming that *familia* has here its narrow sense, the meaning might be: 'May the Sages on earth in their legal deliberations always be in accord with the heavenly law court'. There is ongoing speculation in Talmudic literature on the relationship between *halakhah* on earth and *halakhah* in heaven, and on the respective authorities and jurisdictions of the heavenly and earthly Sanhedrins (see *b. Mak.* 23b; *Pes. K.* 5.13, ed. Buber 48a; cf. *Deut. R.* 5.5, *Gen. R.* 26.6). Alternatively, we could understand Rav Safra as praying for harmony between the worshipping community on earth (Israel) and the worshipping community in heaven (the angels who chant the celestial Sanctus). The idea of heaven and earth conjoining in the worship of God is widespread in early Judaism. It finds powerful expression in the Qumran liturgies and in the synagogue *Qedushot*, especially the *Qedushah de-Yoṣer*.[2] If this is the underlying sense, then it is interesting that Rav Safra has chosen to express this idea in distinctively Heikhalot language. This could be a further example of the well-documented influence of the Heikhalot circles on the development and language of the liturgy.

I know of no clear-cut examples of the distinctive Heikhalot use of *familia* in early Jewish texts outside of rabbinic literature. Some have suggested that it is implied in Eph. 3.14-15. This text—a well-known crux—runs as follows in the *textus receptus*

τούτου χάριν κάμπτω τὰ γόνατά μου πρὸς τὸν πατέρα τοῦ κυρίου ἡμῶν Ἰησοῦ Χριστοῦ, ἐξ οὗ πᾶσα πατριὰ ἐν οὐρανοῖς καὶ ἐπὶ γῆς ὀνομάζεται.

1. Cf. *b. Sanh.* 99b:

   R. Alexandri said: 'He who studies the Torah for its own sake makes peace in the *familia* above and in the *familia* below, as it is written, "Or let him take hold of my strength [i.e. the Torah], that he may make peace with me; and he shall make peace with me" (Isa. 27.5)'.

2. Cf. the Preface of the Eucharist:

   Therefore with Angels and with Archangels, and with all the company of heaven, we laud and magnify thy glorious Name; evermore praising thee, and saying, Holy, holy, holy, Lord God of hosts, heaven and earth are full of thy glory: Glory be to thee, O Lord most High.

This almost certainly goes back to an early synagogue *Qedushah*.

The Authorized Version translates thus: 'For this cause I bow my knees unto the Father of our Lord Jesus Christ, of whom the whole family in heaven and earth is named'. A traditional way of interpreting this has been to take it as referring to the church militant and the church triumphant, united into one family under the headship of Christ, whose head is God, the heavenly father. But there are two problems: first, the Authorized Version rendering appears to ignore the fact that πατριά is anarthrous; and second, there are strong textual grounds for omitting τοῦ κυρίου ἡμῶν Ἰησοῦ Χριστοῦ. Hence, starting with the Revised Version, the generally preferred translation has been: 'For this cause I bow my knees unto the Father, from whom every family in heaven and on earth is named'. But in what sense can we talk of 'families' in heaven and on earth which are named after the heavenly Father? Is there a suggestion that God's relationship to the angels may be defined in terms of 'fatherhood'? It is in this context that some have invoked the rabbinic texts which speak of God's celestial and terrestrial families.[1] The problem is that if this sense is intended, then the language is curiously oblique and unclear. Rather, the basic idea seems to be that God is the archetypal 'father': all true 'fatherhood' derives from, and reflects, his 'fatherhood' The polarity of 'heaven' and 'earth' is simply a case of inclusive language: any fatherhood, anywhere, is a reflex of God's fatherhood.

Whatever may be the precise meaning of Eph. 3.14-15, the passage unequivocally attributes 'fatherhood' to God, and we should interpret that 'fatherhood' in terms of the social structures of the first-century Graeco-Roman world. Fatherhood here may not imply paternity in its narrow, modern, biological sense, but rather headship of a great household. Early Christian writers unquestionably invoke analogies between the Church and the great households of their time. Eph. 2.19-22 is clear on this point. Note especially Eph. 2.19, which presents the Church as the *domus* or *familia Dei*:

ἄρα οὖν οὐκέτι ἐστὲ ξένοι καὶ πάροικοι, ἀλλὰ ἐστὲ συμπολῖται
τῶν ἁγίων καὶ οἰκεῖοι τοῦ θεοῦ (cf. Gal. 6.10).

1.	It seems the suggestion is at least as old as Grotius's *Adnotationes in Vetus et Novum Testamentum* (1642). See also Chr. Schoettgen, *Horae Hebraicae et Talmudicae in universum Novum Testamentum* (Dresden and Leipzig 1733), I, p. 1237; and H.L. Strack and P. Billerbeck, *Kommentar zum Neuen Testament aus Talmud und Midrasch* (Munich: Beck, 1954–56), III, p. 594 (cf. I, pp. 743-44).

It may also be relevant to recall here the epithet Χριστιανοί (Acts 11.26). As has often been observed, this term is formed on the analogy of Καισαριανοί and Ἡρῳδιανοί, which could be applied to the members respectively of Caesar's and Herod's households. Does Χριστιανοί, then, suggest that Christians in some sense constitute the *familia Christi*? Do we have here a further example of 'household' language applied to the Church? We have, then, ideas close to those in Heikhalot literature, but the precise Heikhalot usage, involving the Latin loan word and the contrast between the upper and lower *families*, is confined, it seems, to the Heikhalot texts and to rabbinic traditions influenced by Heikhalot ideas.

3. *The* Familia Caesaris

The Heikhalot mystics designated the angels as the *familia caelestis*. But why did they choose a Latin term? What did they want to signify by it? As I have just hinted, they did not mean to imply that the angels are in any way God's offspring: the modern concept of the nuclear family (mother, father and two children) does not apply. As early as the Twelve Tables (V, 4-5) the Latin term *familia* was used in the sense of 'household' to embrace all those persons, including a wife *in manu* and a *filius familias*, as well as slaves (*famuli*), who were under the *potestas* of a *paterfamilias*. No sharp distinction can be drawn, it seems, between the *potestas* exercised by a *paterfamilias* over his son (*patria potestas*) and that exercised by him over a slave (*dominica potestas*). The Digest (L 16,195.2) grants the status of *paterfamilias* even to a man who has no son under his authority: 'pater autem familias appellatur, qui in domo dominum habet, recteque hoc nomine appellatur, quamvis filium non habeat'. So then, the use of term *familia* in the Hebrew texts suggests that God can be seen quite precisely as the celestial equivalent of a Roman *paterfamilias*, with the angels constituting his servants and the members of his household. The *Heikhalot* texts use a wide range of terms (e.g. *'eved, shammash, na'ar*) which describe the angels as God's servants.

However, the analogy is, I believe, more pointed still. It is not any Roman *familia* that is in view, but the greatest *familia* of all—the *familia Caesaris*.[1] The *familia Caesaris* was a vast body of slaves and

1. I have made this suggestion briefly on a number of occasions in the past: see,

freedmen of the emperor who helped run the imperial administration. They constituted the bulk of the imperial civil service and held most of the posts below those of equestrian rank. The social structure of the *familia Caesaris* has been well analysed by Boulvert, Weaver and others.[1] They have shown that it can be divided into two main branches: (a) the domestic palace servants who engaged in personal service to the emperor, essentially in a private capacity, and ran his private establishments (his palaces, villas and so forth), and (b) the imperial civil service proper which helped the emperor to carry out his extensive public duties as a magistrate. The *familia Caesaris* was a complex organisation, with an elaborate career structure, which ranged from menial posts to positions of real power, such as procuratorships. Membership of the imperial *familia* carried considerable social status, particularly if one belonged to the higher echelons. Most of our knowledge of the *familia Caesaris* is due to the fact that so many of its members proudly recorded on their tombstones that they were slaves or freedmen of the emperor, and detailed the jobs that they performed within his 'family'.

The Heikhalot texts, then, by their use of the expression *familia caelestis*, are implicitly drawing a comparison between God and the Roman emperor, and are suggesting that the angels can be envisaged as a complex bureaucracy similar to the one employed by the emperor to administer the empire. As Weaver points out, the comprehensive term *familia Caesaris*, as used by modern historians to designate the totality of the emperor's slaves and freedmen, is not apparently attested in the Latin sources:

> where the phrase does occur without further determination in the inscriptions and literary texts, the reference is to a particular 'familia' or branch of the administration and has purely local significance.[2]

e.g. my note to *3 Enoch* 12.5 in Charlesworth (ed.), *Pseudepigrapha*, I, p. 265. The suggestion has since been repeated by others—sometimes without acknowledgment. Charles Mopsik (*Le Livre Hébreu d'Hénoch* [Paris: Verdier, 1989], p. 230) simply translates into French my note in the Charlesworth *Pseudepigrapha*, without disclosing the source.

1. G. Boulvert, *Esclaves et affranchis impériaux sous le Haut-Empire romain* (Napoli: Editore Jovene, 1970); G. Boulvert, *Domestique et fonctionnaire sous le Haut-Empire romain* (Paris: Les Belles Lettres, 1974); P.R.C. Weaver, *Familia Caesaris* (Cambridge: Cambridge University Press, 1972).

2. Weaver, *Familia Caesaris*, p. 299. The *Thesaurus Linguae Latinae* appears

The emperor's *familia*, then, comprised many individual *familiae*. One might compare this linguistic usage with the apparent division, mentioned above, of the *familia caelestis* into many *familiyyot*. Imperial slaves and freedom were scattered across the length and breadth of the Roman empire, so the Heikhalot mystics presumably got to know of the *familia Caesaris* from their contacts with the Roman administration. Since, as I noted, membership of the *familia Caesaris* carried prestige and, in certain circumstances, considerable privileges, doubtless the emperor's slaves and freedmen would have lost no opportunity of keeping their imperial connections in the public eye.

4. *Image and Reality*

The *familia*-terminology seems to point towards Rome as the inspiration for the picture of the celestial court in the Heikhalot texts, but to what extent are the realities of the Roman court and of Roman imperial practice accurately reflected in these texts? Here we must advance with great caution, for two reasons. First, it is hard to tell how much the Heikhalot mystics would have known about the Roman court, or how imperial practice would have looked from their social and geographical standpoint. Second, our own knowledge of Roman court practice is very incomplete. The only picture which we can reconstruct is inevitably something of a composite, derived from diverse sources which are often of very different date. Moreover, the secondary literature is, it must be said, not very helpful: study of Roman court ceremonial and protocol seems to have advanced little beyond the pioneering work of Andreas Alföldi in the 1930s.[1] However, with

to cite one literary example of the expression *familia Caesaris*, viz., Lactantius, *de mortibus persecutorum* 14.5: 'erant certantes quis prior aliquid inveniret; nihil usquam reperiebatur, quippe cum familiam Caesaris nemo torqueret'. But the sense here is 'the *familia* of *the* Caesar' (Galerius), as opposed to the servants (*domestici*) of the Augustus (Diocletian). The Greek term for the *familia Caesaris* appears to have been ἡ Καίσαρος οἰκία. See: Phil. 4.22, ἀσπάζονται ὑμᾶς πάντες οἱ ἅγιοι, μάλιστα δὲ οἱ ἐκ τῆς Καίσαρος οἰκίας; Philo, *Flaccus* 35, εἰ δὲ μὴ βασιλεὺς ἦν, ἀλλά τις τῶν ἐκ τῆς Καίσαρος οἰκίας, οὐκ ὤφειλε προνομίαν τινὰ καὶ τιμὴν ἔχειν; Linguistically, however, the obvious Latin equivalent for οἰκία Καίσαρος would be *domus Caesaris* (Tacitus, *Hist.* 2. 92).

1. A. Alföldi, 'Die Ausgestaltung des monarchischen Zeremoniells am römischen Kaiserhofe', *Mitteilungen des Deutschen Archaeologischen Instituts*,

these caveats in mind, I would offer the following tentative notes towards correlating the celestial court of the Heikhalot texts with the court of the emperor in Rome.

The first point to be made is that the Heikhalot picture does not fit in easily with the early Principate. It correlates best with the situation that emerged with the reforms of Diocletian in the late third century CE. The reforms of Diocletian may not have been as radical or as new as is sometimes claimed. Many of his supposed innovations in ceremonial are attested earlier, as a close reading of Alföldi reveals. However there seems little doubt that he did transform and reorganize the court, and that the purpose of this exercise was to project a new imperial image to the outside world—the image of an absolute monarch. Earlier emperors, clinging perhaps to the remnants of republican virtue, were at some pains to create the impression that they were accessible to all their subjects, be they ever so humble, especially when they journeyed round their empire. Seneca exhorts Nero to be 'affable in speech, easy of approach and access, and lovable of countenance (*sermone adfabilis, aditu accessuque facilis, vultu...amabilis*).[1] Diocletian, however, sought to stress the emperor's remoteness and inaccessibility. The palace took on, in a way hardly seen before, the character of a temple. The emperor's person, his dwelling and everything connected with him were regarded as sacred. The adjective *sacer* came almost to be synonymous with royalty.

Roemische Abteilung 49 (1934), pp. 1-156; Alföldi, 'Insignien und Tracht der römischen Kaiser', *Mitteilungen des Deutschen Archaeologischen Instituts, Roemische Abteilung* 50 (1935), pp. 1-171. Useful is F. Dvornik, *Early Christian and Byzantine Political Philosophy* (Washington, DC: Dumbarton Oaks Center for Byzantine Studies, 1966), I–II, esp. II, pp. 520-25. A great deal about later Byzantine court ritual can be gleaned from Constantine Porphyrogenitus, *Liber de caeremoniis* (ed. A. Vogt; Paris: Association Guillaume Budé, 1935–40), on which see A. Cameron, 'The Construction of Court Ritual: The Byzantine Book of Ceremonies', in D. Cannadine and S. Price (eds.), *Rituals of Royalty: Power and Ceremonial in Traditional Societies* (Cambridge: Cambridge University Press, 1987), pp. 106-36. Much has, of course, been written on the imperial cult: for a recent study see S.R.F. Price, *Rituals and Power: The Roman Imperial Cult in Asia Minor* (Cambridge: Cambridge University Press, 1984). Little of this, however, is of use to our present inquiry.

1. Seneca, *De clementia* 1.13.4. For the accessibility of the emperor on journeys, see Fergus Millar, *The Emperor in the Roman World* (London: Gerald Duckworth, 1977), pp. 36-37.

The *quaestor Augusti* who advised the *Princeps* on legal matters, was now designated the *quaestor sacri palatii*. The Minister of Finance became the *comes sacrarum largitionum*. The Lord High Chamberlain was known as the *praepositus sacri cubiculi*. The praetorian prefects no longer assisted the emperor, but acted in his 'sacred stead'—*vice sacra*, and so forth.[1] Likewise the Heikhalot texts stress, to a degree that is perhaps unusual in rabbinic Judaism,[2] the remoteness and inaccessibility of the heavenly emperor. They refer to his heavenly dwelling as a *heikhal*—a word meaning both temple *and* palace in Hebrew, which neatly combines notions both of sacredness and of royalty. And the adjective which, perhaps more than any other, characterizes for the Heikhalot mystics the heavenly court is 'holy' (*qadosh*).

The Heikhalot texts depict graphically the problems that face the adept who seeks an audience with the heavenly emperor—how he must pass through the doors of seven palaces, each of which is guarded by armed angelic doorkeepers. They will only unstring their bows, sheathe their swords and let him past, if he shows them the correct 'seals'. He must be interrogated by the archangel Dumi'el, and must have a document drawn up attesting that he is worthy 'to enter before the Throne of Glory'. He appears to carry with him a 'gift' (the Greek term δῶρον is used), and he is finally ushered with fanfares of trumpets into the throne-room by three high, angelic sponsors.[3] There are doubtless elements of real court ritual reflected here. An interesting text in Pliny implies that the Emperor Claudius gave special gold rings engraved with his likeness to those whom he wished to have free access to his presence. It seems that by showing the ring, the wearer could gain an immediate audience.[4] The 'seals' of

---

1. Alföldi, 'Ausgestaltung', pp. 29-33; Dvornik, *Political Philosophy*, pp. 521-22.

2. For a classic statement of the more usual rabbinic emphasis on the immanence of God, see S. Schechter, *Aspects of Rabbinic Theology* (New York: Schocken Books, 1965), pp. 21-45.

3. *Heik. R.* 15.1–22.2, *Synopse* §§198-236.

4. Pliny, *Nat. Hist.* 33.41: 'fuit et alia Claudii principatu differentia insolens iis quibus admissiones liberae ius dedissent imaginem principis ex auro in anulo gerendi, magna criminum occasione, quae omnia salutaris exortus Vespasiani imperatoris abolevit aequaliter publicando principem'. This text incorporates the widely accepted emendations of Th. Mommsen, 'Die Comites Augusti der früheren Kaiserzeit', *Hermes* 4 (1870), p. 129 n. 1.

the Heikhalot texts were probably envisaged as rings: the Hebrew term used (*ḥotam*) could designate a signet ring. Pliny states that Vespasian abolished the practice, but it is surely plausible to suppose that passes of various kinds, allowing entry to the palace, must have been reintroduced in the later empire as security around the emperor tightened and as access to him was increasingly restricted.

The Heikhalot texts describe elaborate forms of *proskynesis* practised in the heavenly court:

> The angels of the first heaven, when they see their Prince, they dismount from their horses and fall prostrate. The Prince of the first heaven, when he sees the Prince of the second heaven, he removes the glorious crown from his head and falls prostrate.[1]

Various forms of *proskynesis*—kneeling, kissing the hand and foot—were practised at the Roman court.[2] The Heikhalot texts give numerous examples of the acclamations with which the angels greeted their Master, and these correspond tolerably well in their bombastic and repetitive style with the acclamations used at the Roman court.[3] There is evidence that Roman court etiquette decreed that silence should be observed in the presence of the emperor: the audience hall was marked by profound tranquillity and quiet.[4]

1. *3 Enoch* 18.1, *Synopse* §23; cf. Rev. 4.10:

πεσοῦνται οἱ εἴκοσι τέσσαρες πρεσβύτεροι ἐνώπιον τοῦ καθημένου ἐπὶ τοῦ θρόνου, καὶ προσκυνήσουσιν τῷ ζῶντι εἰς τοὺς αἰῶνας τῶν αἰώνων, καὶ βαλοῦσιν τοὺς στεφάνους αὐτῶν ἐνώπιον τοῦ θρόνου, λέγοντες κτλ.

2. Alföldi, 'Ausgestaltung', pp. 46-64. The Greeks (Herodotus, Xenophon, Isocrates) from early on remark, with disapproval, on the Persian practice of prostration before the king: see Dvornik, *Political Philosophy*, I, pp. 117-18.

3. Note, e.g. *Synopse* §378: *melekh 'addir, melekh 'abbir, melekh 'amiṣ, melekh 'emet, melekh 'adon*...On this redundant style see P.S. Alexander, 'Prayer in the Heikhalot Literature', in R. Goetschel (ed.), *Prière, mystique et Judaïsme* (Paris: Presses Universitaires de France, 1987), pp. 43-64. Alföldi ('Insignien und Tracht', pp. 79-88) discusses the style of Roman acclamations of the emperor. Constantine Porphyrogenitus, *Liber de caeremoniis*, contains many examples of later Byzantine acclamations: see e.g. ch. 47 (edn. Vogt II.1, p. 3).

4. Alföldi, 'Ausgestaltung', p. 38.

צבא־השמים
A kneeless familia?

G.E. Pallant-Sidaway

The Heikhalot texts speak frequently of God dwelling in the 'palace of silence' *(heikhal demamah).*[1] The word used for 'silence' *(demamah)* recalls the 'still small voice' *(qol demamah daqqah)* of 1 Kgs 19.12, and it illustrates the ingenuity with which the Heikhalot mystics attached their ideas to Scripture. The angel Dumi'el was mentioned earlier. His name probably means 'Silence of God'. Perhaps Dumi'el's original function was seen as ensuring that the proper respectful silence was observed in God's presence. Roman court etiquette, at least from Diocletian's time, seems also to have decreed that one remained standing in the presence of the emperor. According to Dvornik, even the imperial privy council (the *consistorium*) stood when the emperor was present: 'he alone had the right to be seated, while others remained stranding around his "sacred person"'.[2] Rabbinic and Heikhalot tradition asserts that in heaven there is no sitting.[3] This point is made in typically whimsical fashion by claiming that the angels have no knee-joints, and so cannot bend their legs in order to sit down *(Gen. R. 65.21).* Support for this claim is found in the statement in Ezekiel that the Holy Creatures had 'straight feet' (Ezek. 1.7, *ve-ragleihem regel yesharah),* or, as the text just might be translated, 'straight legs'. Only God is permitted to sit. The admonitory tale is told of how once the archangel Meṭaṭron sat down and at that point the adept Elisha ben 'Avuyah arrived, and, seeing Meṭaṭron sitting, mistook him for a second God. Meṭaṭron was chided for not rising to his feet to prevent the confusion; he was taken out and lashed by the archangel 'Anafi'el with sixty lashes of fire *(b. Ḥag.* 15a; *3 Enoch* 16.1-5, *Synopse* §20).

According to the Heikhalot texts the heavenly emperor does not sit permanently on his throne, but descends from hidden regions at set times to hold formal audience. There are hints that it is not God himself who occupies the throne, but rather a kind of representation of

---

1. See e.g. *Synopse* §97, 'the servants of his glory see the glorious king sitting in the chambers of the palace of silence'; *Synopse* §320, 'in the palace of silence you have established your throne'.
2. Dvornik, *Political Philosophy,* I, p. 522. Further Alföldi, 'Ausgestaltung', pp. 42-45.
3. *b. Ḥag.* 15a, on which see P.S. Alexander, '*3 Enoch* and the Talmud', *Journal for the Study of Judaism* 18 (1987), pp. 54-66. Further, C. R. Morray-Jones, 'Hekhalot Literature and Talmudic Tradition: Alexander's Three Great Texts', *Journal for the Study of Judaism* 22 (1991), pp. 17-36.

God, the *Shekhinah* ('Divine Presence'). It is perhaps not too fanciful to compare this with the Roman practice of adoration of the emperor's empty throne (on which might be placed some of the symbols of his power), or of his statues.[1] The *Shekhinah* could be seen in terms of Roman court ritual as a *simulacrum* or *imago* of the hidden emperor.

At the Roman court the emperor was shielded from public gaze during audiences by a curtain.[2] The Heikhalot texts stated that a curtain hangs before the face of God and only the highest archangels, the 'Princes of the Face' (*Sarei panim*) are permitted to go behind it and communicate directly with God. The adept, when he ascends to heaven, receives oracles 'from behind the curtain'. The reason for the curtain, according to the Heikhalot texts, is not to shield God from the gaze of the *profanum vulgus*, but rather to shield the angels and adepts from the destructive radiance of the divine countenance and crown.[3] The word *velum* is used in the Latin (and, indeed, the Byzantine Greek) sources for the screen behind which the Roman emperor sat. *Velum* does, curiously, occur as a loan word in the Heikhalot texts, but it denotes the first of the seven heavens, which by being drawn back and then closed again creates day and night.[4] The normal word used in the Heikhalot texts for the curtain which hangs before the face of God is *pargod*. This is derived from the Persian *pardag*.[5]

1. Alföldi, 'Ausgestaltung', pp. 65-79; 'Insignien und Tracht', pp. 134-39.

2. Alföldi, 'Ausgestaltung', pp. 36-38.

3. *3 Enoch* 45.1 (*Synopse* §64), with my note *ad loc.* in Charlesworth, *Pseudepigrapha*, I, p. 296, note a. Est. 1.14, 'the seven princes of Persia and Media who see the king's face' (*shiv'at šarei paras u-madai ro'ei penei ha-melekh*), may imply the idea of a curtain. For other traditions regarding heavenly curtains, see O. Hofius, *Der Vorhang vor dem Thron Gottes* (Tübingen: Siebeck–Mohr, 1972). Note how the Roman panegyrists speak of being admitted to adore the sacred countenance (*sacros vultus adorare*) of the emperor: Claudius Mamertinus, *Panegyricus genethliacus Maximiano Aug. dictus* 11.1 and 3 in R.A.B. Mynors (ed.), *Panegyrici Latini* XII (Oxford Classical Texts; Oxford: Clarendon Press, 1964), pp. 264-65.

4. *3 Enoch* 17.3 (Synopse §21), with my note *ad loc.* in Charlesworth *Pseudepigrapha*, I, p. 269, note f.

5. Pahlavi *pardag* (D.N. MacKenzie, *A Concise Pahlavi Dictionary* [London: Oxford University Press, 1971], p. 64) = modern Persian *parda* (I.A. Vullers, *Lexicon Persico-Latinum* [1855: rpr. Graz: Akademische Druck- u. Verlagsanstalt, 1962], I, p. 340) = Urdu *parda [purdah]* (J.T. Platts, *Dictionary of Urdū, Classical Hindī and English* [London: Oxford University Press, 1930], p. 246).

The choice of the Persian word is highly significant. Obviously the heavenly curtain could be compared to the curtain in the ancient temple and tabernacle which screened off the holy place from the holy of holies. The Heikhalot traditions do, sometimes, use the biblical term (*parokhet*) for the heavenly curtain, but the Persian loan word predominates. Why? Presumably because the Heikhalot mystics wanted to allude to the practice of the Sasanian court. Mas'ūdī informs us that

> it was the custom of all the kings of Persia since Ardashir to hide themselves from the gaze of their court, and to place themselves at a distance of twenty cubits from those in the first rank of the state. They were separated by a curtain set at ten cubits from the king and at ten cubits from those in the first rank.[1]

Mas'ūdī uses the Arabic term *sitāra* for the curtain, but it is surely a reasonable guess that the underlying Persian word would have been *pardag*.[2]

This strong allusion to Sasanian court practice is a shot across the bows. It reminds us that most, it not all, the Roman court rituals which we have highlighted were not exclusive to Rome. They were found also in the Hellenistic east and in Persia. Diocletian is often accused of orientalizing the court and of turning himself, in un-Roman fashion, into a Persian-style despot.[3] It must be admitted that the Heikhalot picture could broadly fit almost any court in late antiquity.

---

1. Mas'ūdī, *Murūdj al-dhahab* (ed. B. de Meynard and P. de Courteille; rev. Ch. Pellat; Beirut: 1966), I, p. 288. On the Sasanian court see: A. Christensen, *L'Empire des Sassanides: le peuple, l'état, la cour* (Copenhagen: Bianco Lunos Bogtrykkeri, 1907), pp. 88-106; Dvornik, *Political Philosophy*, I, pp. 73-131. A certain amount about earlier Persian court practice can be gleaned from the *Siyāsat-nāma* of Nizām al-Mulk. For a translation, see H. Darke, *The Book of Government or Rules for Kings* (London: Routledge & Kegan Paul, 2nd edn, 1978).

2. It is just possible that the Hebrew expression 'I have heard from behind the curtain' (*shama'ti me-'ahorei ha-pargod*) is Persian in origin, though I have no clear proof of this. The image of receiving an oracle from behind a curtain occurs in Quran, Sura 42.51:

> It is not fitting for a man that God should speak to him except by inspiration, or from behind a veil (*hidjāb*), or by the sending of a messenger, to reveal, with God's permission, what God wills.

3. Alföldi, 'Ausgestaltung', pp. 6-25.

It does not, indeed, fit any court exactly: that would be rather too much to expect; but it fits Roman and Sasanian practice tolerably well, and I would not claim that the Heikhalot mystics had *only* Rome in mind. In the light of the parallels which we have considered I would suggest that it is fair to see the Heikhalot mystics as creating a distorted but nonetheless recognizable imitation of the mysterious rituals of power which were enacted at the heart of the two great empires of their time—the Roman and the Sasanian—which between them held the destiny of the scattered Jewish communities in their hands.

5. *Is there a Political Point?*

There is a final question to be considered. Is the carefully worked out parallelism in the Heikhalot texts between God and the emperor intended to convey a political message?

The parallelism itself can function in two contradictory ways. It could be used to bolster the emperor's position by representing him as God's viceroy on earth. This was the line taken in Byzantine political theory, in which, as in Heikhalot mysticism, God is cast in the image of the emperor. A number of mosaics in Byzantine churches represent this view inconographically: for example, they depict angels in the dress of courtiers carrying banners bearing the inscription ἅγιος ἅγιος ἅγιος.[1] Here the parallelism solemnly legitimizes the emperor's position on earth. But the parallelism could also be used negatively. For example, it could be argued that God alone is king: his kingship alone should be acknowledged. Earthly kings arrogate to themselves powers which belong properly to God. Such anti-monarchic ideas have a long pedigree in Israel: they go back to the time of Samuel and come down in various forms through the Zealots to the Rabbis.[2]

We can be sure of one thing: neither the Rabbis in general nor the Heikhalot mystics in particular were in the business of propping up the emperor in Rome. Their general attitude is well represented by the text which stands as the motto of this paper. Each king on earth is

1. See, e.g. the mosaic from the Church of the Assumption, Nicaea, reproduced in P.R.L. Brown, *The World of Late Antiquity* (London: Thames and Hudson, 1971), p. 172, illustration 111. On the Byzantine ideology of kingship see Dvornik, *Political Philosophy*, II, pp. 659-723, esp. 719-20.
2. A useful place to begin exploring this strand of early Jewish political thought is M. Hengel, *The Zealots* (Edinburgh: T. & T. Clark, 1989), pp. 90-110.

but an eparch in God's far-flung empire. God will humiliate any king who gets above himself and assumes powers and honours that belong to God alone. Rome in the Heikhalot texts is almost invariably 'wicked Rome', and its heavenly prince is Sama'el, the rabbinic equivalent of Satan. The texts make a number of pointed references to the Legend of the Ten Martyrs—the scholars killed by the Romans in the time of Hadrian. The Great Séance passage in *Heik. R.* states that Neḥunyah ben Haqqanah decided to reveal the mysteries of the heavenly palaces and of the throne of God only after he heard that a harsh decree had gone out from Rome to seize the Sages (*Heik. R.* 15.1, *Synopse* §198). And it should always be borne in mind that in the Heikhalot texts the terrestrial counterpart of the *familia caelestis* is not the *familia Caesaris* but the company of the Sages.

Heikhalot literature can be read, at least in part, as a literature of reassurance for the politically powerless. Unable to influence political events, and denied access to the men of power on earth, the mystics created a higher power in heaven after the image and likeness of the power on earth. If they could not speak to the king on earth, they could speak to the king in heaven and be assured of *his* protection. And they knew that in the archangel Michael they had an advocate and champion who was more than a match for Sama'el, Prince of Rome, or Dubbi'el, Prince of Persia. Traditionally Jews had sought comfort in times of oppression and persecution by praying for the coming of the Messiah. In the Heikhalot texts, however, messianism is curiously vestigial. Instead of projecting their hopes forward in time to a messianic age, the mystics projected them upwards through space to a supra-terrestrial, hidden world in which the relationships that pertain in this world are reversed. From the perspective of this world they are at the bottom of the pile; from the perspective of the other world they are at the top. The Heikhalot literature can, therefore, be seen as subversive, but unlike some forms of messianism it is in no sense a programme for practical political action. Had they been told the visions of the mystics the Roman emperor and his officials would probably have dismissed them as the inventions of deluded fanatics who had lost touch with reality. That may also be our reaction. But we may be missing an important point. Empires can physically coerce their subjects, but they cannot easily compel the imagination or storm the citadel of the mind. The Heikhalot mystics doubtless believed literally in their vision of the world, with its reversal of visible relationships, and that belief may have saved them from despair and helped them to remain true to their own traditions and culture. Their vision can, consequently, be seen as an effective strategy for resisting the imperialism of 'wicked Rome'.[1]

1. The late rabbinic *aggadot* regarding Solomon's throne and hippodrome (J.D. Eisenstein, *Ozar Midrashim* [J.D. Eisenstein: New York, 1915], pp. 526-30) show a certain amount of knowledge of life at the Byzantine court. These traditions have been too readily dismissed as fanciful and absurd. But they may represent another strategy for saving Jewish pride. The message is: 'We too once had political power under a great emperor—King Solomon!' On Roman and Byzantine thrones, see Alföldi, 'Insignien und Tracht', pp. 124-134; further Alföldi, 'Die Geschichte des Throntabernakels', *La Nouvelle Clio* 1–2 (1949–50), pp. 536-66.

Since completing this article my attention has been drawn to the interesting study of D.E. Aune, 'The Influence of Roman Imperial Court Ceremonial on the Apocalypse of John', *Biblical Research* 28 (1983), pp. 5-26. Also useful is M. Hengel and A.M. Schwemer (eds.), *Königsherrschaft Gottes und himmlischer Kult* (Tübingen: Siebeck–Mohr, 1991).

INDEXES

INDEX OF REFERENCES

OLD TESTAMENT

NEW TESTAMENT

INDEX OF AUTHORS

JOURNAL FOR THE STUDY OF THE OLD TESTAMENT

Supplement Series